Legal Foundations of EU Economic Governance

Since the economic crisis unfolded in 2008, the European Union economic governance framework has been profoundly transformed from a legal perspective. The EU has adopted new tools, institutions and rules to tackle the changes and is arguably better prepared to combat any future crises. This book analyzes the basic legal framework of EU economic governance and considers the legal underpinnings which underlie economic institutions in this area. It uses analytical dialectics as a method of analysis and the paradigm of "law as credibility" as the main model through which the substantive parts of EU economic governance are accounted for. Important issues such as access to and exit and expulsion from the euro, the independence of the European Central Bank, the Stability and Growth Pact, bailouts to Member States and the EU's economic strategy are addressed in a clear, critical, and innovative way.

Antonio Estella is Associate Professor of Administrative Law and holds a Jean Monnet Chair "ad personam" of Law and European Economic Governance at the University Carlos III of Madrid (Spain). He was a Jean Monnet Professor of European Union Law from 2006 to 2010. He completed his PhD at the European University Institute (Italy, 1997). He has a Master's degree in European Community law from the Université Libre de Bruxelles (Belgium, 1992) and graduated in law at the Autonomous University of Madrid (Spain) in 1991. Estella has been a Visiting Fellow at Berkeley University (1999), at Princeton University (2012), and at the University of Oxford (Institute of European and Comparative Law, 2014–2015). He was elected a Senior Member of St. Antony's College, Oxford, in June 2014.

The Law in Context Series

Editors: William Twining (University College London),
Christopher McCrudden (Queen's University Belfast), and
Bronwen Morgan (University of Bristol).

Since 1970 the Law in Context series has been at the forefront of the movement to
broaden the study of law. It has been a vehicle for the publication of innovative
scholarly books that treat law and legal phenomena critically in their social, political,
and economic contexts from a variety of perspectives. The series particularly aims to
publish scholarly legal writing that brings fresh perspectives to bear on new and
existing areas of law taught in universities. A contextual approach involves treating
legal subjects broadly, using materials from other social sciences, and from any other
discipline that helps to explain the operation in practice of the subject under discussion.
It is hoped that this orientation is at once more stimulating and more realistic than the
bare exposition of legal rules. The series includes original books that have a different
emphasis from traditional legal textbooks, while maintaining the same high standards
of scholarship. They are written primarily for undergraduate and graduate students of
law and of other disciplines, but will also appeal to a wider readership. In the past, most
books in the series have focused on English law, but recent publications include books
on European law, globalization, transnational legal processes, and comparative law.

Books in the Series
Ali: *Modern Challenges to Islamic Law*
Anderson, Schum & Twining: *Analysis of Evidence*
Ashworth: *Sentencing and Criminal Justice*
Barton & Douglas: *Law and Parenthood*
Beecher-Monas: *Evaluating Scientific Evidence: An Interdisciplinary Framework for
    Intellectual Due Process*
Bell: *French Legal Cultures*
Bercusson: *European Labour Law*
Birkinshaw: *European Public Law*
Birkinshaw: *Freedom of Information: The Law, the Practice and the Ideal*
Brownsword & Goodwin: *Law and the Technologies of the Twenty-First Century*
Cane: *Atiyah's Accidents, Compensation and the Law*
Clarke & Kohler: *Property Law: Commentary and Materials*
Collins: *The Law of Contract*
Collins, Ewing & McColgan: *Labour Law*
Cowan: *Housing Law and Policy*
Cranston: *Legal Foundations of the Welfare State*
Darian-Smith: *Laws and Societies in Global Contexts: Contemporary Approaches*
Dauvergne: *Making People Illegal: What Globalisation Means for Immigration and Law*
Davies: *Perspectives on Labour Law*
Dembour: *Who Believes in Human Rights?: The European Convention in Question*

Stewart: *Gender, Law and Justice in a Global Market*
Tamanaha: *Law as a Means to an End: Threat to the Rule of Law*
Turpin & Tomkins: *British Government and the Constitution: Text and Materials*
Twining: *Globalisation and Legal Theory*
Twining: *Rethinking Evidence*
Twining: *General Jurisprudence: Understanding Law from a Global Perspective*
Twining: *Human Rights, Southern Voices: Francis Deng, Abdullahi An-Na'im, Yash Ghai and Upendra Baxi*
Twining & Miers: *How to Do Things with Rules*
Ward: *A Critical Introduction to European Law*
Ward: *Law, Text, Terror*
Ward: *Shakespeare and Legal Imagination*
Wells & Quick: *Lacey, Wells and Quick: Reconstructing Criminal Law*
Zander: *Cases and Materials on the English Legal System*
Zander: *The Law-Making Process*

International Journal of Law in Context: A Global Forum for Interdisciplinary Legal Studies

The *International Journal of Law in Context* is the companion journal to the Law in Context book series and provides a forum for interdisciplinary legal studies and offers intellectual space for groundbreaking critical research. It publishes contextual work about law and its relationship with other disciplines including but not limited to science, literature, humanities, philosophy, sociology, psychology, ethics, history, and geography. More information about the journal and how to submit an article can be found at http://journals.cambridge.org/ijc.

Legal Foundations of EU Economic Governance

ANTONIO ESTELLA

Universidad Carlos III de Madrid

CAMBRIDGE
UNIVERSITY PRESS

University Printing House, Cambridge CB2 8BS, United Kingdom

One Liberty Plaza, 20th Floor, New York, NY 10006, USA

477 Williamstown Road, Port Melbourne, VIC 3207, Australia

314–321, 3rd Floor, Plot 3, Splendor Forum, Jasola District Centre, New Delhi – 110025, India

79 Anson Road, #06–04/06, Singapore 079906

Cambridge University Press is part of the University of Cambridge.

It furthers the University's mission by disseminating knowledge in the pursuit of education, learning, and research at the highest international levels of excellence.

www.cambridge.org
Information on this title: www.cambridge.org/9781107141018
DOI: 10.1017/9781316493243

First published 2018

Printed and bound in Great Britain by Clays Ltd, Elcograf S.p.A.

A catalog record for this publication is available from the British Library.

Library of Congress Cataloging-in-Publication Data
Names: Estella de Noriega, Antonio, author.
Title: Legal foundations of EU economic governance / Antonio Estella,
    Universidad Carlos III de Madrid.
Other titles: Legal foundations of European Union economic governance
Description: Cambridge [UK] ; New York, NY : Cambridge University Press, 2018. | Series: The
    law in context series | Includes bibliographical references and index.
Identifiers: LCCN 2017055919 | ISBN 9781107141018 (Hardback : alk. paper) |
    ISBN 9781316506226 (pbk. : alk. paper)
Subjects: LCSH: European Union countries–Economic policy. | Eurozone. | Monetary policy–
    European Union countries. | Monetary unions–European Union countries. | Financial crises–
    European Union countries. | Bailouts (Government policy)–European Union countries.
Classification: LCC KJE6415 .E825 2018 | DDC 343.2407–dc23
    LC record available at https://lccn.loc.gov/2017055919

ISBN 978-1-107-14101-8 Hardback
ISBN 978-1-316-50622-6 Paperback

To my English memories

JACK CADE:
... there shall be no money; all shall eat and drink on my score ...

DICK:
The first thing we do: let's kill all the lawyers.

William Shakespeare, *Henry VI, Part 2*, Act IV, Scene 2

Contents

List of Figures

List of Tables

List of Boxes

Preface and Acknowledgments

As in the painting *Duelo a garrotazos* (*Duel with Cudgels*), Europe, the European Union, *seems* today on the brink of falling apart, as was Spain when Goya painted this masterpiece of modern (contemporary, I would even argue) art. The list of challenges that the EU confronts today is not exactly short; to cite but some of the most important ones, we have Brexit, the refugee crisis, the EU's position in the world, its relationship with the USA, China and Russia, terrorism, and the aftermath of the 2008 financial crisis. This book only addresses the last of these, the legal aspects of what we could call the economic governance system of the European Union; however, of course this cannot and must not obscure the more general landscape in which European economic governance occurs, which is punctuated by all of these – and still other – challenges.

One of the striking things about Goya's painting, which I have contemplated so many times on my recurrent visits to El Prado, is the violence that it depicts. In a way, using this image as the front cover of this book makes us think of the past, present, and future of Europe.[1] The European past is formed by countries, such as Spain in the nineteenth century, that most likely confronted dilemmas similar to those that the EU must address today. The past comes, though, with a positive message in its hands, because European history tells us that these dilemmas, at least in part, were overcome with time. It is true that European history is written in blood, but precisely because of this fact, the European Union carries with it an optimistic lesson according to which even the most fractious stories can end well.

That being said, the future projects its dark shadow on this rather brilliant, but complex, past. Confrontation, clash, division, and conflict, even in the worst versions that these words might represent, might return in the future. The once "united in diversity" Europe could become a sordid place in which there is not one Europe but two (or even more) Europes, in which Member States distrust each other and the major source of distrust frequently comes

---

[1] See the excellent account of *Duel with Cudgels* by Foradada (2010).

from the EU's institutions. Goya's painting therefore represents a warning, signal of what our common future could become.

However, what about the present? Where are we precisely in this moment? We could draw a parallel here between history and economics; as economists teach us, one of the most difficult things to know is where a unit of analysis (a country, for example) is in the economic cycle. We know about the past, and we can more or less try to anticipate the future, but knowing where we are at exactly this moment is one of the trickiest questions in economics.

The same is true of Europe. We can read the past, and we can have a more or less objective representation of the European future. However, in this particularly convoluted moment in the European course of human events, the main problem is that we just do not know where we are.

This book will not be able to answer this question, of course. Providing such an answer is not its main purpose. It is, once again, mostly about the past (how things were, what did they tell us) and the future (how they should be, how they should be interpreted in a more correct, rational, and analytical way). The present is another matter. It is very difficult to grasp what the present is with respect to the legal aspects of European economic governance – first, because this is a reality, as shown in this book, that is very much in the making. The economic crisis that began in 2008 is far from over. Therefore, the responses to the new events that the aftermath of the crisis is bringing to us occur in real time. Trying to track these *just in time* changes is one of the purposes of this book. The second reason why it is difficult to currently fix a point in time with respect to the legal foundations of European economic governance is perhaps more compelling: indications exist that this might be more than just another economic and above all monetary crisis (grave as it might be, but nonetheless a crisis) and that we could be on the verge of a more profound change, of a real transformation of the economic model that Europe, the European Union, has known to date.

Considering both limitations that, as has been said before, bring us to reflect on our common history as Europeans, this book attempts to tell the reader, in the most clear and parsimonious way, what are the main legal tenets upon which the EU system of economic governance rests. To this end, Chapter 1 sets the method that will be used throughout this book. This method is what I call "analytical dialectics," which is no more (and no less) than a very particular way to proceed in legal reasoning through the use of opposites. Chapter 1 speaks about rationality. I still remain bewildered that legal academics very rarely make explicit the rational (or other) premises that they use when analyzing a given legal phenomenon. This book tries not to fall into the same trap and is very explicit about the rational foundations upon which it rests. Chapter 1 also speaks about trust, which is the main problem that law tries to solve; trust – or rather, the lack of it – is at the basis of the legal system.

Chapter 2 sets the particular understanding of law that I will use in the rest of the book to analyze specific aspects of what could be called the "law of

European economic governance." This understanding is what I usually refer to as "law as credibility." In this model, law is seen as a functional tool whose primary aim is to solve the trust problems that occur with the making of commitments. Credibility is a key issue in European economic governance, above all in monetary governance; therefore, law, understood as a practical way to solve credibility dilemmas, is especially apt to reflect on the legal foundations of European economic governance.

From Chapter 3 onwards, I leave the theoretical terrain of methods and models and delve into the specific material aspects of European economic governance. I start with the euro and address the problems of access to and exit and expulsion from the Eurozone. What I try to offer in this chapter is a novel vision – one that departs from conventional wisdom, or so it is hoped – of what have become some of the most acute problems of EU economic governance since the crisis exploded. Then, in Chapter 4, I discuss the European Central Bank (ECB) and its conduct of Eurozone monetary policy. I also try to give a new interpretation of how to solve the issue of credibility and monetary policy from a "law as credibility" perspective. In turn, Chapter 5 speaks to the (incomplete) European framework of financial regulation and supervision and the banking union. Chapters 6 and 7 address the Stability and Growth Pact before the 2008 crisis and as it has been reformed after the crisis. Here, again, the issue of credibility is crucial. In Chapters 8 and 9, I address one of the most important – and polemic – aspects of EU economic governance, namely EU financial bailouts. I explain why I believe that the current system is not an equilibrium from a "law as credibility" perspective. Finally, Chapter 10 attempts to fill a lacuna found in many legal texts that treat the juridical aspects of European economic governance, namely that they do not normally address European growth strategy. I believe this is a mistake. Any account of the specifics of the law of European economic governance must integrate this perspective to present a more complete picture of the topic.

More generally, the book has one main theme and one main purpose that tie all its different bits together. The main theme is that of credibility and the law. As explained in Chapter 2, most analysts equate credibility with rigidity. From this perspective, the most rigid norm (for example, the Constitution or the Treaties) would be the most credible one. However, the book shows specifically that this is not always true. In fact, the crucial aspect of credibility through law is not rigidity but that the norm represents an equilibrium point between two competing and dialectical aims: rigidity and flexibility. A credible norm is not (always) a rigid norm but a norm that finds its equilibrium point between rigidity and flexibility. Some legal arrangements in the EU system of economic governance reach that equilibrium point, whereas others do not.

The professed aim of this book is to bridge the gap that currently exists between two ongoing, but separate, conversations on the topic of European economic governance: the lawyers' and the economists' conversations. For the latter, credibility is a main concern with regard to the EU system of European economic governance; however, among lawyers, a discussion on credibility and trust is almost systematically absent in this field. Economists only occasionally explore law as an important driver for credibility, while lawyers usually see economic institutions as being of only secondary importance compared to legal commitments. My claim is that economists must integrate law into their credibility analyses of the European system of economic governance, whereas lawyers need to integrate the crucial discussion of credibility and trust when they address the legal institutions of European economic governance. This double link is attempted in this book.

This book was conceived at Oxford University, where I also started to write the first drafts of some of its chapters during a sabbatical year spent there in the academic year 2014–2015. I can think of no better place to undertake a project of this kind. I therefore dedicate this book to my subjective recollections of this important period of my life that I spent in England, and which changed my point of view in many different ways. The UK was then an established part of the European Union. As I write this book, the country is negotiating its exit from the Union. This is a development that I deeply regret. And it is another reason why this book is dedicated to my English memories, which come from a time when the UK was still a member of the EU.

The book was enriched through a number of talks that I gave on drafts of different chapters at the Seconda Università di Napoli; at Oxford University (European Studies Centre); at the University of Miami (Law School); at the Università del Sannio (Benevento); and at the Dublin City University. I want to thank the conveners of these seminars and talks for hosting me in their respective home universities and for giving me the opportunity to discuss different aspects of this book with other experts and academic colleagues.

To complete this preface, I would like to make particular reference to the following persons who were crucial in the making of this book in different capacities. First and foremost, I would like to thank Professor Paul de Grauwe not only for giving me advice on different aspects of the economic side of the European Union system of governance but also for being a lighthouse in the field of EU economic governance. Without his support, this book would probably not have seen the light of day. As usual, the following disclaimer applies: all errors and mistakes that the reader might find in the following belong only to me.

I also very warmly thank Jenny Dix, the administrator of the Institute of European and Comparative Law at Oxford, for her generosity in giving me wide access to the myriad resources of Oxford University during the making of this book, particularly during its last phases. I also want to thank the following individuals, who read different drafts of this book and took seriously the task of making comments on them: Kalypso Nicolaidis, Stephen Weatherill, Paul Craig, Federico Fabbrini, Joaquín Roy, Carmen Pérez-Llorca, Dorian Singh, Camilla Crea, Tanya Ni Mhuirthile, Sergio Cámara, Gerardo Caffera, Julio Guinea Bonillo, and, last but not least, Alessia Fachechi. Iñaki, Andrea and

Guillermo Estella have been, as always, the best support I could ever have for this enterprise. I am also grateful to Sylvia Fernández-Cuervo for her research assistance during the last phases of completion of this book. I also want to thank the commissioning editor of this series, Marta Walkowiak, and the content manager Catherine Smith, for their patient editing work. Finally, I would like to thank the academic editors of the series, Professors Twining, McCrudden, and Morgan, for their feedback on different drafts of this project. This book has received the generous financial support of research project DER2016–76986-P, whose director is Professor Julio González García, whom I also thank for his generosity.

BIBLIOGRAPHY

Foradada, C. 2010, "La observación recíproca. Nueva interpretación de 'Duelo a garrotazos'," *Artigrama*, vol. 25, pp. 123–142.

1

Analytical Dialectics, Rationality, and Trust

Introduction

"Credibility" is an important concept for European economic governance (EEG henceforth). In fact, it could even be argued that this concept is the crucial idea upon which the entire EEG edifice is built. The concept of credibility emerged and has been developed in the area of political economy. Although economists acknowledge the importance of law as a driver for credibility, they have not systematized or explored this connection in depth. In turn, lawyers only very rarely approach law from the perspective of credibility. To the best of my knowledge, there has not been any serious attempt to configure a legal theory of law as credibility. I will leave that discussion for the next chapter of this book. In this chapter, I will establish the ground – the infrastructure – on which the concept of credibility can be better understood.

To this end, I shall proceed as follows. Since the idea of law as credibility is based on a very particular method or approach to social sciences in general and to law in particular, I shall start by addressing that method in the first section of this chapter. I shall refer to this method or approach as "analytical dialectics." The idea of law as credibility is also based upon a particular model of rationality; this model will be presented in the second and third sections of this chapter. In the fourth section, I shall address the problem of trust in social interaction. This discussion will allow us to dive deeper, in Chapter 2 of this book, into the waters of the concept of law as credibility.

1.1 Analytical Dialectics

Let us start by saying a few words about the method that underlies this work. I call this method "analytical dialectics."[1] For clarity, I will treat its two components, the analytical part and the dialectical part, separately, and then I will establish a number of links between them.

---

[1] For an example of the application of this method in other areas of social sciences, see Medina (2014).

From a first, more superficial perspective, I use an analytical methodology in the sense that it tries to be as clear and as direct as possible. One of the best expressions of this idea is a statement by Eugene d'Ors (1941: 124): "between two explanations, choose the clearest one; between two expressions, choose the briefest." This advice primarily relates to language; the language that the reader will find in the following is (or tries to be) clear language. I believe that social sciences in general and law in particular would be better served if academics abandoned rhetoric and embraced clarity as their main guiding principle when expressing arguments. Rhetoric, occasionally in its obscurest form (Elster, 2011), which is so common in legal studies, is a way to make access to analysis and comprehension of arguments more difficult and is thus a path to legitimize other, nonscientific, purposes. Academics, particularly lawyers, should strive for clarity, not only to abandon medieval domination practices but also to create fine-grained arguments. To Albert Einstein is generally attributed the statement, "if you can't explain it simply, it is because you don't understand it well enough." Self-understanding of an argument is the first premise for scientific evolution in social sciences.

Clarity of language is not the opposite to complexity of argument. On the contrary, according to the analytical method, the only way to address complex arguments is to clarify the different strands of an argument as much as possible. Again, language has an important role here: to understand a complex argument, one must be able to express it in clear language. Complex arguments, expressed in the clearest possible way, are what the reader should find in the following pages.

Clarity also has to do with the number of variables employed to explain or understand a complex phenomenon ("the briefest" in d'Ors' terms). When two explanations lead to the same explanatory outcome, the one that includes fewer variables should be chosen. This principle is known as Occam's razor, or the *parsimonious* principle (Estella, 2005). In law, there are not variables but rather arguments. However, the same principle holds; arguments can be divided into subarguments or strands of arguments. Therefore, I should choose, all other things being equal, that argument that includes fewer strands but has the same explanatory or interpretative potential.

From a second, more profound, perspective, the analytical method implies using natural science methods. To understand exactly what I mean by this statement, I recommend reading Watson's *Double Helix* (1968) – the story of how the application of the scientific method led to a revolutionary discovery, the discovery of the structure of DNA. Thus, when a phenomenon can be measured, such measurement will be done in this book. However, I will not make extensive use of quantitative methods (statistical analysis, in particular), which implies a major qualification of what was said previously; the reason for this qualification is that social sciences are not natural sciences. I believe that this reality implies a very severe limitation on the extent to which we can use more sophisticated quantitative methods in the analysis of law and economics.

Some degree of scientific humility is due here. This point is made by Elster in his latest work (2009, 2011), and I believe that he is essentially correct. I therefore propose to use a "soft" scientific method that is essentially argumentative but that uses basic quantitative data to illustrate certain phenomena.

Third, this book uses what is referred to as "methodological individualism," which is based on the assumption (that is, on the fiction, as in legal fictions) that institutions can be reduced to the level of the individual. Therefore, the basic unit of analysis is the individual, and, more particularly, the individual's behavior. The point is to understand the "microfoundations," or mechanisms, of her conduct. From there, it is more plausible to construct hypotheses of the behavior of larger units, such as institutions, if adequate precautions are taken.

Mechanism is therefore another important concept from an analytical perspective. According to Elster, a mechanism is not a scientific law but rather a probability that takes the following form: "If C, then X, with probability P." Mechanisms are micro, in the sense that they allow explaining what a particular individual is doing. The following example, given by Krugman (2007), is illustrative of the idea of mechanism:

> Suppose that a flu epidemic breaks out, and later analysis suggests that appropriate action by the Centers for Disease Control could have contained the epidemic. It would be fair to blame government officials for failing to take appropriate action. But it would be quite a stretch to say that the government *caused* the epidemic, or to use the CDC's failure as a demonstration of the superiority of free markets over big government.

Mechanisms are, therefore, the concrete, direct, and specific causes that explain outcomes. Thus, once a mechanism has been identified, the analyst must attempt to understand the extent to which this mechanism is more generalizable. To use Elster's words, the point is then to pass from the "micro" level to the "macro" one. For that purpose, counterfactual thinking is an essential tool in the analytical method.

A counterfactual (Tetlock & Belkin, 1996) is a thought experiment that takes the following form: "What if instead of X, Y had occurred?" We do this type of experiment in normal life all the time. "If I had married John instead of Tom, I would be happier now." However, in analytical terms, a counterfactual has very strict and demanding rules. According to Elster (1985: 37), these are, at a minimum, internal consistency between the antecedent and the consequent and historical possibility. Concerning the first – internal consistency – the rules of logical reasoning are applicable. The second aspect (historical possibility) implies that the counterfactual story must be as close as possible to the factual one. If I argue that "America's Southern states would have experienced more economic growth without slavery before 1861," I must start reconstructing the counterfactual from the moment prior to the one slavery started to be generalized in America. This approach rules out worlds that do not exist (the type of reasoning that would be ruled out here would be, "If we were living on Mars, bailouts would not have occurred," because living on Mars is not a historical possibility, at least currently). Finally, it is also important to keep in mind that counterfactuals are neither true nor false but rather assertible or nonassertible.[2]

Counterfactuals play, as shown later in this book, a crucial role in the "law as credibility" theory. Suffice it to say at this point that the role of counterfactuals is the proposed test to try to understand whether a norm is an equilibrium from the perspective of this legal theory. To be sure, the necessary adaptations must be done from counterfactuals in the world of social sciences to counterfactuals in a world that has its particular characteristics, as in law. However, I leave this discussion for Chapter 2.

Second, concerning dialectics, this book proposes a particular method of thinking that is based on considering the concepts or notions or terms in opposition to those that we are trying to explain. The use of counterfactual analysis is, from my point of view, a very good illustration of the dialectical method; if to understand a norm we consider only the opposite state of affairs to that which the norm is in fact considering, we are then thinking in dialectical terms. However, there are more examples of this type. For example, as will be shown in Chapter 8, to understand the concept of bailouts, the best intellectual strategy is to consider bail-ins, which are the opposite of bailouts. Later in this chapter, we will discuss how to understand the concept of trust; it is important to compare it with the notion of distrust. The idea behind this intellectual strategy is that by opposing contradictory concepts, or notions, we can upgrade our level of understanding of complex phenomena and climb further steps all the way up the so-called "intellectual ladder" until we believe that we reach a clear understanding of a particular phenomenon. The analytical approach and the dialectical one need not be in contradiction; rather, the opposite is true. As noted by Van Parijs (1994: 1),

> Marx is often interpreted as having used a "dialectical" mode of thought which he took over, with modifications, from Hegel and which can be contrasted with conventional, "analytical" thinking. Marx himself may have said and thought so. But according to analytical Marxists, one can make sense of his work, or at least of the main or best part of it, while complying with the strictest standards of analytical thought. This need not mean that all of what is usually called "dialectics" should be abruptly dismissed. For example, the study of the typically "dialectic" contradictions which drive historical change constitutes a challenging area for the subtle use of analytical thought.[3]

---

[2] According to the Merriam-Webster dictionary, assertible means, "Capable of being asserted or affirmed: non-contradictory."

[3] This idea is further explored in Elster (1978).

1.2 Rationality

The basic unit of analysis of rational choice (henceforth RC) is the individual, the human being. For the RC tradition, this individual has, or possesses, certain "traits" that make her distinctive from other animal species, the most important of which is her rationality. Individuals are humans because they are rational. Other animals are not humans because they lack this characteristic. This trait is, in other words, what makes a human a singular being.[4]

The problem starts right after the previous point is made. Granted, humans are singular and therefore distinct from other animals because they are rational. However, what is to be understood by rationality? There is a very wide discussion about what rationality really is and what we mean by it, both within and without the RC domain. My purpose in the following is not to reproduce this discussion but rather to take a particular stance in that discussion and at the same time warn the reader that other authors might hold different paradigms of rationality; what is presented here is but a version, or a particular understanding, of rationality.

In neoclassical economics, the individual is rational in, at the very least, two senses: (1) in the sense that she is self-interested; and (2) in the sense that she maximizes her utility function (in other words, she implements the strategies that are best suited to fulfill her preferences). Let us examine a very simple and classical example. An individual has a preference for chocolate ice creams, then for vanilla ice creams and then, in the third place, for banana ice creams. She only has €1, and chocolate ice creams cost €2, whereas the other two each cost €1. For her, the rational thing to do would be to use her euro to buy a vanilla ice cream, or failing this, a banana ice cream. If she used her euro to buy a banana ice cream as a first choice, then her action would be inconsistent with her preferences, and therefore irrational. She should use the means at her disposal to serve her self-interest the best she can, which in this case would amount to buying the vanilla ice cream.

Despite its elegance, the neoclassical model of rationality will not be the model that will be followed in this book, primarily because it is rather unrealistic. It assumes, at the very least, that individuals have perfect and complete information, that individuals are perfectly rational in the making of their preferences, that individuals always contemplate all strategies to maximize their utility, and that they are driven by self-interest in the narrow sense of this word (see my reflections on this point later on). All of these aspects are very difficult to maintain in real-life situations. Such real-life situations are precisely characterized by a lack of complete and perfect information (even in what can

---

[4] This discussion is much wider and in-depth than can be reproduced here. For example, Bentham (1996 [1789]) argued that the main divide between humans and nonhuman species could not be made based on reason but should rather be based on their capacity to suffer, which they both share. See also Singer (1990, and 1993). In my opinion, suffering involves a certain type of "automatic rationality"; for example, plants do not have it, as far as we can tell.

appear the most simple of situations), by the difficulty that human beings have in building up (and keeping) a consistent set of preferences, or utility function, by the incapacity of human beings to devise all possible strategies to maximize their preferences, and by the complex mix of motivations that drive human behavior. For example, laboratory experiments have shown that human beings tend to be more altruistic than the standard, rational choice, game-theoretical models would imply. Cameron (1999) thus reports that experiments on the so-called "ultimatum game" tend to contradict the outcome predicted by game theory; people are therefore more "just" when they divide a pie than the models tell.[5] In my opinion, this and other observations should not cause us to dismiss RC as a valid approach to the understanding of human interactions but should rather compel us to adopt more realistic and refined paradigms of rationality. They also must lead us to understand the limits of this approach; I very much doubt that it has predictive potential, but it does have a certain explanatory role. In the words of Krugman (2007),

> For most of the past two centuries, economic thinking has been dominated by the concept of *Homo economicus*. The hypothetical Economic Man knows what he wants; his preferences can be expressed mathematically in terms of a "utility function." And his choices are driven by rational calculations about how to maximize that function: whether consumers are deciding between corn flakes or shredded wheat, or investors are deciding between stocks and bonds, those decisions are assumed to be based on comparisons of the "marginal utility," or the added benefit the buyer would get from acquiring a small amount of the alternatives available.
>
> It's easy to make fun of this story. Nobody, not even Nobel-winning economists, really makes decisions that way. But most economists – myself included – nonetheless find Economic Man useful, with the understanding that he's an idealized representation of what we really think is going on. People do have preferences, even if those preferences can't really be expressed by a precise utility function; they usually make sensible decisions, even if they don't literally maximize utility. You might ask, why not represent people the way they really are? The answer is that abstraction, strategic simplification, is the only way we can impose some intellectual order on the complexity of economic life. And the assumption of rational behavior has been a particularly fruitful simplification.

In particular, the paradigm of rationality adopted here has the following strands. First, it assumes that individuals are self-interested. However, the concept of self-interestedness that best complies with reality is, from my point

---

[5] In the ultimatum game, there are two players: the dictator and the citizen. The dictator can allocate resources to the citizen however she pleases; in turn, the citizen can only accept or reject the dictator's proposal. Game theory predicts that the dictator will allocate €100 in the following way: she will keep approximately €99 for herself and give the citizen €1. This outcome is contradicted by laboratory experiments. In general, the dictator tends to be much fairer; "there are many 50:50 splits and there are frequent rejections of small offers," Cameron (1999: 48) reports.

of view, one that integrates things such as altruism and even certain aspects of disinterestedness. To make the point clearer, one might want to distinguish between self-interest and sheer egoism. An egoist is someone who would never do anything for other people unless there was a clear and tangible payoff for her. By contrast, a self-interested person is someone who can do things for others, even in a disinterested way, to the extent that she obtains in exchange an abstract sensation of internal approval. Only completely disinterested actions would fall outside this model and therefore would be irrational. For example, in my opinion, it is very difficult to understand actions such as Mandela's recurrent refusals to leave Robben Island and in general his twenty-seven years of imprisonment were it not that his self-esteem increased due to his altruistic behavior. This point is, of course, very difficult to prove, but in his book *Long Walk to Freedom* (Mandela, 1994), it transpires that he experienced such an emotion (the emotion of increased self-esteem as the time in prison went by) when he says that this period of his life "made him stronger."

Therefore, the model of rationality that I uphold here does not aim to explain everything. Occasionally human beings do act in very irrational ways. For example, as Elster (2006) states, the behavior of suicide-mission killers, which is not explained by the promise of a better life in heaven or by, more concretely, the promise of a better life for the suicide's relatives but only by "patriotism," can only be ascribed to irrationality. Here, the neoclassical school's "reduction urge," by way of which everything is explained out of egoism (implicating that the suicide would experience a "warm glow" sensation the second before she kills herself), is most likely absurd and in any case quite impossible to validate empirically for obvious reasons.

A second important strand in the model of rationality that I will use here is that rationality is bound. Human rationality is bound both in the sense that the capacity of human beings to construe their utility function is limited and in the sense that their capacity to devise strategies to maximize (or to satisfy, as shown later) their preferences is also limited. To start with, the capacity of human beings to build up their utility function is limited by one crucial exogenous factor, which is information. Information is imperfect and incomplete, at least in the majority of cases. Therefore, in my opinion, it is very difficult to think of a 100 percent endogenous preference. All of our preferences are related, in one way or another, directly or indirectly, to some strand of information. In other words, one cannot "invent" new preferences completely out of the blue.

Therefore, with the limited amount of information we have at our disposal, we humans attempt to build up our utility function. In turn, the capacity to gather and process more or less information is determined, or at least severely conditioned, by both internal and external factors. With respect to the latter, it clearly is not the same to live in New York as to live in a secluded part of the world, for example. Concerning the former, it is also clear that not all human beings have the same physiological and psychological capabilities to gather and, above all, process information (Hastie & Dawes, 2010). A number of examples will suffice to drive home the point of what otherwise appears a rather abstract discussion. Imagine for a second a tribe living in a secluded place of the world that did not know about chocolate. In fact, a YouTube video that has gone viral[6] shows how cocoa-bean collectors from M'batto, Ivory Coast, do not know what the final result of what they are collecting is – which is chocolate bars. The video shows a journalist making them taste chocolate bars. The collectors are surprised because not only did they not know what the final product of their collection was but also they like chocolate – a product and a taste that they did not know before. This case would be of the first sort (lack of external information to build up your utility function). If the inhabitants of M'batto had known about chocolate, they would most likely have included it in their utility function. A more metaphysical example can also be given. If we knew for sure of the existence of an "afterlife" – and not as a product of our beliefs – many of the preferences that we have in this life clearly would change.

An example of the second type (internal factors that impede gathering or processing information) would be a case in which one of the M'batto inhabitants suffered from "ageusia" (the lack of the sense of taste). In this case, she would not be able to integrate chocolate into her utility function due not to an external lack of information but rather due to an internal incapacitating state of affairs.

A crucial part of the internal factors that affect the human capabilities to gather and process information is beliefs. I include here, not to further complicate things, a very wide definition of beliefs, which also includes biases. In my opinion, the best way to understand beliefs is by saying that they are what mediate between the individual and the gathering and processing of information. Beliefs are an internal mechanism through which individuals trump information up. I will provide a number of examples to drive the point home. Imagine once again our inhabitant in M'batto. This inhabitant is different from the one who had "ageusia"; therefore, she is perfectly capable of "tasting." However, she believes that if she eats this new product (chocolate), she will die. Therefore, she refuses to try it. Had she not refused, she would most likely have liked it and therefore would have integrated it into her utility function. However, she will not – only because she firmly believes in the fatal effects of eating chocolate.

From a different perspective, an excellent metaphor of the role of beliefs in rationality is employed by the John Carpenter movie *They Live* (1988). The plot is rather simple: an alienated drifter by the name of John Nada (John Nothing) discovers a pair of sunglasses that, when donned, allow him to see

---

[6] See www.wimp.com/cocoafarmers.

reality. For example, he examines a city advertisement of a woman suntanning in a hip holiday resort, but when he dons the glasses, he sees instead the following word: "procreate." In the film, the sunglasses have a type of reverse function to the one for which the metaphor of sunglasses is normally used. In fact, the sunglasses allow the blocking of our beliefs and the viewing of reality as it really is. Without the sunglasses, our beliefs would be that which mediates between us and the real world.

Concerning beliefs, there are two more points I wish to make here. The first is that I leave out of this discussion the question of why we have the beliefs (in the wide sense of the word "beliefs" I am using here) that we have. This question is likely one of the most fascinating in the overall discussion of rationality. Suffice it to say here that there are a number of answers to it: our context, the place we were born, the education we had when children, the people we met, the experiences we had – they all help to shape our beliefs. An important point is that, in my opinion, most of our beliefs are determined, not chosen. Only very marginally can we change the core of the beliefs we have. Education, of course, plays a role here, however, again, only a marginal one. As I said, beliefs are exogenous; they are a given, not chosen.

The second important thing to be said at this point is that it is crucial to differentiate between beliefs and emotions or passions. Beliefs are not passions. Beliefs are one of the internal mechanisms through which we human beings shape the gathering and processing of information. Emotions, or passions, are one of the motives for our actions (the other two being reason and self-interest, understood in a sense that I will explain in a later section). However, at this point, differentiating these two notions (beliefs and emotions) suffices.

I also said previously that human beings' rationality is bound in the sense of their capacity to devise all possible strategies to attain particular aims or preferences. Strategies are determined by information shortages. Furthermore, individuals are not so superhumanly clever as to think of all possible strategies that would best serve their purposes. Perhaps if what is referred to by natural scientists and anthropologists (and also by science fiction novelists) as the *Homo singularis* (an evolutionary step of the human being – or, rather, a quantum leap – because of the fusion of human and artificial intelligence) occurred, we would acquire that extra-human capacity to think of all possible options to attain our aims. However, until then, we must accept our limited capacity to think about alternatives. A further point in this sense is that even were the *Homo singularis* already here, many of the strategies we could think of would be out of scope, for example, for technological reasons. If I had a passion to visit the moon, then the best thing I could do would be to wait until the technology to make faster and cheaper trips to the moon is developed. This wait might be for ages, in fact longer than my lifetime. Therefore, I must either change my preference or accept that I will never be able to visit the moon. In any case, this example would be not of an inability to build up a utility function (I have a passion, and I cannot help it) but rather of a lack of available strategies to fulfill it.

A third point, which is connected with the previous one, is associated with the idea of maximizing. Maximizing one's preferences means that I will use the best available strategy to attain my first preference, then my second choice, and so on, as with the example of ice creams.[7] However, in laboratory experiments, individuals are generally rather accommodating. They do not strive for their first preference – chocolate ice cream; they are content if they obtain any ice cream that belongs to their utility function. Therefore and in this case, we should speak, as for example Philip Pettit (1996) does, more of "satisficing" than of "maximizing." In other words, I will assume that individuals do not make the optimum decision, but more often than not they accommodate to "good enough" decisions. If we connect point two, above, and this last point, the following seems to be true: people have more or less clear preferences, and they do more or less what it takes to attain them. However, in the majority of cases at least, it would be rather unrealistic to say that people have clear and robust preferences and that they always implement the best strategies they have at their disposal to attain them. This statement simply is not true in close-to-real-life situations.

There are of course exceptions to the above. For example, when making very important decisions, either personal or professional, people *tend to be* as rational as they can. Therefore, a division as a function of the "nature" or "importance" of the decision emerges here. If decisions are dramatically important, people *tend* more to the "hard" sense of rationality that, for example, the neoclassical school defends. If decisions are trivial ones, people tend to "softer" models of rationality. One could even take the argument a step further and say, as Damasio (2006) has proven, that there are many human decisions that are not only trivial but also automatic and that therefore the model of rationality here is even softer. The main reason for this softness is that being rational is not effortless; it requires a great deal of energy. Note, however, that the accent must be placed on the italicized words above. To "tend" to a harder or softer model of rationality is not the same as to openly embrace one or the other. Therefore, even with this qualification that I am making, my own approach to rationality is in reality very distanced from what the neoclassical school would accept as valid.

This point is an important one. All rationality models assume a "one-fits-all" model of individual rationality. People are either "maximizers" or "satisficers." They always go either for the optimum or for the "good enough" outcomes. They hold either a robust model of rationality or only a soft one. However, it might well be true that it all entirely depends upon the nature of the decisions that are to be made, as we said previously. Other things being

---

[7] I leave aside for the moment the discussion on whether utility increases or decreases marginally.

equal, people will be more or less rational depending upon the decision they must make. Therefore, the model I defend here is not a constant model of rationality but rather a variable or flexible one. In the same way that it is difficult to say that individuals only have one permanent and invariable personality or character, I believe it is difficult to maintain that they only have one type of rationality all of the time. Because there are, at least in many cases, a number of persons in one person, there are also several rationalities in the same individual's reason.

1.3 Motives behind Our Actions: Reason, Passion, Interest

Human beings undertake actions out of specific motives. We could say that motivation is the juice that moves individuals to act. Without motives, human beings would not act, and they would ultimately die. Therefore, it is very important to understand human beings' motivations.

In standard rational choice, there are three main motivations: reason, passion, and interest. However, not everyone understands these in exactly the same way, so for understanding and defining each of them, I will follow Jon Elster hereafter. For him, reason is understood in two senses: as a general way to refer to the motives behind an action and in the more particular sense of "common good" or "common interest" as a specific type of motive. Common interest or common good should be differentiated from altruism. Altruism implies doing things for others, whereas common interest implies doing things for a group in which the agent is included. Therefore, common interest does not necessarily imply altruism, although it occasionally might. In any case, we observed in the previous section that altruism can also be explained in a self-interested way: altruistic actions are self-interested if they generate a vague feeling of increase in the agent's self-esteem. Actions motivated by reasons that are completely disinterested, that is, that do not even produce this vague sense of self-esteem increase (for example, because they produce the reverse feeling), fall outside the model of rationality that is upheld here and therefore can be deemed irrational.

Passion is the second type of motivation behind human beings' actions. Passion is, in my opinion, equivalent to emotions. Elster has systematized in a very complete way the study of human emotions, what they are, and how they interact with human behavior. I therefore refer the reader to his analysis on emotions (Elster, 1999). Suffice it to say here that we are talking about emotions such as love, hatred, envy, guilt, and shame. Elster includes addictions in emotions; however, from my perspective, addictions have a very different nature from the other types of emotion I mentioned a moment ago. Addictions imply the intake of an external, material, substance (be it for example alcohol or heroin), which the others do not. In other words, in my opinion, the behavior of an addict implies a different model of rationality (or if one prefers, of behavior) than does that of a person who is not under the influence of a particular substance. To cut a long story short, I want simply to say at this point that we should distinguish in this context between two different modes of behavior: the passionate one (as a particular way of irrational action) and the addicted one.

The individual who acts under the influence of her emotions, or passions, is not always an irrational individual. This misunderstanding is a common one that must be clarified from the outset. In fact, many rational behaviors can be explained by passion; it can even be said that, under certain conditions, passion is the major driver for rational action. An example could be the lover who is completely carried away by his love for another person but who can still devise and implement very cold strategies to gain her attention. Literature provides very good examples of this behavior. In *Les liaisons dangereuses*, Laclos (2008 [1782]) describes in all sorts of detail what apparently is a domination game between two partners (the Marquise de Merteuil and the Viscount of Valmont) but that in reality hides unbridled love. The Marquise feels passionate love for the Viscount, her old lover; however, she cannot say so because she not only is a woman in an eighteenth-century society but also knows that if she revealed her passion, then she would lose the Viscount. It is very possible to believe that, in reality, the Viscount is also infatuated with the Marquise, although he also coldly hides his passion for her to avoid staining his Don Juan reputation. Thus, passion functions as does any other rational motivation, if and only if the individual experiencing such feeling remains able to devise and implement rational strategies to attain the object of her passion. Only individuals incapable of doing that, completely dominated by their passions in a way that would make them lose even the object of their strong feelings, would be acting in an irrational way.

Interest, or self-interest, is the basic motivation in a rational choice setting, even in a setting such as this one, which has many qualifications and nuances. At the end of the day, there is always a connection, be it indirect or otherwise, between the other two motivations and self-interest. The basic assumption is that human beings always undertake actions out of self-interest: if not, they cannot be deemed rational from a technical perspective.[8] However, as has already been said, self-interest is understood here in a different sense from sheer egoism. A vague feeling of "warm glow," as Elster states, can be sufficient to explain self-interested actions without the need to seek more-robust explanations that incorporate more-tangible payoffs for the agent. Only actions that fall outside self-interestedness, even in the vague sense that I previously mentioned, could be deemed irrational.

Two points are important when talking about self-interest. The first is that if, as stated previously, "there is always a connection, be it indirect or

---

[8] Speaking about this connection, Elster says, for instance, that the link between emotions and reason or rationality is "enthusiasm." See his intervention at www.youtube.com/watch?v=aBfrWUXI9ns.

otherwise, between the other two motivations and self-interest," we could ask ourselves why then do we need passion and reason as motivators of rational behavior. If at the end of the day everything is explained by self-interest (since we have given a very wide and ample definition of self-interest), is reason or passion necessary at all to explain human behavior? The question is legitimate; however, the answer is positive. Yes, we do need reason and passion to make a more complete and complex picture of human rational behavior. In other words, if we reduced everything to self-interest, then we would lose part of the explanation behind an agent's action. At the same time, it is particularly important, when trying to account for human action, to specify the concrete mechanism that connects the other two motivations (reason and passion) with self-interest. This connection is precisely what can round out explanations, that is, make explanations of human behavior more plausible and realistic.

The second point to be made is that the expression "irrational action or behavior" is not a moral category. Irrational is often made equivalent to something "bad," morally or ethically speaking. However, the approach adopted in this book is meta-ethical; to say that a human action is irrational is not to say, at least in the sense I am using this term in this book, that it is morally reprehensible.

1.4 Trust and Distrust

Trust is the cement of society, both in an interpersonal sense and in a social and political sense.[9] In other words, those interpersonal relationships or societies in which distrust is pervasive do collapse. By contrast, relationships and societies in which trust abounds do progress. To understand the importance of trust in both interpersonal relationships and social or political relations, it is key to think about its opposite, distrust. This point is a very good example of how the approach taken in this book, analytical dialectics, works in practice. Thus, we can define trust as the absence of distrust. More specifically, trust would be the belief held by an agent that individual I would undertake action A. Distrust would therefore be the opposite belief, that is, the belief that individual I will not do action A (or, if we want to employ positive terms, that individual I will do action B, which is the opposite of action A).

Therefore, trust and distrust are in a continuum, from 0 (distrust, or total lack of trust) to 1 (trust, or total lack of distrust). If viewed from this perspective, we then understand that we must qualify our previous understanding of trust "simply" as a belief. Thus, if a person were placed at 1 and had total trust in another person, we would talk of "blind trust." Conversely, if a person is placed at 0, then we can say that she has total distrust in another individual. In

---

[9] Elster calls it "the lubricant of society" (Elster, 2007: 344), and Stiglitz calls it a "kind of glue that makes society function" (www.sciencespo.fr/en/news/news/joseph-stiglitz-importance-trust-economics/2232).

my opinion, blind trust and total distrust are closer to emotions than to beliefs. We said in a previous section that beliefs were what mediated between information and us. Through beliefs, we gather and process the limited information we have. However, when we experience either blind trust or total distrust in a person, it is difficult to say that we have a "belief" in that person's trustworthiness. Thus, for example, we want to believe in that person, but we experience, for reasons we cannot perhaps explain or even understand, a feeling of complete and total distrust. The other way around also works. For reasons we cannot understand, we can experience a feeling of blind trust in a particular person. The general point I want to make is that to characterize trust or distrust as only a belief can be misleading. At their respective extremes, blind trust and total distrust can be better grasped as "feelings" rather than as beliefs (the feeling of blind trust in a person can be better understood as closer to the emotion of passionate love, for example). Only when we experience more trust than distrust, or more distrust than trust, but not blind trust or total distrust, can we say that we are in the domain of beliefs. Precisely the interesting thing about trust and distrust is that they represent an element that is at the fringes between beliefs and emotions.

A second point to be made is that it is not necessary to choose between Hobbes and Rousseau to view in general and in epistemological terms the issue of trust. We observe societies that have a great deal of both interpersonal and political trust and societies that have a great deal of interpersonal and political distrust. For example, according to the Organization for Economic Cooperation and Development (OECD) *Society at a glance* report of 2011,[10] the citizens of Nordic countries tend to trust each other more than do citizens in southern countries (with some exceptions: Spain appears to be quite a trusting society and is in fact located, in the OECD survey, well above the mean of OECD countries – ahead of France, for example). Furthermore, interpersonal trust appears to be correlated to political trust; therefore, in those countries in which citizens trust each other more, citizens also trust in their institutions more (with exceptions such as, once again, Spain, which ranks low in terms of political trust).[11] Even in the same polity, trust can be

---

[10] Available at www.oecd-ilibrary.org/sites/soc_glance-2011-en/08/01/index.html?itemId=/content/chapter/soc_glance-2011-26-en&_csp_=7d6a863ad60f09c08a8e2c78701e4faf.

[11] Jonathan Jackson, Mike Hough, Ben Bradford, Tia Pooler, Katrin Hohl, & Jouni Kuha, "Trust in Justice: Topline Results from Round 5," available at www.europeansocialsurvey.org/essresources/findings.html. Spaniards award low scores to the Spanish judicial system (3.1) and political system (1.9), and relatively low ones to the police (5.4). Values range from 0 (no trust) to 10 (total trust). Economic determinants might not explain this disgruntlement with Spanish institutions since, in the same survey, Spaniards show a higher level of satisfaction with the economic situation (5.8), even in the aftermath of the economic crisis. Concerning trust in people, the mean value is 6.3. See Instituto Nacional de Estadística, "Encuesta de Condiciones de Vida 2013. Módulo de Bienestar," available at www.ine.es/dyngs/INEbase/es/operacion.htm?c=Estadistica_C&cid=1254736176807&menu=resultados&secc=1254736194824&idp=1254735976608.

observed in some parts of it and distrust in others, as occurs, according to Gambetta's analysis of the Mafia (Gambetta, 1988), in southern Italy. Perhaps the story behind the whole problem of trust is initially closer to Hobbes[12] (societies in a state of nature experience a great deal of distrust, thereby giving rise to institutions to overcome this problem), and then, in a second step, to Rousseau[13] (once institutions are created, societies come to distrust them). Nevertheless, what is clear is that institutions are created (principally, as shown later) to overcome problems of trust; at the same time, however, their very creation generates novel problems of trust concerning the same institutions that were created to overcome social and political problems of trust.

When we talk about trust and distrust, we must differentiate among a different set of questions. First is the trustor's perspective. Second is the trustee's perspective. Third are the reasons behind trusting and being the recipient of trust from another person. First is the trustor. The trustor is someone who trusts that I will do A. She can trust me for a variety of reasons; however, they all are associated, directly or indirectly, with her self-interest. The trustor trusts because it is in her interest to trust. Again, this interest can be very tangible (I trust my brother that he will lend me €1,000) or more indeterminate (I trust that my brother would "help me" if I needed it). In the second case, we could talk about trust as a potential but not an actual behavior from my brother that, however, creates in the trustor a "warm glow" feeling. In other terms, if trust hurt us, we would not trust. The exception would be blind trust. Blindly trusting someone can hurt us. We do not want to trust but, for whatever reason, for example because we are in love, we do it, even when we know that that blindness does have negative payoffs for us, even in an emotional sense; I cannot escape from blindly trusting anyone, although my rational side tells me that I should most likely not do so. The same goes for total distrust. Both blind trust and total distrust are very close to passionate emotional states, as I argued before. However, beyond these two extremes, we trust out of self-interest because it makes us feel good, at a minimum. In other words, we must trust (someone, at least) to survive (Revuelta, 2005).

Second is the trustee. To be trusted is, once again, to be connected to self-interest. We like to be trusted because, at a minimum, being trusted increases our self-esteem. Someone telling me that she trusts me makes me feel good. Someone telling me that she distrusts me instead makes me feel bad. We want

---

[12] "Hereby it is manifest, that during the time men live without a common power to keep them all in awe, they are in that condition which is called war; and such a war, as is of every man, against every man" (Hobbes, 1998 [1651]).

[13] "It therefore appears to me incontestably true that not only did governments not begin by arbitrary power, which is but the corruption and extreme term of government and at length brings it back to the law of the strongest, against which governments were at first the remedy, but even that, allowing they had commenced in this manner, such power being illegal in itself could never have served as a foundation to the rights of society nor of course to the inequality of institution" (Rousseau, 2005).

to be the object of others' trust because trust is a self-esteem enhancer. Furthermore, when we are trusted, we can obtain more-concrete, material payoffs. For example, because I am trusted, the trustor might offer me a very good business that will make me rich. In summary, it is in our interest to be trusted, to generate the belief in others that we can be trusted. Only sociopaths (people with very low or nonexistent levels of empathy) would be immune to such things as trust.

Different from having the trustee being the recipient of trust is what the trustee does with that "capital." She might or might not use it as the trustor expects. In other words, she might or might not cooperate with the trustor. Thus, it is important to differentiate "trust" from "cooperation." Trust is the basis (the most important one) for cooperation. I am not saying that it is the *sine qua non* (cooperation can stem from sheer interest), but it rather facilitates cooperation. The opposite occurs with distrust. It complicates cooperation, but it is not the *sine qua non* for noncoordinated action. In any case, it is important to differentiate between a trustee's actions that are observable and those that are not. For example, he might trust that his wife will not cheat on him. However, she does, but she is so discreet that he never knows and keeps trusting her. In contrast, if I trust that you will donate to my campaign to save the earth from climate change, and you do not, this behavior is observable. It will be difficult to maintain trust in you when your observable behavior was not the one that I, the trustor, expected. Therefore, trust and cooperation are different concepts, but here again there is a problem of information concerning the extent to which cooperation is observable.

In turn, observable cooperation, or the lack of it, engenders trust or distrust. Therefore, trust facilitates cooperation, but cooperation, when it is observed, reinforces trust, and so on and so forth. Observable noncooperation engenders distrust, and so on and so forth. Therefore, the observation of cooperation is crucial in this setting. On many occasions, such an observation will be easy to obtain. In others, it will not. Thus, credibility is a key issue, above all, when the observation of cooperation is difficult or impossible to obtain. We can say in general terms that the more difficult this observation is, the more important the use of credibility technologies becomes. But this discussion is left for the ensuing chapter.

BIBLIOGRAPHY

Bentham, J. 1996 [1789], *An Introduction to the Principles of Morals and Legislation*, Clarendon Press, Oxford.

Cameron, L. 1999, "Raising the stakes in the ultimatum game: experimental evidence from Indonesia," *Economic Inquiry*, vol. 37, no. 1, pp. 47–59.

Damasio, A. 2006, *Descartes' Error: Emotion, Reason and the Human Brain*, Vintage, London.

d'Ors, E. 1941, *Gnómica*, Colección Euro, Madrid.

Elster, J. 2011, "Hard and soft obscurantism in the humanities and social sciences," *Diogenes*, vol. **58**, no. 1–2, pp. 159–170.

2009b, "Excessive ambitions," *Capitalism and Society*, vol. **4**, no. 2, pp. 1–30.

2009a, *Reason and Rationality*, Princeton University Press, Princeton, N.J.

2007, *Explaining Social Behavior: More Nuts and Bolts for the Social Sciences*, Cambridge University Press, New York.

2006, "Motivations and beliefs in suicide missions" in *Making Sense of Suicide Missions*, ed. D. Gambetta, Oxford University Press, Oxford.

1999, *Strong Feelings: Emotion, Addiction, and Human Behavior*, MIT Press, Cambridge, Mass. & London.

1985, *Making Sense of Marx*, Cambridge University Press, Cambridge.

1978, *Logic and Society: Contradictions and Possible Worlds*, Wiley & Sons, Chichester & London.

Estella, A. 2005, "La navaja de Occam y la complejidad en el derecho," *Claves de Razón Práctica*, vol. **155**, pp. 26–33.

Gambetta, D. 1988, *Trust: Making and Breaking Cooperative Relations*, Basil Blackwell, Oxford & Cambridge, Mass.

Hastie, R. & Dawes, R. 2010, *Rational Choice in an Uncertain World. The Psychology of Judgment and Decision Making*, Sage Publishing, Thousand Oaks, Calif.

Hobbes, T. 1998 [1651], *Leviathan*, Oxford University Press, Oxford.

Krugman, P. 2007, "Who was Milton Friedman?," *The New York Review of Books*, February 15.

Laclos, P. Choderlos de. 2008 [1782], *Les Liaisons dangereuses*, trans. Douglas Parmée, intro. David Coward, Oxford University Press, Oxford.

Mandela, N. 1994, *Long Walk to Freedom*, Abacus,, London.

Medina, L. F. 2014, "Red Phoenix: Notes for the Resurgence of Socialism," unpublished draft.

Pettit, P. 1996, *The Common Mind: An Essay on Psychology, Society and Politics*, Oxford University Press, New York.

Revuelta, P. 2005, "Una cuestión de confianza," *Sociedad y Utopía. Revista de Ciencias Sociales*, vol. **25**, pp. 407–413.

Rousseau, J. J. 2005 [1761], *A Discourse upon the Origin and Foundation of the Inequality among Mankind [electronic resource]*, Thomson Gale, Farmington Hills, Mich.

Singer, P. 2011, *Practical Ethics*, 3rd edn., Cambridge University Press, New York.

1995, *Animal Liberation*, 2nd edn., Pimlico, London.

Stern, R. 2013, *The Routledge Guidebook to Hegel's Phenomenology of Spirit*, Routledge, London & New York.

Tetlock, P. & Belkin, A. 1996, "Counterfactual thought experiments in world politics: logical, methodological and psychological perspectives" in *Counterfactual Thought Experiments in World Politics. Logical, Methodological and Psychological Perspectives*, eds. P. Tetlock & A. Belkin, Princeton University Press, Princeton, N.J., pp. 1–38.

Van Parijs, P. 1994, "Analytical Marxism," unpublished draft.

Watson, J. D. 1968, *The Double Helix. A Personal Account of the Discovery of the Structure of DNA*, Touchstone, New York.

2

Law as Credibility: Basic Traits

Introduction

In this chapter, I propose that law can be better understood and indeed conceptualized in terms of credibility. As noted in Chapter 1, the problems of trust and credibility are a key question with regard to the legal foundations of the European economic governance system. The idea of institutional credibility emerged in the field of political economy, but law played only a minor role in this discussion (Schelling, 1956; Elster, 1984 and 2000). For their part, lawyers have only very occasionally considered law from the perspective of credibility.[1] The point is that the idea of law as credibility is under-systematized. However, to better engage with the following chapters of this book, it is crucial to understand law in terms of credibility. In fact, what follows is but an application of this conceptual structure – law as credibility – to the EU economic governance system. In turn, the issue of credibility and the law can only be understood if approached from a rational setting, like the one that we have established in Chapter 1. To this end, to understand the basic traits of the model of law as credibility, I will proceed as follows. In the next section, I will define a number of concepts that are key to understanding the idea of law as credibility. In the second section, I will examine in more depth the idea of law as a credibility institutional technology. In the third section, I will address the notion of equilibrium in the "law as credibility" paradigm. In the fourth section, I will address a number of legal puzzles and how the concept of law as credibility and equilibrium attempts to solve them. Finally, I will devote the fifth section to the question of the conditions (both in terms of democracy and in terms of the courts) that must be fulfilled to sustain the concept of law as credibility and to the problem of legal reasoning and counterfactual analysis.

---

[1] See however vol. 81, issue 7 (June) of the *Texas Law Review*, which was entirely devoted to the issue of law and credibility, mostly from a legal perspective.

2.1 Concepts

Law is a commitment institutional technology; indeed, it can be viewed as the most sophisticated commitment institutional technology that human beings have created thus far. In its simplest sense, a commitment is a promise that is made by one actor to do or not to do something in particular. We – human beings – make commitments all the time. Joe commits himself to being truthful to his best friend for the rest of his life, or Jacqueline commits herself to not eating candies from tomorrow morning onwards. Both undertakings are commitments. Both of them are promises that the respective individuals make to themselves. However, the nature of the commitment is very different in each case. In the first case, the promise that Joe makes to himself is of a *hetero-referential character*. In the second case, we would simply be talking of a *self-referential* commitment. Hetero-referential commitments are commitments that I make to myself but that are intended to have a primary effect on other people. In this sense, they are strategic commitments. Self-referential commitments are not primarily oriented towards affecting other people (although they can ultimately purport to have consequences for others). If Joe commits himself to being truthful to his best friend, this promise is to himself but is intended to affect his friend (or their relationship). If Jacqueline commits herself to not eating candies, this promise is to herself and primarily aimed at herself (she wants to lose weight); however, in the second case, the promise can have an indirect (and perhaps unintended) effect on others. For example, Jacqueline's partner might like her more if she were slimmer.

Thus, understanding the difference between hetero- and self-referential commitments rests on the intention of the commitment. In the first case, this intention is external to the actor who makes the commitment, whereas in the second case it is internal. Not all commitments, however, aim to solve problems of trust or credibility. In the previous examples, the first commitment is intended to address a problem of credibility: Joe would like to make credible his commitment not to cheat. The second commitment is intended to solve a very different type of problem, in particular, the problem that psychologists call *akrasia* or weakness of will. In general, we can say that self-referential commitments are very common in the world of addictions, be they drugs, alcohol, or even other human desires such as passionate love. Commitments can play an important role here in avoiding or trying to avoid such irremediable desires. However, they have little to do with law, as argued further below.

Legal norms are commitments of the first type; they are hetero-referential commitments. They are promises whose primary purpose is to have a direct effect on others. In other words, they attempt to solve not problems of will but rather problems of credibility. The clearest example would be penal law; penal law is a commitment made by the public authorities to do X when someone does Y. Even procedural rules have a hetero-referential connotation. The clearest example is constitutional law, in particular, constitutional procedural rules. For example, a Constitution might impose a certain majority threshold for its amendment. It might even require that certain parts of the Constitution be unamendable, as in the German Constitution's so-called "eternity clauses" (art. 79.3 of the German Constitution) or the "intangibility" clauses of the Italian Constitution (art. 139 of the Italian Constitution). These procedural rules are commitments that are made by the *pouvoir constituant* to itself but that clearly bind the *pouvoir constitué*. One of their aims might be to avoid problems of will (the temptation to modify the Constitution in the ruler's favor, as with Louis Napoleon Bonaparte in 1852) (Marx, 1926 [1852]). However, they always have a clear credibility dimension. Thus, their fundamental aim is to solve problems of credibility by binding public authorities (both present and future) to a certain course of action (the respect of fundamental rights, for example). Thus, norms are *always* of a hetero-referential character.

All commitments are commitments to myself (to the actor who makes the self-commitment). This point is intrinsic to the very idea of commitment. One cannot commit "others" to doing something. One can commit one's self to react in a certain way if others do something (or to prevent others from doing something). The same is true for law, a point often overlooked when conceptualizing the nature of law. When penal law says that A will be hanged to death (as in some US states) if she blows up the Empire State Building, it is in reality committing the public authorities to hang A to death if she blows up the Empire State Building. The point is that they (the public authorities) are not committing A in any meaningful sense of the word committing. A remains free to blow up the Empire State Building.

All commitments are therefore commitments to oneself. In the same vein, all commitments encapsulated in law are public authorities' commitments to themselves. The remaining question is, of course, who "they" are in the framework of a legal commitment, what I have called for reasons of simplicity up until now "public authorities." Public authorities are what can be identified in a broad sense with "the State" (or for our current purposes, the European Union). The State (the EU) comprises its constitutional and administrative organs, i.e., the legislature, the government, the administration and its agencies (the European Parliament and the Council, the European Commission, and the rest of the EU agencies).[2] These entities are the main public actors who make commitments to themselves. These commitments are, as has been argued previously, hetero-referential commitments and are therefore addressed to two types of addressees: the citizens and the markets. There is no need to say much concerning citizens as addressees of the law.

---

[2] I leave until Chapters 3 and 4 the question of how to conceptualize the European Central Bank. Suffice it to say for the time being that I do not consider it a "regular" administrative agency but rather the very nucleus of governance of the constitutional subsystem that is the EU monetary structure.

This construction is canonical from at least republican Roman law. It is however much more controversial to initially mention the markets as addressees of legal commitments and, above all, to place them on the same footing as citizens. One could attempt to solve this controversy simply by appealing to the legal fiction according to which "the markets" are in reality formed by legal persons. Legal would be equal to natural persons; therefore, the problem would be solved this way. However, this solution is defective, if only because it is only with a high degree of imagination and goodwill that it can be said that legal persons are equivalent to natural persons. Legal persons, firms, companies, and undertakings in general are a very different type of subject from natural persons. If we have accepted this fiction up until now, doing so has been for pragmatism alone.

The real reason why markets are one of the two addressees of law understood as a commitment technology is that markets are a constitutive part of our legal systems. It is not only that very important portions of our legislation are concerned in one way or another with the markets; importantly, markets transform and condition how we live in our democracies. Even legal commitments addressed to the citizens are mediated and strongly conditioned by the markets. Therefore, a more adequate model to understand and conceptualize legal commitments addressed to the citizens would be to integrate the markets' response to those types of commitment. However, were we to do so, the resulting model would lose elegance and parsimony; in other words, it would be too complex. Therefore, for both elegance and parsimony, I differentiate between citizens and markets as the two major addressees of legal norms, knowing that the truth is somehow more complex and accepting the risk of schematicism.

To close this preliminary reflection on concepts, it is important to stress that there is a difference between the commitment itself (the promise I make to myself) and the technology used to render it credible. Joe promises himself that he will never cheat again. In turn, Jacqueline promises herself that she will never eat candies again. Those statements are promises, not credibility technologies. To make these promises credible, both Joe and Jacqueline take certain courses of action. Concerning Joe, he decides that his friend will have full access to his bank account, so that each time Joe cheats on his friend, she will be entitled to retrieve £1,000 from Joe's bank account. Concerning Jacqueline, she decides to place the box of candies in her cellar, so that each time she craves a candy, she must make the effort of going down to the cellar. The point is that both courses of action make breaking each of their promises costly. A credibility technology can thus be defined as a course of action that imposes costs on the agent who makes the commitment. As Sánchez Cuenca (1998) suggests, the higher the costs, the more credible the commitment. However, it is very difficult to think of technologies imposing costs that have no turning point. For example, Hernán Cortés sank his ships in Veracruz so that there was no turning back; his commitment to defeat the Aztecas was thus made credible. However, according to other accounts, Cortés did not destroy his ships but simply drilled holes in them. In fact, it appears that he subsequently repaired his vessels and was able to reuse them (Murado, 2013). In other words, no-turning-point costs are materially difficult to envisage. Moreover, when they are envisaged, there is always the temptation to keep an ace up one's sleeve. I will return to this point when we discuss commitments through legal technologies.

2.2 Law as a Credibility Institutional Technology

I have differentiated thus far between commitments and institutional technologies aimed at rendering credibility to commitments. Law belongs to the second category, not to the first. It is a credibility technology, not a commitment as such. I will provide a number of examples to make the point clearer.

As I have discussed elsewhere (Estella, 2008), presidential term limits are a very good example of how law functions as a credibility device. The following example is extracted from a real case. In 1996, the Spanish would-be prime minister José María Aznar promised that were he elected prime minister, he would remain in power for only two terms. Aznar won the 1996 election, and then the next (the 2000 election). When the 2004 elections were approaching, doubts started to emerge concerning whether Aznar would stand by his promise. There was a credibility issue here, not because Aznar's credibility was low but above all because he had made a political promise. Only when the Popular Party designated another candidate – Mariano Rajoy – did the skeptical voices about Aznar's promise fade.

Compare this situation – the Spanish situation – with the situation of the United States of America. The 22nd amendment of the US Constitution established in 1951 a two-term presidential limit. After that amendment was introduced, the question of whether the person who occupies the White House could run for a third term was no longer an issue in the American political context. Before that amendment was enacted, the presidential term limit (PTL) was simply a tradition (a "custom," we would say in legal terms) in the US. However, Franklin Delano Roosevelt broke this constitutional tradition. Once FDR's second mandate was approaching its end, the Second World War broke out. This war, according to all chronicles, underlay FDR's decision to break with the PTL American tradition. FDR went on to win not only a third mandate but also a fourth. Thereafter, the US Constitution was therefore reformed to prevent such a trend occurring again. Another good example, which will be discussed in Chapter 8, is provided by the EU Treaty rules on sovereign bailouts, in particular, art. 125 TFEU (Treaty on the Functioning of the European Union) (see also my remarks in Section 2.3 in this chapter).

More generally, the point that I wish to make here is the following. I view the relationship between institutions and the people as a game in which both have particular preferences, strategies, and motives. As in Hobbes

(1998 [1651]), people establish institutions to overcome their state of nature. However, as in Rousseau (2005 [1761]), once they establish institutions, they eventually start mistrusting them. There is a principal–agent problem here: they, the people (let us leave the markets aside for a moment), are not certain that institutions will attend to the objectives for which they were set up (which is essentially to help reduce the problems that collective action involves). Here is an example: in a state of nature that is dominated by violence, the people decide to create institutions that have a monopoly on violence. They decide to withdraw all weapons from the society and give them to the institutions so that people will no longer kill one another. However, the institutions have their own preferences, e.g., to become wealthy. Moreover, the institutions use strategies to attain this objective. Thus, institutions, once the guardians of peace, use the weapons that the society gave them to dominate the people with the purpose of becoming wealthy. Because the people are aware of this pattern and are mistrustful of what institutions can do once they have such weapons, they establish a number of safeguards to try to ensure that this result will not occur. The "law as credibility" model proposes to make the point that the most important of these safeguards, the most refined and complex one, is law. Law is a basic tool to ensure that institutions will do what they are supposed to do. The law's main function is, therefore, to overcome the problems of trust that exist between the people and the institutions.

2.3 The Idea of Equilibrium in "Law as Credibility"

The nuclear part in the model of law as credibility is the idea of equilibrium. In this sense, a common mistake among political scientists and political economists (and some lawyers) alike is to equate credibility with rigidity. According to them, the most credible norm is the most rigid one (Keleman & Teo, 2012; Moessinger et al., 2013). This proposition, however, is not completely accurate; as argued below, it does not explain why there are different types of norms in the legal system. Instead, I propose to connect the idea of credibility with that of equilibrium; the most credible norm is not the most rigid but rather is the norm that establishes an optimum equilibrium point between rigidity and flexibility concerning a particular commitment (see Figure 2.1). Thus, there is not a single equilibrium point in the abstract; the equilibrium point depends upon each specific commitment. Further, one can also view multiple equilibria with respect to a given commitment, although this approach also depends on each specific case (Azariadis, 2008).[3] A final point is that the idea of

---

[3] The question of single or multiple equilibria concerning the theory of law as credibility is a complex one that would lead us to very detailed discussion on the nature of the concept of equilibrium. Suffice it to say that, considering that the rationality model that I have adopted in Chapter 1 is a heterogeneous one, multiple equilibria are not discarded in the theory of law as credibility. This will depend upon each case and upon each specific commitment.

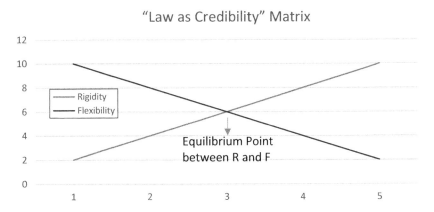

Figure 2.1: "Law as credibility" matrix

equilibrium must be viewed as a function of both the commitment itself and the legal form that is specifically chosen to encapsulate the commitment in law. In my opinion, a good expression of this idea – of the idea of equilibrium in a norm – is provided by Buiter & Grafe (2004):

> An optimal rule is both credible and flexible. Flexible need not mean opportunistic. Credible need not mean rigid and inflexible. Indeed, arbitrary and inflexible rules are not credible. Commitment is not necessarily sacrificed when a rule is made contingent on observable, verifiable events or outcomes – preferably events or outcomes that cannot be manipulated by those implementing the rule or by those judging performance under the rule.

In the "law as credibility" model, equilibrium is defined as implying a Nash equilibrium (Nash, 1950; 1953; see also Myerson, 1999); in a two-person game, the commitment encapsulated in law by one actor will be an equilibrium (and therefore, credible) if the other actor expects that the commitment will be enforced. It would not be an equilibrium if the other actor expected that the commitment will not be enforced. A Nash equilibrium is therefore a situation in which neither of the players in a game has an incentive to modify strategies, considering the strategies available to the other player. However, an equilibrium is something different from an optimum. A situation can be in equilibrium (there are no incentives to change) but be suboptimal. The idea of optimum that I use in this book is that of Pareto's efficiency (Pareto & Bonnet, 1927; Shor, 2014). Therefore, the equilibrium will not be modified if one of the players cannot obtain an improvement in terms of credibility without the other player suffering a cost for that improvement. That would be the ideal situation in terms of credibility. However, as has been said, a norm can be an equilibrium but suboptimal (for example, because the players cannot agree on how to articulate that specific improvement; or for example because player B has certain beliefs that prevent her from understanding that she will not suffer any cost if A's situation is improved).

In summary, the entire point that I want to make in this section is that a credible norm is a norm in equilibrium – neither a rigid nor an inflexible norm. This credibility in turn depends upon how the commitment is drafted and upon which type of norm is selected to encapsulate a given commitment. For example, Chapters 6 and 7 of this book show why the Stability and Growth Pact (SGP) is not an equilibrium – and therefore is not credible. It is not an equilibrium not because the SGP is insufficiently rigid but because, despite its rigidity, the entire regulatory scheme generates many incentives for its change, and even room for Pareto improvements.

2.4 Legal Puzzles

Conceptualizing law as a credibility device and the idea of equilibrium allows us to address a number of legal puzzles, three at the very least. All of them are cases of what could be called "institutional selection." The first relates to what I call "law versus non-law selection"; the second, to the "normative pyramid," or the problem of legal validity; and the third, to the "relationships between public law and private law." All of these cases are legal puzzles in the following sense. The first is a puzzle because one should be able to explain through any legal theory what the reasons are behind a public actor's choice between law and its alternatives (a political pact, a custom, or even morals) to encapsulate a given commitment. The second is a similar puzzle to the first but inside the legal field; one should be able to answer through any legal theory why an actor would make a choice between the different types of norms (for example, constitutional or legal) of any given legal system. The third poses, again, a similar question, although this time the question refers to the choice between two very different normative worlds, those of public and private law.

2.4.1 Law versus Non-Law Selection

There are a number of technologies to encapsulate commitments to render credibility to them. To simplify this issue, let us assume for the time being that the choice is between law, political pacts, custom, and morals. The example that I gave above is a good illustration of how this problem of institutional selection is posed in this context. A political actor must choose between law and a political pact to render her commitment on a term limit credible. Why choose law instead of politics? Why did José Maria Aznar choose a political institution instead of a legal one to encapsulate his commitment not to run for a third mandate? Why, instead, have the Americans chosen law after 1951? Concerning morals, the question is most likely more complex, but in essence, a similar argument is also valid in this field. For example, one approach to making credible your commitment not to run for a third presidential mandate would be to say that you adhere to a specific moral scheme (for example, a religion) that very severely punishes its members for cheating (the punishment

could be that those members who cheat are sent not to heaven but to hell, a
horrible place to spend the rest of one's afterlife).

If the politician who announced her commitment not to run for president
more than twice reveals herself in public as a fervent believer in this religion,
then this characteristic might in turn enhance the credibility of her commitment. The question is, when then to opt for law instead of any of the other
alternatives (politics, custom, or morals). The traditional answer to this question is that law is preferred due to what I call rigidity. Under certain circumstances, it will be difficult not to abide by law. A political pact can be broken, a
custom can be changed, and morals can be reframed. To be sure, such
behaviors will not be without cost. In the case of politics, the cost will be
electoral (see Chapter 10); in the case of customs, the cost will be in terms of
legitimacy; in the case of morals, the cost will be reputational. Instead, in the
case of law, the cost is a transaction cost, and, more specifically, a procedural
cost. If a political actor wants to run for a third term, against what the
Constitution of the country establishes, she must either face a court complaint
or modify the Constitution. Therefore, even under the best of circumstances
(imagine all political parties agree that the Constitution must be modified), she
must follow a certain procedure to do so. This procedure incurs a cost; this
cost might be a minor one, but one need not follow any procedure to modify a
political pact, change a custom or reframe one's morals. This cost is what I call
rigidity, the need to follow a certain legal procedure to modify the law as it
stands. Rigidity is what renders law more credible than its alternatives. This
statement is however not free from qualifications, as shown later.

2.4.2 The Normative Pyramid

Under this heading, I refer to the problems of norm selection. The normative
pyramid is the famous Kelsenian metaphor that helps to understand how legal
systems address norm validity and solve problems of norm clashes.[4] At the tip
of the pyramid, we find the Constitution (or the EU legal order). After the EU
legal order and the Constitution, we find the laws, then the regulations, and so
on and so forth. Clashes between norms of a different pyramid level are thus
automatically solved; the norm that is placed at a superior normative level
sweeps away the norm that is placed at an inferior normative level. What
differentiates norms placed at different levels relates, once again, to rigidity. It
is more onerous procedurally speaking to make or reform a constitution (a
Treaty) than to make or reform a law, a regulation, and so forth. However,
rigidity is not sufficient to understand the so-called normative pyramid.

This point is crucial. In reality, what we want to say when we say that what
explains the difference between normative levels is rigidity is, as discussed in

---

[4] However, the expression "normative pyramid" was coined not by Kelsen (who adopted it later)
but rather by one of his main disciples, Adolf Merkel.

Figure 2.2: Norm selection: the tradeoff between rigidity and flexibility

Section 2.3, above, that every normative level strikes a different balance between two competing goals or objectives: that of rigidity and that of flexibility. Therefore, the problem of norm selection can be more accurately framed *as a tradeoff between rigidity and flexibility*. Rigidity helps to explain the choice between a norm and a nonlegal technology such as customs or politics or morals, as was shown previously. However, it does not serve to understand the problems of norm selection. Only when we frame this entire issue as a problem between rigidity and flexibility can we understand how norm selection works. One idea helps to drive the point home; if the entire problem of norm selection were reduced to a problem of rigidity, then there would be only one norm (for example, the Constitution or the Treaties).

Political economists addressing law as credibility think predominantly of constitutional texts when tend to considering the legal order, as though nothing else mattered normatively speaking in the legal spheres. However, as we lawyers know perfectly well, there is an ample variety of legal norms cohabiting in both the national and the international legal universe. To make sense of how this universe of norms cohabits, it is insufficient to bring rigidity to the fore. Flexibility is also needed here.

To make the point in graphic terms, it is as though a horizontal axis existed that tended to rigidity at one extreme and flexibility at the other (see Figure 2.2). The Constitution would be more rigid and less flexible; the law would be less rigid and more flexible than the Constitution; and regulations would be less rigid than constitutions and laws and therefore more flexible than both constitutions and laws.

This scheme is thus what explains norm selection. Norm selection would depend upon the ruler's blend of rigidity and flexibility that she would be seeking to encapsulate a given commitment. Were she to prefer the highest degree of rigidity (and therefore the lowest degree of flexibility), she would then opt for encapsulating her commitment within the Constitution; conversely, were she to prefer the lowest degree of rigidity but the highest degree of flexibility that the legal order would allow for, she would opt instead for a regulation. From this perspective, the different levels in the normative pyramid would be explained not as a means of providing solutions to norm clashes but, more strategically, as reflecting different equilibrium points between rigidity and flexibility to encapsulate commitments. In short, they would reflect different approaches to solving problems of credibility rather than a pragmatic means of solving the problems of clashes among norms.

2.4.3 Public Law versus Private Law

The structure of the problem of "institutional selection" between public law and private law is similar to the cases that we have examined previously. The ruler will make a choice between public law and private law on grounds of credibility. Her decision will depend on the degree of credibility she wants to give to her commitment.

The reason for this difference in credibility terms between private law and public law rests on the fact that private law is less rigid and therefore much more flexible than is public law. Its implementation depends largely upon the will of private parties that engage in a contract. This effect is precisely that sought when the choice is for private law instead of public law – to obtain more flexibility than that which public law would appear to allow. Instead, public law (under certain conditions) implies a binding duty on the part of public authorities to follow a certain course of action. In legal terms, this implication is referred to as the principle of legality, or the rule of law. Public authorities cannot escape from the specific path that public law has signaled for them; in fact, they have a duty to follow this course of action and to avoid a different one. For instance, in administrative law, this duty is referred to as the public administration's self-executing decision-making powers. Based on the self-executing character of administrative law, public administration acts enjoy a presumption of validity and can be imposed coercively upon citizens without the intervention of the courts. Private law does not enjoy this legal status.

Therefore, if we return to Figure 2.2, private law would be at the fringes between law and other nonlegal commitment technologies. Private law would thus be the very last connection with the legal universe. Thereafter, we would find a void in legal terms, i.e., nonlegal commitment technologies. Stated in different terms, private law would be an instance in which the tradeoff between rigidity and flexibility would involve the lowest possible content of rigidity and the greatest possible content of flexibility we can find in the legal universe, *if and only if* (as is always true for legal commitments) rigidity is greater than flexibility, or

$$R > F$$
Being R(Rigidity) and F(Flexibility)

Adding private law, the resulting figure is Figure 2.3.

The structure according to which private law is the least rigid and most flexible type of legal structure has no "moral" connotation but rather only a functional one. The "law as credibility" concept is (and this point is important) simply a functional structure. Thus, the concept does not mean that private law is "worse" than public law or that it is in any meaningful sense of "less quality" than public law. In fact, as has been noted previously, public actors might be searching for the flexibility provided by private law and

Figure 2.3: Public law versus private law (R > F)

might want to escape the rigidity of public law in specific contexts. In some cases (in purely functional terms), private law can be viewed as a "better option" than public law. There is an excellent example that serves to illustrate the choices that the public and other actors might be facing when trying to decide between public law and private law, namely public procurement laws. In reality, there is no compelling reason for subjecting public agencies to public law when they act as contracting agents. In principle, public agencies could use only private law for contracting, as other actors do. In fact, the new revision of the EU public procurement legislative framework gives a larger role to private law in public procurement (and in fact this change has been criticized by some legal commentators as just another instance of the "flight from public law to private law") (Endicott, 2015). Why then is public law adopted on public procurement? Why subject public agencies to public law when they act as contracting agents? The traditional answer to this question has been that the reason relates to the special status of one of the contractors, the public administration. However, it is also possible to answer this question from the perspective of credibility. In reality, private law could be chosen in the field of government procurement. However, this choice would imply more flexibility and therefore less rigidity. Because the ruler wants to give a higher degree of rigidity to contracts signed by the public administration, it chooses public law instead of private law. A different question is, however, whether this choice is *really* more or less credible. As was discussed previously, this credibility will depend on whether this choice is an equilibrium.

2.5 Conditions

I have referred throughout the above paragraphs to the conditions with which the legal system must comply to render credibility to promises. Thus, the law as credibility theory adopts an exigent standard concerning the conditions under which the legal system should work. The theory is, however, also realistic; remember that we are talking here about men, not angels.[5] Thus, the legal system requires that the law be disclosed, abstract, and general; that public authorities are subject to the law's empire;

---

[5] See *The Federalist* no. 51.

and so on and so forth. In this sense, law as credibility is not different from other legal positivist theories. However, the theory requires both a compelling citizens' democracy and courts that are as independent as they can be in the real world. I will examine these last two points more closely below.

2.5.1 Democracy

Let us start with democracy. Game theory uses a very well-known example to illustrate the trust problems that arise in strategic relationships. The example is taken from the movie *Rebel Without a Cause*. Although the reader may well have seen the film, I will briefly describe its most popular scene. Two men (James Dean, who plays the role of Jim in the film, and Corey Allen, who plays the role of Buzz) are fighting for the affections of a girl (Natalie Wood, who plays Judy). To settle the issue, Buzz proposes a "chicken run" game. The two men will drive their respective cars to the edge of a cliff, and the first one to jump from the car will be a "chicken" – and will therefore lose the girl. Once the run starts, Buzz's jacket sleeve becomes trapped in the car-door handle; he therefore cannot jump from the car, which goes over the edge of the cliff. Buzz dies. Jim, at a certain point prior to the edge, jumps from his car and survives.

Game theory uses the so-called chicken game to illustrate how problems of credibility can be solved. In the case at hand, Buzz's commitment not to jump is made credible through his becoming trapped in the car. Other versions of the chicken game say that the driver of one of the cars would be tied to his seat and then break his steering wheel – just to show a commitment to avoid jumping out and to go straight to the edge of the cliff. The idea is, however, always the same – all of these strategies would be aimed at showing each driver's intention not to jump from the car before the other driver does. The game is a way of solving a credibility problem. The problem that this structure poses is of course that neither driver knows what the other one is doing to make a commitment not to jump credible. In the case at hand, Jim cannot see that Buzz's sleeve is trapped in the car-door handle. In other words, a commitment, to be credible, must be visible. If the credibility technology one of the players is using is not visible to the other player, then a problem of imperfect information arises. In this context, credibility is clearly undermined. The improvement that law makes is that credibility technologies through law are visible to everyone. One of the main tenets of the rule of law is, as I mentioned previously, that law be disclosed through its publication in official journals. This tenet is why I argued at the beginning of this paper that law is the most sophisticated credibility technology that exists. One does not "need to discover" whether Buzz is trapped by the door handle to determine whether his commitment not to jump is sufficiently credible. Law solves this problem through being transparent for all.

However, a reality check is needed to complete this argument. Remember that we are talking here about law (a man's – not an angel's – product). One aspect is what law says and another aspect is the reality of its implementation. Thus, a ruler commits herself to a certain course of action, for example, to a two-term limit. However, after some time, she regrets making that commitment and decides to withdraw it and run for a third mandate. However, the law (for example, a constitutional norm) is an obstacle to this change. She must change the Constitution to remake her commitment. However, she cannot do so; she lacks the necessary votes to change the constitutional text. She therefore decides simply to disregard the constitutional norm and run for a third term. Courts in a well-functioning rule of law system are an additional obstacle to preventing the ruler from not abiding by the constitutional two-term limit norm, as in our example. However, I will address courts in the next subsection. For the time being, what interests me is to focus on democracy. Democracy is another obstacle here. In reality, it is the most important obstacle in this context. Democracy, the rule of the people, by the people, and for the people,[6] is the most important receptacle of law understood as credibility. If the people do not let the ruler violate her previous commitment, the ruler must abide by it. Conversely, if the people are against a given commitment, the ruler will not be able to maintain it. As Elster (1989) states, "there is nothing external to a polity." However, for this statement to be true, one condition must be fulfilled: the polity must be formed by "vigilant" citizens (Pettit, 1997; 2012). The role of citizens as guardians of the system is crucial in the context of law as credibility. Thus, the concept of law as credibility relies upon an exigent vision of democracy that demands active and not merely "rule-book-complier-with" citizens. It should be acknowledged that this probably is the system's most fragile point. In complex societies, in which individuals are burdened with a very large number of different mundane responsibilities, to demand constant vigilance on the part of the citizenry (except, perhaps, in extreme situations) is most likely to demand too much from them. The republican model of active citizenship might therefore appear too idealistic. However, one should view this exigent republican model of democracy, on which the concept of law as credibility is based, more as a tendency than as a fixed point.

The problem in our example (the ruler wants to disregard the two-term limit norm and run for a third time) is that although law might be disclosed and be therefore visible, the ruler's behavior in trying to circumvent that particular norm might not. For example, the ruler might bribe the mass media to create a state of opinion that causes a third term to appear to be an irreversible necessity, or the ruler might threaten other potential candidates so they ultimately give up running for the next presidential term. The list of examples of nonvisible actions that the ruler can adopt to take the upper hand is most likely very large and need not be cited here *in extenso*. The point is,

---

[6] Abraham Lincoln's Gettysburg Address (November 19, 1863).

however, clear: only an active citizenship might be able to unearth all of these "invisible" actions that the ruler might be undertaking to break her previous commitment.

2.5.2 Courts

Courts are, as was noted previously, the other crucial element for a vision of law as credibility to be sustained. I will not insist here on the idea that courts should be independent of the ruler. However, this independence is a must in the construction of law as credibility; as with the neo-republican vision of citizens, the understanding of courts' independence should also be viewed here more as a tendency towards an absolute ideal (complete independence) than as a fixed point.

I will therefore address a different problem in this domain; that is, the problem of courts' legal reasoning. Law courts, judges in particular, have a crucial role in ensuring the law's credibility. We delegate to courts the role of interpreting and applying, in the last resort, the law, as a means to "close" legal systems. The same would be true if we were to hold a view of law as credibility. Thus, delegation to a different agency of the role of interpreting and applying the law is a legal institutional commitment that attempts to render credibility to the entire rule of law construction. If the ruler and only the ruler interpreted and applied the law in the last resort, the entire system would lose credibility.

We do delegate the final legal word to independent bodies, the courts, primarily for reasons of credibility. In Section 2.1 of this chapter, when I was discussing law as a commitment technology, I said that law is the most sophisticated institutional technology that human beings have created to render credibility to the promises that public actors make. We can now refine this idea a little bit further.

In reality, more than generating a factual state of credibility, as though law were physics, what law generates is an *expectation for credibility*. Let us go back to our example of PTL. The country's Constitution binds the ruler's hands by establishing a two-term mandate limit. Actually, what this norm is generating in other actors (for example, the citizens and the markets) is an expectation that the ruler will not run for a third presidential term. The question is not only how credible that norm is but also, more subtly, how credible is the expectation that this norm has generated? Can the people believe, because of the existence of that constitutional norm and other factors, that the ruler will not run for a third term?

2.5.3 Counterfactual Legal Analysis

The only way to answer that question is through a counterfactual analysis (Estella, 2016). This point is crucial in this domain. As mentioned in Chapter 1, "counterfactual" is a concept that comes from social sciences and psychology. In its most basic sense, it implies asking about facts that are contrary to what actually occurred. Its most usual expression is the "what if" formula. We human beings use counterfactual thinking all the time. To return to the examples that were examined earlier on, we could ask, what if Joe had not cheated on his friend? What if Jacqueline had not eaten the candies? Another example: what if Louis Napoleon Bonaparte had not modified the French Constitution in his favor in 1852? The idea is clear: a counterfactual is a thought experiment through which we human beings contemplate possible alternatives to the one that actually occurred. It is for the legislator, in the first instance, to make a counterfactual analysis when she is elaborating a credible commitment. In reality, the natural locus for counterfactual analyses *is* the phase in which the norm is elaborated – and not the phase in which it is interpreted or implemented. The legislator, the ruler, is the one who should ask herself about counterfactuals when she is designing a credible commitment. It must be clarified that a counterfactual thought experiment is not an admonition to the ruler to think about *all possible alternatives* to which the factual basis of a commitment might be subject; it is simply an admonition to think about the *contrary facts* concerning the factual basis that a given norm is contemplating. Thus, the ruler considers not only credibility through law but also expectations of legal credibility.

Let us provide an example just to drive home the point, which is further discussed below in Chapter 8. I referred to art. 125 of the TFEU in Section 2.2 of this chapter. This TFEU provision establishes the so-called no-bailout clause. It is a clear prohibition: if a Member State runs amok with its public debt, neither the Union nor its Member States can rescue it. However, if we consider that there have been eight bailouts since the crisis erupted in 2008, that the drafters of this provision made a counterfactual analysis when they were writing this legal commitment into the Treaty is at least doubtful. The counterfactual analysis here would have been the following: what if a bailout (or bailouts) were necessary? If the counterfactual had been contemplated, then perhaps a different legal answer would have been given. For example, art. 125 TFEU could have introduced a number of qualifications, such as an exception that said that bailouts would be prohibited *unless* the survival of the euro was at stake. The important point that I want to stress here is that, if the ruler does not perform the counterfactual analysis, then courts are legitimated to do so. This point is, again, crucial in this context. Counterfactual analysis acquires a very important role in judge-made law. First, judges must try to detect whether the ruler performed a proper counterfactual analysis. If they detect that the ruler did not, then they should substitute themselves for the ruler in this particular task and ask themselves about the counterfactual. Thus, in a "law as credibility" framework, legal interpretation is primarily about judges answering counterfactuals when the ruler has not done so.

Therefore, judges must provide interpretations of norms that not only hold to the letter of the law but also contemplate the counterfactual, *if and only if* they detect that the ruler did not do this exercise. There are rules for answering to counterfactuals. On top of these rules, judges are constrained by a method – legal reasoning – to answer counterfactuals. Judges' discretion is therefore amplified by the potential need to make counterfactual analyses but at the same time constrained by the formal requirements of legal discourse. We will revisit this issue in Chapter 4 of this book, in which the *Gauweiler* case of the European Court of Justice will be extensively analyzed.

In conclusion, the credibility of a norm is related to the expectations of the actors (to which the norm is addressed) concerning the norm's own credibility. If the expectations of a norm's credibility are low, no matter how rigid or clear the norm might be, the norm will lose its effect in terms of credibility. A counterfactual analysis can be the key to revealing problems of expectations concerning the credibility of a given norm. Ultimately, a norm will be credible if it reflects an optimum equilibrium between rigidity and flexibility. In certain circumstances, and given a counterfactual analysis, the equilibrium point will tend more to rigidity than to flexibility; in other circumstances, it will be the other way around. This balancing is the essence of the concept of legal credibility – the idea of finding the right expected equilibrium point between these two contrasting objectives.

BIBLIOGRAPHY

Azariadis, C. 2008, "Multiple equilibria in macroeconomics" in *The New Palgrave Dictionary of Economics*, 2nd edn., Palgrave Macmillan, Basingstoke.

Buiter, W. & Grafe, C. 2004, "Patching up the Pact: some suggestions for enhancing fiscal sustainability and macroeconomic stability in an enlarged European Union," *Economics of Transition*, vol. 12, no. 1, pp. 67–102.

Elster, J. 2000, *Ulysses Unbound: Studies in Rationality, Pre-commitment and Constraints*, Cambridge University Press, New York.

1989, *Solomonic Judgements. Studies in the Limitations of Rationality*, Cambridge University Press, Cambridge.

1984, *Ulysses and the Sirens*, Cambridge University Press, Cambridge.

Endicott, T. 2015, *Administrative Law*, 3rd edn., Oxford University Press, New York.

Estella, A. 2016, "Rationality and counterfactual legal analysis," *Italian Law Journal*, vol. 2, no. 1, pp. 105–129.

2008, "Law as credibility: the case of Presidential Term Limits," *European Journal of Legal Studies*, vol. 2, no. 1, pp. 116–142.

Hobbes, T. 1998 [1651], *Leviathan*, Oxford University Press, Oxford.

Kelemen, D. & Teo, T. K. 2012, "Law and the Eurozone Crisis," American Political Science Association (APSA 2012) Annual Meeting Paper.

Marx, K. 1926 [1852], *The Eighteenth Brumaire of Louis Bonaparte* (translated from the German by Eden & Cedar Paul), George Allen & Unwin, London.

Moessinger, M., Feld, L., Kalb, A., & Osterloh, S. 2013, "Sovereign Bond Market Reactions to Fiscal Rules and No-Bailout Clauses: The Swiss Experience," CESifo Working Paper no. 4195, ECONSTOR.

Murado, M. A. 2013, *La invención del pasado: Verdad y ficción en la historia de España*, Debate, Madrid.

Myerson, R. 1999, "Nash equilibrium and the history of economic theory," *Journal of Economic Literature*, vol. 37, no. 3, pp. 1067–1082.

Nash, J. 1953, "Two-person cooperative games," *Econometrica*, vol. 21, no. 1, pp. 128–140.

    1950, "The bargaining problem," *Econometrica*, vol. 18, no. 2, pp. 155–162.

Pareto, V. & Bonnet, A. 1927, *Manuel d'économie politique*, 2nd edn., Marcel Giard, Paris.

Pettit, P. 2012, *On the People's Terms: A Republican Theory and Model of Democracy*, Cambridge University Press, New York.

    1997, *Republicanism: A Theory of Freedom and Government*, Oxford University Press, Oxford & New York.

Rousseau, J. J. 2005 [1761], *A Discourse upon the Origin and Foundation of the Inequality among Mankind [electronic resource]*, Thomson Gale, Farmington Hills, Mich.

Sánchez-Cuenca, I. 1998, "Institutional commitments and democracy," *European Journal of Sociology*, vol. 39, no. 1, pp. 78–109.

Schelling, T. 1956, "An essay on bargaining," *American Economic Review*, vol. 46, no. 3, pp. 281–306.

Shor, M. 2005, "Pareto optimal," in Dictionary of Game Theory Terms, www.gametheory.net/dictionary/ParetoOptimal.html.

3

The Eurozone: Accession, Exit, and Expulsion – Revisited

Introduction

We move in this chapter onwards to the analysis of the substantive parts of the EU legal system of economic governance. I start with an examination of issues related to access to and exit and expulsion from the Eurozone. Mainstream legal literature on the euro area argues that a Member State's accession to the euro area is an automatic process. Furthermore, it argues that a Member State's exit from the euro area is forbidden. Finally, it also argues that expulsion from the euro area would be possible, at least under certain conditions. In turn, economic analyses of the Eurozone also provide arguments that uphold the previous three propositions. Economic governance is in fact clearly one of the areas in which legal and economic analyses of the Eurozone meet each other. However, legal analyses of these three issues very rarely rely on economic considerations, which is indeed striking. The converse is also true: economic analyses of access to and exit and expulsion from the Eurozone hardly ever consider legal aspects.

This chapter will argue that a different approach to this problem can be adopted. Although I will primarily address the legal aspects related to access to and exit and expulsion from the Eurozone, I will also refer to economic considerations to show the previously noted coincidence and to remark that the legal and economic conversations on this issue reinforce each other, which makes their reciprocal neglect even more surprising. Therefore, this chapter will argue the following:

1) Incorporation into the euro area is not an automatic process; rather, the process is voluntary throughout its phases.
2) Exit from the euro area is permitted, provided certain conditions are met.
3) Expulsion from the euro area is forbidden. This proposition is absolute and universal.

The structure of the chapter is as follows. In the first section, I will address a number of considerations related to the intrinsic logic of the argument that will be developed later. In the second section, I will present and analytically discuss the mainstream legal literature on access to and exit and expulsion from the Eurozone. I will supplement the previous analysis by showing the position of mainstream economic thinking on these three issues. In the third section, the first argument (access is a voluntary process) will be sustained. In the fourth section, the second argument (exit is possible if certain conditions are met) will be sustained. In the fifth section, the third argument (expulsion from the Eurozone is prohibited) will be presented. Finally, in the sixth section, I will link the previous discussion to the issue of credibility.

3.1 Preliminaries

Before going to the heart of the discussion on access to and exit and expulsion from the Eurozone, I will start by making a more general point on its intrinsic logic. Note that the three aspects listed above are in reality three different dimensions of the same problem, which is how to understand membership in the Eurozone. Therefore, the answer that we provide to the first problem (whether accession is voluntary or automatic) determines or, at the very least, greatly conditions the answer that we must provide to the other two (exit and expulsion). If accession to the Eurozone is automatic, then it logically follows that unilateral exit cannot exist and that a Member State can be expelled from the Eurozone. These problems are logically connected because if the process were voluntary, then a Member State that joined on a voluntary basis would retain its freedom to exit whenever it considered doing so appropriate and could not be expelled unless being expelled was expressly foreseen.

Many private clubs or associations work similarly. Joining is an act of will of the joiner; therefore, the joiner is free to decide whether she wants to remain in the club. For expulsion, unless it is expressly contemplated, no one can expel anyone from a club.[1] The reason for this limitation is precisely that membership in the club or association is always *based on and only on* a free act of will from the member that adheres therein. To be sure, it can be argued that the EU is not a private club. Nevertheless, international organizations work similarly. Access implies a free decision on the side of the State that wants to take part in the international organization. Therefore, exit is also free, and expulsion is only possible if it is expressly contemplated as a sanction in the treaty that

---

[1] See Ashton & Reid (2011). According to them, "the first criterion of a club is the voluntary nature of the association of the members who compose the club. From this criterion follows the proposition that a member may at any time voluntarily retire from a club by his resignation or withdrawal from it" (p. 165). Furthermore, on pages 169–170, they say, "If the rules of a members' club are silent on the topic of expulsion of a member of the club, no such power will be implied into the rules. Provided there is provision to amend the rules, they would first have to be amended to give the club the necessary power to expel a member. In the absence of an expulsion rule, it will not be possible as an alternative to convene a special meeting of all the members to discuss and then pass a resolution to expel a member ... The power of expulsion must always be expressly given in the rules."

brings about the international organization (Magliveras, 1999; 2011).[2] In the case of the Eurozone, we would not be talking about access to and exit or expulsion from the whole organization, in this case, the EU, but to or from one particular policy (its monetary policy). However, this policy is of such importance that it has been described by some analysts as constituting "a subsystem" within the constitutional system of the Treaties (Alonso Garcia, 1994). For this reason, the analogy with membership in an international organization can be a useful one.

However, what interests me here is not so much the praxis of either private associations or international organizations on access, exit, and expulsion but rather the intrinsic logic of the argument that will be unfolded in the following sections. It is not by chance that for private associations and public bodies (such as international organizations) the sequence "free access, free exit and non-expulsion unless contemplated" is correct. We have here a logically deductive structured argument. If States (or individuals) are free throughout their membership, then exit should be permitted. Similarly, if States/individuals are free throughout their membership, then expulsion should be barred. The opposite argument should also be valid. If States/individuals are not free throughout their membership, then unilateral exit should be ruled out. Again, if States/individuals are not free throughout their membership, then expulsion should be possible. The difference is that in the first case, States/individuals have a certain margin of freedom after access, whereas in the second case, they do not. This stance conditions the answer

---

[2] The Vienna Convention on the Law of the Treaties foresees withdrawal in article 56: "Denunciation of or withdrawal from a treaty containing no provision regarding termination, denunciation or withdrawal

1. A treaty which contains no provision regarding its termination and which does not provide for denunciation or withdrawal is not subject to denunciation or withdrawal unless:

(a) it is established that the parties intended to admit the possibility of denunciation or withdrawal; or

(b) a right of denunciation or withdrawal may be implied by the nature of the Treaty."

It also foresees suspension of a Member's rights in article 57. However, it is silent on the issue of expulsion of a member to a Treaty. In turn, Magliveras says (1999: 35), "Thus, and this argument applies to all international organisations, membership may be terminated permanently if the state wishes (withdrawal) or if the organisation, applying the relevant provisions, orders it". He adds (2011: 93), "It should be noted that not all international organizations have been endowed with the right to address violations perpetrated by members. This omission should not be attributed to an oversight by drafters. On the contrary, it should be interpreted as an intentional decision of the original members not to envisage the imposition of punitive measures. In its turn, this could mean that they prefer to solve instances of transgression through diplomatic and similar means but outside the formal environment of the organization. This pattern has been followed in a not insignificant number of international institutions (including the European Community). However, it seems to have been abandoned. Indeed, since the early 1990s there has been a trend to amend the constitutive instruments of existing institutions and allow them to impose measures of a punitive nature, especially for violating democratic and human rights norms (e.g., Organization of American States, Commonwealth of Nations, European Union, etc.)."

that we should be giving to exit and expulsion thereafter. In other words, both arguments are logical units. What cannot be maintained, at the same time, is, for example, that access is voluntary but that exit is ruled out or that access is automatic but exit is possible. For this reason, all of the theories that do follow a logical argumentative path will be considered in this chapter. However, I will disregard those arguments that do not hold to either one or the other logical sequence.[3]

3.2 The Mainstream Legal (and Economic) Literature on Access to and Exit and Expulsion from the Eurozone

We can now turn to the analysis of the mainstream legal literature on accession to and exit and expulsion from the euro. As has been said, the legal literature indicates that accession to the Eurozone is from the very beginning of this process an automatic decision, exit is forbidden, but a Member State could be expelled from the Eurozone. In turn, the economic literature on all three issues essentially provides support to the previous legal stance. It is of crucial importance to emphasize the idea that the irreversible character of the euro is maintained for reasons of credibility. The general argument of the mainstream literature is that if the euro were reversible, this status would in turn undermine the credibility of the Eurozone (Buti, Franco & Ongena, 1998; see, in general terms, Bordo & MacDonald, 2012).

3.2.1 Accession

For most lawyers, accession to the euro area is far from being a voluntary act of the European Union's Member States. Once a Member State has joined the Union, it has an obligation to join the Eurozone. This obligation would not just be a "common" obligation; in fact, lawyers do qualify this obligation as a legal commitment. One of the clearest examples of this school of thought is the work of Jean-Victor Louis and Rosa M. Lastra. According to these authors,

> The participation in the euro area is a right but also an obligation for each Member State except for the UK and Denmark, to which protocols have conferred a special status.
>
> (Louis & Lastra, 2013: 72)

Therefore, for Louis and Lastra, the right and the obligation to accede to the Eurozone would be but two sides of the same coin. It would be a right in the sense that no one (neither the Union nor other Member States) could ever

---

[3] See Dammann (2013: 139) making a similar argument on these logical units: "This duty [the duty to join the euro] has obvious implications for the withdrawal right question; to the extent that the TFEU imposes a duty to join the Eurozone, it makes little sense to grant a withdrawal right."

deny entry to Member States complying with the convergence criteria.[4] How-ever, it is an obligation in the sense that, once in the EU, Member States would be legally committed to accede to the Eurozone. Hofmeister (2011: 127) joins Louis and Lastra in this position. For this author, "membership in the EU is voluntary, i.e., states can apply to become members of the EU or decide to remain outside. However, once a state has made the decision to join and eventually becomes a Member State, that state is subject to a number of obligations. One of these obligations is the requirement to participate in the EMU [Economic and Monetary Union]."

In turn, the Tuori brothers agree with the previously noted stance and state, "the provisions on EMU were premised on the assumption that Member States would join as soon as they fulfilled the convergence criteria. Indeed, this was considered a *legal obligation*, except for the UK and Denmark who had negotiated opt-outs confirmed in separate Protocols attached to the Maastricht Treaty. Moreover, in Maastricht the general expectation was that the opt-outs would be merely temporary and that the UK and Denmark, too, would enter sooner or later" (Tuori & Tuori, 2014: 28).

More specifically, the mainstream legal literature on access to the Eurozone supports its position on the following arguments. First, the main argument is that of the importance and significance that the Treaties give to the EMU. For the Treaties, the EMU would have such relevance that the main implication derived from it would be its irreversible character. Second, a more specific basis for upholding this argument would be found in the "Protocol on the Transition to the third stage of Economic and Monetary Union" attached to the Maastricht Treaty, which declares "the irreversible character of the Community's movement to the third stage of economic and monetary union." Finally, a third basis in support of its position would be the Acts of Accession of the Member States that entered the Union since 1994, which indicate that "Member States shall participate in Economic and Monetary Union from the

---

[4] The process of accession of new members to the Eurozone is regulated in article 140 TFEU and in the Protocol to the TEU and TFEU no. 13 "on the Convergence Criteria." In essence, a candidate must comply with the following four criteria to accede to the Eurozone: (1) price stability: the candidate must show an average rate of inflation, observed over a period of one year before the examination, that does not exceed by more than 1½ percentage points that of, at most, the three best-performing Member States in terms of price stability. (2) Government budgetary position: the candidate must show a government deficit not exceeding the 3 percent limit and a public debt not exceeding the 60 percent limit over its GDP at market prices at the time of the examination. (3) ERM-II: the candidate must accede to the ERM-II prior to accession to the Eurozone; within the ERM-II, the candidate must have respected the normal fluctuation margins provided for by the exchange-rate mechanism of the European Monetary System without severe tensions for at least the last two years before the examination. (4) Interest rates: the candidate must have had an average nominal long-term interest rate that does not exceed by more than two percentage points that of, at most, the three best-performing Member States in terms of price stability. Interest rates shall be measured based on long-term government bonds or comparable securities, considering differences in national definitions.

date of accession as a Member State with a derogation" (these points will be developed in greater detail in Section 3.2).

For their part, mainstream economic analyses on accession to the Eurozone supplement legal ones in different ways. For example, de Grauwe (2012: 144), when commenting on why Sweden is not only not a member of the Eurozone but also not a member of the Exchange Rate Mechanism II (ERM-II), argues the following:

> Another EU country that has not adhered to the ERM-II is Sweden . . .. *Entering this exchange rate arrangement would legally bind Sweden also to enter the Eurozone (provided the other convergence criteria are satisfied).*
>
> [my emphasis]

De Grauwe is making two points here: (1) entry into the ERM-II is a voluntary decision of the Member State that wants to join. (2) However, once a Member State is in the ERM-II, it has an obligation to join the euro (which he qualifies as a legal obligation), provided of course that the convergence criteria are met.

De Grauwe is not precisely alone in his understanding on how the accession process to the euro works. If anything, he is even surpassed by other authors. For example, Jürgen Stark[5] said the following in an address he delivered before the Icelandic Chamber of Commerce on February 13, 2008:

> A country that has joined the EU has eventually the obligation to join the euro.

In a further passage of the same speech, Stark remarked as follows:

> Once a country is able to fulfil these legal and economic criteria in a sustainable manner, it joins the euro area.

Therefore, there appear to be two economists' positions on the issue of accession, a soft one and a harder one. The soft one (exemplified by de Grauwe) would imply that accession would be voluntary until a country decided to join the ERM-II. The harder one (Stark's) would be the position according to which the mere fact of joining the EU would imply an obligation to join the euro once the convergence criteria were met.[6]

Mainstream legal analysis, examined above, appears therefore to be closer to what I have called the "harder" view on accession. As seen, mainstream legal authors argue that there is a legal obligation to join the EMU once a State is a member of the EU. To accede is not only an obligation; it is a legal commitment for Member States that joined the EU. Interestingly, Louis and Lastra cite Denmark and the UK (the two Member States that enjoy opt-outs from the EMU) as the only Member States to which this obligation would not apply, but

---

[5] Jürgen Stark is a German economist who served on the executive board of the ECB from June 1, 2006, to December 31, 2011.

[6] Barroso supported what I have called "the harder" stance on accession. See his statement in November 2010: "If you are in the EU, you should join the euro." www.express.co.uk/news/uk/282825/Barroso-If-you-are-in-the-EU-you-should-join-euro.

not Sweden (the country that provoked de Grauwe's comments on the automaticity of the accession process). Sweden, for Louis and Lastra, would also be
obliged to enter the EMU; however, Sweden (and other countries) would have
a certain margin of discretion concerning when.[7]

3.2.2 Exit

Exit from the Eurozone is not expressly foreseen in EU law. Only exit from the
whole Union is foreseen in article 50 of the EU Treaty (EUT) (Tatham, 2012),
as Brexit illustrates well. However, lawyers' conventional interpretation is that
this clause is "all-or-nothing"; it does not allow for selective withdrawal from
specific EU policies in general, and even less from the Eurozone specifically.
For example, Hofmeister (2011) argues that there would not be such a thing as
a separate right to withdrawal from the EMU and a right to withdrawal from
the EU. Therefore, either a Member State exits the EU, as article 50 of the EU
Treaty allows for, or it remains in the EU. Therefore, cherry-picking of different
policies (in particular, monetary union) would be legally barred due to the
irrevocable character of the EMU and to the fact that the process of accession to
the Eurozone is an automatic one. Hinajeros (2015: 5) also argues, "there are no
express provisions on the Treaty on terminating EMU as a whole, or on a
Member State leaving EMU, voluntarily or otherwise – presumably unless the
Member State decides to leave the EU altogether, pursuant to article 50 TEU."

In turn, in a lengthy and widely cited article on withdrawal and expulsion
from the EMU, Athanassiou (2009: 4) argues, "a Member State's exit from
EMU, without a parallel withdrawal from the EU, would be legally inconceiv-
able." Athanassiou's arguments in support of his position are the following.
First, withdrawal from the EMU is not foreseen by the Treaties. Second,
therefore, although negotiated withdrawal would be in principle possible,
unilateral withdrawal would not. The reason for this opinion appears to be a
mix of economic and, above all, legal considerations. "Among other things,"
Athanassiou argues, "commentators focus on the continuity of contracts and
on the uncertainty surrounding the extent to which foreign courts would
recognize the validity of the redenomination of contracts between debtors
established in the withdrawing NCB's jurisdiction and their foreign creditors."
He however does not clarify why all of these issues would evaporate in the case
of a negotiated withdrawal. The bottom line is, however, clear: exit (unilateral
exit) is forbidden by EU law.

---

[7] See however their remarks on the Swedish question on p. 90. For these authors, "to submit the
compliance of an obligation imposed upon the State by the Treaty to the approval of either
Parliament or the people is not compatible with the Treaty" (Louis & Lastra, 2013: 90). The
Swedish people rejected joining the euro in a referendum held on September 14, 2003. In the face
of this rejection, these authors must recognize the following: "Obviously, the Commission
did not wish to adopt a legal position in this respect. How can you enforce upon a State a change
of its currency?"

For other authors such as Scott (1998), "a partial [i.e., unilateral] withdrawal from a continuing monetary union is unlikely because a withdrawing country would find it exceedingly difficult to re-establish control over its monetary supply." Therefore, Scott's position seems to be that the definitive argument for advocating against unilateral withdrawal would rather be of an economic type – namely, the difficulty the withdrawing Member State would have in regaining control of its monetary supply. However, he does not explain why doing so would be difficult or, above all, why in those cases in which countries have left currency unions in the past, they have been able to regain control of their monetary supply – at least over time.[8]

Scott revisited his argument on euro-exit in an article dated 2011. In this paper, the author appears to uphold the arguments that he advanced in his article of 1998, although in a more nuanced way. He also adds new arguments to his previous ones. In particular, he argues that a Treaty amendment would be the "clearest path" for unilateral withdrawal. Therefore, even when it is unilateral, a Member State exit from the Eurozone would imply, according to his view, a certain degree of coordination among Member States and the EU institutions. This expectation can be interpreted in the sense that this author is discarding a Member State's plain, unilateral exit.

In turn, in an article published in 1998, Proctor and Thyeffry argue, "a unilateral withdrawal from the Maastricht Treaty would constitute a clear breach of a Treaty obligation owed to other Member States" and therefore would be illegal. To be sure, these authors were writing before the Lisbon Treaty introduced article 50 into the TEU. For this reason, in a more recent article, Thyeffry (2011) qualifies his previous stance and argues, "Withdrawal [from the EMU] would have to be negotiated," thus supporting Scott's position of 2011 in this respect.

In the same vein, Lastra (2006: 29, 242) and Seyad (1999: 262) preclude exit due to the irreversible character of the EMU. They accept termination of the euro only in the case in which Member States unanimously amend the Treaties. Treves (2000: 116) and Herrmann (2002) employ a similar argument; the euro is irreversible and irrevocable. Zilioli and Selmayr (2000) agree on the irreversible character of the euro but add qualifications. According to these authors, "the Member States have never, not even for a juridical second, transferred their monetary sovereignty to the legal person EC – which then could have delegated the powers in this monetary field to the ECB – but have chosen to directly transfer it, without using the Community institutions as an intermediary, to the newly established ECB on 1 January 1999, and thus to constitutionalize this (irreversible) transfer of sovereign power." Therefore, according to these authors, the bearer of this irreversible transfer of sovereignty would be not the EU but the ECB. Herrmann (2002) disagrees with this

---

[8] Argentina would be a case in point. See Eichengreen (2007: 19).

position; the Union – and not the ECB – would be the bearer of this irreversible transfer. However, all of these authors agree on the point that the sovereignty transfer is irreversible.

In turn, for economists, adoption of the euro also has an "irreversible" character. Therefore, unilateral exit is impossible. In other words, once the euro is adopted by a country, this commitment cannot be unmade. One of the best illustrations of this stance is given by the first president of the ECB, Jean-Claude Trichet. According to him,[9]

> ... to enter the euro zone there must be an overwhelming sentiment within society that the country is preparing to achieve a common destiny with the other members ... One cannot jump in and jump out of the euro area as one hops on and off from a bus; *participation in EMU commits the destiny of a country.*
>
> [my emphasis]

Since then, Trichet's "bus metaphor" has been repeated countless times. Other metaphors have also been used to refer to the same idea (Charteris-Blacka & Musolffb, 2003). The point is always the same: because the EU Treaty "makes no provision for exit [from the EMU]," the euro is irreversible. More specifically, Einchgreen (2007), who is one of the economists who have worked more extensively on the break-up of the euro area, points to the economic, political, and legal obstacles to a euro break-up (i.e. unilateral withdrawal). Concerning the economic obstacles, he argues that departure from the euro would "be associated with a significant rise in spreads and debt-servicing costs." Concerning the political obstacles, he argues that "diplomatic tensions and acrimony" would follow exit. Finally, concerning the legal obstacles, he mentions the fact that the EU Treaties do not foresee exit, together with the legal obstacles that would be related to the re-establishment of the new national currency. He however recognizes that in cases such as Argentina in 2001 (a country that broke the dollarization of its currency, the peso), the ensuing litigation did not "force re-dollarization of previously 'pesified' contracts or force other compensation to aggrieved creditors."

Another good illustration of the traditional economists' stance on euro-exit is given by the current president of the ECB, Mario Draghi. In the worst moment of the euro crisis, Draghi spoke of the irreversibility of the euro as follows:

> We think the euro is irreversible. And it's not an empty word now, because I preceded saying exactly what actions have been made, are being made to make it irreversible.[10]

---

[9] Cited by Louis (2010).

[10] Speech by Mario Draghi, president of the European Central Bank, at the Global Investment Conference in London, July 26, 2012.

In summary, the irreversible character of the euro explains for economists why unilateral exit would be barred. The credibility of the euro would be at stake were it otherwise – that is, if economic operators and policymakers did not consider the euro to be an irreversible project. To this position they add other considerations, such as the difficulties with reintroducing a new currency or the rise in spreads and debt servicing if exit occurred; however, such difficulties would be of a more contingent nature and therefore not totally insurmountable.

3.2.3 Expulsion

Expulsion from the EMU is, as with exit, not expressly foreseen by EU law. Only "suspension of Member States' voting rights" is foreseen by article 7 of the TEU. However, as will be shown later, no one argues that suspension can amount to expulsion. Here, both lawyers and economists are more nuanced in their stance towards expulsion, but in general, their position might indirectly be interpreted as amounting to recognition of the possibility of expulsion from the EMU.

To start with, the main reference with respect to expulsion is again Athanassiou, who extensively addresses this issue in the article cited above. For him,

> [E]xpulsion ... from the EMU ... may be possible in practical terms – even if only indirectly.
>
> (Athanassiou, 2009: 7)

This statement represents common ground at least in the legal literature that addresses expulsion. For example, Scott (1998; 2011) reaches a similar conclusion. He assumes that expulsion is a viable legal option, although he speaks of a "cooperative" solution to this problem, in which all Member States and the expelled one would be required to collaborate. In turn, Proctor (2006) is even more nuanced. Expulsion would be an option, but it would have decayed in the case, for example, of Greece, because the failure of this Member State to provide the Union with "accurate" statistics on its macroeconomic performance before joining the euro would already have been remedied through other means (the EU law regular infringement procedures). Therefore, the possibility for expulsion would "have been lost." My interpretation of Proctor's stance is that the option of expulsion would be a type of sanction available in EU law, but that option would be pre-empted once other – less radical – remedies were enforced.

Concerning economists, Buti, Franco and Ongena (1998: 87) state, "Once in the euro, incentives to pursue budgetary retrenchment may weaken considerably as ... expulsion from the Eurozone is not contemplated by the Treaty." These authors wrote in 1998, one year before the euro was formally adopted. In other words, expulsion was very much in the economists' mindset when the

EMU was brought about. It is interesting to note that although the previously cited authors say that expulsion is not foreseen by the Treaties, this statement does not immediately cause them to discard this option. If anything, they remain silent on this point.

The most forceful expression of expulsion as a viable economic alternative is that of German economists Sinn and Sell. In July 2012, in a very polemical article published in the *Financial Times* (Sinn & Sell, 2012), both authors advocated the possibility of a "temporal exit" from the Eurozone for the most economically distressed members of the EMU. Once their public finances were restored, these countries would have a "return ticket" to the Eurozone. In this article, Sinn and Sell only refer indirectly to expulsion. However, in a number of interviews that Sinn has given to different media, he explicitly refers to the expulsion of some Eurozone members (Greece in particular). For example, Credit Writedowns, a well-known site on finance and financial markets, published in 2011 an interview with Sinn whose title leaves little grounds for doubt: "There is no alternative but Greece's Eurozone expulsion" (Sinn, 2011). True, Sinn's position was proclaimed in the midst of the euro-crisis and as an answer to it at least for some peripheral countries. In other words, expulsion was most likely considered more of a pragmatic response to a specific situation of extreme difficulty than as a matter of principle. However, the point is that these economists (Sinn in particular) now explicitly view expulsion as a feasible alternative in economic terms.

3.3 Incorporation into the Euro Area is not an Automatic Process; Rather, it is a Voluntary Process throughout its Phases

As has been argued previously, mainstream economic analyses on the issue of accession is divided in two strands (the soft one and the harder one), whereas legal analyses are closer to the harder one. Let me now review this stance.

3.3.1 The Harder Thesis on Accession

I will start with the harder thesis on accession. For most lawyers and many economists, EU accession determines EMU accession. Member States are thus obliged to join the euro. The only margin of discretion they have is to decide (but not completely unilaterally) when they want to join and at what pace.

The accuracy of this stance is, however, unclear – at least from a legal perspective and most likely from an economic one. First, there is no provision in the EU Treaty that expressly obliges Member States to join the euro. The Treaty makes clear that the EMU is a crucial policy for the Union at many points – for example, when the TFEU declares monetary policy an EU "exclusive competence" for the Eurozone Member States (article 3.1(c) TFEU) or when it establishes a specific Chapter for Monetary Policy (Chapter II, Title VIII, FTEU), differentiated from the Chapter on Economic Policy. However, the importance of the EMU cannot be made equivalent to an express legal obligation to join the euro once a Member State has joined the EU.

Second, it is often argued that the Maastricht Treaty (the Treaty that introduced the EMU) legally obliged Member States of the Union to join the euro. In connection with this argument, it is argued that the Accession Acts of Member States that joined the EU after the enactment of the Maastricht Treaty also reference this obligation. To start with the first argument, its defenders[11] cite the "Protocol on the Transition to the third stage of Economic and Monetary Union" to the Maastricht Treaty in their support. This Protocol states the following:

> The High Contracting Parties declare the irreversible character of the Community's movement to the third stage of economic and monetary union by signing the new Treaty provisions on economic and monetary union.

What is to be understood by the expression "irreversible character"? The Protocol itself later provides clarification:

> Therefore all Member States shall, whether they fulfil the necessary conditions for the adoption of a single currency or not, respect the will for the Community to enter swiftly into the third stage, *and therefore no Member State shall prevent the entering into the third stage.*
>
> [my emphasis]

Thus, the only concrete and specific obligation that Member States had was a negative one – not to impede accession of those Member States that wanted to enter into the third phase of the EMU (Seyad, 1999: 245). Considering that the EMU was conceived as an enhanced cooperation mechanism *ex tractatu*, this part of the wording of the previous Protocol is perfectly understandable. A systematic analysis of the Maastricht Treaty reinforces this interpretation; it is not by chance that the two Protocols that come after the Protocol on the transition to the third stage of the EMU were the British and the Danish opt-outs from the EMU. The UK and Denmark were given this choice; in exchange, both countries legally committed themselves not to impede other Member States from adopting the euro. This situation might appear exaggerated today. However, if one performs a careful reading of the negotiations that led to the incorporation of the EMU into the Maastricht Treaty, it is very clear that some Member States, in particular Britain, not only did not want to join the EMU but were also opposed to the whole EMU project.[12] It is in this light that the wording of the Protocol, previously transcribed, must be interpreted.

---

[11] See Lastra (2006), Seyad (1999), and Zilioli & Selmayr (2000), for example.

[12] See James (2012: 237), commenting on the meeting of the Delors Committee on the EMU: "Delors also had some luck on his side. The three central bankers who came to play a dominant role in the committee all had very firm views ... From the outset it looked as if Leigh-Pemberton [Bank of England], *whose government was firmly opposed to the whole project*, might wreck the discussion" (my emphasis). On p. 262, he reports, "Indeed, in November [1990], the

According to the second argument previously mentioned (joining the euro would be an obligation for the new acceding Member States), an analysis of the different Acts of Accession of new Member States since 1994 provides grounds to conclude that such an obligation did not exist. First, the Act of Accession of Austria, Sweden and Finland (and Norway)[13] is completely silent on this point. However, the Act of Accession of the countries that acceded to the Union in 2004 (the Czech Republic, Estonia, Latvia, Lithuania, Hungary, Poland, Slovenia, and Slovakia, plus Cyprus and Malta)[14] is not. In particular, article 4 of this Act says,

> Each of the Member States shall participate in Economic and Monetary Union from the date of accession as a Member State with a derogation within the meaning of article 122 of the EC Treaty.

For advocates of the "harder" thesis, the above is the acid test that confirms that joining the EU implies an obligation to join the euro. However, if the previous provision is carefully read, one can realize that the answer is exactly the opposite; what article 4 simply says is that new Member States will become, for the EMU, States "with a derogation." In other words, those new Member States were out of the EMU. It is difficult to read article 4 as creating any "obligation." The article is more on what the status of new Member States is vis-à-vis the euro than on anything else. If one were to read article 4 as creating an obligation, the only obligation that could stem from this article would be to keep these Member States away from the EMU, at least in principle. This point is precisely the one that de Grauwe makes; the enthusiasm for Member States' accession to the euro in the first EMU years has been much less visible after the 1995 enlargement.[15] The "new" EU policy for these new countries was more one of stopping, rather than encouraging, their accession to the EMU. The previous article is a clear proof of the new EU mood towards the new

---

Bank of England issued a statement to the other European central banks: 'The Governor of the Bank of England records that the UK authorities do not accept the case for a single currency and a monetary policy." In general, James' account provides ample evidence of the extent to which the UK was opposed to the EMU project.

[13] Act concerning the conditions of accession of the Kingdom of Norway, the Republic of Austria, the Republic of Finland, and the Kingdom of Sweden to the European Union and the adjustments to the Treaties on which the Union is founded (94/C 241/08). OJEC, 29.8.94, at p. 21.

[14] Act concerning the conditions of accession of the Czech Republic, the Republic of Estonia, the Republic of Cyprus, the Republic of Latvia, the Republic of Lithuania, the Republic of Hungary, the Republic of Malta, the Republic of Poland, the Republic of Slovenia and the Slovak Republic and the adjustments to the Treaties on which the European Union is founded; Official Journal of the European Union (OJEU), September 23, 2003, p. 33.

[15] De Grauwe says, in particular, the following: "Things are different for the new Member States. The political will to allow [them] into the Eurozone is weak, and suddenly the Treaty numbers are used with great precision to block entry. Although the principle of equal treatment applies to the old and new Member States, in practice this does not seem to be the case." (de Grauwe, 2012: 145).

entrants. The same is true for the accession of Bulgaria and Romania[16] and for the accession of Croatia.[17]

The third major argument that the harder thesis makes is connected to the "irrevocability" mentioned by article 140.3 TFEU. This article reads as follows:

> If it is decided, in accordance with the procedure set out in paragraph 2, to abrogate a derogation, the Council shall, acting with the unanimity of the Member States whose currency is the euro and the Member State concerned, on a proposal from the Commission and after consulting the European Central Bank, irrevocably fix the rate at which the euro shall be substituted for the currency of the Member State concerned, and take the other measures necessary for the introduction of the euro as the single currency in the Member State concerned.

I will not tire the reader with an analysis of an article that has received much attention in the legal and economic fields.[18] However, because it stems from the wording of article 140.3, "irrevocability" is referring to the fixing of exchange rates. Only a voluntary interpretation could link it to the process of incorporation of the euro – and not only to the fixing of exchange rates. From an economic perspective, the irrevocable fixing of the exchange rates is a necessary step that must be taken prior to the abandonment of the national currency in favor of the European one; exchange rates must be frozen at a given time before the new currency is adopted. When the freezing should occur is, of course, open for debate. However, that it should occur is not able debate (Dammann, 2013: 140).

3.3.2 The Soft Thesis on Accession

I will now discuss the arguments of what I have called the "soft" thesis. As will be recalled, its advocates say that the process of joining the EMU is a voluntary process until a Member State joins the ERM-II. Once in, the Member State in question would have a legal obligation to join the euro.

To address this issue, it is important to recall the Resolution of the European Council of Amsterdam of June 16, 1997.[19] This Resolution established the so-called ERM-II (Exchange Rate Mechanism-II, the successor to the EMS). According to point 1.6 of the Resolution, "participation in the

---

[16] See article 5 of the Protocol concerning the conditions and arrangements for admission of the Republic of Bulgaria and Romania to the European Union, OJEU L 157/29 of June 21, 2005.

[17] Again, see article 5 of the Act concerning the conditions of accession of the Republic of Croatia and the adjustments to the Treaty on European Union, the Treaty on the Functioning of the European Union and the Treaty establishing the European Atomic Energy Community, OJEU L 112/21 of April 24, 2012.

[18] See, *inter alia*, Hofmeister (2011) and de Grauwe (2012).

[19] Resolution of the European Council on the establishment of an exchange-rate mechanism in the third stage of economic and monetary union Amsterdam, 16 June 1997 (97/C 236/03), OJEC no. C 236/5 of August 2, 1997.

exchange-rate mechanism will be voluntary for the Member States outside the euro area." The question is whether this Resolution is legally binding or only incorporates a political commitment. The European Court of Justice of the European Union (ECJEU) has thus far not pronounced on the issue of the legal nature of European Council resolutions. However, according to Alonso Garcia (2001: 84), the Court of Justice is in general concerned with material reality rather than with formal reality. It therefore is not formalistic in the following respect: if, according to the content of the measure, an EU act is legally binding, then the ECJ will rule that the act deploys its full legal effects.[20]

If this case law were to be followed, then one most likely would conclude that the European Council resolution of June 16, 1997, amounts to a legally binding act. This conclusion would be reached because the content of this resolution (the setting-up of the ERM-II to facilitate access to the third and definitive phase of the monetary union) is so crucial that it could not be otherwise. Furthermore, such a conclusion would possibly be reinforced by the fact that at least part of the Resolution of June 16, 1997, was taken up by the agreement of March 16, 2006, between the ECB and the national central banks of the Member States outside the euro area on an exchange rate mechanism.[21] Thus, the preamble of this agreement incorporates, in the fourth indent of its third recital, the principle according to which access to the ERM-II is voluntary. This agreement is a legally binding act beyond any possible doubt. As Louis and Lastra remark, the ECB is competent to conclude these sorts of agreements as an expression of its "international legal personality," as framed by article 23 of the ESCB Statute.[22] The only remaining question would be that of the legal nature of the agreement's preamble. In principle, legally binding acts' preambles have an interpretative force. This point is consistent with the case law of the ECJ.[23] However, we also know that the line separating acts that function as an interpretation parameter from acts that function as a validity parameter is rather fine.[24] Therefore, recitals of preambles should be used to interpret the substantive part of a legal act – in this case, the agreement

---

[20] This case law can be traced back to the *ERTA* case of March 31, 1971, Case 22/70.

[21] This agreement replaces the first agreement that was made in this field, which was adopted on September 1, 1998. In turn, the 2006 agreement has been amended each time that a new national central bank has become party to the Agreement on the ERM-II. Therefore, it has been amended four times thus far. See Agreement of 16 March 2006 between the European Central Bank and the national central banks of the Member States outside the euro area laying down the operating procedures for an exchange rate mechanism in stage three of Economic and Monetary Union (2006/C 73/08), OJEU C 73/21 of March 25, 2006.

[22] Which says, "The ECB and national central banks may: establish relations with central banks ... in other countries ..."

[23] Case C-162/97 *Nilsson* [1998] ECR I-7477, paragraph 54. See also Case C-412/93 *Edouard Leclerc-Siplec* [1995] ECR I-179, paragraph 47; Case C-308/97 *Manfredi* [1998] ECR I-7685, paragraph 30; Case C-136/04 *Deutsches Milch-Kontor* [2005] ECR I-10095, paragraph 32; Case C-110/05 *Commission v Italy* [2008] ECR I-0000, first Advocate General's Opinion, paragraphs 64–65, and second Advocate General's Opinion, paragraphs 174–175.

[24] See BRAC Rent-a-car [2003] EWHC Ch 128, paragraph 26.

of 2006 – with the exclusion of *contra legem* interpretations. In this case, it is fairly obvious that the preamble recital on the voluntary character of accession to the ERM-II has a regulatory character; be that as it may, it is also clear that the preamble goes neither against any of the norms that are contained in the substantive part of this agreement nor against other norms of the rest of the EU legal order.

To summarize, there are at least two indications that appear to imply that voluntary access to the ERM-II is not only a political commitment but also a legal one. The first indication is the fact that the Resolution of June 16, 1997, most likely contains a substantive regulation. The second indication is that the ECB agreement of 2006 is without any doubt a legally binding act. Its preamble could never take precedence over the substantive part of the agreement but, as has been argued, the preamble does not go against the substantive part of the agreement (or against other EU norms). In other words, the preamble would appear to give grounds to the "soft" thesis – and not to the "harder" thesis – when it says that if access to the ERM-II is voluntary, then mere membership in the EU is not sufficient to generate an obligation for Member States to join the euro. To be sure, membership would be a condition to join, but it would be a necessary condition, not a sufficient one.

The main consequence derived from this stance is that Member States of the EU would not be required to expressly opt out of joining the EMU. They would simply need not to accede to the ERM-II if they wanted not to join the Eurozone.

However, coincidence with this part of the "soft" thesis does not imply coincidence with the second part of the soft thesis. As will be remembered, the second part of the soft thesis was that once a Member State had joined the ERM-II, it would be obliged to join the euro. In the following, I proceed to explain why this interpretation cannot be correct.

As seen previously, article 140.3 of the TFEU is the Treaty provision that regulates the last phase of the accession process to the EMU of the Member States of the Union that did not belong to the euro area. In particular, this article establishes the decision-making procedure through which Member States will decide to "irrevocably fix" the rate at which the old currency will be set vis-à-vis the euro. The relevant part of article 140.3 I want to emphasize is the following:

> ... the Council shall, *acting with the unanimity of the Member States whose currency is the euro, and the Member State concerned*, ... irrevocably fix the rate at which the euro shall be substituted for the currency of the Member State concerned ....

> [my emphasis]

It is particularly interesting to note that, different from other provisions in which the EU Treaties establish unanimity as the decision-making procedure, article 140.3 refers to unanimity of the Member States of the Eurozone *and of the* Member State that is not (yet) in the Eurozone. This wording cannot be a mere coincidence; it can only be understood in the sense that a Member State that is not yet in the Eurozone holds a right to veto the particular exchange rate which the other members of the Eurozone might want to establish. In other words, this article foresees the emergence of a possible discrepancy on this point. The clearest example of this potential discrepancy would be the case in which the members of the Eurozone would want to fix an exchange rate at a different level from that preferred by the Member State outside the Eurozone. Imagine, for example, that the members of the Eurozone preferred to fix the exchange rate between the euro and the other currency at par (1 unit of the old currency = €1), whereas the Member State outside the Eurozone would prefer an exchange rate at 2 units of the old currency = €1. In other words, the Member State outside the Eurozone would prefer a competitive devaluation of its currency before adopting the euro. If both players (the members of the Eurozone and the Member State outside the Eurozone) did not reach an agreement, then the latter would exercise its right to veto; therefore, it would not enter the Eurozone. This final exit door from the whole process of accession to the euro makes complete sense if the process of accession is seen as voluntary, even once the accessing Member State is in the ERM-II system. A different interpretation would imply that article 140.3 would be devoid of any legal substance. The conclusion is that both accession to the ERM-II *and* accession to the final stage of the euro are acts of will of the Member State that is outside the Eurozone.

3.4 Exit from the Euro Area is Permitted, Provided Certain Conditions are Met

As I have argued previously in the second section of this chapter, the answers that we should be giving to the question of exit and expulsion are largely conditioned by the answer that we provide to the problem of access to the Eurozone. As shown previously, access to the Eurozone is a voluntary decision of the Member State in question, voluntarism that is maintained right up to the final step of the accession process. This point provides a preliminary indication that the answer that must be given to the question of exit is that unilateral exit is also permitted in EU law. As argued previously, the whole argument is built in a logical sequence. Therefore, unilateral exit would not contradict the premise according to which access to the EU is voluntary throughout this process. On the contrary, the possibility of exit would be its logical consequence.

However, further arguments can be advanced in favor of unilateral exit from the Eurozone. The argument that I will develop in the ensuing pages is the following: the *"permissum videtur in omne quod non prohibitum"* principle (the principle according to which all that is not prohibited is permitted) is of application in this context.

As a first point, it is important to recall once again that exit from the Eurozone is not contemplated in the EU Treaties. It is therefore not prohibited, at least explicitly. Only withdrawal from the entire Union is foreseen, as seen above, in article 50 of the EU Treaty.[25] Therefore, and on the contrary, the silence of the Treaty might be an indication that unilateral withdrawal is possible. As shown in the following, this interpretation would be further reinforced through the application of the *permissum videtur* principle, mentioned above, to this problem.

3.4.1 Origin of the *Permissum Videtur* Principle

According to Kolb (2001), the *permissum videtur* principle or, as this author refers to it, the "*règle residuelle de liberté en droit international*,"[26] was unknown to Roman law. From this author's perspective, "*une règle mécanique et générale n'a pas de place dans la pensée problématique et topique romaine.*" This statement might be true for the immediate origin of the rule, but perhaps not for its remote and conceptual origin. More particularly, it appears that the maxim had its origin in the civil glossator Andrea Bonello (from Barletta, also known as Andreas de Barulo[27]), who taught in Naples University around the second half of the thirteenth century. However, as noted previously, the intellectual root of this maxim can be traced back to Roman law. For example, the Roman jurisconsult Florentinus referred to liberty in the following terms:[28]

> Libertas is the natural faculty of doing what one wants, unless it is prohibited by force or by law.

This maxim was incorporated in the Justinian Digest (*Digesto*, I.5.4) and in the Justinian Institutions (*Instituta*, I.3.1). The connection between this principle and the *permissum videtur* maxim is, to the best of my knowledge, not explicitly made by the Roman law experts who have explored this issue, although it is, in my opinion, possible. In fact, the *permissum videtur* principle developed initially in the private law realm and was thereafter incorporated into public law. This sequence provides indirect proof of the connection between the two.[29]

---

[25] Hofmeister (2011: 126) explores the eventual use of an argument "*a maiore ad minus*"; if a State can leave the whole Union, then *a fortiori*, it can leave one of its subsets, in this case, the EMU. This rationale is however not the argument I wish to pursue here because to consider the EMU a "minus" would be, in my view, essentially misleading. The EMU cannot be compared with any other EU policies; rather, as part of the legal doctrine argues, it is of such importance that it must be rather understood as a whole system within the system of the Treaties. See Alonso Garcia (1994).

[26] Residual or subsidiary law of liberty in international law.

[27] BONELLO DE BARULO, Commentaria ad Codicem, 10.1.7, page 8.

[28] See on this point Ando (2010: 195).

[29] I am indebted for their advice to trace back the origin of the *permissum videtur* maxim (and its reverse, the "*quae non sunt permissae prohibita intelliguntur*" maxim) to Cosimo Cascione

In the public law realm, the *permissum videtur* principle is one of the cornerstones of, in particular, administrative law. It underlies what is referred to as the principle of public administration's "negative bond" (*negative Bindung* in German, *vinculación negativa* in Spanish). In this domain, there are two approaches to understanding the application of this principle: concerning the relationship between the administration and the individuals and in relation to the administrative action outside its relationship with individuals. Concerning the first approach, the principle protects individuals' freedom vis-à-vis administrative interference, above all when this interference has a negative effect upon the citizens' rights. Therefore, citizens are free to act unless their actions are expressly forbidden. The administration cannot impinge upon the citizens' rights unless doing so is expressly provided for in the laws and regulations. The second dimension implies that the administration is free to act unless doing so is forbidden by the law of the land, thus implying a wider margin of maneuver for the administration, which would deploy its activity always within the limits of the first dimension we have mentioned previously. This dimension would also be in sharp contrast to the principle of "positive bond" (*positive Bindung* in German, *vinculacion positiva* in Spanish), which is amalgamated in the Latin maxim *quae non sunt permissae prohibita intelliguntur*. This (the reverse of *permissum*) would imply that the administration could only act when doing so was expressly permitted. In administrative law, there is a lively debate about which of these strands of the *permissum videtur* principle (the negative or the positive) should regulate the public administration's activity.[30]

3.4.2 Application of the *Permissum Videtur* Principle in Public International Law

In the public law domain, the *permissum videtur* principle also finds application in public international law. Kelsen, for example, had a very expansive understanding of the application of this principle in public international law. For him, the States could act freely in the international sphere unless doing so was expressly prohibited. In his opinion,

> *S'il n'y a aucune norme du droit international conventionnel ou coutumier imposant l'obligation de se conduire d'une manière déterminée, le sujet est au point de vue du droit international juridiquement libre de se conduire comme bon lui semble.*
>
> (Kelsen, 1953: 121, 122)

(Federico II University, Naples), Pierangelo Buongiorno (University of the Salento, Lecce), and Fernando Reinoso (Complutense University, Madrid). See, in general, Domingo (2006: 328, principle number 740) and Fernandez de Bujan (2008: 973).

[30] The principle is known not only in the legal "continental" tradition but also in the "common law" tradition. See, in particular, Tomkins & Scott (2015).

Furthermore, for Kelsen,

> *L'absence de telles normes signifie seulement que l'Etat ou un autre sujet du droit international n'est pas, dans le cas concret, obligé de se conduire d'une manière déterminée. Ceux qui prétendent que dans un tel cas le droit existant ne peut pas être appliqué oublient le principe fondamental **selon lequel ce qui n'est pas interdit par le droit est permis par lui**.*
>
> [my emphasis]³¹

However, authors such as Kolb, previously cited, are opposed to this extensive application of the principle into the realm of international relations. His arguments are important to consider in this context because this author is one of those who have made the most fundamental contributions in this field.

As a starting point, it is important to recall the following platitude: States can act in the international sphere because they have legal personality. In other words, States are to public international law what individuals are in the civil law realm. Other actors are legal persons recognized legally to act in the international sphere. However, as Shaw (2008: 197) remarks, "despite the increasing range of actors and participants in the international legal system, States remain by far the most important legal persons, and despite the rise of globalization and all that it entails, states retain their attraction as the primary focus for their social activity of the humankind and thus for international law." The legal fiction according to which States are similar to persons is fundamental to understanding the extent to which the *permissum videtur* principle might have a role in this context.³²

Having said this, Kolb understands that the *permissum videtur* principle has a role in international relations, although only a subsidiary one. Briefly, his arguments in favor of this stance are the following. His main departing premise is that public international law is public law according to its content but private law according to its structure. Thus, the identification between the sovereign state and the individual, mentioned previously, emerges here again. Accordingly, the application of the *permissum videtur* principle should be an *ultima ratio*; it should be a "*règle très subsidiare*" and not a "*prius*" but a "*posterius.*" In the absence of a clear regulation on a particular matter, the law implementer should apply first the legal order in its entirety, then the general principles of law, then use legal analogies, and even the fundamental values on which law rests to fill the lacunae. Only thereafter would the application of the *permissum videtur* principle be possible.

It is important to remember that when Kolb writes, he is considering the case in which a State would unilaterally act in the international sphere, and not

---

³¹ For an in-depth understanding of the context of ideas (not only legal) in which Kelsen's stance on public international law was developed, see the excellent book by Bernstorff (2010).

³² According to Kolb (2001: 125), "*le droit public est un droit publique par son contenu ... mais prive par son structure.*"

so much the case of a State action within an international organization. The references that Kolb makes to this second case are very few in his chapter. In this sense, he argues the following:

> *Une autre distinction importante est celle entre le droit international de coexistence ... et le droit international modern de cooperation . . ... Cette cooperation se réalise notamment à travers des organisations internationals. Les finalités communes impriment ici aux Etats des devoirs de prise en compte, de bonne foi, de partage, axes sur la réalisation du but recherché. De lors, comme on l'a dit, le droit ne peut, dans ces brances moins encore qu'allieurs, se satisfaire d'un règle residuelle de droit, qui contredirait l'essence même de l'effort commun.*
>
> (Kolb, 2001: 119)[33]

To summarize, although Kolb understands that the *permissum videtur* principle has some application in public international law, he would restrict this application to cases in which (1) there would be no express norm; (2) there would not be an implicit order or norm applicable to the case at hand; and (3) the possibility of making a valid legal analogy would be foreclosed. However, in cases in which (1) the general principles of law would operate and, above all, (2) in cases in which the general values of the legal order would find application to fill a lacuna, the *permissum videtur* principle might find its natural *locus* for application. This restriction would be even stricter in the case of the relationships between states and the international organization to which they belong, although this situation is not the primary focus of Kolb's analysis.

3.4.3 Application of the *Permissum Videtur* Principle in European Union Law, in Particular, in the Case of Eurozone Exit

I intend in the following to reverse Kolb's argument and explain why the *permissum videtur* principle would have a wider application in EU law with respect to Eurozone exit. In other words, I will try to explain why, for the EU law case, Kelsen was right and Kolb's restrictions might be in need of further qualification. The arguments that I will develop henceforth are the following three:

1. The ECJ case law concerning competences is very clear in this respect: competences have been delegated to the EU "albeit within limited fields."
2. Article 5(1) of the EU Treaty very clearly expresses the principle of attributed competences.
3. The subsidiarity principle also finds application here.

My point of departure is that the whole EU constitutional law competence edifice rests upon the premise that Member States can do everything that is not expressly prohibited to them by EU law (and by national law, but this is a

---

[33] See in the same vein Kolb (2001: 127).

different matter in this context). First, the ECJ case law with respect to competences is very clear on this point. Competences have been delegated to the EU "albeit within limited fields."[34]

Second, article 5(1) of the EU Treaty very clearly expresses the principle of attributed competences.[35] And third, the subsidiarity principle would also find application here.[36] All three arguments, which I need not develop at length here because they are all well-known tenets of EU constitutional law, are the main pillars upon which an expansive reading of the *permissum videtur* principle in EU law can be based. The first argument (the EU would have a restricted ambit of delegated competences) would mean that outside that field, there would be the presumption that the Member States could act, at least *a priori*. This point would be reinforced by the principle of attributed competences; for the EU to act would require an expressly attributed competence rather than the other way around. Outside the field of competences that have expressly been attributed to the EU, Member States would be entitled to act, even in their relationship with the Union, and in their relationship with other Member States.

Finally, subsidiarity as it is enshrined in article 5(2) of the EU Treaty would concern more the exercise than the attribution of EU competences, as I have argued elsewhere (Estella, 2002). Nevertheless, as a general principle of EU constitutional law, it is clear that subsidiarity establishes a presumption in favor of Member State action and against EU action, which would be required

---

[34] See *Van Gend en Loos* (Judgment of 5. 2. 1963 – case 26/62, at page 12): "The conclusion to be drawn from this is that the Community constitutes a new legal order of international law for the benefit of which the states have limited their sovereign rights, albeit within limited fields."
A different question is whether the ECJ has respected its own self-imposed limitation (according to which Member States have made a restricted delegation of competences to the EU). Weiler (2001: 5) indicates that it has not done so: "There is a widespread anxiety that these fields are limited no more." Craig (2011) and Weatherill (2004) appear to point in the same direction. However, Lenaerts (2011: 1367) adopts a more nuanced stance: "Far from being a sign of inconsistency, this jurisprudence shows that the ECJ pays full respect for the competences retained by the Member States in [areas] so fundamental to national sovereignty." In my opinion, the ECJ, once an activist Court in the field of competences, would have adopted a much more cautious approach to this issue in more recent times, at least in crucial areas of national sovereignty. As Lenaerts & Gutierrez-Fons (2010: 1668) stated, "Vertically, the ECJ must be respectful of the constitutional traditions of the Member States, but not to the extent of giving up the basic constitutional tenets of the Union. This is what appears to transpire by contrasting the outcome of Omega with that of Viking and Laval. Beyond the bounds of a core nucleus of key, shared values vital to the Union's integrity, however, the ECJ should have recourse to a 'margin of appreciation' analysis that would strike the right balance between 'European commonality' and 'national particularism'. Thus, the national identities are preserved as the Union continues to be based upon a model of 'value diversity'." This point is in sharp contrast with the following much-cited sentence in Lenaerts (1990): "There simply is no nucleus of sovereignty that the Member States can invoke, as such, against the Community." Lenaerts was writing in the 1990s. This contrast with Lenaerts' more recent approach to the issue of EU competences exemplifies particularly well the new mood that presides today over the ECJ on this matter.
[35] For an in-depth analysis, see Craig (2012) and Craig (2011).   [36] See Estella (2002).

to justify why its action would be more effective than individual Member State action. Therefore, *a fortiori*, what is true for the exercise of EU competences would be even truer concerning their attribution. Competences that have not been attributed to the EU (such as the competence to prohibit Member States from leaving the Eurozone) would be Member States' competences, unless the Treaties expressly provided otherwise. The fact that we would be talking here about a competence "not to do," about a prohibition, further reinforces the force of all three arguments in this context; the EU would have a restricted ambit of competences, EU competences should be expressly attributed to the EU for it to act, and subsidiarity would imply a presumption against EU action. However, this presumption would be even more true for EU interventions with the aim of preventing Member States from taking action. In summary, all three arguments would give grounds for the *permissum videtur* principle to softly land in EU law. The *permissum videtur* principle would regulate the relationship between individual Member States and the Union, a *sui generis* international organization. Legal commitments encapsulating prohibitions against Member States should therefore be explicit. Outside this framework, Member States would be free to do as they please vis-à-vis other Member States and vis-à-vis the European Union itself. In other words, as exit from the Eurozone is not expressly prohibited, then Member States are free to unilaterally exit if and when they please. If one wants a metaphor to try to drive the following point home definitely, single Member States would be akin to individuals and the EU would be the public authority in this context. Therefore, the *permissum videtur* principle as applied to the EU and Member States would mirror the relationship between public power and individual relationships.

3.4.4 Restrictions on the Application of the *Permissum Videtur* Principle

Would there be any restrictions on the application of this principle in the Eurozone context? The answer is affirmative; there would be certain restrictions. The point is, rather, how extensive would these restrictions be. Would they impede the application of the *permissum videtur* principle to the Eurozone? Let us first consider the answer that Kolb provides to this problem from a general (public international law) perspective. According to this author,

> en généralisant ... on peut dire que la théorie de l'autorisation doit au moins l'emporter sur celle de la liberté résiduelle à chaque fois que le comportement d'un sujet affecte les droits subjectifs du tiers ... On a par ailleurs proposé de ne pas étendre la protection de la théorie de l'authorisation à tout comportement qui a des conséquences sur dessimples interest ... des tiers, car dans un monde de plus en plus interdépendant cela revient à inhiber trop largement les sphères d'action.

(Kolb, 2001: 118)

Applied to the EU context, the idea would then be the following: the application of the *permissum videtur* principle would find its limits when the subjective rights of other Member States (or the EU) were at stake. Simple "interests" would not be sufficient to definitively paralyse its application.

It is obvious that no other Member State or EU subjective rights (in the legal sense of this expression) would be affected if a Member State decided to exit the Eurozone. Not even the most extreme legal and or economic theses against unilateral exit elaborate on this idea. Similarly, it is however clear that if a Member State decided to exit, other Member States' interests or the European Union's (the Eurozone's) interests could be at stake. As Kolb says, this point would not be a definitive argument to stop the rule from being applied. However, it is also true that it should have some relevance for understanding how the *permissum videtur* principle should be applied in this context. In this sense, the idea would be that a Member State could unilaterally leave the Eurozone *if, and only if,* before making that decision, it had done everything it could to try to solve the situation in a cooperative manner with the EU and the rest of the Eurozone members. Once this approach had been tried with no positive results, then the Member State in question would be free to leave the Eurozone. EU or Member States' interests would only be a temporal stop for a Member State's unilateral exit. It would also be a brake that would imply that the potential exiter would do, to the best of its ability, what is possible to solve the issue cooperatively with the rest of the involved actors. Thereafter, it would be free to leave the Eurozone.

This stance is further reinforced by the analysis that Klamert (2014) performs, more specifically, on the EU principle of "loyal cooperation," which is enshrined in article 4(3) of the EU Treaty. According to Klamert,

> ... the Union interest in the form of a qualified expression of a concrete interest of one or several Union institutions should be the determining criterion for activating duties of action or abstention. While duties of conduct based on loyalty exist, they have shown to be the exception, while duties of result are the rule.

Klamert is speaking here of duties and not of plain legal commitments. Clearly, duties would be more than a political or a moral commitment[37] (to consider the Union's or other Member States' interests) but less than a legal obligation.[38] Second, Klamert also argues that in many cases, rather than speaking of a duty of result or of a duty of conduct, one should speak of a

---

[37] On the difference between legal, political, and moral commitments, see Estella (2015).

[38] Klamert appears to suggest that specific duties could stem directly either from the principle of loyal cooperation or from article 4(3) of the EUT. In my opinion, this provenance could only be correct if other articles (either of the Treaties or of EU secondary legislation) supported the creation of those duties. In the rest of the cases, either the principle or article 4(3) of the EUT would generate, at most, a general duty to cooperate, or a "best-effort" duty as Klamert refers to it.

"best-effort" duty. This commitment would exist, as I have suggested previously, concerning the area of exit from the Eurozone. Member States would have a sort of "duty" to make the best possible effort to find a cooperative solution before they decide to leave the euro. After that "duty" had been satisfied, they would be free to leave the Eurozone.

3.5 Expulsion from the Euro-Area is Forbidden. This Proposition is Absolute and Universal

As shown previously, expulsion from the Eurozone is not expressly foreseen in EU law. Moreover, mainstream legal and economic analyses, although more nuanced about expulsion, do accept the possibility of a member being expelled from the Eurozone. However, I will argue in the following that expulsion from the Eurozone is illegal in EU law. Moreover, this proposition is universal and does not admit further qualification.

Neither the TFEU nor the TEU foresees expulsion from the Union or from a particular EU policy. Nor does secondary EU law foresee expulsion. At most, EU constitutional law provides, as has already been mentioned in Section 3 of this chapter, for a system of "suspension" of Member States' voting rights in article 7 of the TEU.[39] However, such a sanction would be the consequence of a systematic violation by a Member State of article 2 of the TEU, an article that incorporates the main values and principles on which the EU is based such as democracy, the rule of law, human rights, and the equality principle. Article 7 raises the following points: first, because it establishes a sanction, it must be interpreted restrictively. Therefore, it applies only to cases in which a clear breach of article 2 TEU has occurred. Second, suspension of voting rights does not amount to expulsion from the Union. In fact, article 7(3) *in fine* states very clearly that the "suspended" Member State remains bound by EU law obligations derived from its membership in the Union. Third, it is unclear whether this article could provide a legal ground to suspend the voting rights of a Member State selectively concerning a particular policy; the wording of the article appears to indicate that this sanction is *all-or-nothing*. Finally but perhaps most importantly, this article poses very fundamental legitimacy issues, which most likely causes its potential application to become a very exceptional one, if it is ever applied at all. Thus, the structure of this article relies on the assumption that the Union is a perfect democracy, in which the rule of law, human rights, and the rest of the list included in article 2 are fully respected. However, and to say the least, this assumption is rather cavalier. In fact, were article 7 applied at all, we would then face a Kafkaesque conundrum in which an entity that is being constantly challenged from the perspective of its own legitimacy would also be suspending the rights of a Member State for

---

[39] On the genesis of article 7 EUT and its incorporation into the Treaty, see Sadurski (2010).

reasons of legitimacy. This contrast may explain why, irrespective of the fact that some Member States have recently undertaken a path that is at least dubious from the perspective of democracy and human rights, this article has never been implemented (Müller, 2013).

If suspension of voting rights is, as described by former president of the European Commission Barroso, "a nuclear option" solution (therefore, unusable) (Müller, 2013: 17) and expulsion is not foreseen by the EU Treaties, then it should be concluded that expulsion from the Eurozone is also barred. However, in the case in which both arguments were deemed to be of a rather formal type and therefore not completely convincing, there would be an additional argument against expulsion (from the Eurozone but also from the Union as a whole). I turn to this argument in the next pages.

The argument to which I refer is the reverse argument to the *permissum videtur* principle, which was mentioned in Section 3.4.1, above. In Latin, this second maxim would be "*quae non sunt permissae prohibita intelliguntur*," which means that all that is not permitted is prohibited. Because I have devoted an important part of this chapter to the *permissum videtur* principle, I will not tire the reader with a lengthy explanation of the origins and development of this principle, which can also be traced back to Roman law. The point I would wish to recall here is that, in public law, this principle is also called the principle of "positive bond," according to which public authorities, and in particular the public administration, would only be entitled to act when doing so is expressly permitted. Therefore, and applied to EU law, if expulsion is not expressly foreseen, then the EU public authorities could not simply expel a Member State. Here, the parallelism that we observed in Section 3.4 between public authorities (the Union) and individuals (single Member States) would also be applicable.

Let us develop this argument further. The first point to be noted is that the principles of both negative bond and positive bond, or *permissum videtur* and *permissae prohibita*, are but two sides of the same coin. Both would be applied to the Union in its relations with single Member States. From this perspective, the combination of both principles would imply a double restriction upon the Union. The first restriction (*permissum videtur*) would mean that the Member States are free to do everything that is not expressly prohibited. Therefore, the Union would not be legally entitled to prevent them from doing what is not expressly prohibited. The second restriction (*permissae prohibita*) would be that the Union could not do something when doing so is not expressly permitted. As occurred in the case of the *permissum videtur* principle, this point would be even truer in the area of sanctions of Member States.[40] In this

---

[40] According to Craig & de Burca (2011: 77), the ECJ has adopted both a narrow and a wider formulation of the "implied powers" theory. The narrow one connects the implied power to a preexistent, express, power or competence. The wider one connects it to a preexistent EU

field, the lack of permissions in favor of the Union to sanction should be more restrictively interpreted. Because expulsion from the Eurozone would be a type of sanction to a Member State that is not behaving well inside the Eurozone (as the conventional legal and economic view on expulsion argues), this restrictive interpretation should also be applied here. The interpretation should be that expulsion could only be accepted if it were expressly permitted. Lacking this particular permission, the Union could not expel any of its Members either from the Union or from particular policies. Recall that the two principles, "*permissum*" and "*permissae*," are thus applied to the Union due to the three major arguments that were previously advanced (competences have been delegated to the Union "albeit in limited fields," principle of attributed competences, and principle of subsidiarity).

A second point to be noted in the structure of the argument is that it assumes that the Union is "the public authority" and that single Member States are "like" individuals. It is clear that this proposition is a legal fiction, above all with respect to single Member States. However, as has been shown in a previous section of this chapter, public international law takes this assumption for granted in the sphere of international relations. Therefore, this part of the argument is not over-stretched to its logical limits. In other words, it does not assume anything that classical international relations or public international law does not. The metaphor according to which single Member States are similar to individuals in their relationships with the Union is a valid one if we want to obtain a better analytical insight into the problems associated with membership of and exit and expulsion from particular policies or areas, such as the Eurozone.

The third point to note is that the prohibition on expelling members from the Eurozone is a universal proposition with no exceptions. In this sense, it differs from the interpretation that was given to exit. We observed in a previous section that exit is subject to certain conditions, in particular, to the duty to make "a best effort" to solve the issue in a cooperative manner before a Member State proceeds to exit. However, the reason for this difference is clear: whereas *permissum videtur* is in reality thinking in terms of a single Member State's freedom to do or not to do, *permissae prohibita* is thinking in terms of the freedom of the Union to do or not to do. What the Union can do under the first (*permissum videtur*) is only a mirror reflexion of what Member States can or cannot do. Member States are free to leave; therefore, the Union cannot

objective. Although the "implied powers doctrine" has developed more extensively in the sphere of EU external action (see Konstadinidies, 2014), there are instances in which it has also found application in purely internal (EU) situations (see the case law cited by Craig & de Burca, *supra*). Expulsion would be closer to an internal EU situation than to the development of an EU external power. However, an "implied powers" argument could not be constructed here, because it is very difficult to see to which preexistent competence or even objective the power to expel could be linked. The closest option would be to link it to article 7 of the EUT, which, as I have argued in the text, clearly excludes expulsion.

impede them from doing so. However, because a single Member State's freedom to leave might affect either other Member States of the Union or the Union as a whole, the exercise of this freedom should be handled with care. Conversely, in the case of *permissae prohibita*, we are only discussing the relationship between the Union (a public authority) and a single Member State (the individual who could be expelled). If not expelled, one could argue that the rest of the Union or other Member States could be negatively affected.[41] However, this argument could not justify the acceptance of the Union's capacity to expel. The parallelism here is with the death penalty; if it is not legal, a particularly bad wrongdoing that a person might have done could not make it legal.

To summarize, because expulsion from the Eurozone is not expressly foreseen by EU law, it follows that Member States cannot be expelled from the European monetary union. The *permissae prohibita* principle, according to which all that is not expressly permitted is prohibited, would be of application to the Union authorities here. Furthermore, that the expulsion would have a "sanction" dimension would imply that a broad interpretation should be given to this restriction on the EU. Therefore, the Union could not derive a supposed right to expel members from the Eurozone indirectly from other legal bases of EU law, such as, for example, article 7 of the EU Treaty.

3.6 Access to and Exit and Expulsion from the Eurozone, and Credibility

To conclude this chapter, let me now turn to making general remarks concerning access, exit, and expulsion and the issue of credibility. The argument that has been developed thus far, above all concerning exit (exit from the Eurozone is legally possible), might appear counterintuitive from a credibility perspective. In fact, as seen, economists belonging to the classical tradition have linked the euro's credibility with the prohibition of exit from it. The euro would be credible insofar as it is perceived by citizens and above all by the markets as a definitive, irrevocable project. In other words, the strength of the euro would rely on its infinitude. To argue that the euro is a sort of hop-on/hop-off project would have amounted to inserting a time bomb in its very core.

From this perspective, lawyers' argument that because exit was not foreseen by the Treaties, this option was legally barred is but a reflection of the

---

[41] However, there should be an exercise of comparison of sufferings; for the same reason that a Member State exit could cause the rest of the Union or single Member States to suffer, expulsion could also have the same effect. Therefore, if expulsion were accepted, then the Union would have to consider whether it would suffer more with or without that Member State being expelled. In other words, expulsion, were it to be accepted, would necessarily cause the Union to engage in a similar comparative analysis of the relative costs and benefits that it would have, which we saw with respect to exit.

economists' idea according to which the credibility of the euro rested on its definitive and irrevocable character. In a way, the lawyers' arguments were tailor-made, perhaps unconsciously, to serve the purposes of the economists' perspectives about how to give to the euro the highest degree of credibility. In short, economists and lawyers coincided on this point, although their respective conversations rarely crossed each other.

The point that this chapter makes is the contrary one. A more credible interpretation of this issue would be that, because accession to the euro is voluntary, exit is possible and expulsion is barred. It is not by asserting (in economic and legal terms) that the euro is irrevocable – and, therefore, that no one can step away from it – that the EU would render this project more credible.

In my opinion, the following counterfactual drives the point home: what if a Member State exited the Eurozone? This possibility cannot be completely discarded. Even now that the crisis appears to have entered into a less hard phase, the truth of the matter is that Greece currently remains very much on the verge of exiting the Eurozone. If a Member State exited the Eurozone, the conventional interpretation could not make sense of this development; that is, of why the euro ceased to be irreversible, at least for one Member State. By contrast, the interpretation that is maintained in this book could take stock of this change; a Member State's exit would be understood, if not as a desirable state of affairs, then at least as normal business in a framework in which accession to the Eurozone is seen as merely voluntary. In other words, the interpretation according to which accession to the euro is voluntary (and therefore exit is also voluntary, but expulsion is barred) would be an equilibrium point in terms of credibility because it would consider the counterfactual better than the alternative interpretation. In fact, the credibility of the euro would have been better served had a more realistic approach to the issues of accession, exit, and expulsion presided over the minds of the drafters of the Treaty's provisions on the Eurozone, and above all over those who later endeavored to interpret them in a very particular way.

The role of interpretation (legal and economic) is of crucial importance in this domain. In fact, the Treaty's provisions on accession, exit, and expulsion are, as seen in this chapter, rather open-ended. The Treaty offers room to interpret these provisions, as has been done in this chapter, without stretching their logical and analytical chords to their limits. In other words, this chapter should not be viewed as a suggestion to modify the Treaty rules on the Eurozone to, for example, foresee the possibility of exit. The matter is, instead, one of exegesis, rather than one of Treaty reform. In terms of credibility, the Eurozone Treaty rules would be fine as they stand now *if and only if* a new conversation emerged on the issues of access, exit, and expulsion among both lawyers and economists. This new conversation should most likely give way to a new interpretation of these provisions that in turn better reflects the optimum state of affairs in this domain.

BIBLIOGRAPHY

Alonso Garcia, R. 2011, "El soft law comunitario," *Revista de Administración Pública*, no. 154, pp. 63–94.

   1994, *Derecho comunitario : sistema constitucional y administrativo de la Comunidad Europea*, CEURA, Madrid.

Ando, C. 2010, "'A dwelling beyond violence': on the uses and disadvantages of history for contemporary republicans," *History of Political Thought*, vol. 31, no. 2, pp. 183–220.

Ashton, D. & Reid, P. 2011, *On Clubs and Associations*, 2nd edn., Jordan, Bristol.

Athanassiou, P. 2009, "Withdrawal and expulsion from the EU and EMU. Some reflections," *ECB Legal Working Paper Series*, vol. 10, pp. 1–48.

Bernstorff, J. 2010, *The Public International Law Theory of Hans Kelsen*, Cambridge University Press, Cambridge.

Bordo, M. & MacDonald, R. 2012, *Credibility and International Monetary Regime. A Historical Perspective*, Cambridge University Press, New York.

Buti, M., Franco, D., & Ongena, H. 1998, "Fiscal discipline and flexibility in EMU: the implementation of the Stability and Growth Pact," *Oxford Review of Economic Policy*, vol. 14, no. 3, pp. 81–97.

Charteris-Blacka, J. & Musolffb, A. 2003, "'Battered hero' or 'innocent victim'? A comparative study of metaphors for euro trading in British and German financial reporting," *English for Specific Purposes*, no. 22, pp. 153–176.

Craig, P. 2012, "Competence and member state autonomy: causality, consequence and legitimacy" in *The European Court of Justice and the Autonomy of the Member States*, eds. H. W. Micklitz & B. de Witte, Intersentia, Cambridge, pp. 11–62.

   2011, "The ECJ and ultra vires action: a conceptual analysis," *Common Market Law Review*, no. 48, pp. 395–437.

Craig, P. P. & De Burca, G. 2011, *EU Law: Text, Cases, and Materials*, 5th edn., Oxford University Press, Oxford.

Damman, J. 2013, "The right to leave the Eurozone," *Texas International law Journal*, vol. 48, no. 2, pp. 125–155.

De Grauwe, P. 2012, *Economics of Monetary Union*, 9th edn., Oxford University Press, Oxford.

Domingo, R. 2006, *Principios de derecho Global. 1000 reglas, principios y aforismos juridicos comentados Aranzadi*, Thomson Aranzadi, Cizur Menor.

Draghi, M. 2012, Speech by Mario Draghi, President of the European Central Bank at the Global Investment Conference in London July 26, 2012.

Durden, T. 2015, "UBS Says 'A Market Dislocation Is Necessary To Focus Minds' And Stop 'Underestimating Grexit Risks'," June 2, www.zerohedge.com.

Eichengreen, B. 2007, "The breakup of the Euroarea," NBER (National Bureau of Economic Research) Working Paper 13393.

Elster, J. 1989, *Solomonic Judgements. Studies in the Limitations of Rationality*, Cambridge University Press, Cambridge.

Estella, A. 2015, "Law as credibility: an outline," *Il Foro Napoletano*, no. 1, pp. 40–63.

   2002, *The EU Principle of Subsidiarity and Its Critique*, Oxford University Press, Oxford.

Fernández de Buján, F. (dir.) 2008, *Diccionario Juridico El Derecho*, El Derecho Editores, Madrid.

Garcia de Enterria, E. 1958, "Observaciones sobre el fundamento de la inderogabilidad singular de los reglamentos," *Revista de Administración Pública*, vol. 27, pp. 63–86.

Herrmann, C. W. 2002, "Monetary sovereignty over the euro and external relations of the euro area: competences, procedures and practice," *European Foreign Affairs Review*, vol. 7, no. 1, pp. 1–24.

Hinajeros, A. 2015, *The Euro Area Crisis in Constitutional Perspective*, Oxford University Press, Oxford.

Hofmeister, H. 2011, "Goodbye Euro: legal aspects of withdrawal from the Eurozone," *Columbia Journal of European Law*, vol. 18, pp. 111–134.

James, H. 2012, *Making the European Monetary Union*, Harvard University Press, Cambridge & London.

Kelsen, H. 1953, "Théorie du droit international public," *Collected Courses of the Hague Academy of International Law*, vol. 84, pp. 1–201.

Klamert, M. 2014, *The Principle of Loyalty in EU Law*, Oxford University Press, Oxford.

Kolb, R. 2001, 'La règle résiduelle de liberté en droit international public ('tout ce qui n'est pas interdit est permis'). Aspects théoriques.," *Revue Belge de Droit International*, no. 1, pp. 100–127.

Konstadinidies, T. 2014, "EU foreign policy under the doctrine of implied powers: codification drawbacks and constitutional limitations," *European Law Review*, vol. 39, no. 4, pp. 511–530.

Lastra, R. M. 2006, *Legal Foundations of International Monetary Stability*, Oxford University Press, Oxford & New York.

Lastra, R. M. & Louis, J. 2013, "European economic and monetary union: history, trends, and prospects," *Yearbook of European Law*, vol. 32, no. 1, pp. 57–206.

Legrain, P. 2014, *European Spring: Why Our Economies and Politics are in a Mess – and How to Put Them Right*, CB Books, London.

Lenaerts, K. 2011, "Federalism and the rule of law: perspectives from the European Court of Justice," *Fordham International Law Journal*, vol. 33, no. 5, pp. 1338–1387.

1990, "Constitutionalism and the many faces of federalism," *The American Journal of Comparative Law*, vol. 38, no. 2, pp. 205–263.

Lenaerts, K. & Gutierrez-Fons, J. A. 2010, "The allocation of powers and general principles of EU law," *Common Market Law Review*, vol. 47, pp. 1629–1669.

Louis, J.-V. 2010, "Guest editorial: The no bail-out clause and rescue packages," *Common Market Law Review*, vol. 47, pp. 971–986.

Magliveras, K. 2011, *Membership in International Organisations*, Edward Elgar, Cheltenham.

1999, *Exclusion from Participation in International Organisations. The Law and Practice Behind Member States' Expulsion and Suspension of Membership*, Kluwer Law International, The Hague.

Merler, S. 2015, "Who's (still) exposed to Greece?," Bruegel, 29 January. http://bruegel.org/2015/02/whos-still-exposed-to-greece/.

Mody, A. 2013, "Sovereign debt and its restructuring framework in the euro area," Bruegel Working Paper 2013/05.

Müller, J. 2013, "Defending democracy within the EU," *Journal of Democracy*, vol. 24, no. 2, pp. 138–149.

Proctor, C. 2006, "The future of the Euroarea: what happens if a Member State leaves?," *European Business Law Review*, no. 4, pp. 909–937.

Proctor, C. & Thyeffry, G. 1998, "Thinking the unthinkable – The break up of Economic and Monetary Union," www.nortonrosefulbright.com/knowledge/publi cations/68769/thinking-the-unthinkable-the-break-up-of-economic-and-monetary-union.

Sadurski, W. 2010, "Adding bite to a bark: the story of article 7, E.U. enlargement, and Jorg Haider," *Columbia Journal of European Law*, vol. 16, pp. 385–426.

Scott, H. 2011, "When the Euro falls apart – A sequel 5," Harvard Public Law, Working Paper no. 12-16, available at http://papers.ssrn.com/sol3/papers.cfm?abstract_id= 1998356.

1988, "When the Euro falls apart," *International Finance*, vol. 1, no. 2, pp. 207–228.

Seyad, S. M. 1999, *European Community Law on the Free Movement of Capital and EMU*, Kluwer Law International, The Hague & London.

Shaw, M. 2008, *International Law*, Cambridge University Press, Cambridge.

Sinn, H. 2011, "There is no alternative but Greece's euro zone expulsion," www.creditwritedowns.com/2011/09/sinngreece-eurozone-expulsion.html.

Sinn, H. & Sell, F. 2012, "Our opt-in opt-out solution for the euro," *Financial Times*, July 31, p. 9, www.ft.com/cms/s/0/b2c75538-da35-11e1-b03b-00144feab49a .html#axzz3LP3MQJht.

Stark, J. 2008, Speech by Jürgen Stark, Member of the Executive Board of the ECB, delivered at the Icelandic Chamber of Commerce Reykjavik, February 13, 2008.

Tatham, A. 2012, "'Don't mention divorce at the wedding, darling!': EU accession and withdrawal after Lisbon" in *EU Law after Lisbon*, eds. A. Biondi, P. Eeckhout & S. Ripley, Oxford University Press, Oxford, pp. 129–154.

Tayler, D. 2015, "White House Refutes European Complacency: Warns Grexit Threatens Global Economic Recovery," May 7, 2015, www.zerohedge.com/news/ 2015-04-21/white-house-refutes-european-complacency-warns-grexit-threatens-global-economic-reco.

Thieffry, G. 2011, "Thinking the probable: the break-up of monetary union," *Journal of International Banking Law and Regulation*, no. 3, pp. 103–104.

Tomkins, A. & Scott, P. 2015, *Entick v Carrington: 250 Years of the Rule of Law*, Hart Publishing, Oxford and Portland.

Treves, T. 2000, "Monetary sovereignty today" in *International Monetary Law: Issues for the New Millennium* ed. M. Giovanoli, Oxford University Press, Oxford, pp. 111–121.

Tuori, K. & Tuori, K. 2014, *The Eurozone Crisis: A Constitutional Analysis*, Cambridge University Press, Cambridge.

Weatherill, S. 2004, "Competence creep and competence control," *Yearbook of European Law*, vol. 23, no. 1, pp. 1–55.

Weiler, J. H. H. 2001, "Federalism without constitutionalism: Europe's Sonderweg" in *The Federal Vision: Legitimacy and Levels of Governance in the United States and the European Union*, eds. K. Nicolaïdis & R. Howse, Oxford University Press, Oxford, pp. 1–17.

Zilioli, C. & Selmayr, M. 2000, "The European Central Bank: an independent specialized organization of Community Law," *Common Market Law Review*, vol. 37, no. 3, pp. 591–643.

4

The ECB and European Monetary Policy

Introduction

In this chapter, I will analyze one of the key institutions (if not the most important) of the EU system of economic governance: the European Central Baulc [ECB]. I will also analyze how it has conducted European monetary policy since the euro came into being, and will make particular reference to how it has handled Eurozone monetary policy during the crisis that started in 2008.

The main justification that underlies the setting up of independent monetary authorities, not only in the EU but also in general terms, relates to credibility. Thus, it is usually argued that the only approach to conducting a credible monetary policy is to isolate it from the normal political circle. This position is why democracies delegate monetary policy to independent, technocratic agencies. This chapter revisits this argument concerning the ECB and offers a new reading of the delegation of monetary policy to this EU agency from the perspective of the "law as credibility" paradigm. As we will see, the issue of trust (or distrust) of the normal political system in democracies is at the basis of this move towards delegation. I will therefore start with this crucial point.

4.1 Why Delegate Monetary Policy to Independent Agencies?

According to its statute, the ECB is an independent authority. As Martin Shapiro states when he speaks of independent agencies (Shapiro, 1997), the ECB is independent from "all," at least in theory; it is independent from the markets, from the citizens, but above all, it is independent from politicians and political-democratic institutions. Thus, the EU does not escape from the trend, generalized in the 1990s, towards the delegation of monetary policy to independent and technocratic institutions: rather, it is but another example of the same species. In the following, I will review the main arguments why this should be.

The idea that monetary policy should be isolated from politics was born in the 1980s. In a number of seminal papers, Barro and Gordon (1983a; 1983b) and Rogoff (1985) defended the idea that monetary policy should be conducted not by the government but by an independent agency. The main tenets of this literature are the following.

First, there exists a tradeoff between unemployment and inflation, as illustrated by the so-called "Philips curve."[1] Therefore, to curb unemployment, the government might be tempted to implement "surprise inflation." This tactic has a short-term benefit (growth is enhanced and unemployment lowered) but a medium-and long-term cost (inflation increases even beyond equilibrium). Governments' commitments that they will not use surprise inflation are not credible because they face a time-consistency problem; they have incentives to deviate from the original commitment over time. These incentives are primarily of an electoral type; if, in the short term, they can raise growth and lower unemployment to secure reelection, voters will forget about the longer-term negative effects on inflation that can derive from an activist monetary policy. Furthermore, society rationally expects that the government will behave as described. Therefore, the government will accommodate its behavior to society's expectations, since it has an incentive to do so.

Second, the only approach to credibly commit not to implement surprise inflation and to effectively change society's expectations is to delegate monetary policy to an agency independent from the government, which should be run by a conservative policymaker. In turn, this independent agency, the central bank, would be legally committed to follow a given inflation target. Thus, the society would modify its expectations and would know that the government could not use monetary policy for the purposes of steering growth and combatting unemployment.

However and in the third place, as Rogoff contends, this commitment to a given inflation target should not be too rigid. There should therefore be "intermediate" inflation targets, and the central bank should be run by a conservative policymaker, although she should not be "too conservative." Such targets would introduce a certain range of flexibility within the capacity of the central bank to address sudden economic shocks.

As seen, there are at least three main ideas in this seminal literature: first, the idea of delegating to an agency independent from the government because governments cannot be credibly trusted not to implement surprise inflation; second, the idea of legally committing to specific inflation targets (although for some authors, these targets should be intermediate and not infinite in any case) that the agency should implement and that the government cannot modify; and third, the idea that the central bank should be run by a conservative policymaker (although according to some authors, she should not be too conservative).

As de Grauwe explains (2016: 158), the idea that monetary policy should be delegated to independent agencies was not born in a vacuum. It was a reaction

---

[1] The "Philips curve" denotes an inverse relationship between the unemployment rate and the inflation rate. See Philips (1958).

to the Keynesian turn that occurred after the Great Depression and lasted until
the 1960s. However, the mid 1970s and 1980s witnessed in a number of
countries (such as the UK and the US) what was referred to as "stagflation"[2] –
a situation of low or no growth, high unemployment, and high inflation, that
is, the worst of all possible economic worlds. The so-called "monetarist school"
now took the lead, arguing against Keynesianism and in favor of strong
control over inflation through implementation of a strict monetary policy.
The main advocate of this point of view was a University of Chicago
economics professor, Milton Friedman:

> My own prescription is ... that the monetary authority go all the way in
> avoiding such swings by adopting publicly the policy of achieving a steady rate
> of growth in a specified monetary total. The precise rate of growth, like the
> precise monetary total, is less important than the adoption of some stated and
> known rate. I myself have argued for a rate that would on the average achieve
> rough stability in the level of process of final products, which I have estimated
> would call for something like a 3 to 5 percent per year rate of growth in currency
> plus all commercial bank deposits or a slightly lower rate of growth in currency
> plus all commercial bank deposits only. But it would be better to have a fixed
> rate that would on the average produce moderate inflation or moderate defla-
> tion, provided it was steady, than to suffer the wide and erratic perturbations ...
> experienced.
>
> (Friedman, 1968: 16)

The importance of money as a fundamental economic driver was thus redis-
covered. For Friedman, money mattered. Not only did it matter, but its
mismanagement could also provoke severe recessions, such as the Great
Depression. Keynes had explained the Great Depression as a fiscal (public
spending) problem. Instead, Friedman labeled the Great Depression the Great
Contraction; the supply of money had been contracted and this led, in turn, to
the depression. If the monetary authorities had reacted differently, the slump
would not have been as severe.[3] Therefore, it was for the monetary authority to
manage monetary policy rather strictly and conservatively.

---

[2] The term was coined by Samuelson (1977), who defined it as involving "inflationary rises in
prices and wages at the same time that people are unable to find jobs and firms are unable to find
customers for what their plants can produce."

[3] This conclusion is criticized by Krugman (2007): "In interpreting the origins of the Depression,
the distinction between the monetary base (currency plus bank reserves), which the Fed controls
directly, and the money supply (currency plus bank deposits) is crucial. The monetary base went
up during the early years of the Great Depression, rising from an average of $6.05 billion in
1929 to an average of $7.02 billion in 1933. But the money supply fell sharply, from $26.6 billion
to $19.9 billion. This divergence primarily reflected the fallout from the wave of bank failures in
1930–1931: as the public lost faith in banks, people began holding their wealth in cash rather
than bank deposits, and those banks that survived began keeping large quantities of cash on
hand rather than lending it out, to avert the danger of a bank run. The result was much less
lending, and hence much less spending, than there would have been if the public had continued
to deposit cash into banks, and banks had continued to lend deposits out to businesses. And

The monetarist school had its intellectual roots in the Hayekian tradition. In fact, the controversy between the neo-Keynesians and monetarists from the 1970s onwards replayed the previous debate between Keynes himself and Hayek, a duel that had been fought for much of the first half of the twentieth century (see Wapshott, 2011). In a way, we remain today, in 2018, in the middle of this controversy.

For Friedman, "the elementary truth is that the Great Depression was produced by government mismanagement."[4] However, an overall mistrust of government and in general of public intervention as a means of efficiently managing the economy had been argued by Hayek in *The Road to Serfdom* (originally published in 1944), almost four decades before Friedman wrote the previous statement. Hayek was Friedman's mentor in the Mont Pelerin Society, a think-tank that was founded by the Austrian school and aimed to spread neoliberal ideas around the world.[5] "Most planners who have seriously considered the practical aspects of their task have little doubt that a directed economy must be run on more or less dictatorial lines," said Hayek in *The Road to Serfdom*. Government's intervention in the economy should not be considered of secondary importance but instead the "crux of the matter" of freedom; "the authority directing all economic activity would control not merely the part of our lives which is concerned with inferior things; it would control the allocation of the limited means of all our ends. And whoever controls all economic activity controls the means for all our ends and must therefore decide which are to be satisfied and which not."

Concerning monetary policy, Hayek said, "With government in control of monetary policy, the chief threat in this field has become inflation" (1960: 285). Therefore, he contended, the supply of money should be privatized and become part of a competitive process, as are all other supply processes of goods and services in a free economy: "Why should we not rely on the

since a collapse of spending was the proximate cause of the Depression, the sudden desire of both individuals and banks to hold more cash undoubtedly made the slump worse. Friedman and Schwartz claimed that the fall in the money supply turned what might have been an ordinary recession into a catastrophic depression, itself an arguable point. But even when we grant that point for the sake of argument, one has to ask whether the Federal Reserve, which after all did increase the monetary base, can be said to have caused the fall in the overall money supply. At least initially, Friedman and Schwartz didn't say that. What they said instead was that the Fed could have prevented the fall in the money supply, in particular by riding to the rescue of the failing banks during the crisis of 1930–1931. If the Fed had rushed to lend money to banks in trouble, the wave of bank failures might have been prevented, which in turn might have avoided both the public's decision to hold cash rather than bank deposits, and the preference of the surviving banks for stashing deposits in their vaults rather than lending the funds out. And this, in turn, might have staved off the worst of the Depression." Available at www.nybooks.com/articles/2007/02/15/who-was-milton-friedman.

[4] Cited by Krugman (2007).

[5] "Though not necessarily sharing a common interpretation, either of causes or consequences, [the Mont Pelerin Society] see[s] danger in the expansion of government, not least in state welfare, in the power of trade unions and business monopoly, and in the continuing threat and reality of inflation," reads the Mont Pelerin Society's website. See www.montpelerin.org.

spontaneous forces of the market to supply what is needed for a satisfactory medium of exchange as we do in most other respects?" he asked (ibid.: 282). However, he warned that the previous proposal was not feasible in the current state of affairs: "Perhaps, if governments had never interfered, a kind of monetary arrangement would have evolved which would not have required deliberate control ... this choice, however, is now closed to us" (ibid.: 282). Consequently, he advocated central banks' independence as a second-best approach. According to Hayek (ibid.: 290–293),

> ... an independent monetary authority, fully protected against political pressure and free to decide on the means to be employed in order to achieve the ends it has been assigned, might be the best arrangement. The old arguments in favor of independent central banks still have great merit ... the argument against discretion in monetary policy rests on the view that monetary policy and its effects should be as predictable as possible. The validity of the argument depends, therefore, on whether we can devise an automatic mechanism which will make the effective supply of money change in a more predictable and less disturbing manner ... this means, in practice, that under present conditions we have little choice but to limit monetary policy by prescribing its goals rather than its specific actions.

To summarize, the advocates of central banks' independence made their point acutely clear; the normal political process could not be credibly trusted to control inflation. The temptation to inflate to make the economy grow and thereby combat unemployment was deemed too strong to be resisted. Therefore, the control of inflation, and in general terms, monetary policy, should be taken out of the hands of politicians and given to independent, technical agencies whose proclaimed legal goal should be the control of inflation. At the beginning of the 1990s, there was a basic consensus in the academic economic world that central bank independence was a key factor for controlling inflation.

4.2 Evidence on the Correlation between Independence and the Control of Inflation

In accord with the previous consensus, the 1990s witnessed an increasing trend towards the delegation of monetary policy to central banks and towards a reinforcement of their respective statutes. To the best of my knowledge, the latest and broadest analysis that exists on central banks' independence reforms is that of Carolina Garriga (2016). She coded central bank legislation in 182 countries. Her results do not differ much from conventional wisdom on the issue (Cukierman, 2008: 725), but her study qualifies it to a certain extent. According to the author, "the percentage of observations coded as reforms is 5.3% for the 1970s, 3.2% for the 1980s, 7.9% for the 1990s, 5.5% for the 2000s, and 5.9% for the first three years of the 2010s." Therefore, in relative terms, the period in which more advances towards independence were made was the 1990s, although this does not mean that reforms were absent in other periods.

Because the proof of the pudding is in the eating, since the 1990s, a growing empirical literature has emerged on the correlation between independence and inflation control. This literature falls into two groups: a mainstream group that in fact found a correlation between the two, and a more modern one that casts doubts upon it. This division is important because if a lack of correlation were evidenced, this would have consequences in terms of credibility. I will therefore review this literature in the following.

The literature measuring the correlation between independence and inflation starts with Cukierman (1992; 2008) and Cukierman, Webb, and Neyapti (1992). Cargill (2016) claims that, in reality, Bade and Parkin (1982) constitute the paleo-literature in this field: "Interestingly, the 1982 paper by Bade and Parkin is probably the most cited paper because it provides the framework for constructing indices of central bank independence; yet the paper has never been published, nor is the original version even available. The only available version of the 1982 paper is a revised version dated 1988 [Bade and Parkin, 1988]." Other authors who have worked along the same lines are Alesina and Summers (1993), Grilli, Masciandaro, and Tabellini (1991), Gutierrez (2003) and Carlstrom and Fuerst (2009). This work represents the conventional wisdom on the issue.

In essence, this strand of literature finds a robust negative correlation between independence and inflation; thus, more independence results in less inflation. Cukierman (1992) and Cukierman, Webb, and Neyapti (1992) constructed an index of central bank independence. This index is based on what they refer to as "*de iure*" independence; that is, to construct their index, they focused on the extent to which the law has granted independence to monetary agencies. This focus has been criticized by some authors as biasing the results. Cukierman (2008) has addressed such criticisms and has found similar results: independence and inflation control are highly negatively correlated even when we control for "*de facto*" independence. He cites the Bank of Israel as a case in point. Cukierman also finds similar results for both industrialized and developing countries. However, he admits that the explanation must rely also on other variables: in particular, he says, "Countries that entrench the legal independence of the [central bank] in the constitution have lower inflation than those that do not." This point is crucial for our analysis of this issue from a "law as credibility" perspective, as will be seen later.

Grilli, Masciandaro, and Tabellini (1991) find a correlation between independence and low inflation in OECD countries. For them, monetary independence is similar to a free lunch because monetary independence has no negative side effects on macroeconomic variables. In much the same vein, Alesina and Summers (1993) find a correlation between central bank independence and inflation, and, again, find no correlation between independence and other "real" economic variables such as unemployment, growth, and real interest rates. Gutierrez (2003) builds up an independent index based on constitutional delegation of monetary policy to independent agencies. However, he confines his analysis to Latin American countries. He finds a correlation between central bank independence as enshrined in constitutions and inflation central. Even more important for our purposes, he finds a higher degree of correlation between independence and inflation when independence is entrenched in constitutions rather than in laws.

> There are several reasons why constitutional provisions regarding the central bank might reflect the true degree of autonomy of the institution better that the central bank charter ... the constitution is likely to be better enforced than ordinary statutes due to its higher legal rank. Claims on the violations of constitutional provisions can only be addressed by the Constitutional court, typically including the most respected judges in the country. The members of the court hold long term positions, which help detach them from government influence. In addition, constitutional entrenchment might enhance central bank independence, particularly in environments where the government or the governing coalition with a legislative majority attempts to influence central bank policies. This is so because modifications in the constitution tend to require qualified majorities, eliminating potential threats to make changes in the legal status of the central bank. Furthermore, constitutional entrenchment of central bank independence reflects a wide political and social consensus regarding the status and objectives of the central bank, which is likely to be translated into de facto central bank independence.
>
> (Gutiérrez, 2003: 3)

Finally, Carlstrom and Fuerst (2009) analyze independence with respect to a number of industrialized countries in two periods (1955–1988 and 1988–2000). In these two periods, inflation decreased as independence increased. On average, the authors conclude that "increased independence explains ... 63% of the decline in average inflation rates."

This strand of research has been questioned from the late 1990s onwards. Posen (1995; 1998) was the first to raise the so-called "endogeneity" question; perhaps low inflation could be explained not by exogenous variables (and in particular by the independence of central banks) but by endogenous ones. In particular, he explored the extent to which the financial sector's opposition to inflation played a primary role in explaining low inflation outcomes, and he found a correlation, which in turn downplayed the importance of institutional factors such as independence. However, the significance of this variable (financial sector opposition to inflation) has also been explored by a number of authors in more recent analyses, and they have found no correlation with inflation (Campillo & Miron, 1997; Haan & Kooi, 2000).

In turn, Campillo and Miron (1997) show evidence that independence does not by itself appear "to be of much help to achieve low inflation." Other variables, such as openness of the economy, political instability, and tax policy, appear to play a much larger role in explaining inflation outcomes. In much the same vein, Ismihan and Ozkan (2004) develop a model in which public debt and inflation are correlated. Therefore, the control of public spending is, according to the authors, a much better predictor of inflation outcomes than is independence. Haan and Kooi (2000) qualify the finding that independence, as measured by central banks' governor turnover, is a better predictor of inflation outcomes "only if high inflation countries are included in the sample." Garriga (2016: 852) questions this index as a proxy for independence because it can simply indicate that central bankers unable to control inflation are replaced more often; therefore, a high turnover is perhaps indicative of a strong commitment to low inflation rather than a symptom of government control over the central bank. The same author puts her finger on the wound when she argues that the dynamics of independence as an explanatory variable are very much influenced by the availability of data on central bank independence and how these data are construed. "It is possible that results on global samples are biased." Although she finds associations between independence and low inflation, she concludes, "The global effect of central bank reforms seems less dramatic on samples including more countries, especially because the previously excluded countries show less variance in Central Bank Independence." In other words, the larger the sample, the less the association between independence and inflation control.

Finally, Cargill (2016) summarizes all of the problems with the "conventional wisdom" literature on the correlation between independence and low inflation. According to this author, the problems are threefold: (1) this literature mostly relies on "*de iure*" measures of independence, which are far from perfect. (2) "*De facto*" independence is a more appropriate variable; however, it is difficult to systematize (what is to be understood by "*de facto*" independence?) and, above all, measure. (3) Most of the studies ignore the so-called "Japan" problem, which is a case of a central bank with high political dependence on the government and low inflation outcomes; for Cargill, this case is so significant that any account of the relationship between independence and inflation should be able to explain it. Finally, Cargill finds that other, endogenous variables, such as culture (societal aversion to inflation) and politics (self-sustained commitment to low inflation by political institutions), are better predictors of inflation outcomes.

To summarize this review of both strands of the academic literature that has addressed the empirical issue of independence and inflation, we can say that, at the very least, the most recent research on the topic should lead us to take at least a prudential approach to this complex matter. Central banks' independence is most likely a factor that affects inflation control – although not the only or the most decisive one. To my knowledge, a counterfactual experiment has not been done in this area; one would most likely add more information on the relationship between independence and inflation than what is provided by the state-of-the-art research on this matter. It is also very striking to see that, above all, the strand of literature that shows evidence of a strong relationship between independence and low inflation does not explain the mechanisms that could underlie this relationship. If a relationship between independence and low inflation were shown, a fine-grained explanation of the reason for this relationship would remain to be given. It is also unfortunate that the idea that constitutional independence of the central bank yields better results than other legal entrenchments of independence has not been further explored.

4.3 Legal Statute of the ECB

The legal statute of the ECB is fixed in the Treaty on the Functioning of the European Union. In particular, the provisions that shape the basic trends of its statute are scattered in the Treaty itself and in Protocol no. 4 on the "Statute of the European System of Central Banks and of the European Central Bank." This Protocol was originally annexed to the Treaty on European Union (Maastricht Treaty, 1992). Therefore, the Protocol also has the same legal status as the Treaty itself. In other words, the basic and most important elements forming the legal statute of the ECB have constitutional rank. The legal statutes of central banks are not always entrenched in constitutions or constitution-like texts such as the EU Treaties. For example, the statute of the Federal Reserve of the United States was established in an Act of the US Congress in 1913. In turn, the German Basic Law provides for the setting up of a central bank and the delegation of its monetary powers to the ECB in its article 88. However, even the German Basic Law is rather cursory concerning this aspect; it simply says that the federation shall set up a Federal Bank.[6] Interestingly, article 88 of the German Basic Law speaks of independence and price stability but concerning the ECB – not the Bundesbank. The other aspects that form the legal statute of the Buba are developed in the Bundesbank law of 1957.

I will review in turn how the EU Treaties (in particular, the TFEU) delineate the legal statute of the ECB. The main pillars of the ECB statute are (1) the ECB's independence, (2) the ECB's mission, (3) the election of the ECB's president, and (4) the prohibition imposed on the ECB with respect to bailouts.

4.3.1 Independence

Article 130 TFEU says:

> When exercising the powers and carrying out the tasks and duties conferred upon them by the Treaties and the Statute of the ESCB and of the ECB, neither

---

[6] "The Federation shall establish a note-issuing and currency bank as the Federal Bank. Within the framework of the European Union, its responsibilities and powers may be transferred to the European Central Bank, which is independent and committed to the overriding goal of assuring price stability."

the European Central Bank, nor a national central bank, nor any member of their decision-making bodies shall seek or take instructions from Union institutions, bodies, offices or agencies, from any government of a Member State or from any other body. The Union institutions, bodies, offices or agencies and the governments of the Member States undertake to respect this principle and not to seek to influence the members of the decision-making bodies of the European Central Bank or of the national central banks in the performance of their tasks.

This point is repeated at least twice more. The first time is in article 282.3 of the TFEU, when it says that the ECB "shall be independent in the exercise of its powers and in the management of its finances. Union institutions, bodies, offices and agencies and the governments of the Member States shall respect that independence." The second time is in article 7 of the Protocol on the ECB statute, which repeats article 130 almost verbatim.

To the best of my knowledge, there is not such a bold and redundant declaration of a central bank's independence in any other constitutional text. As seen previously, the US Constitution does not even mention the Federal Reserve, and the German Basic Law only refers indirectly to Bundesbank independence in article 88. The aim of the drafters of the ECB statute, when including the ECB's independence at different points in the Treaty, was clear: to provide the highest degree of credibility to the ECB's independence, even higher than what two of the most successful central banks in the world, the Federal Reserve and the Bundesbank, had obtained.

In terms of the particular commitment to monetary independence (that is, independently of its effect on inflation control), this movement is in principle understandable (see however my remarks in the final section of this chapter). The EU Treaties are particularly rigid to amendment (above all, now, with 28 Member States), and the best approach to make credible the proposition that the new bank would be independent from all (but above all from the governments of the Member States) was to entrench its independence in the Treaties. The counterfactual (what if this particular commitment had been placed in a regulation?, for example) would have given the commitment to independence a lesser degree of credibility. In other words, credibility here amounts to the maximum degree of rigidity that a system (in this case, the EU system) could afford. I will, however, revisit this argument later.

We are speaking, of course, of legal or "*de iure*" independence. A different thing is whether the EU central bank has achieved "*de facto*" independence not with respect to the governments of the Member States (or even the EU's government) but with respect to one of its most powerful counterparts, the Bundesbank. Because this issue demands the consideration of other variables (such as how the president of the ECB is elected), I will leave this discussion for a different section. Suffice it to say that by now there are indications that the ECB could be acting under what I will refer to as "the shadow" of the Bundesbank.

4.3.2 Mission

Article 127 TFEU reads as follows:

> The primary objective of the European System of Central Banks (hereinafter referred to as "the ESCB") shall be to maintain price stability.

The European System of Central Banks is defined by article 282 TFEU as follows: "The European Central Bank, together with the national central banks, shall constitute the European System of Central Banks (ESCB)." The ECB presides over the ESCB (in particular, the Eurosystem); it is *primus inter pares*. This preeminence is made clear by the second sentence of article 282, which says that "The European Central Bank, together with the national central banks of the Member States whose currency is the euro, which constitute the Eurosystem, shall conduct the monetary policy of the Union." The ECB is therefore at the epicenter of the EU system of monetary governance.

Price stability is therefore the primary mission of the ECB. However, article 127 adds the following:

> Without prejudice to the objective of price stability, the ESCB shall support the general economic policies in the Union with a view to contributing to the achievement of the objectives of the Union as laid down in Article 3 of the Treaty on European Union.

In turn, article 282.2 TFEU and article 2 of the Protocol repeat exactly the wording of article 127 TFEU.

The socio-economic objectives of the Union are set, in particular, in article 3.3 TFEU. These are:

- Economic growth and price stability
- A highly competitive social market economy, aiming at full employment and social progress
- A high level of protection and improvement of the quality of the environment
- The promotion of scientific and technological advance.

There are two possible interpretations of this reference to the (larger than price stability) objectives of the Union that article 127 makes. The first, more ample one would be to say that the ECB's mission of price stability must be achieved such that the other objectives that article 3.3 establishes are also achieved. The second, more restrictive one would be to say that the overriding objective is price stability, which should have priority over the rest of the EU's economic objectives. In other words, both interpretations assume that there is a tradeoff between price stability and the other objectives, in particular, the (full) employment objective. Therefore, the first interpretation would imply that the ECB must try to accommodate these objectives, even at a certain expense in terms of inflation control, whereas the second interpretation would imply that the tradeoff must be resolved, always, in favor of inflation control.

Which of the two interpretations has been retained? Clearly, the second, more restrictive one is the one that has triumphed, or at least, it has guided the conduct of monetary policy by the ECB. The ECB website reads, where this institution describes its own "tasks," that "the primary objective of the European System of Central Banks . . . shall be to maintain price stability. This provision is the critical one in the monetary policy chapter of the Treaty on the Functioning of the European Union."[7] Further, in "The Monetary Policy of the ECB" (2011), a document in which the ECB describes its mission and how it has conducted monetary policy since the inception of this institution, the ECB says,

> The Treaties thus establish a clear hierarchy of objectives for the Eurosystem, which clarifies that price stability is the most important contribution that monetary policy can make to achieving a favorable economic environment and a high level of employment.

The control of inflation is therefore the ECB's mission. This mission locates this institution closer to the Bundesbank and further away from the Federal Reserve. In effect, the Bundesbank Basic Law says, as seen elsewhere (article 88), that the "overriding" objective is price stability. This objective is confirmed by article 3 of the Bundesbank law, which says that the primary objective of the Bundesbank is "maintaining price stability." Neither article 88 of the German Basic Law nor article 3 of the Bundesbank law references other objectives, whereas article 2A of the Federal Reserve Act has a very different tone: "The Board of Governors of the Federal Reserve System and the Federal Open Market Committee shall maintain long run growth of the monetary and credit aggregates commensurate with the economy's long-run potential to increase production, so as to promote effectively the goals of maximum employment, stable prices, and moderate long-term interest rates." Maximum employment, stable prices and moderate long-term interest rates are placed on the same footing; this approach has allowed the Fed to act more flexibly during economic slowdowns, without at the same time placing its own statute in jeopardy. I will return to this crucial point when I analyze the issue of the ECB's mission and credibility.

Although the mission of the ECB is the control of inflation, what the Treaties and the Protocol do not set up is a *particular* inflation target. This omission could have been made as a proof of flexibility; on the one hand, the Treaties were set up very clearly such that the primary objective is inflation control. On the other hand, they did not specify any particular inflation target. The ECB could have taken this flexibility to "adapt" the inflation target to the specific point of the economic cycle in which the EU might be. This point is

---

[7] www.ecb.europa.eu/ecb/tasks/html/index.en.html.

similar to the one about "intermediate" inflation targets that Rogoff (1985) made.

However, the ECB, following the majoritarian vision on inflation targeting and credibility that has been examined above, set up a general specific inflation target for the whole Eurozone in 1998. In particular, at the ECB's Governing Council meeting of October 13, 1998, the ECB stated that[8]

> Price stability shall be defined as a year-on-year increase in the Harmonised Index of Consumer Prices (HICP) for the euro area of below 2%.

This statement generated a certain amount of confusion, because the expression "an inflation target below 2%" appeared to set a maximum limit, but not a minimum one. Therefore, the ECB further clarified its monetary strategy in another statement on May 8, 2003, according to which[9]

> The Governing Council agreed that in the pursuit of price stability it will aim to maintain inflation rates close to 2% over the medium term. This clarification underlines the ECB's commitment to provide a sufficient safety margin to guard against the risks of deflation. It also addresses the issue of the possible presence of a measurement bias in the HICP and the implications of inflation differentials within the euro area.

Therefore, the fixed, once-and-for-all, inflation target for the Eurozone is an objective that is "below, but close, to 2% over the medium term." The importance of the expression *medium term* must also be stressed because it provides a certain margin of maneuver to the ECB to adapt to changing economic circumstances; "to retain some flexibility, it is not advisable to specify *ex ante* a precise horizon for the conduct of monetary policy, because the transmission mechanism spans a variable, uncertain period of time. Additionally, the optimal monetary policy response to ensure price stability always depends on the specific nature and size of the shocks affecting the economy," says the ECB.[10] This point has become even truer during the 2008 crisis.

4.3.3 Election

Article 283.2 TFEU states:

> The President, the Vice-President and the other members of the Executive Board shall be appointed by the European Council, acting by a qualified majority, from among persons of recognised standing and professional

---

[8] "A stability-oriented monetary policy strategy for the ESCB." ECB Press Release, October 13, 1998, available at www.ecb.europa.eu/press/pr/date/1998/html/pr981013_1.en.html.

[9] "The ECB's monetary policy strategy." ECB Press Release, May 8, 2003, available at www.ecb.europa.eu/press/pr/date/2003/html/pr030508_2.en.html.

[10] See www.ecb.europa.eu/mopo/strategy/princ/html/orientation.en.html.

experience in monetary or banking matters, on a recommendation from the Council, after it has consulted the European Parliament and the Governing Council of the European Central Bank.

In other words, the president of the European Central Bank shall be elected by the European Council by a qualified majority vote. This point is reiterated by article 11.2 of the Protocol to the ECB.

I will make two points concerning this important issue. The first addresses the voting procedure that is established to elect the ECB's president, and the second is related to the technical profile that he or she must have.

Concerning the first point, a qualified majority is defined by article 16 TEU through four criteria:[11]

- 55 percent of the members of the Council
- Representing 15 members
- 65 percent of the population of the Union
- A blocking minority must include at least four Council members.

In other words, a single Member State cannot veto an election of the president of the ECB; conversely, it also means that one single Member State cannot impose or determine the imposition of its candidate through the threat of vetoing the other Member States' candidate or candidates. On its own, Germany cannot oppose the preferred candidate of the rest of the Member States; nor can it impose its own preference acting under the shadow of its veto power. This structure would indicate, in principle, that a great deal of consensus among Member States is necessary to elect the president of the ECB.

However, the information that has been made public on this issue arguably means that it will be very difficult for a candidate to be elected without the support of the two most important Member States of the Union, France and Germany. For example, concerning the election of Mario Draghi, the current ECB president, Bastasin (2015: 245–246) reports the following. It appears that the preferred candidate of the German chancellor Angela Merkel was Alex Weber, the (then) president of the Bundesbank. However, Weber was well known for being an austerity hawk, and President Sarkozy of France strongly opposed his nomination. During the process of selecting a candidate, Sarkozy had met with Draghi and had become persuaded that he was the right candidate for the post. Later, Weber communicated to Angela Merkel that he did not want to play the game of politics: "I want to remain independent." Thus, Merkel had no other choice than to accept Mario Draghi.

This story illustrates two points. First, as has been mentioned previously, a single Member State (even the most powerful one, Germany) cannot impose its own candidate. Second, however, the deal on this matter must be struck

---

[11] Article 16 defines a qualified majority vote at the Council level. However, this article applies, by analogy, to the European Council.

between Germany and France. This point has also been true for the election of the other two presidents of the ECB, Duisenberg and Trichet (Belke, 2011; Landleraug, 2005).

The profile of the president of the ECB has to be of a technical kind. As hinted previously, article 283.2 TFEU explicitly says that the president must be selected "from among persons of recognized standing and professional experience in monetary or banking matters." Does this requirement mean that the president must be selected from the most conservative members of the profession; that is, from the members most committed to controlling inflation?

If we examine the three presidents that the ECB has had to date, Willem Frederik "Wim" Duisenberg, Jean-Claude Trichet, and Mario Draghi, we can say the following. First, the three of them had long worked in the financial industry or in public positions related to it before they took up their posts at the ECB. Duisensberg worked for the International Monetary Fund (IMF), was then finance minister in the Dutch government and was then the president of the central bank of the Netherlands (Landleraug, 2005). Trichet had a more mixed background that combined positions in the financial industry ("he worked in the competitive sector from 1966 to 1968," his CV at Bruegel reads) and in the public sector (he was also president of the French central bank).[12] Draghi also had a mixed career in the private sector (he was the vice chairman and managing director at Goldman Sachs International) and in the public sector (president of the Italian central bank).[13] The three of them had, therefore, a reputation as central bankers and technocrats in monetary affairs. Second, concerning the extent of their conservatism, Duisenberg was known for pegging the guilder, the old Dutch currency, to the German frank to stabilize the monetary stance of the country,[14] while Trichet was notorious for his defence of a *franc fort* and was a committed anti-inflation fighter. Both of them can therefore be considered rather conservative central bankers. Draghi was most likely the most flexible of the three. He earned his PhD at the Massachusetts Institute of Technology under the supervision of two well-known neo-Keynesians, Modigliani and Sollow.[15] His candidacy was initially opposed by Germany. However, after he was proposed by Sarkozy for the post, he professed his faith in monetary stability and inflation control all over Europe and, above all, in Germany. "All this looks quite German-centric. But is this just a roadshow in which he enacts every effort to get the job? How German the heart of the Italian really beats with respect to monetary policy issues, nobody can actually tell," said an analyst in September

---

[12] "Jean Claude Trichet," http://bruegel.org/author/jean-claude-trichet.

[13] "The President of the European Central Bank," www.ecb.europa.eu/ecb/orga/decisions/html/cvdraghi.en.html#education.

[14] "Wim Duisenberg," *The Telegraph*, August 2, 2005, www.telegraph.co.uk/news/obituaries/1495301/Wim-Duisenberg.html.

[15] "Mario Draghi," Banca d'Italia, October 8, 2011, https://web.archive.org/web/20111008134839/http://www.bancaditalia.it/bancaditalia/direttorio/governatore.

2011 before Draghi took up the post on November 1, 2011 (Belke, 2011). Therefore, we can conclude that the first two were rather conservative central bankers, whereas the third was, to use Rogoff's words, conservative but not "too" conservative.

4.3.4 Bailouts

Article 123.1 TFEU reads as follows:

> Overdraft facilities or any other type of credit facility with the European Central Bank or with the central banks of the Member States (hereinafter referred to as "national central banks") in favour of Union institutions, bodies, offices or agencies, central governments, regional, local or other public authorities, other bodies governed by public law, or public undertakings of Member States shall be prohibited, as shall the purchase directly from them by the European Central Bank or national central banks of debt instruments.

Article 123 TFEU establishes two rules: it prohibits the ECB from bailing out Member States and from buying sovereign bonds directly from the Member States.

Thus, the first rule is an extension of the overall prohibition that the EU Treaties have imposed on the EU and on the Member States against performing bailouts of Member States in difficulty, which will be analyzed in Chapters 8 and 9 below. It is obvious that this prohibition would have been circumvented had the Treaty not included any reference to the ECB. Therefore, the EU, the ECB included, cannot grant bailouts to the Member States' governments.

The second rule is more difficult to interpret. If the ECB cannot buy sovereign bonds from the Member States directly, then, *a contrario*, it could buy them indirectly on the open market. Would this option not amount to the possibility of performing indirect ECB bailouts?

De Grauwe (2016: 175) provides the following interpretation. There is no contradiction between the first and the second rule because what article 123 prohibits is providing credit to Member States but not providing liquidity. Therefore, the ECB could inject liquidity into Member State governments indirectly by buying sovereign bonds on the open market.

The truth of the matter is that it is very difficult to differentiate between liquidity and credit monetary operations, as Zilioli argues (Zilioli, 2015: 5). Even were we to argue that the ECB could provide liquidity to the markets, it would do so by giving credit (through the purchase of securities), which is what banks do. Be that as it may, the point is that the second rule reinforces the first. As a further brake on the ECB's prohibition on bailouts, the ECB cannot purchase sovereign bonds directly from Member States' governments without passing through the normal market channels. Therefore, if a Member State were in dire straits and the financial markets were closed, the ECB could not come to its rescue and buy sovereign bonds. If that Member State wanted to augment its revenues, it could only do so through a tax increase.

According to Garbade (2014), the prohibition on buying sovereign bonds directly was established in the United States in 1935. "Until 1935, Federal Reserve Banks from time to time purchased short-term securities directly from the United States Treasury to facilitate Treasury cash management operations," says the author. The rationale for the 1935 prohibition was "to prevent excessive government expenditures." Therefore, this prohibition was not strictly necessary, as the same author argues (Garbade, 2014: 6). From a different perspective, if the prohibition on buying sovereign bonds directly had not been introduced in the TFEU, de Grauwe's argument about liquidity would have been more plausible. The sense of the second rule is therefore to make the prohibition against ECB bailouts more strict and bold. It follows that, according to article 123 TFEU, the only reason why the ECB could buy Member State sovereign bonds in the open market would be for the sole purpose of controlling inflation, not to provide credit (or liquidity) to the Member States.

4.3.5 Acting under the Shadow of the Bundesbank?

We can conclude this section by wrapping up some of the arguments made so far and by discussing one of the points that is generally made by observers of the ECB's behavior, which is that, independent as the ECB might be legally speaking, it acts under what could be called "the shadow" of the Bundesbank.

As seen, the ECB's independence is established at the highest normative hierarchical level of the EU's legal order; that is, in the EU Treaties. This commitment is very rigid, rigidity that is further reinforced by how the ECB`s president is elected (France and Germany have a *de facto* veto power), by the emphasis placed on the control of inflation as the ECB's sole mission, and by the bold prohibition on Member State bailouts. All of these commitments are written into the EU Treaties, which reduplicates the rigidity with which the ECB statute is designed.

Some analysts argue that, irrespective of what the Treaties say, the ECB in reality navigates along the lines of the Bundesbank's dictum. It is not only that Germany is a key player in the election of the ECB's president, as seen previously. What this stance unearths is, more profoundly, a question of legitimacy. The ECB's legitimacy would rest upon the Bundesbank's support.

Dornbusch et al. (1998) raised the issue a year before the euro was initially put in circulation in 1999. According to these authors,

> The ECB will need to do a lot of explaining. It will have to explain to all those who hoped that the transition from the Bundesbank Zone to EMU meant a more relaxed monetary policy that this cannot be so. It needs to establish the legitimacy of a serious monetary policy as a desirable European objective rather than an automatic continuation of Bundesbank policy. At the same time, the ECB has to offer decisive assurance to the sceptics, demonstrating its

commitment to price stability without compromises. Most importantly, to be successful the ECB needs to create a constituency that understands and supports its conception of policy.

(Dornbusch et al., 1998: 12)

Starting from that initial paper, a corpus of empirical literature has emerged on the issue of the Bundesbank's influence over the ECB. For some analysts, there are no clear signals of such influence. For example, Hayo and Hofman (2005) find that "the Bundesbank regime can be characterized, both before and after German reunification, by an inflation weight of 1.2 and an output weight of 0.4. The estimates for the ECB are 1.2, and 1, respectively. Thus, the ECB, while reacting similarly to expected inflation, puts significantly more weight on stabilizing the business cycle than the Bundesbank did." This point is confirmed by Belke and Polleit (2006): "The empirical estimates for the euro area suggest that the ECB put a larger weight on the output gap relative to inflation." In turn, Rühl (2015) argues that the ECB is not reacting to inflation as strongly as does the Bundesbank. Finally, Ersoy and Antment (2016) find that the determinants of long-term interest rates in the Eurozone are inflation gaps, political stability, the absence of violence/terrorism, government effectiveness, and regulatory quality (thus, implicitly, not the Bundesbank's influence).

However, these findings sharply contrast with another strand of literature that finds a link between the Bundesbank's preferences and the ECB's conduct of Eurozone monetary policy. For example, Smant (2002) argues that after an initial period of lower interest rates, the ECB aligned its policy to the Bundesbank's from mid 2000 onwards. This point is confirmed and enlarged on by Rotondo and Vaciago (2007), who provide new evidence "supporting the hypothesis of an ECB with Bundesbank preferences." Finally, Odendahl (2014) criticizes the Bundesbank's behavior during the 2008 crisis for "torpedoing reasonable ECB decisions," thus assuming the former's influence over the latter.

The most that can be said about this issue is that it is a difficult one and that insufficient time has elapsed since the euro was put into circulation to allow much certainty about the influence of the Bundesbank (or of other factors) on the ECB's conduct. Nonetheless, it can be ascertained that the issue most likely goes beyond how the ECB makes decisions. In fact, article 10 of the ECB Protocol states, "Save as otherwise provided for in this Statute, the Governing Council shall act by a simple majority of the members having a voting right. In the event of a tie, the President shall have the casting vote." In other words, the Bundesbank cannot impose its views on policy decisions on the rest of the members composing the ECB Governing Council via the German representative on the Council.[16]

---

[16] According to article 283 TFEU, the Governing Council is composed of the governors of the national central banks whose currency is the euro plus the members of the Executive Board of the ECB. The Executive Board is composed of the president of the ECB, the vice-president and

However, there are qualitative symptoms that appear to indicate that the Bundesbank's influence over the ECB, although perhaps exercised indirectly (through policy announcements, for example), is very real when the issues that must be decided by the ECB are of primary importance. An example of this situation is given by the OMT (Outright Monetary Transactions) program that the ECB announced on September 6, 2012, when the 2008 crisis was at one of its peaks. The Bundesbank publicly announced that it was against this program. In a note delivered on September 6, 2012, it stated the following:

> In the most recent discussions, as before, Bundesbank President Jens Weidmann reiterated his frequently substantiated critical stance towards the purchase of government bonds by the Eurosystem. He regards such purchases as being tantamount to financing governments by printing banknotes. Monetary policy risks being subjugated to fiscal policy. The intervention purchases must not be permitted to jeopardise the capability of monetary policy to safeguard price stability in the euro area. If the adopted bond-purchasing programme leads to member states postponing the necessary reforms, this will further undermine confidence in the political leaders' crisis-resolution capability. This underscores the crucial importance of ensuring both credibility in the promised condition-ality and the resolute determination to immediately terminate intervention purchases if the underlying conditionality is no longer assured. The announced interventions in the government bond market carry the additional danger that the central bank may ultimately redistribute considerable risks among various countries' taxpayers. Such risk-sharing, however, can be legitimately authorised solely by democratically elected parliaments and governments.[17]

This note did not provoke, by itself, the bringing of an action for the annul-ment of the OMT program before the German Constitutional Court; however, it most likely had an effect (Petch, 2013). In effect, after the Bundesbank note, a number of private plaintiffs, together with a faction of the German left political party Die Linke, brought an action on November 13, 2012, for annulment against the OMT program,[18] in what would become the *Gauweiler* case.[19] That case will be analyzed later. The point that I want to make now is that although the ruling of the German Constitutional Court did not oppose the program, the ECB never in fact implemented it (it implemented

---

four other members. The meetings of the Governing Council are confidential, according to article 10.4 of the ECB Protocol. The Governing Council sets interest rates for the Eurozone.

[17] See https://mninews.marketnews.com/content/bundesbank-text-weidmann-reiterated-bond-buy-criticism. The president of the Bundesbank, Jens Weidmann, voted against the OMT program in the vote that occurred at the ECB Governing Council. However, the Bundesbank was not one of the plaintiffs in the *Gauweiler* case; it only intervened in the proceedings as a witness. The entire story is well-recounted at www.dw.com/en/fight-over-ecb-bond-buying-returns-to-german-court/a-19050494.

[18] For a very detailed analysis of who the plaintiffs in this case were, see Schiek (2014).

[19] See case C-62/14, *Gauweiler and others*, Judgment of the Court (Grand Chamber) of June 16, 2015, ECLI:EU:C:2015:400. See the German Constitutional Court's press release on the *Gauweiler* case at www.bundesverfassungsgericht.de/SharedDocs/Pressemitteilungen/EN/2016/bvg16-034.html.

quantitative easing programs through other means, as seen below, but not through OMT). One possible hypothesis would be that the ECB did not implement the program precisely because the Bundesbank opposed it. This omission, in turn, would provide indirect evidence of the ECB acting under the shadow of the Bundesbank, at least when the policy stakes are high.

4.4 Conduct of Monetary Policy by the ECB

Let us start this section by making a number of general and preliminary points that relate directly to the conduct of the ECB's monetary policy.

The first point to be stressed is that a central bank is defined by Samuelson and Nordhaus as "a bank of bankers" (Samuelson & Nordhaus, 2010). This definition is the simplest and most elegant that I have found because it focuses on the very essence of what central banks are and do. In essence, they act like any other bank: they lend money at an interest rate to financial institutions. The difference with other banks is that central banks are public banks. Therefore, they are bound to a public policy goal. The ECB is no exception to this rule.

Second, the ECB's particular public policy goal is, according to the Treaties, price stability, the control of inflation. Above all, after the crisis that began in 2008, academia and experts, even those who espouse the orthodox view on European monetary matters, have tried to justify the conduct of monetary policy by the ECB on the basis that the ECB is bound by a larger goal; that is, financial stability and not only price stability. Price stability is thus balanced against financial stability. The truth of the matter is that article 127 is radical in its clarity and does not admit any different interpretation. The unique mission of the ECB is price stability, legally speaking at least.

The third aspect relates to the task of "lender of last resort" of the ECB, which in turn relates to the bailout prohibition. Again, many legal and economic interpretations have arisen during the crisis with the aim of justifying this task for the ECB. However, the truth of the matter is, once again, that this task is clearly excluded by the Treaties, first, because the difference between liquidity and solvency is very blurred, as has been said previously (Zilioli, 2015: 5). The second reason is that a lender of last resort, in its simplest understanding, is someone who lends to you when no one else is ready to do so. Article 123.1, when barring the possibility of directly buying Member States' bonds, is clear on this point; it bans the lender of last resort task. Moreover, that the Treaties do not mention this task concerning financial institutions at all must be interpreted in the same direction. In other words, the ECB's mission is to control price stability, not to inject liquidity into the markets per se.[20]

---

[20] Nor can this conclusion be altered by using the "constructive ambiguity" argument, according to which "the Central Bank must have the highest discretion possible when intervening in the capacity of lender of last resort, in order to be in a position to appropriately weigh the risks and act accordingly to each case" (Gortsos, 2015: 56). This argument would justify the absence of

As a final point, I understand the sense of these new, more open interpretations of the Treaty concerning the objectives and tasks of the ECB. However, the truth of the matter is that they are all very *voluntaristic*. This point does not mean that the Treaty was correct when it decided to implement such a rigid framework. Nevertheless, from a "law as credibility" perspective, the important thing is to ascertain what the legal statute of the ECB really is, as a means of understanding where the credibility problems of the institution and, in general, of the conduct of the ECB's monetary policy actually reside. We discuss this point in the next subsections.

4.4.1 Institutional Features

The ECB is at the epicenter of the Eurosystem, which is part of the so-called European System of Central Banks (see Box 4.1). The Eurosystem is composed of the ECB plus the central banks of the Member States whose currency is the euro; in turn, the ESCB is composed of these plus all of the Member States' central banks. This "triadic" structure denotes a certain decentralization of the system; in fact, some authors ask whether the system is not, perhaps, too decentralized (de Grauwe, 2016: 170). This stance also relates to how decisions are made inside the ECB's governing structure, a question that will be addressed below. The point is that, generally speaking, the system is one in which the ECB makes the main decisions and the national central banks implement them.

The main governing structures of the ECB are the Executive Board and the Governing Council. They are also the governing structures of the whole ESBC (article 282.2 TFEU). The Executive Board is defined by article 283.2 of the TFEU in the following terms: "It shall comprise the President, Vice-President [of the ECB] and four other Members." In turn, the Governing Council is defined by article 283.1 as follows: "It shall comprise the members of the Executive Board of the ECB and the Governors of the national central banks of the Member States whose currency is the euro."

The tasks of each of these institutions are defined in the Treaties and in the ECB statute Protocol. In essence, they conform to the following rule: the Governing Council decides and the Executive Board implements those decisions and monitors the implementation by national central banks of the orders issued by the ECB (see article 12 of the ECB Statute). It is important to stress that the key decision that the ECB must adopt, which is the setting of interest rates, is made by the Governing Council.

The Governing Council adopts decisions by a simple majority (article 10.2 of the ECB statute, 4th paragraph), as has been mentioned in Section 4.3.5.

---

any reference whatsoever to the lender of last resort task of the ECB in the Treaties. However, in my opinion, the mission of the ECB to control inflation and the prohibition on buying government bonds directly by the ECB are established in such a bold way in the Treaties that they exclude the "constructive ambiguity" argument.

Box 4.1: ESBC, Eurosystem, European Central Bank

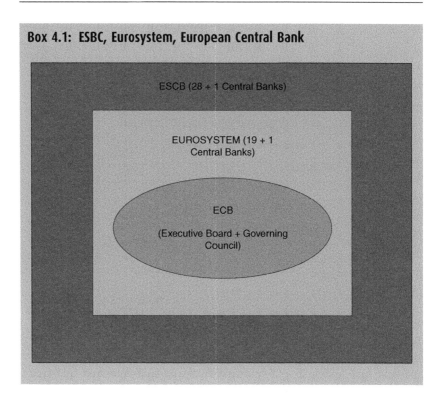

However, as de Grauwe notes, the problem posed by the simple majority rule was that as the Eurozone enlarged, the Governing Council could become dominated by small and medium-sized Member States. Therefore, the simple majority voting rule is further qualified by the second and third indents of article 10.2 of the ECB statute, which establishes a rotating system. This provision has been implemented by the following legal acts: (1) Decision of the Council to amend article 10.2 of the ECB statute of March 21, 2003;[21] (2) the ECB's decision to postpone the rotating system until the number of governors exceeds eighteen of December 18, 2008;[22] and (3) the ECB's decision on the implementation of the rotation system of March 19, 2009.[23] As foreseen by all of these decisions, the accession of Lithuania to the euro

---

[21] Decision of the Council, Meeting in the Composition of the Heads of State or Government of March 21, 2003, on an amendment to Article 10.2 of the Statute of the European System of Central Banks and of the European Central Bank. OJEU 1.4.2003, L 83/66.

[22] Decision of the European Central Bank of December 18, 2008, to postpone the start of the rotation system in the Governing Council of the European Central Bank (ECB/2008/29) (2009/5/EC). OJEU 7.1.2009, L ¾.

[23] Decision of the European Central Bank of March 19, 2009, amending Decision ECB/2004/2 of February 19, 2004, adopting the Rules of Procedure of the European Central Bank (ECB/2009/5) (2009/328/EC). OJEU 18.4.2009, L 100/10.

area in 2015, as Member State number 19 of the Eurozone, started the implementation of the new, rotating system. This system is fully explained by the ECB in the document "Rotation of Voting Rights in the Governing Council of the ECB" (ECB, 2009).[24]

4.4.2 Legal and Para-legal Instruments

According to article 132 TFEU and article 34 of the ECB statute, the ECB can adopt

- Regulations
- Decisions
- Recommendations, and
- Opinions.

Furthermore, the ECB statute speaks of two further legal acts that the ECB can adopt:

- Guidelines and
- Instructions.

Starting with the first group of legal acts previously mentioned, their definition is exactly the same as the general definition that article 288 TFEU gives to these acts.[25] Therefore, legally speaking, there is no difference between a regulation adopted by the Council and a regulation adopted by the ECB. The same holds for decisions, recommendations, and opinions.

At least two main qualifications must be made with respect to the previous rule. These nuances refer to decisions and the publication of the ECB's decisions, recommendations, and opinions. Concerning the first, the ECB statute differentiates between decisions of a regulatory nature and decisions of an administrative nature. An example of the first would be article 30 of the ECB statute, which says that the ECB will decide on the national central banks' percentage shares of the ECB's capital. Accordingly, the ECB has adopted decision ECB 2013/28 of August 29, 2013.[26]

---

[24] For a good summary, see the ECB website www.ecb.europa.eu/explainers/tell-me-more/html/voting-rotation.en.html.

[25] Article 288 TFEU states the following: "To exercise the Union's competences, the institutions shall adopt regulations, directives, decisions, recommendations and opinions. A regulation shall have general application. It shall be binding in its entirety and directly applicable in all Member States. A directive shall be binding, as to the result to be achieved, upon each Member State to which it is addressed, but shall leave to the national authorities the choice of form and methods. A decision shall be binding in its entirety. A decision which specifies those to whom it is addressed shall be binding only on them. Recommendations and opinions shall have no binding force."

[26] Decision of the European Central Bank of August 29, 2013, on the national central banks' percentage shares in the key for subscription to the European Central Bank's capital (ECB/2013/28) (2014/30/EU). OJEU L 16/53 of January 21, 2014.

> ## Box 4.2: ECB decision on interest rates on January 19, 2017
>
> **Press Release**
>
> Monetary policy decisions
>
> *19 January 2017*
>
> At today's meeting the Governing Council of the ECB decided that the interest rate on the main refinancing operations and the interest rates on the marginal lending facility and the deposit facility will remain unchanged at 0.00%, 0.25% and –0.40% respectively. The Governing Council continues to expect the key ECB interest rates to remain at present or lower levels for an extended period of time, and well past the horizon of the net asset purchases.
>
> Regarding non-standard monetary policy measures, the Governing Council confirms that it will continue to make purchases under the asset purchase programme (APP) at the current monthly pace of €80 billion until the end of March 2017 and that, from April 2017, the net asset purchases are intended to continue at a monthly pace of €60 billion until the end of December 2017, or beyond, if necessary, and in any case until the Governing Council sees a sustained adjustment in the path of inflation consistent with its inflation aim. The net purchases will be made alongside reinvestments of the principal payments from maturing securities purchased under the APP. If the outlook becomes less favourable, or if financial conditions become inconsistent with further progress towards a sustained adjustment in the path of inflation, the Governing Council stands ready to increase the programme in terms of size and/or duration.
>
> The President of the ECB will comment on the considerations underlying these decisions at a press conference starting at 14:30 CET today.

An example of the second is set out in article 12 of the ECB statute, which says that the Governing Council shall adopt decisions relating to key interest rates. An example of the second type of decisions is the decision on interest rates of January 19, 2017 (see Box 4.2).

Concerning publication, article 110 TFEU and article 34.2 of the ECB statute indicate that the ECB "may decide" to publish decisions, recommendations, and opinions. The issue is (slightly) less important concerning recommendations and opinions because they have a non-legally binding character. It is however more important concerning decisions, even were we to restrict the wording of articles 110 TFEU and 34.2 to the second type of decisions that we mentioned previously (administrative decisions). For example, the decision setting interest rates, that the Governing Council adopts approximately every six weeks in Frankfurt,[27]

---

[27] "The Governing Council usually meets twice a month at the ECB's premises in Frankfurt am Main, Germany. The Governing Council assesses economic and monetary developments and takes its monetary policy decisions every six weeks." See ECB at www.ecb.europa.eu/ecb/orga/decisions/govc/html/index.en.html.

is only published through an ECB press release. Suffice it to say at this point that the situation is very odd; for reasons of both transparency and accountability, all legal acts (binding or not) of the ECB, such as decisions setting interest rates, should be published in the Official Journal of the European Union (OJEU). Above all, for reasons of both accountability and transparency, the publication of such acts should not be left to the discretion of the ECB.[28]

The second group of legal acts that we previously mentioned are guidelines and instructions. Despite their respective nomenclatures, they both have, as Zilioli and Selmayr (2001; 2006) have noted, a legally binding character. Guidelines are normally addressed either to the Executive Board (which must implement the Governing Council's monetary decisions according to its guidelines) or to the national central banks (which must enact the ECB's monetary decisions according to its guidelines). The translation into other EU languages appeared to indicate that they had a sort of soft-law legal nature.[29] However, as Zilioli and Selmayr note, one must stand to their "legal nature in each individual case"; therefore, there can be no doubt that the ECB's guidelines are "meant to be legally binding instruments" (Zilioli & Selmayr, 2001: 106). One example of an ECB guideline is set out in article 12.1 of the ECB statute, which says, "The Governing Council shall formulate the monetary policy of the Union including, as appropriate, decisions relating to intermediate monetary objectives, key interest rates and the supply of reserves in the ESCB, and shall establish the necessary guidelines for their implementation." Accordingly, the ECB has adopted Guideline 2011/14 of September 20, 2011, on monetary policy instruments, which will be commented on later.[30]

Instructions are adopted by the members of the ECB Executive Board that have as addressees one or more national central banks. Zilioli and Selmayr do not question their legal nature as legally binding acts; they "allow for a very detailed legal description of the addressee's behavior" (Zilioli & Selmayr, 2001: 108). Instructions are, in principle, not published, which, again, is very odd given their legally binding nature and importance for daily monetary policy

---

[28] Article 17.7. of the ECB Rules of Procedure (Decision of the European Central Bank of February 19, 2004, adopting the Rules of Procedure of the European Central Bank (ECB/2004/2) (2004/257/EC) – 02004D0002 – EN – 24.09.2016 – 004.001 – 1) states, "All ECB legal instruments shall be numbered sequentially for ease of identification. The Executive Board shall take steps to ensure the safe custody of the originals, the notification of the addressees or consulting authorities, and the publication in all of the official languages of the European Union in the Official Journal of the European Union in the case of ECB Regulations, ECB opinions on draft Community legislation and those ECB legal instruments whose publication has been expressly decided."

[29] In Spanish, they are translated as *orientaciones*; in French, *orientations*; in Italian, *indirizzi*; and in Portuguese, *orientaçoes*. All of these terms appear to point to a non-legally binding act.

[30] Guideline of the European Central Bank of September 20, 2011, on monetary policy instruments and procedures of the Eurosystem (recast) (ECB/2011/14) (2011/817/EU). OJEU L 331/1 of December 14, 2011.

operations.[31] An example of instruction is found in article 12.1 of the ECB statute, which says, "[The] Executive Board shall give the necessary instructions to national central banks." I have not been able to trace back an example of an Executive Board instruction.

As a further note relating to the ECB's legal instruments, it is important to stress that article 35.1 of the ECB statute says, "The acts or omissions of the ECB shall be open to review or interpretation by the Court of Justice of the European Union in the cases and under the conditions laid down in the Treaty on the Functioning of the European Union." It could not be otherwise. In my opinion, this provision must be interpreted extensively due to the rigidity with which the status of independence of the ECB is set in EU law. Thus, for example, even ECB decisions on the setting of interest rates might be challenged before the Court of Justice. This position is very controversial, but considering that the ECB is probably the most independent monetary agency in the world, its accountability should be streamlined by other means; in this case, by legal means. Even if the Court should only annul a decision of the ECB setting interest rates when it is manifestly out of sync with the monetary and economic conditions of the euro area, or when the ECB manifestly did not provide sufficiently good reasons for its decision, one should not discard this last-resort legal control. Conversely, the ECJ could also declare, for example, an omission by the ECB to raise or lower interest rates in the same circumstances.

I will conclude this section by making a final observation on a policy instrument that, although lacking legal content, can be even more important for the purposes of conducting ECB monetary policy than legal acts. I am referring to the ECB's policy announcements. As seen later, when we review the ECB's monetary instruments, the ECB does not use an inflation-targeting strategy. The only reference to a target is the one we already know – below (but close to) 2 percent inflation over the medium term. However, what the ECB does is to "announce" an inflation forecast (we will see exactly how the ECB performs this task in a later section). For example, the ECB's inflation forecast for the first quarter of the year is 1.4 percent (current calendar year). Another example is that the ECB can announce particular monetary programs or actions. A case in point is the announcement of the implementation of the OMT (Outright Monetary Transaction) program by President Draghi in a press conference on August 2, 2012. This announcement was followed by an

---

[31] Article 17.6 of the ECB Rules of Procedure (Decision of the European Central Bank of February 19, 2004, adopting the Rules of Procedure of the European Central Bank (ECB/2004/2) (2004/257/EC) – 02004D0002 – EN – 24.09.2016 – 004.001 – 1) states, "ECB Instructions shall be adopted by the Executive Board, and thereafter notified, in one of the official languages of the Union, and signed on the Executive Board's behalf by the President or any two Executive Board members. Notification of the national central banks may occur electronically, by means of telefax or in paper form. Any ECB Instruction that is to be officially published shall be translated into the official languages of the Union."

ECB press release on "Technical Features of Outright Monetary Transactions" on September 6, 2012.

From a strictly legal point of view, the problem posed by announcements is whether they can be challenged before the ECJ. In principle, the answer should be a clear and resounding "no" if the fact that announcements are not legal acts is considered. For example, the ECB's press release that announced that the Governing Council of the ECB had "taken decisions on a number of technical features regarding the Eurosystem's outright transactions in secondary sovereign bond markets" was only that – an announcement. To my knowledge, these decisions have never been published, and no one has seen them.

The question appears, however, to have been solved in the opposite direction by the ECJ in the *Gauweiler* case. This preliminary reference was sent by the German Federal Court to the ECJ concerning the OMT program. One of the admissibility points raised by some of the parties in the proceedings related to the fact that the OMT program had simply been announced by the ECB:

> Ireland, the Greek, Spanish, French, Italian, Netherlands and Portuguese Governments, the Parliament, the Commission and the ECB submit that the first question is inadmissible since a question concerning validity cannot, in their submission, be directed at an act which, like the OMT decisions, is preparatory or does not have legal effects.
>
> [paragraph 23]

Instead, for the ECJ,

> The fact that the OMT decisions have not yet been implemented and that their implementation will be possible only after further legal acts have been adopted is not a ground for denying that the request for a preliminary ruling meets an objective need for resolving the cases brought before that court.
>
> [paragraph 28]

In other words, ECB policy announcements can be reviewed by the ECJ.

The second issue posed by the ECB's policy announcements relates to their credibility. In fact, there is significant debate in economic academic circles concerning this point. For example, de Grauwe argues that the mere announcement of the OMT program by the ECB was sufficiently credible to calm financial markets, irrespective of the fact that the program was not only never implemented but also not adopted, at least formally speaking (de Grauwe, 2016: 128). The issue is a complex one because for one strand of the economic literature, policy announcements might enhance the credibility of the ECB, but for another strand they might undermine it. In fact, the main reason why the ECB does not follow an inflation intermediate targeting strategy relates to the following point: if targets were not reached, then the credibility of a (young) institution like the ECB would be undermined in general terms (Solans, 2000). From a "law as credibility" perspective, it is important to stress that policy announcements are placed in the nonlegal world; in other words, the condition $R > F$ does not hold here (in fact, $R < F$ holds). Flexibility is therefore the main reason the ECB can choose, as in the OMT program, a policy announcement rather than adopting a legal decision. In fact, this flexibility is what allowed the ECB not to adopt the OMT program, later. Under specific circumstances (no clear ECB competences to adopt a particular program, as in the OMT case), the use of policy announcements can be an optimum from a credibility perspective when compared with its alternative, the use of law. In other words, under specific circumstances, markets can believe a policy announcement more than a bold decision from the ECB. This fact can enhance the credibility of the ECB. However, whether markets did so concerning the OMT decision is something that is very much under discussion (Altavilla et al., 2014).

4.4.3 Monetary Instruments

To better grasp the main foundations of ECB monetary policy operations, it is important to start by understanding what monetary economics refers to as the "transmission mechanism of monetary policy."[32]

In principle, this mechanism is easy to understand. Money markets work just like any other commodity market: they are subject to the laws of supply and demand. The main difference between the market of money and the market for commodities is that central banks have a monopoly on issuing money. Therefore, they have a monopoly on setting "official" interest rates. It is as though the government had a monopoly of the meat stock of a country and could set minimum prices for this product (imagine for the sake of argument that meat was imperishable). The market participants could sell and buy meat in the market, under the laws of supply and demand, but they would always know that the government decides on the stock and the price of meat. They could always, as a last resort, go to the government and buy meat at the price that the government sets. A money market works exactly similarly. The price for money that is set by the central bank affects money market prices directly.

This basic model becomes slightly more complicated when we introduce into it the issue of rational expectations. In essence, as seen below, central banks do two things: they set the price of money in the short term (official interest rates) and set inflation targets. For example, they can set intermediate inflation targets or medium-term inflation targets. We have said already that the ECB only does the latter; it only sets a medium-term inflation target. The point is that market operators take the information available to them (the information on short-term interest rates and the information on inflation

---

[32] The ECB explained this point very well at www.ecb.europa.eu/mopo/intro/transmission/html/index.en.html.

targets) and elaborate expectations on future inflation and therefore on future prices. Their behavior will be affected by their beliefs. If they believe that short-term prices are in sync with inflation targets, they will not change their behavior. If they believe that prices are out of sync, they will change their behavior. For example, they might believe that inflation in the medium to long term will be higher and that official money prices will therefore be augmented; therefore, they might charge higher prices to borrowers. Conversely, they might believe that inflation will be lower than expected and that prices will be lower; therefore, they might provide more credit or charge lower prices to borrowers. The issue of money market expectations works very similarly to a love relationship: fear plays a crucial role.

The question is, what generates markets' fears that today's decisions are out of sync with future inflation? The answer is simple: the credibility of the central bank.[33] That the answer is simple does not mean that building up a reputation as a credible central bank is an easy thing to do. This point, among others, is why we are devoting a whole book to the issue of credibility, law, trust, and economic governance. However, a short answer to this question would be that the credibility of a central bank largely depends upon its record in controlling inflation – that is, on its capability to align inflation targets with inflation achievements. The point that this book makes is that law can play, under certain circumstances, a crucial role in making this alignment possible.

Once the transmission mechanism of monetary policy is understood, we can move to explain what is usually referred to as the "ECB monetary policy strategy;" that is, how the ECB attempts to achieve its inflation target. Currently, it is a two-pillar strategy: the first pillar is the economic one and the second is the monetary one. In fact, if one examines the president of the ECB's introductory remarks when he announces the ECB's decisions on interest rates, he always starts by using the same expression: "Based on our regular economic and monetary analyses, we decided to set interest rates ...".[34] Furthermore, the fact that the president of the ECB starts with the economic analysis and leaves for second place the monetary analysis signals the fact that the monetary analysis has lost some of the relevance that it had when the ECB started conducting the Eurozone monetary policy. In other words, the ECB appears to have accepted the criticisms according to which the money stock (M3) is a less good predictor of inflationary trends (de Grauwe, 2016: 192). Furthermore, and as hinted above, the ECB does not follow an inter-mediate inflation targeting strategy, although it makes inflation forecasts.

---

[33] Of course, the issue is much more complex, as we saw in Chapter 1. The capacity to conjure fears depends, occasionally, as much on the trustee as on the trusted. A person incapable of trusting would not even trust the most credible human being in the world. Similarly, animal spirits may cause a market operator to hardly ever believe in the most credible central bank. To be sure, in the two cases (cases of total mistrust), the loser will be the trustee.

[34] See, as an example, "Introductory statement to the press conference of the President of the ECB, 19 January 2017" at www.ecb.europa.eu/press/pressconf/2017/html/is170119.en.html.

Therefore, concerning the first pillar (economic analysis), the ECB considers a number of economic variables, such as wages, the exchange rate, and bond prices, to forecast future inflation trends. Concerning the second pillar (monetary analysis), the ECB makes a forecast of the growth rate of the money stock. As indicated above, it uses a broad definition of the money stock, which is M3. M3 is defined by the ECB as the "sum of M2, repurchase agreements, money market fund shares/units and debt securities with a maturity of up to two years."[35]

The final point relates to the monetary instruments that the ECB uses to implement its monetary policy. These instruments are in reality the means that the ECB employs to channel its price decisions to the markets. These instruments are established in the ECB Protocol. The ECB Protocol has been further developed on this point by the following (see for a summary ECB, 2014: 18–30):

- A "permanent framework" of monetary policy instruments, which includes a "minimum reserve" legislation, and
- A "financial crisis" related temporary framework.

I will very succinctly refer to the main aspects of the permanent framework in this subsection and leave for the next section the analysis of the temporary (crisis) framework.

Guideline 2015/510 of the ECB[36] is the so-called "general documentation guideline." This legal instrument sets the main ECB monetary policy operations. In essence, they are

- Open market operations
- Standing facilities
- Minimum reserve requirements.

Open market operations are the "buying and selling of marketable securities with the aim of increasing or reducing money market liquidity." It is the most important instrument of the three. In turn, standing facilities are the instrument that "provides and absorbs overnight liquidity." Furthermore, minimum reserve requirements are "the imposition of minimum reserves for banks" (for a discussion of the practical operation of these instruments, see de Grauwe, 2016: 205–209). Box 4.3 describes the main operations of which these instruments are composed. Concerning minimum reserves, one should also bear in

---

[35] In turn, the definition of M1 "is the sum of currency in circulation and overnight deposits," and M2 is "the sum of M1, deposits with an agreed maturity of up to two years and deposits redeemable at notice of up to three months." See ECB at www.ecb.europa.eu/stats/money_credit_banking/monetary_aggregates/html/index.en.html.

[36] Guideline (Eu) 2015/510 of the European Central Bank of December 19, 2014, on the implementation of the Eurosystem monetary policy framework (General Documentation Guideline) (ECB/2014/60). See the consolidated version in 02014O0060 – EN – 01.01.2017 – 004.001 – 1.

Box 4.3: Monetary policy instruments

- **Open Market Operations** (article. 5)
  - Main Refinancing Operations (MROs) (article. 6)
  - Long Term Refinancing Operations (LTROs) (article. 7)
  - Fine-Tuning Operations (article. 8)
  - Structural Operations (article. 9)
- **Standing Facility** (article. 17)
  - Marginal Lending Facility (article. 18, 19, 20)
  - Deposit Facility (article. 21, 22, 23)
- **Minimum Reserve Requirements** (Annex I)

---

mind Council Regulation 2531/98[37] and ECB regulation 1745/2003.[38] Finally, Title III of the Guideline regulates the procedures for the Eurosystem monetary policy operations.

4.5 Effectiveness of the ECB's Monetary Policy

The ECB's conduct of Eurozone monetary policy has been only partially successful. Even if we use the control of inflation as the sole benchmark, the conclusion is very mixed; the ECB appears to have been able to deliver, but only until the 2008 economic crisis began. Since a picture is worth more than a thousand words, I have plotted in Figure 4.1 the yearly inflation average for the Eurozone since the inception of the euro in 1999.

Figure 4.1 recalls that the inflation target objective for the Eurozone is below, but close to, 2 percent in the medium term, as previously seen. This objective is represented by the orange line. From this perspective, the figure shows that the ECB's performance revolved around this objective, at least until 2008. The year 2008 witnessed a sudden rise in the Eurozone's inflationary trend (3.3 percent), followed by a plunge almost into deflation in the year 2009 (0.3 percent). This pattern provides evidence not only of the severe economic shock that the Eurozone suffered but also of the incapacity of the ECB to handle the situation. The Eurozone little by little recovered from this deflationary trend, until, in 2013, the whole area started experiencing the second part of the crisis, which was fiscal. In 2016, the average inflation rate was 0.2 percent, which is clearly very far from the stated 2 percent objective. The conclusion is therefore clear: under normal economic conditions, the ECB has

---

[37] Council Regulation No 2531/98 of November 23, 1998, concerning the application of minimum reserves by the European Central Bank. L 318/1 of 27.11.98.

[38] Regulation (EC) no. 1745/2003 of the European Central Bank of September 12, 2003, on the application of minimum reserves (ECB/2003/9). It has lately been amended by Regulation (EU) 2016/1705 of the ECB of September 9, 2016, amending Regulation (EC) No 1745/2003 (ECB/2003/9) on the application of minimum reserves (ECB/2016/26), OJ L 257/10 of 23.9.2016.

Figure 4.1: Eurozone yearly inflation rate

been able to control inflation, but it has been much less able to do so under extraordinary economic conditions.

As hinted previously, this difficulty most likely relates to the many doubts and hesitations that the ECB has shown when facing the crisis. I will analyze in the following the main aspects of the ECB's strategy during the crisis.

The most important measures that the ECB took to combat the crisis were the following (for a detailed and clear discussion of the whole array of measures that the ECB took during the crisis, see Micossi, 2015). The first one was decision 2010/5 of May 14, 2010, which established a securities market purchase program.[39] In other words, it took not more and not less than two years after the crisis started for the ECB to take the first important measure to face the situation. The second measure that the ECB took was to relax the conditions for accepting collateral from the markets in exchange for the liquidity that the ECB was injecting. The ECB accomplished this relaxation through a number of guidelines and decisions.[40] The third main measure that the ECB took was to relax the minimum reserve requirements with which financial institutions had to comply. It made this change through regulation 2011/26 of December 14, 2011.[41,42]

---

[39] Decision of the European Central Bank of May 14, 2010, establishing a securities markets programme (ECB/2010/5) (2010/281/EU). L 124/8 of 20.5.2010.

[40] See Guideline of the European Central Bank of March 20, 2013, on additional temporary measures relating to Eurosystem refinancing operations and eligibility of collateral and amending Guideline ECB/2007/9 (recast) (ECB/2013/4) (2013/170/EU). L 95/23 of 5.4.2013; Decision of the European Central Bank of September 26, 2013, on additional measures relating to Eurosystem refinancing operations and eligibility of collateral (ECB/2013/35) (2013/645/EU) L 301/6 of 12.11.2013; Decision of the European Central Bank of September 26, 2013, on additional temporary measures relating to Eurosystem refinancing operations and eligibility of collateral (ECB/2013/36) (2013/646/EU). L 301/13 of 12.11.2013.

[41] Regulation (Eu) No 1358/2011 of the European Central Bank of December 14, 2011, amending Regulation (EC) No 1745/2003 on the application of minimum reserves (ECB/2003/9) (ECB/2011/26). L 338/51 of 21.12.2011.

[42] Additionally, the ECB Governing Council made, on October 16, 2013, the decision to make the procedural rules on ELA (Emergency Liquidity Assistance, provided by national central banks) public. The rules of procedures are dated October 17, 2013. Technically speaking, ELA is not an ECB program but an NBC program, which must be implemented in the framework of the procedural rules set by the ECB. See ECB at www.ecb.europa.eu/press/govcdec/otherdec/2013/html/gc131018.en.html.

In 2012, the economic crisis experienced one of its worst peaks. Due to the situation in Greece, the financial markets seemed to be persuaded that the euro would collapse and attacked other periphery countries, notably Spain and Italy, the two major Eurozone economies after Germany and France. The president of the ECB leapt to the fore and, in a public intervention in London, pronounced these famous words, which are now part of the European Union's epic tale: "the ECB is ready to do whatever it takes to preserve the euro. And believe me, it will be enough."[43] Thus, approximately two months later on September 6, 2012, the ECB announced its OMT program, as has been hinted previously.[44] This program was part of the measures that the ECB took to combat the crisis. In fact, one could even argue that it was the main measure thus far adopted. Due to its importance (and regardless of the fact that the program has not been and will most likely not be implemented), I will start with its analysis (see Fabbrini, 2016: 94–98).

In effect, the main peculiarity of the OMT program was that it provided for the unlimited purchase of sovereign bonds in secondary markets. "Unlimited" was meant in two senses: concerning the volume of bonds that the ECB would buy[45] and concerning time.[46] The ECB committed itself to maintaining the program until the financial markets returned to normality.

As has been said already, this program was challenged before the German Constitutional Court, which, in turn, sent a referral for a preliminary ruling to the ECJ. The ECJ's preliminary ruling, in what has become the *Gauweiler* case, said that the OMT program was legal from the perspective of the Treaties. The ECJ divided the substance of its judgment into four parts: (1) powers of the ESCB, (2) delimitation of monetary policy, (3) proportionality, and (4) violation of article 123.1 TFEU.

First, concerning powers, the ECJ recalled that the main mission of the ECB was to maintain price stability and that, to that end, the Treaties had set a number of instruments. Second, concerning the delimitation of monetary policy, the ECJ said, "It is apparent that a programme such as that announced in the press release, in view of its objectives and the instruments provided for achieving them, falls within the area of monetary policy." Third, concerning proportionality, the ECJ deemed the program to be proportionate to its

---

[43] Speech by Mario Draghi, President of the European Central Bank, at the Global Investment Conference in London, July 26, 2012. See the text at www.ecb.europa.eu/press/key/date/2012/html/sp120726.en.html.

[44] Technical features of Outright Monetary Transactions. See ECB at www.ecb.europa.eu/press/pr/date/2012/html/pr120906_1.en.html.

[45] The crucial paragraph is this one: "No ex ante quantitative limits are set on the size of Outright Monetary Transactions."

[46] The crucial paragraph is this one: "Following a thorough assessment, the Governing Council will decide on the start, continuation and suspension of Outright Monetary Transactions in full discretion and acting in accordance with its monetary policy mandate."

objective, because "in economic conditions such as those described by the ECB at the date of the press release, the ESCB could legitimately take the view that a program such as that announced in the press release is appropriate for the purpose of contributing to the ESCB's objectives and, therefore, to maintaining price stability." The ECJ reviewed, within its proportionality assessment, the most controversial aspect of the OMT program, which was the purchase of sovereign bonds in unlimited volumes. According to the ECJ, "a programme whose volume is thus restricted could legitimately be adopted by the ESCB without a quantitative limit being set prior to its implementation, such a limit being likely, moreover, to reduce the programme's effectiveness." Finally, concerning the violation of article 123.1, the ECJ concluded that the conditions that the OMT program set were the guarantee that article 123.1 would be respected. Under this heading, the ECJ analyzed the question of the unlimited time span of the program. "The programme provides for the purchase of government bonds only in so far as is necessary for safeguarding the monetary policy transmission mechanism and the singleness of monetary policy and that those purchases will cease as soon as those objectives are achieved," said the Court.

The ECJ's *Gauweiler* decision is a perfect example of how a Court's counterfactual reasoning works. This issue has been analyzed in Chapter 2. As we said therein, it is, as a matter of principle, for the legislator to consider counterfactual situations. When drafting a legal commitment, the legislator (or the constituent power, as the case may be) must consider the opposite factual situation to the one that served as a basis for making the legal commitment. In turn, the judicial power must ensure that the legislator made the counterfactual assessment and considered the opposite factual situation to the one the norm finally integrated. If the judicial power becomes convinced that the legislator did consider the counterfactual situation, it should defer to the legislator and should not substitute for it. If, by contrast, the judge becomes convinced that the legislator did not consider the counterfactual situation, then the judge could substitute his or her judgment for the legislator's and even go so far as to regulate the whole area under its scrutiny.

The ECJ did precisely the above in the *Gauweiler* case. From a strictly legal perspective, the OMT program was clearly against the Treaty and, in particular, against article 123.1 TFEU, which prohibits ECB bailouts. The ECJ itself recognizes that the OMT program can be a disguised approach to circumvent this prohibition when it says the following:

> It is true that, despite those safeguards, the ESCB's intervention remains capable of having, as the referring court points out, some influence on the functioning of the primary and secondary sovereign debt markets. *However, that fact is not decisive since such influence constitutes, as the Advocate General has observed in point 259 of his Opinion, an inherent effect in purchases on the secondary market* which are authorized by the FEU Treaty. That effect is, moreover, essential if those purchases are to be used effectively in the framework of monetary policy [paragraph 108; my emphasis].

However, the Court does not stop there. Once it recognizes that, in fact, a program such as the OMT can have an effect equivalent to the outright buying of sovereign bonds in the primary markets, it proceeds to analyze whether doing so could not be excepted if particular economic conditions were in place. According to the ECJ,

> In the situation described in paragraphs 72 and 73 of this judgment, the purchase, on secondary markets, of government bonds of the Member States affected by interest rates considered by the ECB to be excessive, is likely to contribute to reducing those rates by dispelling unjustified fears about the break-up of the euro area and thus to play a part in bringing about a fall in – or even the elimination of – excessive risk premia.
>
> [para 76; ibid. in paras. 72, 73, 74, 77]

The implicit reasoning is therefore the following: (1) article 123.1 prohibits ECB bailouts; (2) clearly, this article did not consider a situation in which the euro could break up; (3) the ECJ therefore considers this situation; and (4) in this (counterfactual) particular situation, the ECB could bail out Member States, even without limitations. The ECJ's reference to the conditions under which the ECB could implement the OMT program should most likely be understood as not more than a concession to the German Constitutional Court; that is, as a way to make the whole *Gauweiler* decision more acceptable to it.

4.6 The ECB and Credibility

I will make in the following a number of concluding remarks concerning the issue of credibility and the ECB. This section wraps up and summarizes many of the arguments made at various points in this chapter but also offers new insights into this important question.

As seen above, the ECB's legal statute is amongst the most rigid that one can find in the world of central banking today. It is more rigid than the statute of two of its most important counterparts, the Fed and the Bundesbank. This rigidity is expressed in two ways. First, the ECB statute is constitutionally entrenched through the EU Treaties. The second expression of rigidity relates to how these legal (constitutional) commitments are made. If one examines how the main elements of the ECB statute are framed (be it for example its independence, mission, election of the president, or prohibitions), it is apparent that these commitments are written in a very clear and unambiguous way; they leave little room for interpretation or exceptions. Clearly, the framers of the Treaties placed themselves in the most rigid of all possible scenarios, by intellectually ruling out any counterfactual situation.

This point is in itself intriguing. The framers of the Treaty could not have ignored the fact that economic crises with a monetary leaning are the daily bread of post-capitalist systems. The Latin American crisis of the 1980s and then the Asian crisis of the 1990s, not to speak of the breakup of the European Monetary System in 1992, gave evidence of this fact. Therefore, their movement towards rigidity cannot be explained as mere chance. It was a very conscious choice on the part of the framers of the Treaty to try to provide the highest possible credibility to the ECB.

By doing so, the main mistake that the framers of the Treaty made was to equate credibility with rigidity. They started from the assumption that by inserting the ECB statute in the Treaties (in the EU's constitution) and by drafting the most important legal commitments that shaped the ECB statute in the most clear and unambiguous way, they were guaranteeing the credibility of the institution; instead, they were paying it lip service. Further, the existing doubts about the correlation between central banks' independence and the control of inflation are a further problem in this domain. Had this correlation been irrefutably proven, constitutionalizing a bold independent statute for the ECB would then have been more credible. However, because this relationship is at least uncertain, rigidity in this field is less understandable in terms of credibility.

The 2008 crisis has revealed the structural importance of this mistake. When the euro was at stake, the ECB had to react to save the Eurozone. With the Treaties in the hands of the ECB, the margin of maneuver of this institution was close to zero. The ECB, not without hesitation, had to "reinterpret" its own statute and the instruments it had available to face the crisis. The reaction was clumsy, full of doubt, and came late almost every time. In other words, the ECB's reaction to the crisis was a consequence of the rigidity with which its statute had been drafted by the framers of the Treaty. The outcome of this story (which has not finished yet, because we remain immersed in the aftermath of the crisis) is most likely that the legitimacy and credibility of this institution has been seriously put to question.

The purpose of this book is not to provide policy recommendations; however, the issue of the ECB's credibility is so important to maintaining the standing of the European economic governance edifice that some remarks on the future prospects of this institution may well be warranted. Two possible alternatives exist for escaping the current suboptimal situation: either the statute of the ECB could be drafted more flexibly in the Treaties (for example, by incorporating economic growth and unemployment into the mission of the ECB clearly and boldly), or the ECB statute could be left as it is but in a downgraded legal *locus*. For example, a regulation, adopted by the Member States by qualified majority, might be the legal act in which the main elements of the ECB statute could be placed. Such a regulation would facilitate amending this statute when the ECB was in need of more flexibility.

Be that as it may, the most important thing is to convey the message that rigidity, important as it can be, is only one element among the complex combination of variables that serve to provide credibility to an institution and the policies it implements.

BIBLIOGRAPHY

Alesina, A. & Summers, L. H. 1993, "Central bank independence and macroeconomic performance: some comparative evidence," *Journal of Money, Credit, and Banking*, vol. 25, no. 2, pp. 151–162.

Altavilla, C., Giannone, D., & Lenza, M. 2014, "The financial and macroeconomic effects of OMT announcements," ECB Working Paper Series no. 1707, August.

Bade, R. & Parkin, M. 1988, "Central Bank Laws and Monetary Policy," Unpublished manuscript. University of Western Ontario, London, Ont. http://economics.uwo.ca/people/parkin_docs/CentralBankLaws.pdf.

Barro, R. J. & Gordon, D. 1983b, "Rules, discretion and reputation in a model of monetary policy," *Journal of Monetary Economics*, vol. 12, no. 1, pp. 101–121.

  1983a, "A positive theory of monetary policy in a natural rate model," *Journal of Political Economy*, vol. 91, no. 4, pp. 589–610.

Bastasin, C. 2015, *Saving Europe: Anatomy of a Dream*, 2nd edn., Brookings Institution, Washington, D.C.

  2012, *Saving Europe: Anatomy of a Dream*, Brookings Institution, Washington, D.C.

Belke, A. 2011, "Change of Guard from Trichet to Draghi – Watch or Not to Watch Money under Political Constraints," Directorate General for Internal Policies Policy Department A: Economic and Scientific Policies Economic and Monetary Affairs, September.

Belke, A. & Polleit, T. 2006, "How the ECB and the US Fed Set Interest Rates," *Hohenheimer Diskussionsbeiträge*, no. 269/2006.

Brown, M., Trautmann, S., & Vlahu, R. 2014, "Understanding Bank-Run Contagion," ECB Working Paper Series no. 1711, August.

Campillo, M. & Miron, J. 1997, "Why does inflation differ across countries?" in *Reducing Inflation: Motivation and Strategy*, eds. C. D. Romes & D. H. Romes University of Chicago Press, Chicago, pp. 335–362.

Cargill, T. 2016, "The Myth of Central Bank Independence," Mercatus Working Paper, October, pp. 1–26.

Carlstrom, C. & Fuerst, T. 2009, "Central Bank independence and inflation: a note," *Economic Inquiry*, vol. 47, no. 1, pp. 182–186.

Cukierman, A. 2008, "Central bank independence and monetary policymaking institutions – Past, present and future," *European Journal of Political Economy*, vol. 24, pp. 722–736.

  1992, *Central Bank Strategy, Credibility and Independence – Theory and Evidence*, The MIT Press, Cambridge, Mass.

Cukierman, A., Webb, S., & Neyapti, B. 1992, "Measuring the independence of central banks and its effect on policy outcomes," *The World Bank Economic Review*, vol. 6, pp. 353–398.

De Grauwe, P. 2016, *Economics of Monetary Union*, 11th edn., Oxford University Press, Oxford.

De Haan, J. & Kooi, W. 2000, "Does central bank independence really matter? New evidence for developing countries using a new indicator," *Journal of Banking & Finance*, vol. 24, pp. 643–664.

Dornbusch, R., Favero, C., & Giavazzi, F. 1998, "Immediate challenges for the European Central Bank," NBER (National Bureau of Economic Research) Working Paper no. 6369.

Ersoy, I. & Antmen, S. 2016, "The determinants of long-term interests rates in eurozone: Taylor rule and governance indicators," *International Business Research*, vol. 9, no. 9.

European Central Bank 2014, "Legal framework of the Eurosystem and the European System of Central Banks: ECB legal acts and instruments 2014 update."

Fabbrini, F. 2016, *Economic Governance in Europe: Comparative Paradoxes and Constitutional Challenges*, Oxford University Press (Oxford Studies in EU Law), Oxford.

Friedman, M. 1968, "The role of monetary policy," *The American Economic Review*, vol. 58, no. 1, pp. 1–17.

Garbade, K. 2014, "Direct Purchases of U.S. Treasury Securities by Federal Reserve Banks," Federal Reserve Bank of New York Staff Reports, no. 684.

Garriga, C. 2016, "Central bank independence in the world: a new data set," *International Interactions*, vol. 42, no. 5, pp. 849–868.

Gortsos, C. V. 2015, "Last resort lending to solvent credit institutions in the euro area before and after the establishment of the SSM," in European Central Bank (ed.) *ECB Legal Conference 2015: From Monetary Union to Banking Union, on the Way to Capital Markets Union: New Opportunities for European Integration*, European Central Bank, Frankfurt, pp. 53–77, www.ecb.europa.eu/pub/pdf/other/frommonetaryuniontobankingunion201512.en.pdf.

Grilli, V., Masciandaro, D., & Tabellini, G. 1991, "Political and monetary institutions and public financial policies in the industrial countries," *Economic Policy*, vol. 6 no. 13, pp. 342–392.

Gutierrez, E. 2003, "Inflation Performance and Central Bank Independence: Evidence from Latin America and the Caribbean," IMF Working Paper 03/53.

Hayek, F. A. 1960, *The Constitution of Liberty*, Routledge, London & New York.
1944, *The Road to Serfdom*, The University of Chicago Press, Chicago & London.

Hayo, B. & Hofmann, B. 2005, "Comparing monetary policy reaction functions: ECB versus Bundesbank," *Marburg Papers on Economics*, vol. 2.

Ismihana, M. & Ozkanb, F. 2004, "Does central bank independence lower inflation?," *Economics Letters*, vol. 84, pp. 305–309.

Krugman, P. 2007, "Who was Milton Friedman?," *The New York Review of Books*, February 15.

Landleraug, M. 2005, "Willem F. Duisenberg, First European Bank President, Dies at 70," *New York Times*, August 1.

Miscossi, S. 2015, "The Monetary Policy of the European Central Bank (2002–2015)," CEPS (Centre for European Policy Studies) Special Report 109/2015.

Odendahl, C. 2014, "The ECB is not the German Central Bank," Centre for European Reform, December 2, www.cer.eu/insights/ecb-not-german-central-bank.

Petch, T. 2013, "The compatibility of outright monetary transactions with EU law," *Law and Financial Markets Review*, vol. 13, pp. 13–21.

Phillips, A. 1958, "The relation between unemployment and the rate of change of money wage rates in the United Kingdom, 1861–1957," *Economica*, new series, vol. 25, no. 100, pp. 283–299.

Posen, A. 1998, "Do better institutions make better policy?," *International Finance*, vol. 1, no. 1, pp. 173–205.
1995, "Declarations are not enough: financial sector sources of central bank independence" in *NBER Macroeconomics Annual, Vol. 10*, eds. B. Bernanke & J. Rotemberg, MIT Press, pp. 253–274.

Rogoff, K. 1985, "The optimal degree of commitment to an intermediate monetary target," *Quarterly Journal of Economics*, vol. 100, no. 4, pp. 1169–1189.

Rotondi, Z. & Vaciago, G. 2007, "Lessons from the ECB Experience: Frankfurt Still Matters!," Universita' Cattolica del Sacro Cuore, vol. IEF0070.

Rühl, T. 2015, "Taylor rules revisited: ECB and Bundesbank in comparison," *Empirical Economics*, vol. 48, pp. 951–967.

Samuelson, P. 1977, *Worldwide Stagflation: The Collected Scientific Papers of Paul Samuelson, Vol. IV*, MIT Press, Cambridge, Mass.

Samuelson, P. & Nordhaus, W. 2010, *Economics*, 19th edn., McGraw-Hill Irwin, Boston, Mass.

Schiek, D. 2014, "The German Federal Constitutional Court's ruling on outright monetary transactions (OMT) – another step towards national closure?," *German Law Journal*, vol. 15, no. 2, pp. 329–342.

Shapiro, M. 1997, "The problems of independent agencies in the United States and the European Union," *Journal of European Public Policy*, vol. 4, no. 2, pp. 276–291.

Smant, D. 2002, "Has the European Central Bank followed a Bundesbank policy? Evidence from the early years," *Kredit und Kapital*, vol. 35, no. 3, pp. 327–343.

Solans, D. 2000, "Monetary Policy under Inflation Targeting," Contribution presented by Eugenio Domingo Solans, Member of the Governing Council and the Executive Board of the European Central Bank, at the Fourth Annual Conference of Banco Central de Chile, Santiago de Chile, December 1.

Wapshott, N. (ed.) 2011, *Keynes versus Hayek: The Clash that Defined Modern Economics*, W. W. Norton & Company, New York; London.

Zilioli, C. 2015, "Introduction" in European Central Bank (ed.) *ECB Legal Conference 2015: From Monetary Union to Banking Union, on the Way to Capital Markets Union: New Opportunities for European Integration*, European Central Bank, Frankfurt, pp. 49–52, www.ecb.europa.eu/pub/pdf/other/frommonetaryuniontobankingunion201512.en.pdf.

Zilioli, C. & Selmayr, M. 2001, *The Law of the European Central Bank*, Hart Publishing, Oxford.

5

The European Framework of Financial Regulation and Supervision: Towards a Banking Union

Introduction

Having examined the ECB and the monetary policy of the Eurozone, we can move in this chapter to an analysis of the institutional system that has emerged, since the 2008 crisis exploded, for financial market regulation and supervision. The new framework primarily implied the reinforcement of the supervisory powers of the ECB. However, it also implied the establishment of new institutions specifically dedicated to the surveillance (and regulation) of financial markets. The following institutions will be examined:

- The European Systemic Risk Board
- The European Banking Authority
- The European Insurance and Occupational Pensions Authority
- The European Securities and Markets Authority.

The entire new system is completed by a Single Supervision Mechanism and a Single Resolution Mechanism (which also includes a Single Resolution Fund) of financial institutions, which will also be examined herein.

We start with a discussion of the rationale behind this new institutional development, which is connected with the issues of trust and credibility.

5.1 Why a European Framework for Financial Regulation and Supervision?

On November 11, 2008, the president of the European Commission, José Manuel Barroso, decided on the establishment of a High Level Group on Financial Supervision. The Group's first chair was Jacques de Larosière, a former governor of the central bank of France, under whose name the Group has passed to posterity (Lannoo, 2011). The Larosière Group delivered its report on February 25, 2009, with recommendations to the Commission on a number of reforms to streamline the regulation and supervision of financial

Figure 5.1: "Trust chain" of financial markets

markets.[1] However, the Group did not limit itself to making recommendations; it also made a thorough analysis of the causes of the near-collapse of the global financial system after the fall of Lehman Brothers. The report went straight to the point in its first paragraph; the main reason underlying the financial meltdown related to trust: "Financial markets depend on trust. But much of this trust has evaporated."

It is therefore important to understand the foundations of what I call "the trust chain" in the financial sector. A simplified version of this chain is represented in Figure 5.1. In effect, financial markets depend, as the de Larosière report correctly states, on a complex chain of trust that involves at least three sets of actors: the citizens, the supervisory institutions, and the financial institutions. The citizens trust that financial institutions work properly because they trust that supervision works properly. In turn, financial institutions lend to and borrow from other financial institutions; thus, they also must trust one another. Furthermore, the financial institutions trust the supervisory institutions; therefore, they lend to and borrow from other financial institutions because they trust that those institutions are correctly supervised. This chain works as a "house of cards": if one card falls, the rest of the trust structure also collapses. To better understand this metaphor, it is important to understand the meaning of the old saying "house of cards": it denotes a structure that not only heavily depends upon its parts but also holds on a very weak basis, so weak that if only one part (one card) falls, the rest of the structure also falls apart.

This collapse is exactly what occurred when Lehman Brothers went broke in September 2008. One part of the trust chain, trust among financial institutions, fell apart. Therefore, the rest of the system also collapsed, or came close to collapse. Citizens started mistrusting the financial institutions, and these and the citizens also mistrusted the supervisors. When this process of

---

[1] "The High-Level Group on Financial Supervision in the EU Report." Brussels, February 25, 2009. See http://ec.europa.eu/internal_market/finances/docs/de_larosiere_report_en.pdf.

cumulative mistrust unfolds, there are two main risks: that credit stops (which almost occurred in 2008) and that a bank run occurs (which did occur, but on a more limited basis and varying by country; see Brown et al., 2014). This situation is a financial perfect storm that might place the entire global financial system on the brink of collapse. As the Larosière report mentions, we were very close to witnessing this situation in 2008, had it not been for the rapid reaction of, above all, the Federal Reserve Bank and Treasury department of the USA.

When the "trust chain" of financial markets collapses, there is only one possible avenue to restore trust, which is to streamline the regulation and supervision of financial markets. This point is even more true in the EU context, in which the subsidiarity principle (Estella, 2002) had meant, until the crisis, that, above all, the supervisory functions over financial markets had been left to the Member States. Our discussion about credibility and law emerges here once again; to restore trust, the EU streamlined both regulation and supervision of the financial markets. However, from a "law as credibility" perspective, the point is not so much to pile up regulation after regulation, procedure after procedure and supervisory agency after supervisory agency but, instead, how credible the new system is. The piling up of new regulations and agencies can help to stop the trust haemorrhage in the very short term; however, in the medium and long terms, trust will be restored only if the new system in place is an equilibrium. The main problem that we have in judging whether the new regulatory and supervisory system for financial markets that emerged after the crisis is an equilibrium is that insufficient time has elapsed since the system came into being to perform a serious analysis of this issue, and also that, as we will see in this chapter, the system is incomplete. However, the "quantitative" signals that we have (the EU appears to be trapped in an unprecedented regulatory spiral in this area) are indeed not very promising. Less but better regulation should most likely have been in place. However, as stated previously, it remains too early to provide a more definitive account of how the new system is working.

Moreover, as said before, the system remains far from complete. As noted by de Grauwe (2016: 178), for the system to be complete, another step must be taken: the creation of a Eurozone deposit insurance mechanism that would avert the risk of a bank run or, in other words, that would address the problem of citizens' mistrust of the financial system. Although actions have been taken in this direction,[2] Germany's opposition casts doubts on the feasibility of this

---

[2] See Directive 2014/49/EU of the European Parliament and of the Council of April 16, 2014, on deposit guarantee schemes (recast), L 173/149 of 12.6.2014. This directive harmonizes Member States' deposit insurance schemes, setting a general coverage level of €100,000 per depositor. The Commission has already proposed the establishment of an EDIS, a European Deposit Insurance Mechanism, but the proposal remains under discussion. See Proposal for Regulation of the European Parliament and of the Council amending Regulation (EU) 806/2014 to establish a European Deposit Insurance Scheme, Strasbourg, 24.11.2015 COM(2015) 586 final 2015/0270 (COD).

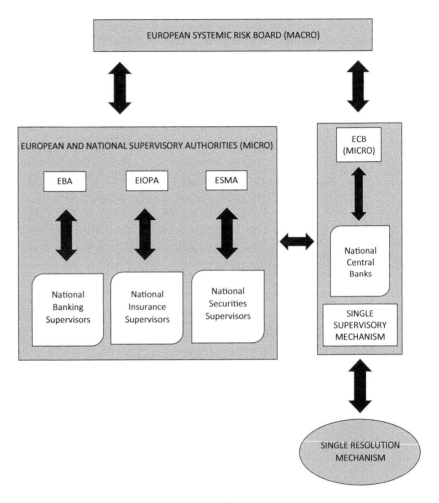

Figure 5.2: European Framework for financial regulation and supervision
(IN ORANGE ESFS, EUROPEAN SYSTEM OF FINANCIAL SUPERVISION)

proposal (Howarth & Quaglia, 2016: 155). At present, deposits are only covered by national mechanisms. An in-depth "law as credibility" assessment can only be made when the whole system is finally completed.

The Larosière report proposed to the Commission of a new institutional system as a solution to the crisis, which in essence was finally put in place. The Commission accepted most of the recommendations through two communications that it adopted in 2009.[3] This scheme is represented in Figure 5.2. I call the whole system the "European framework for financial regulation and

---

[3] Commission Communication "Driving European Recovery" Brussels, 4.3.2009 COM(2009) 114 final and Commission Communication "European financial supervision" Brussels, 27.5.2009 COM(2009) 252 final.

supervision" (see in general Shoenmaker et al., 2014). To understand this system better, it is important to differentiate between the macro- and micro-prudential aspects of regulation and supervision of financial markets. By "macro," we encompass the systemic dimension of financial markets. By "micro," we refer to individual financial institutions. The system therefore works as follows: the European Systemic Risk Board is in charge of macro-prudential regulation and supervision, whereas the European Supervisory Agencies (ESAs), together with the national ones, are in charge of microprudential regulation and supervision. The Board and the European and national authorities constitute the ESFS (European System of Financial Supervision). The whole framework is completed by the ECB, which is in charge of micro-prudential supervision of financial institutions of more than €30 billion in asset value. Therefore, the ECB is also in charge of some microprudential tasks. Once again, although the system is often referred to as a system of "supervision," most of the supervisory agencies also have important regulatory powers. Furthermore, one should view this framework as a whole system; the arrows in Figure 5.2 denote that all of these institutions must be coordinated with one another (which, as shown in the ensuing analysis, will not always be an easy task). Finally, it is important to mention that a Single Resolution Mechanism has been added to this system. Technically speaking, this system is not a regulatory or supervisory mechanism but rather a mechanism that operates once supervision has determined that a financial institution has failed and must be resolved. To differentiate it from the other regulatory and supervisory actors, I have circled this mechanism in Figure 5.2.

In the ensuing sections, I will analyze, one by one, all of these new institutions, with particular reference to the following three main items: (1) composition, (2) voting rules, and (3) functions.

5.2 European Systemic Risk Board

Regulation 1092/2010, of November 24, 2010,[4] establishes the European Systemic Risk Board. Interestingly, the legal basis of this regulation is article 114 TFEU (internal market); however, the Board's tasks clearly go well beyond internal market issues (Fahey, 2011). In reality, the Board is the institution (with no legal personality) entrusted with the task of surveying the EU financial market in its entirety with a view to detecting risks which might imperil the system; that is, risks that might have a systemic dimension.

Article 1 of regulation 1092/2010 starts with a definition of the ESFS, which comprises the following institutions (see Figure 5.2):

---

[4] Regulation (EU) No 1092/2010 of the European Parliament and of the Council of November 24, 2010, on European Union macro-prudential oversight of the financial system and establishing a European Systemic Risk Board. OJEU L 331/1 of 15.12.2010.

- The European Systemic Risk Board
- The ESAs
- The Joint Committee of European Supervisory Authorities
- The competent or supervisory authorities of the Member States.

The Board is the object of this section, and the ESAs are analyzed in the next section. The competent or supervisory authorities of the Member States are the counterparts of the ESAs. Finally, the Joint Committee to which article 1 refers is an institution established by regulations 1093/2010, 1094/2010, and 1095/2010. In essence, this Committee is a forum in which cooperation and coordination among the three ESAs is organized.

The Board has a chair, a first vice-chair, and a second vice-chair. Currently, the chair is the president of the ECB. Article 5.1, in conjunction with article 20 of regulation 1092/2010, states that the modalities for the designation of the chair of the ESRB will be reviewed after the first five years following the entry into force of regulation 1092/2010. However, the president of the ECB has been confirmed as chair of the Board, which illustrates the close connection between the ESRB and the ECB.[5] The Board comprises the following:

- A general board
- A Steering Committee
- A Secretariat
- An advisory scientific committee
- An advisory technical committee.

The general board is the key organ of the five and makes the most important decisions of the ESRB. It comprises the president and vice-president of the ECB, the governors of national central banks, a member of the Commission, the chairpersons of the ESAs, the chair and two vice-chairs of the advisory scientific committee, and the chair of the technical committee. These members have voting rights. Additionally, the general board includes one high-level representative per Member State of the competent national supervisory authorities and the president of the Economic and Financial Committee. These members do not have voting rights but only a voice in the general board meetings.

In principle, the general board makes decisions by a simple majority of the members with voting rights. However, article 10.3 of regulation 1092/2010 says that a two-thirds majority of the votes cast shall be required to adopt a recommendation or to make a warning or a recommendation public. This article is, however, further nuanced by article 18.1 of regulation 1092/2010, which says that a quorum of two-thirds "shall always apply" for the decision to make public warnings and recommendations.

---

[5] See Council Regulation (EU) No 1096/201 of November 17, 2010, conferring specific tasks upon the European Central Bank concerning the functioning of the European Systemic Risk Board, L 331/162 of 15.12.2010.

The main task of the Board is an oversight one, in which the Board does not make legally binding decisions. It monitors the proper functioning of the European Union's financial system. If it detects problems, it can issue warnings and recommendations. Warnings are the instrument that the Board uses when it detects the existence of a menace to the system. Recommendations are the instruments that the Board uses for remedial action. Warnings can be either general or specific. They can be sent to the Union as a whole, to one or more Member States, to one or more ESAs, or to one or more national supervisory agencies. Recommendations can have as addressees the same actors plus the European Commission and must include a specific timeline in which these actors must provide a policy response to the Board. Both warnings and recommendations must always be "transmitted" to the Council and the Commission. In principle, warnings and recommendations are not public, but article 18 of regulation 1092/2010 states that the general board can decide to make them public, according to the voting and quorum rules previously examined.

5.3 European Supervisory Authorities (ESAs)

Regulations 1093/2010, 1094/2010, and 1095/2010 establish, respectively, the EBA, the EIOPA, and the ESMA. I will review them in turn.

5.3.1 European Banking Authority (EBA)

The EBA is established by regulation 1093/2010[6] (Masciandaroa, Nieto, & Quintyn, 2011). Unlike the ERSB, the EBA is a proper administrative agency. It has legal personality and enjoys both enforcement and regulatory powers under terms that will be shown later. It can adopt legally binding decisions whose addressees can be both national agencies and individual financial institutions. Furthermore, the subject area covered by the EBA regulation, as defined by its articles 1.2 and 1.3, is the activities of credit and financial institutions, financial conglomerates, investment firms, payment institutions, and e-money institutions directly or indirectly related to the EU legislation indicated in article 1.2 of the regulation.

More specifically, article 1.5 of regulation 1093/2010 states that the EBA shall contribute to a "sound, effective and consistent" level of regulation and supervision. These main tasks are operationalized through a number of organs that compose the agency (article 6). These are the following:

- A board of supervisors
- A management board

---

[6] Regulation (EU) No 1093/2010 of the European Parliament and of the Council of November 24, 2010, establishing a European Supervisory Authority (European Banking Authority), amending Decision No 716/2009/EC and repealing Commission Decision 2009/78/EC, OJEU L 331/12 of 15.12.2010.

- A chairperson
- An executive director
- A board of appeal.

The board of supervisors is composed of the chairperson (nonvoting), the heads of the national supervisory agencies, one representative of the Commission (nonvoting), one representative of the ECB (nonvoting), one representative of the ESRB (nonvoting), and one representative of the other two ESAs (nonvoting). The executive director of the EBA can participate in the meetings of the board (nonvoting).

The board is the most important organ of the EBA. The board makes Chapter II decisions under regulations 1093/2010, which are the most relevant ones, as seen below. Its decisions are made, in principle, by a simple majority of its members. However, there are exceptions to this general rule because some decisions must be made by a qualified majority of its members (article 44.1, second and third paragraphs).

The management board is composed of the chairperson and six other members of the board of supervisors. Decisions by the management board shall be made "on the basis of the majority of the members present" (article 45.2). The management board has a sort of supervisory mission over the agency; it must ensure that the EBA "carries out its mission and performs the tasks assigned to it in accordance with this Regulation" (article 47.1). It has, for example, the power to propose to the board of supervisors the work program of the Authority for the ensuing year, on which the board must vote.

The chairperson and executive director are defined, respectively, in articles 48 and 51 of the regulation. Although the former represents the agency, the latter manages the EBA.

In turn, the board of appeal is a joint organ of the ESAs (article 58). It is composed of six members and six alternates. All of them shall be individuals of a high professional reputation, including supervisory experience, in the fields of banking, insurance, occupational pensions, securities markets, or other financial services (article 58). The board makes decisions by a majority of four of its six members (article 58.6): "Where the appealed decision falls within the scope of this Regulation, the deciding majority shall include at least one of the two members of the Board of Appeal appointed by the Authority," says article 58.6. The board of appeals works as a quasi-judicial body; decisions adopted by the agency can be appealed before the board according to a procedure set in article 60 of the regulation. The board of appeal's decision can in turn be challenged before the ECJ.

The main tasks of the EBA are defined in articles 8 to 39 of the regulation. These decisions are, in essence, of two types: regulatory decisions and administrative or enforcement decisions. I will analyze them in turn.

Concerning regulatory decisions, the agency adopts

- Draft regulatory technical standards
- Draft implementing technical standards
- Guidelines and recommendations.

Regulatory technical standards are defined in article 10 of regulation 1093/ 2010. First, regulatory technical standards are defined as "technical" (*sic*, article 10.1 second paragraph) and cannot imply strategic decisions or decisions on policy (see Box 5.1 for an example). Second, their content is delimited by the legislative acts on which they are based, following the *Meroni* doctrine,[7] which has recently been updated by the ESMA case[8] (Nicolaides & Preziosi, 2014; Pelkmans & Simoncini, 2014).

The process works as follows: The agency proposes a draft to the Commission. The latter might (or might not) endorse the draft. In the second case, it must provide reasons for its decision and send the draft back to the agency. The agency must inform the European Parliament and the Council of the draft. We are speaking here of the area of delegated powers to the Commission, pursuant to article 290 TFEU.[9] The regulation in turn delegates the capacity to make drafts to the agency. However, the final say is on the Commission's side. If within a given deadline the agency has not sent a draft to the Commission, the Commission can adopt the decision without a draft. Nevertheless, if the agency sends a draft, the Commission cannot just ignore it; "the Commission may not change the content of a draft prepared by the authority without prior coordination with the Authority," says article 10.1 *in fine*.

In turn, implementing technical standards are defined in article 15 of regulation 1093/2010. They are also defined as being "technical" (*sic*) by the first paragraph of that article. Therefore, in administrative law terms, implementing technical standards are normative developments of previous regulatory technical standards (as in the example in Box 5.1; implementing technical standards on "own funds" develop from regulatory technical standards on "own funds"). The process of adoption of implementing technical standards works similarly to the process of adoption of regulatory technical standards,

---

[7] Case 9/56, *Meroni v High Authority*, Judgment of the European Court of Justice of 13.6.1958.
[8] Case C-270/12, *United Kingdom v European Parliament and Council of the European Union*, Judgment of the Court (Grand Chamber) of January 22, 2014.
[9] Article 290 TFEU reads:

1. " A legislative act may delegate to the Commission the power to adopt non-legislative acts of general application to supplement or amend certain non-essential elements of the legislative act. The objectives, content, scope and duration of the delegation of power shall be explicitly defined in the legislative acts. The essential elements of an area shall be reserved for the legislative act and accordingly shall not be the subject of a delegation of power.
2. Legislative acts shall explicitly lay down the conditions to which the delegation is subject; these conditions may be as follows:
   (a) the European Parliament or the Council may decide to revoke the delegation;
   (b) the delegated act may enter into force only if no objection has been expressed by the European Parliament or the Council within a period set by the legislative act.
   For the purposes of (a) and (b), the European Parliament shall act by a majority of its component members, and the Council by a qualified majority.
3. The adjective 'delegated' shall be inserted in the title of delegated acts".

Box 5.1: Example of regulatory and implementing technical standard

EBA final draft technical standards on own funds

27 March 2014

The European Banking Authority (EBA) published its final draft Regulatory Technical Standards (RTS) and final draft Implementing Technical Standards (ITS) on own funds. These final draft RTS and ITS will be part of the Single Rulebook aimed at enhancing regulatory harmonisation in the banking sector in Europe and namely at strengthening the quality of capital.

RTS and ITS on own funds

These draft final RTS and ITS cover different areas of own funds. In particular, the **RTS on own funds part I** specify the different elements of own funds, including Common Equity Tier 1 (CET1) capital, Additional Tier 1 capital, Tier 2 capital, deductions from the different types of capital, and transitional provisions for own funds in terms of grandfathering. **The RTS on Gain on Sale** specify further the concept and the treatment of a gain on sale, defined as any increase (or part of an increase) in equity under the applicable accounting framework arising from future margin income in the context of a securitisation transaction. The **RTS on own funds part II** specify the conditions under which competent authorities may determine that a type of undertaking recognised under applicable national law qualifies as a mutual, cooperative society, savings institution or similar institution for the purpose of calculating own funds. **The draft RTS on own funds part III** set out criteria to deduct indirect and synthetic holdings, to define broad market indices and to calculate minority interest. **The ITS on disclosure for own funds** focus on disclosure requirements and aim at increasing transparency on regulatory capital held by European institutions. Finally, **the RTS on own funds part IV** settle harmonised criteria for instruments with multiple distributions that would create a disproportionate drag on capital, as well as clarifying the meaning of preferential distributions.

Legal basis and next steps

These final RTS and ITS have been developed in accordance with Regulation (EU) No 575/2013 of the European Parliament and of the Council of 26 June 2013 on prudential requirements for credit institutions and investment firms and amending Regulation (EU) No 648/2012 (colloquially known as Capital Requirements Regulation or CRR).

The final standards have been sent to the European Commission for their adoption as EU Regulations that will be directly applicable throughout the EU.

(source: www.eba.europa.eu/regulation-and-policy/own-funds/draft-regulatory-technical-standards-on-own-funds)

whose main traits have been explained previously. However, the Treaty reference is here article 291[10] (and not article 290, as in regulatory technical standards).

Finally, guidelines and recommendations are established in article 16 of regulation 1093/2010. Through guidelines and recommendations, the agency establishes common supervisory practices. Therefore, both are addressed to the national supervisory agencies. Guidelines and recommendations are not legally binding, but the addressees must provide reasons for noncompliance with them.

As stated previously, the agency also enjoys enforcement powers. In particular, it can

- Issue recommendations in specific cases
- Make individual decisions addressed to national supervisory agencies
- Make individual decisions addressed to financial institutions.

First, the power to make recommendations in specific cases is regulated in article 17 of regulation 1093/2010. These are cases of breaches of European Union law by national supervisory agencies, because they failed to apply EU law that directly concerns them, because they applied it incorrectly, or because they failed to implement the regulatory and implementing technical standards that are in force. In these cases, the EBA can address a recommendation to the failing competent authority or agency indicating that it must comply with EU law. If the authority fails to comply with the recommendation, then the issue goes to the Commission, which can issue an opinion addressed to the national agency. If the national agency does not comply with the Commission's opinion, then the Commission has recourse to article 258 TFEU (action for failure to comply with EU law). However, the process does not stop there. Article 17.6 establishes that the EBA can adopt an individual decision against a financial institution in the case that the contested act was an act directly applicable to financial institutions. In other words, in certain circumstances, the agency can substitute itself for its national counterpart if the latter fails to act.

---

[10] Article 291 TFEU reads:

1. Member States shall adopt all measures of national law necessary to implement legally binding Union acts.
2. Where uniform conditions for implementing legally binding Union acts are needed, those acts shall confer implementing powers on the Commission, or, in duly justified specific cases and in the cases provided for in Articles 24 and 26 of the Treaty on European Union, on the Council.
3. For the purposes of paragraph 2, the European Parliament and the Council, acting by means of regulations in accordance with the ordinary legislative procedure, shall lay down in advance the rules and general principles concerning mechanisms for control by Member States of the Commission's exercise of implementing powers.
4. The word "implementing" shall be inserted in the title of implementing acts.

Second, individual decisions addressed to national agencies and financial institutions are regulated in articles 18 and 19 of regulation 1093/2010 (to which one must add individual decisions addressed to financial institutions of article 17.6, *supra*). Article 18 foresees action in emergency situations; that is, in situations in which "adverse developments which may seriously jeopardize the stability of the whole or part of the financial system in the Union" occur. In such cases, the EBA can make individual decisions addressed to the national competent authorities (article 18.3) or financial institutions (18.4). In turn, article 19 regulates cases of disagreement about the measure or measures to be taken in cross-border situations by different national agencies. Article 19 establishes a conciliation process, the failure of which determines the possibility of the EBA making a decision requiring the national competent authorities to adopt a specific action or to refrain from acting (article 19.3). However, if the competent authority does not comply with the EBA's decision, the EBA might directly issue a decision addressed to a financial institution when doing so is necessary to settle the issue (article 19.4).

5.3.2 European Insurance and Occupational Pensions Authority (EIOPA)

The EIOPA is established by regulation 1094/2010.[11] The structure of this regulation follows the lines of regulation 1093/2010 (Busuioc, 2013). The main difference lies in the subject area covered by the EIOPA, which is, according to articles 1.2 and 1.3 of the EIOPA regulation, the supervision and regulation of activities of insurance undertakings, reinsurance undertakings, financial conglomerates, institutions for occupational retirement provision, and insurance intermediaries directly or indirectly related to the EU legislation indicated in article 1.2 of the regulation. As occurs with the EBA, the EIOPA has legal personality; can be considered an EU administrative agency; holds both regulatory and enforcement powers; and can adopt legally binding decisions enforceable against national agencies and financial institutions. The EIOPA organs, decision-making rules and main tasks replicate those established in the EBA's regulation.

5.3.3 European Securities and Markets Authority (ESMA)

Finally, the ESMA is established by regulation 1095/2010.[12] This regulation duplicates the two previous regulations in terms of the organs of this

---

[11] Regulation (EU) No 1094/2010 of the European Parliament and of the Council of November 24, 2010 establishing a European Supervisory Authority (European Insurance and Occupational Pensions Authority), amending Decision No 716/2009/EC and repealing Commission Decision 2009/79/EC, OJEU L 331/48 of 15.12.2010.

[12] Regulation (EU) No 1095/2010 of the European Parliament and of the Council of November 24, 2010, establishing a European Supervisory Authority (European Securities and Markets Authority), amending Decision No 716/2009/EC and repealing Commission Decision 2009/77/EC, OJEC L 331/84 of 15.12.2010.

institution, the voting rules, and the main tasks that are assigned to this agency (Moloney, 2011a; 2011b). The area of competence of the ESMA is defined by articles 1.2 and 1.3 of the 1095/2010 regulation, which covers the activities of financial market participants directly or indirectly related to the EU legislation as defined in article 1.2 of the regulation. Market participants are defined in article 4 rather redundantly; a market participant is a person to whom the legislation indicated in article 1.2 of the regulation is applicable. For example, Credit Rating Agencies and Trade Repositories fall under the direct supervisory and regulatory scope of the ESMA.[13]

5.4 ECB Powers of Microprudential Regulation and Supervision: The Single Supervisory Mechanism

Regulation 1024/2013[14] is one of the two most important pieces of legislation in the area of financial supervision (the other being the regulation on the Single Resolution Mechanism, which will be examined below) (Alexander, 2015). It bestows supervisory (and, as will be shown, regulatory) powers on the ECB over individual financial institutions. More specifically, it creates what is referred to as the Single Supervisory Mechanism (SSM), which shall be integrated into the ECB (but not confounded with the structures of the ECB dedicated to the conduit of monetary policy). I will review the main elements of the SSM in the following.[15]

---

[13] Note that Directive 2010/78, "Omnibus I" and directive 2014/51, "Omnibus II" modify, amend and adapt all of the EU legislation that is affected by the three new ESA regulations. See Directive 2010/78/EU of the European Parliament and of the Council of November 24, 2010, amending Directives 98/26/EC, 2002/87/EC, 2003/6/EC, 2003/41/EC, 2003/71/EC, 2004/39/EC, 2004/109/EC, 2005/60/EC, 2006/48/EC, 2006/49/EC and 2009/65/EC with respect to the powers of the European Supervisory Authority (European Banking Authority), the European Supervisory Authority (European Insurance and Occupational Pensions Authority) and the European Supervisory Authority (European Securities and Markets Authority), OJEU L 331/ 120 of 15.12.2010; and Directive 2014/51/EU of the European Parliament and of the Council of April 16, 2014, amending Directives 2003/71/EC and 2009/138/EC and Regulations (EC) No 1060/2009, (EU) No 1094/2010 and (EU) No 1095/2010 in respect of the powers of the European Supervisory Authority (European Insurance and Occupational Pensions Authority) and the European Supervisory Authority (European Securities and Markets Authority), OJEU L 153/1 of 22.5.2014.

[14] Council Regulation (EU) No 1024/2013 of October 15, 2013, conferring specific tasks on the European Central Bank concerning policies relating to the prudential supervision of credit institutions, OJEU L 287/63 of 29.10.2013.

[15] The granting of regulatory and supervisory microprudential powers to the ECB creates potential problems of demarcation of the respective ECB and EBA's powers in this domain. In this connection, regulation 1022/2013 was adopted to amend the EBA regulation and adapt it to the new ECB's powers under regulation 1024/2013. The aim of regulation 1022/2013 is, in essence, to streamline the coordination between the EBA and the ECB concerning some of their respective microprudential tasks. See Regulation (EU) No 1022/2013 of the European Parliament and of the Council of October 22, 2013, amending Regulation (EU) No 1093/2010 establishing a European Supervisory Authority (European Banking Authority) concerning the

The SSM is defined by article 6 of regulation 1024/2013 as a system composed of "the ECB and national competent authorities." The latter are, in principle, national central banks. However, the ECB is a *primus inter pares* in the Mechanism. The same article says, "The ECB shall be responsible for the effective and consistent functioning of the SSM."

Once defined, the most important point that the regulation makes is the definition of the scope of the SSM. Because the EBA and national supervisory agencies are already in place, not all financial institutions fall under the scope of the SSM. The financial institutions that do are defined in article 6.4 of the regulation:

- Financial institutions whose total asset values exceed €30 billion
- Financial institutions whose ratio of total assets over GDP of the Member State exceeds 20 percent (unless the total value of their assets is less than €5 billion)
- Financial institutions whose national competent authorities have notified the ECB of their significance, and the ECB has confirmed such significance.

Regulation 1024/2013 makes two further remarks on this topic. First, the ECB can also decide that a given financial institution (which does not fall into the other three categories) falls within the scope of the SSM when such financial institution has subsidiaries in another Member State and its cross-border assets and liabilities represent a significant part of its total assets or liabilities. The second remark is that all financial institutions that have been bailed out by the European Financial Stability Facility (EFSF) or the European Stability Mechanism (ESM) will also fall under the supervisory scope of the SSM.

The main question is why the regulation establishes this limit (in essence, the limit of €30 billion) and not a superior or inferior one. The answer is provided by Howarth and Quaglia (2015: 13): "The outcome of the SSM negotiations was a compromise between the main Member States, in which Germany had most (but by no means all) of its preferences on the institutional features of the SSM accommodated because this country had strong bargaining power." In particular, these authors argue, "the German federal government succeeded in resisting direct ECB supervision of the smaller savings and cooperative banks" by setting the threshold at €30 billion (see also Howarth & Quaglia, 2016).

In turn, regulation 1024/2013 establishes a supervisory board that, together with the ECB governing council, constitute the main organs of the SSM. The supervisory board is composed, according to article 26 of the regulation, of a chair, a vice-chair, four representatives of the ECB, and one representative of the national competent authorities of each participating Member State. In essence, the supervisory board performs preparatory works concerning the

conferral of specific tasks on the European Central Bank pursuant to Council Regulation (EU) No 1024/2013, OJEU L 287/5 of 29.10.2013.

supervisory tasks of the ECB. The idea is that the supervisory board *proposes* and the governing council *disposes*; therefore, the board proposes draft decisions that the Governing Council of the ECB adopts as it sees fit (non-objection procedure).[16] Decisions by the supervisory board are made by a simple majority of its members, with the exception of article 4.3 of regulation 1024/2013, second paragraph, *in fine*, which refers to the regulations that the ECB can adopt to the extent "necessary to organize or specify the arrangements for the carrying out of the tasks conferred on it by" regulation 1024/2013. The supervisory board is assisted by a secretariat (article 26.9) and a steering committee (article 26.10). Finally, regulation 1024/2012 foresees the establishment of a mediation panel. This panel must mediate between the supervisory board and the governing council concerning draft decisions upon request of the national competent authorities. The mediation panel was created by regulation ECB/2014/26 of June 2, 2014.[17] Regulation 1024/2012 insists repeatedly that the ECB functions in the conduit of monetary policy and that its banking supervisory powers should be strictly separated (article 25; paragraphs 65, 73, 77, 85 of the regulation's preamble).

The powers that regulation 1024/2013 grants to the ECB are, without any doubt, the most important part of this piece of legislation. We are speaking here of an almost complete takeover by the ECB of the supervisory powers previously exercised by national central banks (and other authorities) on banks (see article 9). On the one hand, this step is necessary if the aim is to create a banking union. On the other hand, it clearly reflects a certain distrust from the EU institutions concerning the supervisory functions in the financial sector and, in particular, on banks, that the national central banks and other institutions were exercising until the 2008 crisis exploded.

Concerning the SSM, the new powers of the ECB can be divided, as was true with the ESAs, into regulatory and supervisory. These powers are only attributed to the ECB concerning the "participatory" Member States in the SSM (although the regulation grants the ECB powers concerning nonparticipatory Member States). The ECB's supervisory powers are, generally speaking, much ampler than the regulatory powers. I will start by addressing the latter.

The regulatory powers are limited to the employment of the supervisory powers that regulation 1024/2013 attributes to the ECB. In this connection, the

---

[16] See articles 13 g to 13 j of the ECB's rules of procedure. Decision of the European Central Bank of February 19, 2004, adopting the Rules of Procedure of the European Central Bank (ECB/2004/2) (2004/257/ EC) (OJ L 80, 18.3.2004, p. 33). Decision as amended by Decision ECB/2009/5 (OJ L 100, 18.4.2009, p. 10), Decision ECB/2014/1 (OJ L 95, 29.3.2014, p. 56), and Decision ECB/2015/8 (OJ L 114, 5.5.2015, p. 11). See the unofficial consolidated version at www.ecb.europa.eu/pub/pdf/other/ecbinstitutionalprovisions2015.en.pdf?8e51827ecf698cd6d7fabd3091ff164a.

[17] Regulation (EU) No 673/2014 of the European Central Bank of June 2, 2014, concerning the establishment of a Mediation Panel and its Rules of Procedure (ECB/2014/26), OJEU L 179/72 of 19.6.2014

Box 5.2: Aggregated statistics on the 2016 contribution cycle

	BAC numerator (including lump sums, with zero floor for negative BAC numerators)	BAC numerator (excluding lump sums, mortgage, Basic, and the first €300m for Art. 8.5)	BAC numerator (as per previous column)* SRM risk factor	BAC numerator (as per previous column)* BRRD risk factor	Final amount notified after 2015 deduction
AT	443.852.249.752	401.780.412.679	491.830.437.759	502.847.399.362	204.285.295
BE	475.635.230.620	471.015.181.125	583.606.671.127	650.136.708.460	277.592.989
CY	33.616.909.980	31.944.637.892	36.892.331.341	37.603.327.021	25.080.489
DE	4.082.152.349.255	3.852.176.617.248	4.623.150.462.200	4.655.560.253.080	1.760.899.426
EE	6.739.098.639	5.700.126.626	5.971.127.478	5.932.831.282	5.179.718
ES	1.519.594.378.725	1.506.566.635.002	1.854.904.940.273	1.826.464.530.269	725.548.134
FI	347.453.322.223	343.327.643.313	413.460.886.261	383.203.525.800	111.549.819
FR	5.000.366.500.064	4.747.706.437.584	5.991.199.245.578	5.527.102.104.952	1.572.935.612
GR	145.588.557.130	144.297.049.557	172.986.255.475	142.474.398.588	97.918.533
IE	275.216.864.572	274.016.085.207	313.874.808.588	350.530.902.202	97.306.469
IT	1.614.066.416.587	1.523.801.056.412	1.864.661.288.032	1.837.795.010.491	762.793.036
LT	5.364.041.579	4.734.833.529	5.203.209.448	4.788.400.634	7.408.276
LU	358.980.746.041	346.352.640.940	392.559.618.743	424.971.313.086	77.280.406
LV	14.753.608.986	11.923.120.392	14.107.411.859	13.773.976.953	7.287.939
MT	14.440.225.967	11.183.565.331	13.802.915.828	11.486.847.958	8.482.052
NL	1.250.955.006.519	1.247.046.861.087	1.528.744.474.774	1.400.242.656.929	503.655.460
PT	195.583.392.471	188.418.004.756	251.596.196.308	258.132.127.613	144.574.916
SI	12.097.717.244	8.930.073.244	10.507.448.621	9.005.024.465	12.534.550
SK	21.594.710.597	19.882.813.440	23.477.099.153	18.753.224.262	21.610.800
Tot	15.818.051.326.951	15.140.803.795.365	18.592.507.128.847	18.060.804.563.409	6.423.923.919

Source: Single Resolution Board (https://srb.europa.eu/en/content/2016-ex-ante-contributions).

ECB can adopt guidelines and recommendations and can even adopt regulations, although such regulations can only be made to the extent necessary to organize or specifically arrange for the implementation of the ECB's supervisory powers.

The ECB's supervisory powers are, as noted previously, the most important ones under regulation 1024/2013. They are divided into investigatory powers and specific supervisory powers (see Box 5.2). The ECB's investigatory powers are threefold: (1) powers to request information, (2) powers to undertake general investigations, and (3) powers to make on-site inspections.

Concerning the first, request of information powers, the ECB can request from financial institutions all of the relevant information concerning their activities that might be related to the powers that the regulation bestows on the

ECB. Financial institutions are obliged to supply this information to the ECB. Concerning the second, powers to undertake general investigations, the ECB can conduct all of the investigations that it considers necessary to perform its duties with respect to the financial institutions that fall under its supervisory purview. Finally, concerning on-site inspections, the ECB can physically enter the premises of any financial institution under its supervision to make on-site inspections, even without previous announcement. Occasionally, these on-site inspections might require a previous judicial authorization under national law. In these cases, the ECB must apply for such authorization. However, article 13.2 of the regulation says that the national judge can only limit the control of the ECB's request with respect to its authenticity, arbitrariness, and excessiveness. The control of the legality of the ECB's request is left by the same article to the ECJ.

In turn, the "specific" ECB supervisory powers are fivefold: (1) authorization (and withdrawal of authorization) powers, (2) powers of assessment, (3) enforcement powers, (4) sanction powers, and (5) evaluation powers.

First, concerning authorization powers, regulation 1024/2013 establishes the procedure through which financial institutions that fall under the supervisory radar of the ECB can be authorized by this institution. Recall that financial institutions must be authorized to operate. In turn, the authorization withdrawal determines the suspension of their activities; finally, if they are resolved, they cease to operate.

The authorization procedure works as follows. First, the financial institution must request the authorization from the national authority of the Member State in which the financial institution is to be established. Second, the national authority makes a proposal to grant the authorization, which is sent to the ECB for final approval. Third, if the national authority rejects the application for an authorization, the procedure ends there. In other words, the ECB only intervenes in this procedure if the national authority certifies that the authorization should be granted.

Two cases must be differentiated in the domain of withdrawal: when the initiative for withdrawal comes from the ECB and when the initiative comes from a national authority. In the first case, the procedure is as follows: the ECB, before making the final decision, consults with the competent national authority. After consultations have occurred, the ECB makes a decision on withdrawal. In particular, the ECB must consider whether the national authority can take other remedial actions, resolution therein included, before making its final decision. Article 14.6 of regulation 1024/2013 contemplates in this context a particular situation, which is when the national authority believes that the withdrawal might undermine actions that it might be adopting to resolve the financial institution in question. We are speaking here of cases in which the national authorities retain the powers of resolution of financial institutions, and only "as long as they keep them." In these cases, the national authority can object to the ECB's intention to withdraw, and the ECB must abstain from proceeding to the withdrawal during a sunset period mutually agreed by both institutions, after which, if the national authority has taken no further measures, the ECB shall withdraw the authorization.

When the national authority initiates the procedure, it must make a proposal for withdrawal to the ECB, which then makes the final decision.

Second, the ECB's assessment powers are related to the acquisitions of qualified holdings by financial institutions. In essence, article 15 establishes a procedure that has three steps: (1) the financial institution notifies the national authority of its decision to purchase, (2) the national authority makes a proposal to the ECB to oppose or not oppose the acquisition, and (3) the ECB makes the final decision.

Third, the ECB's enforcement powers are designed very amply and proceed from the requirement to increment own funds of financial institutions to the decision to remove members from the management bodies of the financial institution. More specifically, the ECB might make decisions to require institutions to take the following actions:

- To hold own funds in excess
- To reinforce the financial institution's own arrangements, processes, mechanisms, and strategies
- To present a plan to restore compliance with supervisory requirements
- To apply a specific provisioning policy or treatment of assets in terms of own funds requirements
- To restrict or limit the business, operations, or network of financial institutions or to request the divestment of activities that pose excessive risks to the soundness of an institution
- To reduce the risk inherent in the activities, products, and systems of financial institutions
- To limit variable remuneration as a percentage of net revenues when it is inconsistent with the maintenance of a sound capital base
- To use net profits to strengthen own funds
- To restrict or prohibit distributions by the institution to shareholders, members, or holders of Additional Tier 1 instruments in which the prohibition does not constitute an event of default of the institution
- To impose additional or more frequent reporting requirements, including reporting on capital and liquidity positions
- To impose specific liquidity requirements, including restrictions on maturity mismatches between assets and liabilities
- To require additional disclosures
- To remove at any time members from the management body of credit institutions who do not fulfil the requirements set out in the acts referred to in the regulation.

Fourth, the ECB can adopt sanctions (penalties, to use the regulation's jargon) according to article 18 of the regulation. There are two modalities at this point:

sanctions that can be imposed directly by the ECB, and sanctions that can be imposed by national authorities upon the request of the ECB. The demarcation line between the two is provided by the definition of the financial institutions that fall under the supervisory radar of the ECB according to the regulation. In other words, the powers of the ECB in the second case are only request powers; the national authority can deny the ECB's application. Because it could not be otherwise, the sanctions that are foreseen by regulation 1024/2013 are established without prejudice to the general system of sanctions that the ECB can impose on financial institutions for violating other norms that emanate from this institution in other sectors.

Article 24 of the regulation establishes an "administrative board of review" to review the decisions made by the ECB under regulation 1024/2013. This review organ is composed of five individuals (plus two alternates) who are appointed by the ECB from the Member States. They must show a "high repute" in the sector. The administrative board of review makes its decisions by a majority of three members. Only decisions adopted by the supervisory board (not by the Governing Council) can be reviewed by this organ, following the procedure established in article 24.7 of regulation 1024/2013. As always, decisions that are made by this organ are reviewable by the ECJ (article 24.11).

Finally, it is important to say a final word on what I have labeled the "evaluation powers" of the ECB. I am referring here, in particular, to the power under which the ECB must undertake stress tests upon financial institutions. Interestingly, regulation 1024/2013 refers to these powers (both in its preamble and in article 4.1 f), but does not develop this important point. The ECB can participate in the stress-testing exercise in cooperation with other agencies, and in particular with the EBA, together with national authorities (see in particular articles 22 and 23 of the EBA regulation).[18] The ECB published a stress test manual in August 2014.[19]

5.5 The Single Resolution Mechanism (SRM)

Regulation 806/2014[20] establishes the Single Resolution Mechanism. As said previously, together with regulation 1024/2013 (Alexander, 2015), this legislation concerning the EU's Banking Union is crucial. Other norms that are

---

[18] The results of the stress tests that have been performed thus far can be consulted on the EBA webpage. See this link: www.eba.europa.eu/risk-analysis-and-data/eu-wide-stress-testing/2016.

[19] See ECB, Comprehensive Assessment Stress Test Manual, at www.ecb.europa.eu/pub/pdf/other/castmanual201408en.pdf.

[20] Regulation (EU) No 806/2014 of the European Parliament and of the Council of July 15, 2014, establishing uniform rules and a uniform procedure for the resolution of credit institutions and certain investment firms in the framework of a Single Resolution Mechanism and a Single Resolution Fund and amending Regulation (EU) No 1093/2010, OJEU L 225/1 of 30.7.2014.

important in the context of the SRM include directive 2014/59[21] and the Intergovernmental Agreement on the Transfer and Mutualisation of Contributions to the SRM of May 2014.[22]

In essence, regulation 806/2014 establishes a Single Resolution Mechanism and a Single Resolution Fund for all participating Member States in the Single Supervisory Mechanism. As recital no. 13 of the regulation says, to restore trust and credibility in the banking sector, both aspects, but above all the second one, were an absolute necessity. I will review the main aspects of this important regulation in the following; however, the main idea to be remembered is what "resolution" means in this context. "Resolution" is defined by article 2.1 of directive 2014/59 as the application of a resolution tool or tools to achieve one or more of the resolution objectives set by the regulation. These objectives include (1) to ensure the continuity of critical functions of the resolved institution; (2) to avoid a significant adverse effect on the financial system, in particular by preventing contagion, including to market infrastructures, and by maintaining market discipline; (3) to protect public funds by minimizing reliance on extraordinary public financial support; (4) to protect depositors; and (5) to protect client funds and client assets. Two ideas stem from this definition: first, resolution is the termination of a bank's activity; and second, the idea behind the whole resolution exercise is to avoid bailouts and use, instead, bail-ins for the purposes of resolution.

In the following, I will describe and analyze the main resolution organs that are established by regulation 806/2014, their decision-making procedures, and how the resolution procedure works. Then, I will discuss the most important mechanism under this regulation, which is the Single Resolution Fund.

To start with, regulation 806/2014 establishes a Single Resolution Mechanism. According to article 1 of the regulation, this Mechanism comprises the Single Resolution Board, the Council, the Commission, and the national resolution authorities.

The key institution of this system is the Single Resolution Board. The Board is defined by article 42 of the regulation as a Union agency "with a specific structure." Recital 31 of the regulation says, somewhat mysteriously, that the board "departs from the model of all other agencies of the Union." It is clear that the regulation wants to give to the board a specific and higher status when compared with other EU agencies and, notably, with the agencies that compose the European Financial Supervision System. In other words, to make the

---

[21] Directive 2014/59/EU of the European Parliament and of the Council of May 15, 2014, establishing a framework for the recovery and resolution of credit institutions and investment firms and amending Council Directive 82/891/EEC, and Directives 2001/24/EC, 2002/47/EC, 2004/25/EC, 2005/56/EC, 2007/36/EC, 2011/35/EU, 2012/30/EU and 2013/36/EU, and Regulations (EU) No 1093/2010 and (EU) No 648/2012, of the European Parliament and of the Council, OJEU L 173/190 of 12.6.2014.

[22] Agreement on the transfer and mutualisation of contributions to the Single Resolution Fund, Council of the European Union, Brussels, May 14, 2014, EF 121 ECOFIN 342.

decision to resolve a financial institution is a serious matter, regulation 806/2014 appears to say. In fact, it is for the Board to decide whether to resolve a financial institution. It also approves the resolution scheme.

The board is composed of the following organs:

- A Chair
- Four further full-time members appointed in accordance with article 56
- A member appointed by each participating Member State, representing their national resolution authorities
- A representative of the Commission and the ECB, respectively, with voice but no voting rights.

Furthermore, the Board's administrative and management structure comprises the following:

- A plenary session
- An executive session of the Board
- A Secretariat.

Concerning the plenary session, all members of the board participate in the plenary session. According to article 52 of the regulation, the plenary session makes, in principle, its decisions by majority voting, but there are important exceptions to this rule. The first exception is that certain decisions shall be made by the majority of the board members who represent at least 30 percent of contributions. Decisions concerning the use of the Single Resolution Fund (articles 50.1(c) and (d)) and decisions concerning the mutualization of the Single Resolution Fund are made under this voting procedure. The second exception is that certain decisions shall be made by a majority of two-thirds of the board members who represent at least 50 percent of the contributions (until the Fund is fully mutualized) and of two-thirds who represent 30 percent of the contributions from then on. These decisions are key decisions such as, for example, the raising of ex post contributions, alternative financing means, and voluntary borrowing between financing arrangements. In other words, the most important Member States of the Union are privileged under these exceptions.

The executive session of the Board is composed of the Chair and the four full-time members referred to previously. It makes decisions based on unanimity. However, if a consensus cannot be reached, the Board makes decisions by a simple majority. The executive session makes the most important decisions within the board, notably the decision to resolve a financial institution and the decision on the resolution scheme, if the amount of the resolution Fund involved in the resolution plan does not reach the threshold of €5 billion. If the amount exceeds this threshold, it is then for the plenary session to make the resolution decision (article 50.1(d)).

The procedure for the resolution of a financial entity is established in article 18 of the regulation. The first point to be stressed concerning this procedure is that the resolution of a financial institution is conceived of by the regulation as a last resort measure that is taken to protect the public interest. Therefore, before resolution is proposed, the EU authorities involved in the resolution procedure must do their best to recover the institution. Only when this recovery is not possible does resolution come to center stage.

The resolution procedure, which has been almost unanimously defined by experts as "convoluted" (Howarth & Quaglia, 2016: 137) (although clearly this criticism is not limited to this area of the Banking Union), works as follows. It starts with an ECB assessment of the troubled financial entity. In this assessment, the ECB indicates that the financial institution is failing or is close to failure. This indication demonstrates the connection between the SRM regulation and the SSM regulation. The ECB plays a primary role here.

Two further conditions must be met for resolution to proceed. First, there are no alternative private sector measures, including early intervention measures, that would prevent the failure of the institution. This assessment is made by the Board in its executive session. Second, the resolution measure must be adopted for the public interest.

If both of these conditions are met, the Board adopts a resolution scheme. The crucial aspect of the resolution scheme is the setting of what regulation 806/2014 refers to as "resolution tools." These tools are established in article 22.2 of the regulation and are the following: (1) the sale of business tool, (2) the bridge institution tool, (3) the asset separation tool, and (4) (the most important one) the bail-in tool. Resolution tools can be applied "either individually or in any combination, except for the asset separation tool which may be applied only together with another resolution tool," says article 22.4.

Right after the adoption of the resolution scheme, the Board transmits it to the Commission. The Commission shall then either endorse the plan or object to it with regard to its discretionary aspects. It then sends it to the Council, with the proposal of either objecting to the resolution scheme on the ground that it does not serve the public interest, or approving (or objecting to) a material modification of the amount of the Fund provided in the resolution scheme. In turn, the Council adopts the Commission proposal by a simple majority. If the Council approves the Commission proposal (or the Commission has objected to the plan), then the Board must modify the plan accordingly.

However, there is a second possibility, which is that neither the Council nor the Commission object to the resolution scheme within twenty-four hours after the transmission by the Board of its plan. In this case, the resolution plan is deemed adopted.

Once the resolution plan has been adopted, the Board has the duty to ensure that the plan is implemented by the relevant national authority or authorities.

Article 85 of regulation 806/2014 establishes an Appeal Panel. The Panel is composed (as occurred with the Administrative Board of Review in the SSM) of five members of "high repute" in the sector (plus two alternates) who shall be appointed by the Board (plenary session: article 50.1(p)). The Appeal Panel can review only certain decisions of the Board.[23] Currently, the regulation does not foresee that the Appeal Panel reviews the Board's decision to resolve a financial institution. Therefore, article 86 applies here: "Proceedings may be brought before the ECJ contesting a decision taken by the Appeal Panel *or, when there is no right of appeal to the Appeal Panel, by the Board*" [my emphasis].

The most important mechanism that the regulation establishes is the Single Resolution Fund. This Fund is solemnly established by article 67 of the regulation: "The Single Resolution Fund is hereby established." This declaration notwithstanding, one should view the establishment of the Fund more as a process than as an immediate outcome of article 67. In effect, article 69 of regulation 806/2014 states that by the end of an initial period of eight years to be counted from January 1, 2016 onwards, the Fund must reach a target level of at least 1 percent of the "amount of covered deposits of all credit institutions authorized in all participating Member States," which totals approximately €55 billion.[24]

The process of progressively constituting the Fund works as follows. The participating Member States must establish "national compartments" to the Fund. The competent national authorities shall feed these national compartments on an annual basis. Contributions are financed from national banks and raised at the national level. This question is key and allows concluding that the Single Resolution Mechanism is a bail-in mechanism. In fact, the whole idea of the SRM is to avoid bailouts, as has been said previously.

Once the national compartments are progressively constituted, they are finally pooled, or mutualized, in a single fund after the period referred to previously has been reached. The Agreement on the transfer and mutualization of contributions to the Single Resolution Fund indicates how this process of mutualization comes about. It also establishes how the Fund and the national compartments should operate during the transition phase.

Concerning the first aspect, article 4.2 of the Intergovernmental Agreement on the Transfer and Mutualisation of Contributions to the SRM says that "the size of the compartments of each Contracting Party shall be equal to the

---

[23] These decisions include the following: (1) decisions on the assessment of the measures proposed by a financial institution to address or remove substantive impediments to the effective application of resolution tools and the exercise of resolution powers by the Board (article 10.10); (2) decisions to apply simplified obligations upon financial institutions; (3) decisions on minimum requirements for own funds and eligible liabilities that financial institutions are required to meet at all times (article 12.1); (4) decisions on fines (articles 38 to 41); (5) decisions on contributions of financial institutions to the administrative expenditures of the board; (6) decisions on extraordinary ex post contributions to cover additional amounts not covered by the Resolution Fund (article 71); and (7) decisions on access to documents of financial institutions (article 90.3).

[24] Statement of the European Commission "European Parliament and Council back Commission's proposal for a Single Resolution Mechanism: a major step towards completing the banking union" of March 20, 2014.

totality of contributions payable by the institutions authorized in each of their territories pursuant to articles 68 and 69 of the SRM Regulation and to the delegated and implementing acts referred to therein." The Board shall make up a list (only for information purposes) detailing the size of the compartments of each contracting party. That list shall be updated every year of the transitional period. For example, for 2016, the total amount of ex ante contributions collected by the SRF at the end of June was of €6.4 billion. Box 5.2 reflects each participating Member State's respective contribution. Once the mutualization process is completed, the national compartments will disappear and will fuse into one single fund (article 1.1(b)) of the Agreement).

Concerning the second point, remember that until the Fund is fully mutualized, the costs of a given resolution are borne by the national resolution fund. National compartments will be used to this end, if recourse to the Fund is so decided. In other words, although the decision to resolve a financial institution has already been delegated to the Single Resolution Board, the costs of resolutions remain imputed to the national authorities. To be sure, this aspect is the most worrisome of the whole system, at least until full mutualization has been reached (Goodhart & Schoenmaker, 2014).

When the Board decides that the Fund will intervene during the transition period, the Agreement establishes how this intervention will work. The Agreement prioritizes national solutions over European ones. This prioritization results in a four-step approach in which, first, the national compartment of the Member State in which the resolved financial institution is placed acts first. Second, the rest of the national compartments act if the funds of the former are insufficient. Third, if the previous means are not sufficient, then the Fund shall activate ex post contributions to the Fund according to article 71 of regulation 806/2014. Finally, if the previous measures do not suffice, then the Board can exercise its power to contract for Fund borrowings or other forms of support in accordance with articles 72 and 73 of regulation 806/2014.

5.6 How the System Works in Practice: The Case of the Italian Bank Monte dei Paschi di Siena

The Italian bank Monte dei Paschi di Siena (hereinafter MdP) has the privilege of being the oldest bank in the world (the first bank in the world ever to exist as such, therefore) and the third largest bank in Italy by assets. The MdP case thus goes well beyond a mere technical problem. It also involves politics, power, and the captivating force that certain domestic symbols have for national identity. MdP is not just a bank; it is a fetish for Italians. The MdP case is also a test of the new banking union rules that have been examined in this chapter. As shown in the following, whether the test will be passed is unclear.

The story of how the MdP got into trouble is well known, so I will only refer to its most fundamental aspects. Although financial problems most likely started for the bank earlier, the line that marked a watershed was the acquisition by MdP of Banca Antonveneta in November 2007, which had previously been bought by the Santander Bank from ABN AMRO. MdP paid €9 billion for the operation. The problem was that the deal amounted more or less "to MPS' total equity at the time the deal was announced." As de Groen reports, the acquisition itself had a negative effect on the capital positions of the bank (de Groen, 2016). Although the acquisition was made before the 2008 crisis officially began, there were already winds in 2007 that indicated an overheated global economy situation. When the crisis broke, it caught MdP in a very weak position. The bank had to make recourse to the Italian government, which helped with the purchasing of the so-called "Tremonti Bonds" that the bank had previously issued (€1.9 billion). This action can be considered a (first) bailout, occurring before the SSM and SRM rules were in place. However, the whole issue took a definitive twist when it was made public in November 2012 that the bank had incurred large losses with the Santorini and Alessandria operations and that, to hide the losses, the bank had undertaken creative derivative construction. The documentation concerning these operations was never communicated to the bank's own auditors or to the Italian central bank. It was only made public when new managers took over control of the bank.

When the EBA operated the 2011 stress tests on EU banks in 2011, MdP was only approved due to "tricks" (de Groen, 2016: 3). However, it failed the capital exercises; the European supervisors noted a capital shortfall of €3.3 billion due to a sovereign portfolio whose market value was below the book value. MPS also failed the combination of the EBA EU-wide stress test and ECB's asset quality review in 2014. This sequence ended (for the time being) with the stress tests that were published in July 2016, in which MdP was found to be the "weakest" financial institution of a list of 51 banks. According to the Bank of Italy (2016), the MdP would need a capital injection of €5 billion; however, the ECB did not agree with its national counterpart and believed that because the MdP financial situation was rapidly deteriorating, it would need a superior injection of €8.8 billion. At the end of 2016, the MdP tried to raise approximately €5 billion from the markets, but the operation failed. Therefore, the bank requested precautionary recapitalization under directive 2014/59 from the Italian government.

This request is currently at the epicenter of the storm. On the one hand, the German government does not want to send the signal that the new SSM and SRM rules, which, I cannot emphasize sufficiently strongly, place the principle of "bail-in goes first" at center stage, are watered down. On the other hand, the Commission and the ECB are also quarreling about the details of the recapitalization plan. The whole situation is wonderfully summarized by Barker, Jones, and Sanderson (2017), writing for the *Financial Times*:

> The Single Supervisory Mechanism, the ECB's supervisory wing, believes it is waiting for Brussels to agree a plan to restructure MPS and approve state aid.

Yet Brussels, in turn, thinks it is waiting for the supervisors to agree a capital plan with MPS before it can finalise restructuring terms. One person involved in the process called the situation "surreal."

Only the future will tell how the MdP issue is resolved. This resolution would be a first indication that could serve as a basis of a more detailed analysis of the credibility of the entire new system from the perspective of the law as credibility model. Until then, we can only wait. The truth of the matter is, however, that as the story of the MdP unfolds, ever more shadows are cast upon the entire new European system of supervision and resolution.

BIBLIOGRAPHY

Alexander, K. 2015, "European Banking Union: a legal and institutional analysis of the Single Supervisory Mechanism and the Single Resolution Mechanism," *European Law Review*, vol. 2, pp. 154–187.

Bank of Italy. 2016, "The 'precautionary recapitalization' of Banca Monte dei Paschi di Siena," www.bancaditalia.it/media/approfondimenti/2016/ricapitalizzazione-mps/precautionary-recapitalization-MPS.pdf?language_id=1.

Barker, A., Jones, C., & Sanderson, R. 2017, "Brussels and ECB split on Monte dei Paschi's capital proposals," *Financial Times*, February 23.

Brown, M., Trautmann, S., & Vlahu, R. 2014, "Understanding Bank-Run Contagion," ECB Working Paper Series no. 1711, August.

Busuioc, M. 2013, "Rule-making by the European financial supervisory authorities: walking a tight rope," *European Law Journal*, vol. 19, no. 1, pp. 111–125.

De Grauwe, P. 2016, *Economics of Monetary Union*, 11th edn., Oxford University Press, Oxford.

De Groen, W. P. 2016, "A Closer Look at Banca Monte dei Paschi: Living on the Edge," CEPS (Centre for European Policy Studies) Policy Brief no. 345.

Estella, A. 2002, *The EU Principle of Subsidiarity and Its Critique*, Oxford University Press, Oxford.

Fahey, E. 2011, "Does the Emperor have financial crisis clothes? Reflections on the legal basis of the European Banking Authority," *The Modern Law Review*, vol. 74, no. 4, pp. 581–595.

Goodhart, C. & Schoenmaker, D. 2014, "The ECB as lender of last resort?," VoxEU.org, October 23. www.voxeu.org.

Howarth, D. & Quaglia, L. 2016b, "Internationalised banking, alternative banks and the Single Supervisory Mechanism," *West European Politics*, vol. 39, no. 3, pp. 438–461.

2016a, *The Political Economy of European Banking Union*, Oxford University Press, Oxford.

2015, "The Political Economy of the Single Supervisory Mechanism: Squaring the 'Inconsistent Quartet'," Paper presented to the EUSA (European Union Studies Association)Biennial Conference, Boston, Mass., March 5–7.

Lannoo, K. 2011, "The EU's Response to the Financial Crisis: a Mid-Term Review," CEPS (Centre for European Policy Studies) Policy Brief no. 241.

Masciandaro, D., Nieto, M., & Quintyn, M. 2011, "Exploring governance of the new European Banking Authority – a case for harmonization?," *Journal of Financial Stability*, vol. 7, pp. 204–214.

Moloney, N. 2011b, "The European Securities and Markets Authority and institutional design for the EU financial market – a tale of two competences: Part (2) Rules in action," *European Business Organization Law Review*, vol. 12, no. 2, pp. 177–225.

2011a, "The European Securities and Markets Authority and institutional design for the EU financial market – a tale of two competences: Part (1) Rule-making," *European Business Organization Law Review*, vol. 12, no. 1, pp. 41–86.

Nicolaides, P. & Preziosi, N. 2014, "Discretion and Accountability: The ESMA Judgment and the Meroni Doctrine," Bruges European Economic Research Papers 30/2014.

Pelkmans, J. & Simoncini, M. 2014, "Mellowing Meroni: How ESMA Can Help Build the Single Market," CEPS (Centre for European Policy Studies) Commentary, vol. 18, February.

Shoenmaker, D. (ed.) 2014, *Macroprudentialism*, VoxEU, e-book. VoxEU.org.

6

The Stability and Growth Pact before the Crisis

Introduction

If there is an area in which the "law as credibility" model is particularly useful, that area is the Stability and Growth Pact. This chapter and the next address the description and analysis of this nuclear piece of the EU economic governance system.

The Stability and Growth Pact (SGP hereinafter) was established as a way to reinforce the credibility of the Eurozone. However, we will show that the SGP is not only about rigidity, it is also about flexibility (Schelkle, 2007). In fact, the SGP attempts to establish an equilibrium point between these two competing – dialectical – goals. From this perspective, what will be shown is how the SGP has evolved, since its inception, within the margins of rigidity and flexibility – occasionally approaching rigidity, other times approaching flexibility. In addition, we will show that there have been instances of flexibility within general turns to rigidity, and instances of rigidity within general moves towards flexibility. In other words, the SGP's life is not a picture of either blacks or whites but a more complex one.

Briefly, the SGP's history can be divided into four stages or periods. The first period went from Maastricht to 2005. In this period, the SGP's rigidity was reinforced. The second period went from 2005 to 2011. In this period, the SGP was made more flexible. The third stage of the evolution of the SGP was a period that occurred right in the middle of the crisis that started in 2008. This period went from 2011 to 2014 and implied a new turn to rigidity. Finally, currently, we can discern on the horizon the start of a new period, which would imply a new bounce towards flexibility, although this new movement in the opposite direction has taken the form of a simple Commission communication – at least for the time being. Because the changes brought about since 2008 are so salient, I will analyze them at length. The analysis of the evolution of the SGP until the 2008 crisis will be done in this chapter, and the evaluation of the SGP since the 2008 crisis will be left for the next chapter. The entire discussion is preceded by a succinct analysis of the economic rationale underlying the SGP.

6.1 Economic Rationale of the SGP

As seen in Chapters 3 and 4 above, Eurozone Member States have relinquished their monetary sovereignty in favor of the European Union; in particular, in favor of the ECB. In other words, Member States are no longer capable of manipulating their currency in the event of an economic shock. One means by which States address an economic crisis, above all if the economic crisis has a strong financial or monetary component, is through the manipulation of their currency's exchange rate.[1] They can devalue their currency to become more competitive and thereby try to reverse a negative economic trend, or at least to stop it. This approach was used by the Member States of the European Union in the 1990s crisis; even when they were inside the European Monetary System, the crisis was so strong that some Member States had to devalue their currency, which, in turn, eventually spelled the end of the EMS. Devaluing a State's own currency is a standard practice by which governments address economic crises having a strong international component.

However, as stated previously, Eurozone Member States can no longer use this instrument. Therefore, if an economic crisis arises, the only action that they can take is to manipulate their fiscal policy, because the Eurozone fiscal policy (in general, the EU Member States' fiscal policy) has not been delegated to the EU. Therefore, in the absence of a centralized and strong EU budget, the only alternative that Member States have is to use their own budgets to accommodate the shock. In particular, they have three alternative ways to fight against the shock: they spend more, they alleviate the fiscal burden of citizens and firms, or they do both. Normally, they do both: they spend more and grant tax credits to citizens and firms, using the budget to steer the economy upwards. Thus, people and firms have more money to spend, which in turn helps to boost the economy. However, to simplify what is a complex discussion (because tax cuts can affect the budget and, therefore, the capacity of the government to spend), let us assume that governments only use the first strategy: they raise public spending to combat an economic depression.

The problem with this concrete (and peculiar) application of the subsidiarity principle (delegation of the monetary policy to the ECB, on the one hand, but Member States' retention of their fiscal competences, on the other hand) is that raising public spending in one Member State to overcome an economic downturn might have a negative spillover effect on other Member States,

---

[1] In an open market, which money markets are, a country's currency can be devalued through monetary authorities' increasing the monetary mass. This action in turn lowers interest rates (because the money amount offered is greater), which then has the effect of depreciating a country's currency. Other things being equal, the exchange rate between the country's currency and other countries' currencies is incremented. The second means of producing a similar effect is by monetary authorities' lowering interest rates without affecting the monetary mass. A combination of both techniques (increasing the monetary mass and lowering interest rates) is a third possibility. See Krugman, Obstfeld & Melitz (2015).

above all when they share a currency. The mechanism is the following. Imagine that Member State A is hit by a crisis. To combat the crisis, the State raises public spending. By doing so, it risks attaining an unsustainable fiscal stance and ultimately defaulting on its debt. Financial markets observe this risk; therefore, the risk premium of this country increases. In other words, selling public debt on the markets will have a higher price. In turn, this result might have a negative spillover effect on other Member States either because they are the holders of Member State A's debt or because they must pay for a bailout (or both). Markets start distrusting not only country A – the country in which the crisis started – but also country B, which also belongs to the monetary union, to the Eurozone in our case. If this sequence occurs, then country B will also be affected by the crisis, although its macroeconomic fundamentals might be superior to those of country A.

As hinted previously, contagions are further reinforced in monetary unions because the members of a monetary union are locked into the same monetary policy stance. Therefore, the monetary authority, in our case the ECB, will not have the flexibility to adopt measures for the particular Member State that is experiencing difficulties. It must act for all of the Member States of the Eurozone, which might be in different situations if the crisis is asymmetric. Paradoxically, the monetary authority will be able to react when the crisis affects all or most of the members of the monetary union but not (or less) when the crisis affects one of them; otherwise, its credibility as an institution will be at stake. The ECB's management of the Eurozone is a case in point, as was seen above in Chapter 4. Not all Eurozone members were happy with how the ECB reacted to the crisis. This condition is structural in economic crises of countries belonging to monetary unions. There is no way to escape it.

The important point is to stress that the SGP assumes that contagions occur. This point is the justification for having a Stability and Growth Pact. Briefly, the SGP ensures, or attempts to ensure, the credibility of the entire Eurozone. Because contagions do occur, it is in the best interest not only of particular Member States but also of the Eurozone as a whole to manage the public finances of all members of the group well.

More specifically, the whole point of having common rules for the competent management of euro area fiscal policies is therefore that, in boom times, Member States are able to create a fiscal buffer that is sufficiently large to let the economic stabilizers work when a crisis hits that particular country. If country A is in a sound fiscal position – for example, it has a surplus of 2 percent and a debt of 50 percent of its GDP – then it could weather the downturn much better than if it had an already fiscally compromised situation of, for example, a deficit of 3 percent and a public debt of 70 percent GDP. In turn, if country B were in a sound fiscal position, it would be better placed to react to a possible contagion from country A.

Let us analyze this negative spillover effect in more detail. As de Grauwe (2012: 218–219) notes, those who believe in contagions assume that markets

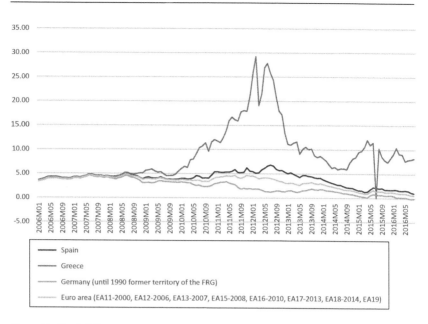

Figure 6.1: Bond yields
Source: Eurostat (September 2016)

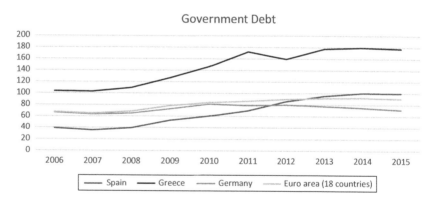

Figure 6.2: Government debt
Source: Eurostat (September 2016)

are efficient and can discriminate between States that are in financial difficulty and those that are not. However, de Grauwe argues that one should most likely be suspicious about the financial markets' capacity to discriminate. To validate his argument, he uses the following evidence: When the euro was established, the spreads of senior bonds of the Eurozone members became virtually the same. There was no difference between buying a German ten-year bond and a Spanish one, as Figure 6.1 shows (cf. Figures 6.2 and 6.3). However, with time

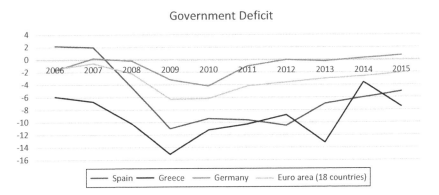

Figure 6.3: Government deficit
Source: Eurostat (September 2016)

and the 2008 crisis, spreads between Eurozone Member States' bonds increased, as though markets had realized that, in fact, there were large differences among the fiscal policies of the different Eurozone members. De Grauwe does not deny contagions; he simply disputes how rational contagions are. However, this point is important because *if contagions were irrational, then it would be useless to implement tight fiscal rules throughout the Eurozone.*

Nevertheless, one could also argue that markets have at least a certain learning capacity. Therefore, when the euro started, they just did not know whether the fiscal policies of Eurozone Member States were converging. We could argue that they expected that the policies would converge, which is why the markets priced different Member States' public debts equally. With time and with the crisis, the markets realized that the debts had not converged. Therefore, the markets priced the government risk of Eurozone Member States differentially, placing a higher price on Member States that presented more risk (basically, those on the periphery) and a lesser price on those at the center of the system. This matter is, however, complex and will not be resolved here. Economists continue to discuss this important issue. Therefore, for simplicity, let us assume that contagions do occur and that the SGP attempts to fight against them to inject credibility into the entire Eurozone.

6.2 From Maastricht to 2005

6.2.1 Maastricht Rules

The history of the SGP has the Maastricht Treaty (1992) as its starting point. After long debates among the Member States, it was decided that the Treaty would establish two rules on fiscal discipline: one concerning a government deficit ceiling and the other concerning a public debt limit. Thus, article 104c (1) of the Maastricht Treaty established the following:

Member States shall avoid excessive government deficits.

In turn, paragraph 2 of article 104c granted competences to the Commission to monitor Member States' fiscal policies, or "budgetary discipline," to use its own wording. In particular, the Commission was to monitor whether the public deficit *and debt* levels of Member States exceeded a reference value. Therefore, besides the deficit criterion, Maastricht established a second criterion: the public debt criterion. The reference values would be established, as the same article announced, by the Protocol on Excessive Deficit Procedure attached to the Treaty on European Union.

Two points are worth mentioning here with respect to the Treaty of Maastricht. The first is that the Treaty clearly establishes a certain preference for the control of government deficits as the main fiscal governance criterion. Granted, the public debt criterion is also important, but the fact that indent 1 of article 104c specifically speaks of government deficit (without mentioning public debt) nicely illustrates this preeminence. As seen later, this point has in fact been true: the main criterion for fiscal governance has been that of the deficit rather than the public debt criterion, at least until the 2008 crisis exploded. We will examine later whether this situation is neutral economically speaking or is,[2] rather, the crystallization of a very particular approach to viewing fiscal governance.

The above-mentioned Protocol sets both limits (both reference values) as follows:

- 3 percent government deficit
- 60 percent government debt.

It is important to recall that the two limits were completely discretionary; there is no particular economic reason why the ceilings should be these ones and not others, either higher or lower. De Grauwe (2016: 148–149) explains that the reason why they were chosen is that at the time the Delors report (which is the basis of the SGP) was agreed, the average public debt and deficit in Member States were 3 percent and 60 percent respectively. Furthermore, the EU economy was growing, at the time, at an average rate of 5 percent GDP. From there, we arrive at the following (simple and elegant) formula:

$$d = gb$$

where

$$d = public\ deficit$$
$$g = nominal\ growth$$
$$b = public\ debt.$$

---

[2] See Section 7.3.1 of Chapter 7.

Therefore, considering that the nominal growth was 5 percent and the public debt was 60 percent, the deficit should be 3 percent. As the same author notes, "there is no scientific justification for this." In fact, many Member States did not respect these limits in the run-up to the euro (see for data Briotti, 2004: 9). Therefore, Member States, above all those on the periphery, had to make almost quixotic efforts to respect these limits to enter the Eurozone.[3] Lacking any clear economic rationale, these limits work as a sort of self-fulfilling prophecy; if a Member State does not respect them, then it will be punished by the markets (de Grauwe, 2016: 226). At the same time, the markets use these ceilings as signals to orient their own economic behavior; in other words, other limits would have prompted different economic behavior.[4]

The second important aspect introduced by Maastricht was a system of sanctions that would be imposed upon those Member States that failed to respect the above limits. In essence, article 104c of the Maastricht Treaty established a procedure that contemplated the imposition of either non-interest-bearing deposits or fines. It is important to stress that this possibility was foreseen only for Eurozone Member States. In effect, article 109k (3) of the Maastricht Treaty exempted Member States "with a derogation" (therefore,

[3] Article 3 of the "Protocol on the Convergence criteria referred to in article 109 j of the Treaty establishing the European Community" includes both the 3 percent and 60 percent limits. Therefore, to accede to the euro, Member States had to respect both criteria, among others. There is a common misunderstanding with respect to the application of this Protocol and the application of the "Protocol on the excessive deficit procedure": Member States must not only respect both limits to accede to the euro (Protocol on convergence) but do so once they are in the Eurozone (Protocol on excessive deficit procedure). Recall that Italy and Greece constitute a good case of periphery countries that made intensive consolidation efforts to accede to the euro. However, whereas the efforts of the former were successful, Greece did not reach the Maastricht limits and therefore did not accede to the euro in the first round. Periphery countries were not the only ones in difficulties with respect to the Maastricht deficit and debt criteria; another example is Belgium.

[4] There is another story of from where the 3 percent deficit limit came; see "3% de déficit: Le chiffre est né sur un coin de table," *Le Parisien*, September 28, 2012, at www.leparisien.fr/economie/3-de-deficit-le-chiffre-est-ne-sur-un-coin-de-table-28-09-2012-2186743.php. According to the French economist Guy Abeille, the rule was invented in May 1981 at the request of the then President of the French Republic, François Mitterrand. In Abeille's account, the rule was given to Mitterrand "without any sort of economic theoretical reflection." Then it was theorized by economists and made its own headway until it was finally retained by the Maastricht Treaty. With respect to the 60 percent criterion, Werner Sinn (2014: 31) explains that the reason why this mark was retained was to make it more difficult for the southern Member States to accede to the Eurozone: "The German government and the Bundesbank naturally inferred as much. They wanted to exclude the southern European countries, because they were afraid of the high level of public debt of such countries . . . That was the reason behind its insistence on incorporating in the Maastricht Treaty the condition that, to accede to the euro, public debt was not to exceed 60% of GDP." When Maastricht was negotiated (1991), Germany respected this threshold; it had a public debt of 42 percent GDP. See Fergusson (2002: 113). These stories, coupled with de Grauwe's narrative, coincide on one point; there is no specific economic basis for these numbers to be retained.

Member States not in the Eurozone) from the application of article 104c (11) (the Treaty article establishing the possibility for the Council to impose sanctions). Under Maastricht, sanctions for an excessive deficit were only contemplated for Eurozone Member States.[5]

The Maastricht rules raised a number of fundamental questions. The first was whether the reference values (3 percent and 60 percent) were nominal values (that is, whether they had to be calculated considering the economic cycle). This is especially important with respect to the deficit, as seen below. The second question was temporal (that is, the question whether Member States must comply with these objectives at the end of the year, in the medium term, or in the long term). The third question was procedural (that is, how the sanction scheme foreseen by Maastricht would be specifically articulated).

Therefore, immediately after the entry into force of the Maastricht Treaty, some Member States, and in particular Germany, argued that the Maastricht rules were insufficiently clear and that, for the credibility of the euro area, they should be further streamlined. According to this view, the previous questions needed a clear answer, giving rise to the Stability and Growth Pact, which was adopted, as analyzed in the next section, at the Amsterdam European Council of 1997. However, under a different reading, the SGP was the price that periphery Member States had to pay for joining the Eurozone in the first round (Sinn, 2014). Nevertheless, the SGP is in reality an extension of the rules originally established in the Maastricht Treaty, which have been described here. Therefore, formally speaking, the SGP is the pact that Member States agreed to in Amsterdam in 1997. However, materially speaking, it is much more than that. Thus, the Maastricht rules can still can be deemed the beating-heart core of the SGP.[6]

6.2.2 Amsterdam European Council of 1997

Once the German insistence that the Maastricht rules should be streamlined was accepted by the rest of the Member States, there was a philosophical quarrel between two camps on the future EU (and in particular, the Eurozone) fiscal rules' exact content. As Brunnermeier, James, and Landau (2016) have argued, we can say that the two camps were led on the one hand by the French, who wanted a flexible SGP, and on the other hand by the Germans, who wanted a much more stringent pact. Although one might believe that the

---

[5] This language is now reproduced in paragraph 22 of regulation 1177/2011 and article 136 TFEU.

[6] I will use the past tense in the following discussion of the SGP before the crisis; however, it is important to emphasize that many of the aspects that will be analyzed henceforth are still, wholly or partially, in force. The new SGP rules adopted after the 2008 crisis do not repeal, but only amend, the SGP as it was originally conceived; they must be viewed as a continuation of the original rules rather than as a rupture with them. Therefore, the only way to make sense of the SGP as it now stands is to understand how the SGP was in its original formulations.

respective positions of these Member States were a little bit more complex than that (see Bastasin, 2015), we assume this simplification of things for clarity. The important point, is to stress that these two philosophies on what the SGP should be, and in general on what the EU fiscal rules should be, have permeated this debate throughout the life of the SGP since its very inception. That is why the correct approach to examining the SGP is as a set of rules that navigate between the margins of flexibility and rigidity.

The SGP took the form of a Resolution of the European Council.[7] Resolutions, even Council Resolutions, do not have a legally binding character, although they can be used as fundamental interpretative parameters of other areas of EU law. Furthermore, the Amsterdam resolution was supplemented by two Council regulations, which will be analyzed below.

The SGP established a major amendment with respect to the Maastricht Treaty original rules, an amendment that "was little noticed at the time the SGP was signed" (de Grauwe, 2016: 224). Arguably, precisely the fact that it was unnoticed at that time may provide a clue about its significance. This amendment was inserted in point 1 of the SGP, which said the following:

> The Member States commit themselves to respect the medium-term budgetary objective of positions close to balance or in surplus set out in their stability or convergence programmes.

The change, which was prompted by the previous rule, was the following: whereas in Maastricht, the rule was that Member States should respect the ceilings of 3 percent and 60 percent, under Amsterdam, they were to achieve a budgetary position "close to balance or in surplus." Close to balance means approximately a 0 percent deficit, which also determines whether we apply the previous mathematical formula ($d = gb$), a public debt of 0 percent in growth periods. This change was a radical departure from the original Maastricht rules, which allowed for a margin of maneuver for Member States' fiscal policy.

Time was an important consideration here, and the SGP in point 1 spoke of a "medium-term" objective (MTO). Then the question arose concerning what the medium term was (Buti, Franco & Ongena, 1998). According to Regulation 1466/1997 (see below), the MTO was three years.[8] Therefore, the fiscal plans that Member States were to design had to be committed to the objective of having their budgets close to balance, at the very least, and if possible, in surplus, in the next three years. Thus, if we combined the Maastricht and SGP rules, the only possible means of accommodating them was to conclude that

---

[7] Resolution of the European Council on the Stability and Growth Pact, Amsterdam, June 17, 1997. OJEC no 236/1 of 2.8.97.

[8] Article 3.3 of Council Regulation 1466/1997, of July 7, 1997, OJEC L 209/1, of 2.8.97. This has become the Commission's common definition; see http://ec.europa.eu/economy_finance/economic_governance/sgp/preventive_arm/index_en.htm.

Member States could have a deficit of approximately 3 percent in a particular year. However (and the *however* is important here), this deficit could only be justified if they could convince the European Union institutions that the deficit would be brought down to close to balance or in surplus in the next three years. With the SGP, Member States were only on the safe side if they brought their fiscal balances close to zero. Even when they were within the margin of 3 percent, they had to make improvements.

This turn to rigidity that the SGP made, if compared to the original Maastricht rules, was supplemented by other measures that were also not in Maastricht. These were the following. First, whereas Maastricht spoke of two rules, deficit and public debt, the Amsterdam resolution only mentioned the first one (which remained 3 percent) and omitted the second. Granted, as was said previously, Maastricht established a certain preference for the first. Nevertheless, the omission of the second, public debt rule, was remarkable in itself. I will comment further on this point later in this chapter; suffice it to say here that by focusing solely on the deficit criterion, the SGP was planting the seeds of yet another rigidity turn later on, when other reforms of the Pact spoke of structural rather than nominal deficit.[9]

The second reform that Amsterdam brought about was the deadline that it granted in favor of Member States to correct their budgetary situation. Maastricht was more flexible on this point; it only spoke of "a period" and a "time limit" that the Council granted to the defective Member State to place the budget back on track. Instead, the SGP established a limit of one year; it said in point 5, "correction should be completed no later than one year following the identification of the excessive deficit" unless special circumstances existed. Third, another SGP change, which also went in the direction of rigidity, was that it specified that a severe recession be defined as a situation in which a Member State experienced a fall of 0.75 percent per year in its GDP (point 7). This definition was more rigid because Maastricht was quite unspecific on this point[10] and, in any case, did not mention the "severe recession" scenario, a factor that provided more flexibility to both the Commission and the Council to account for the specific economic circumstances that a country might be experiencing to decide whether there was an excessive deficit. Finally, concerning the institutional aspects of the SGP, the Pact added nothing new to the Maastricht rules, although the tone that it employed concerning the guardians of the new SGP rigors was stronger: the Commission was required to

---

[9] This interpretation is precisely that given by Artis & Buti (2000b: 564) of the "close to balance or in surplus" SGP clause.

[10] It applied the three "unlesses" of Maastricht article 104c: the Commission monitors the budgetary position of Member States and takes appropriate measures unless (1) the debt ratio has declined substantially and continuously; (2) the debt ratio is exceptional and temporary; and (3) the debt ratio is sufficiently diminishing and approaching the reference value at a satisfactory pace. Clearly, the aim of these three rules was to give more flexibility to EU fiscal governance.

Table 6.1: Maastricht rules and SGP compared

Item	Maastricht	SGP
Reference value	Reference values: 3% and 60%	CTBOS criterion
MTO	No reference to medium-term objectives	MTO close to balance or in surplus
Deadline to lower deficit	"Given period" and "time limit" to reduce deficits	1 year to correct deficit unless special circumstances
Exceptions	"Unless" vague clauses	Severe recessions: 0.75% drop in GDP (but also mention of "unless ... special circumstances")

implement the SGP in a "strict, timely and effective" way (point 1). Further, the Council was required to be committed to a "rigorous and timely" implementation of the Pact (point 1), was urged to view the deadlines of the SGP as "upper limits" (point 2), and was "always" invited to impose sanctions on defective Member States (point 3).

The victory of the rigidity camp in the SGP was further confirmed by the analysis of the two regulations that were approved right after the Pact was agreed, as seen in the next subsection.

6.2.3 Two Council Regulations of 1997

As the SGP resolution stated in its third paragraph, the "Stability and Growth Pact consists of [the Amsterdam] Resolution and of two Council Regulations." These were regulations 1466/1997[11] and 1467/1997[12] – in the EU jargon, the "preventive" and "corrective" arms of the SGP, respectively.

Concerning the first regulation, its aim was to prevent Member States from running excessive deficits. The point of departure of this regulation was a differentiation between the "stability" (section 2) and "convergence" (section 3) plans that Member States were to submit to the European institutions. The section 2 plans were to be submitted by the Eurozone Member States, and the section 3 plans by the Member States that were not part of the Eurozone. The SGP applies therefore to all of the Member States of the Union. The main difference between those that are in the euro and those that are not is that the

---

[11] Council Regulation (EC) No 1466/1997 of July 7, 1997, on the strengthening of the surveillance of budgetary positions and the surveillance and coordination of economic policies. OJEC L 209/1 of 2.8.97.

[12] Council Regulation (EC) No 1467/1997 of July 7, 1997, on speeding up and clarifying the implementation of the excessive deficit procedure. OJEC L 209/6 of 2.8.97.

latter cannot be sanctioned when they do not comply with the SGP requirements, as seen below.

In terms of prevention of excessive deficits, both "ins" and "outs" are
subject, therefore, to the same rules and procedures. Therefore, in the
following, I will refer to both without differentiating between them. Essentially, Member States were to submit plans to the European Union institutions
with information about how their respective MTOs were close to balance or in
surplus or, if need be, the adjustment paths towards this objective. This
information was to be provided on an annual basis, but Member States were
to make projections for the ensuing three years. This requirement is why the
stability objective was a medium-term objective.

Once the EU institutions received these plans, they were to judge them. In
particular, they were to evaluate whether the plans provided for a "safety
margin to ensure the avoidance of an excessive deficit" (articles 5 and 9). It
is very interesting to note that the 3 percent deficit objective completely
disappeared from the dispositive part of the 1466/1997 regulation.[13] What,
then, was this safety margin?

Artis and Buti (2000a) interpreted this expression as follows. Theirs was an
authoritative interpretation (and one that made headway in the practical
management of the SGP) because Buti is (at the time of writing) the
Director-General (DG) Economic and Financial Affairs (ECFIN), the
Commission service in charge of the implementation of the Pact. According
to them, the "safety margin" point of reference was, precisely, the 3 percent
limit. Interpretations according to which the 3 percent could be overshot
(because this limit is not mentioned in regulation 1466/1997) were therefore
to be barred. Thus, a Member State had to present to the EU institutions a
three-year consolidation plan to make its budget close to balance or in surplus
to have a margin of maneuver up to the 3 percent deficit in the event of an
economic slowdown. This requirement meant a strong constriction: even in
harsh times, Member States could only maneuver *within* that margin. In a
crisis, if they overshot the 3 percent ceiling, they would be violating the SGP. It
was not, therefore, that Member States could safely navigate within the
3 percent margin in good times but then overshoot this margin in bad times;
the correct interpretation was the more rigid or restrictive one.

Once they received Member State plans, the Council delivered an opinion
on the programs; if a Member State was invited to make changes, it resubmit-
ted its plan, which was reexamined by the Council. If necessary, the Council

---

[13] The matter is even more intriguing because the 3 percent limit is mentioned in the declarative
part of the 1466/1997 regulation. In effect, paragraph 4 of the regulation's preface says that
"whereas adherence to the medium-term objective of budgetary positions close to balance or in
surplus will allow Member States to deal with normal cyclical fluctuations while keeping the
government deficit within the 3% of GDP reference value." This language appears to give
credence to Artis and Buti's interpretation.

emitted another Communication (and so on and so forth until the plan convinced the Council).

A second aspect of the preventive arm of the SGP, included in regulation 1466/1997, was that the Council monitored Member States' implementation of the stability or convergence plans (articles 6 and 10). If the Council detected a divergence between plans and implementation, it issued a recommendation, an early warning for the Member State in question to take appropriate measures. If the divergence persisted, then the Council issued another recommendation to the Member State to take "prompt corrective measures." The Council could decide to make this recommendation public.

Neither opinions nor recommendations are legally binding acts.[14] Therefore, the preventive arm of the SGP, as enshrined by regulation 1466/1997, opted for a naming and shaming system, at least in part, because in principle only the last recommendations previously reviewed could be made public. This system apparently provided a larger degree of flexibility to the preventive arm of the SGP. However, as seen next, this flexibility was more apparent than real, because the "corrective" arm of the SGP extracted legally binding consequences from the previous, preventive Council exercise.

Regulation 1467/1997 contains, as has been said previously, the corrective arm of the SGP. Its aim was to deter Member States from falling into excessive deficits and to further their rapid correction, once they had fallen into an excessive deficit. It did so through sanctions. Recall that sanctions were (and are) only imposed on Eurozone Member States.[15]

The main steps of the sanctioning procedure under regulation 1467/1997 were the following. The starting point of this procedure was the Council's decision that declared the existence of an excessive deficit (article 3.3). At the same time that the Council made this decision, it sent a recommendation to the failing Member State establishing a deadline to take effective measures and eliminate the excessive deficit. Second, if the Member State took no effective measures (and the excessive deficit situation continued), then the Council decided to give notice to the failing Member State. The third step, after the Council had given notice, was to adopt sanctions. This decision was not a discretionary decision of the Council; this institution "shall impose sanctions," says article 6 of regulation 1467/1997. In principle, sanctions took the form of non-interest-bearing deposits that could become fines (article 13). The former was preferred over a straight imposition of the latter "as a rule" (article 11), which means that the Council could directly impose fines in particular cases. In my interpretation, in this event, the Council had to provide reasons for such a decision.

---

[14] See article 288 TFEU.

[15] Paragraph 9 of the preface of regulation 1467/1997 recapitulates the Maastricht rules; by effect of article 109k (3) of the Maastricht Treaty, article 104c (11) of the Maastricht Treaty (sanctions) applies only to Eurozone Member States.

As seen, the "corrective" arm was quite straightforward in its rigidity. However, there were also instances of flexibility. In particular, article 2 of regulation 1467/1997 established the so-called "benefit clause." We must turn back for a moment to the Amsterdam Resolution on the SGP; its point no. 7 stated that Member States should refrain from invoking the benefit clause unless they are in "severe recession." Article 2.2 of regulation 1467/1997 defined a "severe economic downturn" as a case in which there was an annual fall of at least 2 percent of real GDP. The problem was how to reconcile this article with point 7 of the SGP because the latter defined a severe downturn as a fall of at least 0.75 percent in real GDP. The answer was provided by article 2.3 of regulation 1467/1997, which said that a fall in real GDP of *less* than 2 percent might nonetheless be considered a symptom of the "abruptness" of a downturn. If we interpret the three dispositions conjointly, the following results occur. When the slump was of 2 percent (or more), then there was no discretion; regulation 1467/1997 stated that a Member State that was in that situation would be experiencing a severe recession. A measure of discretion was given, however, to EU institutions when the slump was within the range of 0.75 percent (Resolution) and less than 2 percent (regulation 1467/1997) of real GDP. In that case, the Council considered further evidence to determine whether an exception could be applied to the failing Member State.

Thus, regulation 1467/1997 generated this instance of flexibility. Recall that this flexibility is less than what the Maastricht rules established and is less flexible yet than what the SGP Amsterdam resolution established. This change amounted to another rigidity turn in the SGP, this time within the overall framework of the more flexible parts of the EU fiscal rules (the exceptions). Another instance of flexibility was that sanctions could be abrogated, "depending on the significance of the progress made" by the Member State concerned (article 12). Moreover, article 15 stated that if the decision declaring the existence of an excessive deficit were abrogated, this action would then determine the abrogation of the sanctions that had been adopted accordingly, without the need to adopt a new decision specifically aimed at the abrogation of the sanctions. The resulting regulatory scheme is summarized in Table 6.2.

6.3 SGP from 2005 to 2011

6.3.1 Economic Situation in 2000

The EU experienced "buoyant" growth from the renewal of the SGP in 1997 until 2000 (European Commission, 2002). The introduction of the euro as an accounting currency on January 1, 1999 seemed to add to the overall optimistic atmosphere of the time. However, in the first half of the year 2000, the growth prospects of both the world and the EU suddenly changed. The new slowdown shared trends with other crises such as, for example, a rise in energy prices, a tightening of monetary conditions, and a correlative

Table 6.2: SGP evolution until 2005

Items	Maastricht	SGP	Regulation 1466/1997	Regulation 1467/1997
Reference value	Reference values: 3% and 60%	CTBOS criterion	3% disappear; safety margin; CTBOS	Idem
MTO	No reference to medium-term objectives	MTO close to balance or in surplus	MTO close to balance or in surplus. Safety margin	Idem
Deadline to lower deficit	"Given period" and "time limit" to reduce deficits	1 year to correct deficit unless special circumstances		1 year to correct deficit unless special circumstances
Exceptions	"Unless" vague clauses	Severe recessions: 0.75% drop in GDP (but also mention of "unless ... special circumstances")		Severe recessions: 2%. From 0.75% to less than 2%, an exception is discretionary

deceleration of internal demand in some countries, as in the US, the world's leading economy. However, the slowdown also had peculiarities; in March 2000, the IT bubble, which had been fed since the 1990s in the US stock market, burst. This event further complicated the world economic outlook and affected the Eurozone (the EU) economy (IMF, 2001) and in particular its fiscal perspectives.

However, in yet another proof of the asymmetrical economic structure of the Eurozone, the crisis did not evenly hit all Eurozone Member States. According to the Commission's account of this episode, the Euro-8 (all Eurozone countries except Germany, France, Italy, and Portugal) performed better in fiscal terms than did the Euro-4. "A notable difference between the Euro-4 and the Euro-8 is the development of cyclically adjusted expenditure," said the Commission in its report (European Commission, 2002: 56). In particular, France and above all Germany were at pains to respect the SGP's rigors. Therefore, the fathers of the beast were now witnessing how their child was turning her fury against them. This behavior particularly affected Germany.

In Germany, GDP growth from approximately the mid 1990s was "lacklustre" (European Commission, 2002: 1) (see Figure 6.4). There were a number of reasons for this situation, but above all Germany was suffering economically from reunification, which had occurred in 1990. The dynamic, pro-exporter, and resilient west German economy had engulfed the east German economy, which was stuck in the 1950s, above all in terms of its labor market. This absorption had a large social and economic impact on the unified country.

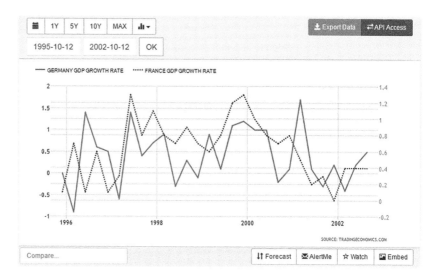

Figure 6.4: Germany and France growth rates
Source: Trading Economics, https://tradingeconomics.com (last visited October 15, 2016)

Despite the euro (which implied a hidden devaluation in real terms for the Germans, if compared with the mark), Germany was still absorbing the costs of reunification when the 2000 crisis hit the country.

The growth prospects, which were not very positive before, suddenly changed for the worse. This change affected Germany's fiscal balances, as Figures 6.5 and 6.6 illustrate; thus in 2001, Germany's deficit was 3.1 percent, in 2002, 3.9 percent, and in 2003, 4.2 percent. In terms of public debt, things were better, but the prospects were somber for a country such as Germany; whereas in 2001 Germany had a public debt of 57.7 percent, in 2005, it reached 67 percent.

Unlike Germany, France had enjoyed a significant growth rate from 1997 until the end of 2000. However, the 2000 crisis hit the country with virulence. According to international observers (IMF 2001; 2002), this effect was largely due to the lack of structural reforms in this country, coupled with a specific problem of population aging. In particular, the size of the public sector was considerable, pension reform had not been undertaken, the labor market showed a lack of flexibility, and the tax burden was considered significant. To address some of these issues, France had undertaken certain reforms before the crisis started, such as the 35-hour working time legislation. However, the effects of this reform on the labor market, and in general on the output growth of the French economy, were debatable, to say the least.

France also entered the crisis with a problem with its fiscal balances. In the run-up to the euro, it had undertaken an important consolidation effort. However, in 2001, the previous positive trend started to reverse (1.4 percent), and in 2002 this Member State overshot the 3 percent limit (3.1 percent).

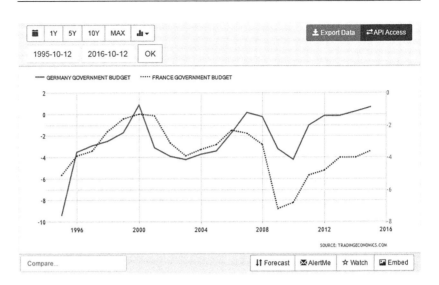

Figure 6.5: Germany and France government deficit
Source: Trading Economics, https://tradingeconomics.com (last visited October 15, 2016)

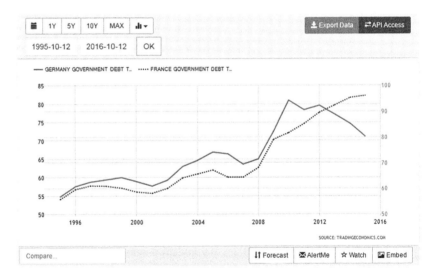

Figure 6.6: Germany and France government debt
Source: Trading Economics (last visited October 15, 2016)

The situation deteriorated further in 2003, when as France's deficit peaked at 3.9 percent, becoming slightly better (but still above the limit) in 2004 (3.5 percent). Concerning public debt, the situation was better, but from 2002 it developed a tendency to increase (60.2 percent). In 2005, France's public debt equaled 67.2 percent.

Considering the fiscal stance of both Germany and France, the European Commission started an excessive deficit procedure against both countries, in November 2002 against Germany and in April 2003 against France. In January 2003, the Council addressed a recommendation to Germany and in June 2003 to France, urging both countries to eliminate their excessive deficits. Germany responded to the Council recommendation by taking a number of measures. However, the Commission, although welcoming these measures, considered them insufficient. Therefore, it recommended that the Council make further decisions under articles 104.8 and 104.9 of the Treaty.[16] In turn, with respect to France, the Commission stated that this Member State had not taken further actions within the deadline established by the Council's decision and requested the Council to act under articles 104.8 and 104.9 of the Treaty.[17]

In the Economic and Financial Affairs Council (ECOFIN) meeting of November 25, 2003, the Council rejected the adoption of decisions against Germany and France because there was not a qualified majority to this effect. In essence, concerning Germany,[18] the Council considered the following facts (see Box 6.1):

- The worsening in cyclical developments was abrupt and unexpected, and therefore the effort to bring the deficit below 3 percent was much greater than expected
- Lower growth expectations than foreseen
- The cumulative loss of real GDP was close to 2 percent in 2003–2004.

For France, the Council considered the following (see Box 6.2):

- The worsening in cyclical developments was abrupt and unexpected, so that the effort to bring the deficit to below 3 percent was much greater than expected
- Lower growth expectations than foreseen
- Loss of real GDP growth over the period 2003–2004 of 1.5 percent.

In turn, the Commission, wary that these decisions could make the SGP's credibility implode, protested. The very text of the Council meeting's conclusions takes up the Commission's stance on this situation and reflects well the tension that this Council meeting undoubtedly had. The Commission deeply regretted "that the Council has not followed the spirit and the rules of the

---

[16] Commission recommendation for a Council Decision giving notice to Germany, in accordance with article 104.9 of the EC Treaty, to take measures for the deficit reduction judged necessary to remedy the situation of excessive deficit. Brussels, November 18, 2003. SEC (2003) 1317 final.

[17] Commission recommendation for a Council Decision giving notice to France, in accordance with article 104.9 of the EC Treaty, to take measures for the deficit reduction judged necessary to remedy the situation of excessive deficit. Brussels, October 21, 2003. SEC (2003) 1121 final.

[18] With Belgium, Denmark, Greece, Spain, Netherlands, Austria, Finland, and Sweden voting in favor, the Presidency concluded that there was not a qualified majority for adopting the Decision.

Box 6.1: ECOFIN November 2003, Germany, page 19

iv. Several important economic and budgetary developments have taken place since the spring: (i) the worsening in cyclical developments was abrupt and unexpected and made the effort to bring the deficit below 3% of GDP in 2004 much greater than expected in May 2003; the Commission spring forecast foresaw a growth rate for Germany of 0.4% in 2003 and 2.0% in 2004; in autumn, the forecast was revised to 0.0% in 2003 and 1.6% in 2004; (ii) the cumulative loss of real GDP growth over the period 2003–2004 compared to what was expected in the spring now amounts to nearly 2 percentage points.

v. The following arguments, which the Commission stressed, should be given the appropriate relevance: (i) too great a consolidation effort in one single year might prove economically costly in view of the prolonged stagnation in Germany over the last three years and the expected slow recovery; and (ii) government proposals for structural reforms would boost potential growth and reduce the deficit in the medium to long term.

vi. Taking into account these factors, and in order to provide the conditions for a balanced correction, the Commission considered that it appears that the deadline set in January 2003 for the elimination of the excessive deficit in Germany should be extended by one year, provided that effective measures are taken by the German authorities as from 2004.

Box 6.2: ECOFIN November 2003, France, page 16

iii. Several important economic and budgetary developments have taken place since spring 2003, which the Commission recommended be taken into account: (i) the worsening in cyclical developments was abrupt and unexpected and made the effort to bring the deficit below 3% of GDP in 2004 much greater than expected in June 2003; the Commission spring forecast foresaw a growth rate for France of 1.1% in 2003 and 2.3% in 2004; in autumn, the forecast was revised to 0.1% in 2003 and 1.7% in 2004; (ii) the cumulated loss of real GDP growth over the period 2003–2004 compared to what was expected in the spring now amounts to about 1.5 percentage points; (iii) the budgetary plans for 2004 submitted to Parliament in September are targeted at a reduction in the cyclically-adjusted deficit of 0.7 percentage points of GDP, slightly more than the 0.5 recommended by the Council in June. Consideration was also given to the fact that the French Government committed to implementing in 2004 a structural reform of health insurance, with the aim of curbing the dynamic of health expenditure, which constituted a major problem in controlling general Government expenditure in recent years.

iv. The argument stressed by the Commission, that too great a consolidation effort in a single year might prove economically costly, in particular in the light of the downward revision of growth forecasts, should be given the appropriate relevance. On the basis of this argument, the Commission considered that the deadline which was set in June for the elimination of the excessive deficit in France should be extended by one year, provided that effective measures are taken by the French authorities as from 2004.

Treaty and the Stability and Growth Pact that were agreed unanimously by all Member States" and reserved for itself the eventual bringing of an action for annulment against ECOFIN's conclusions before the ECJ.

The Commission did the above on January 27, 2004. For the Commission, the Council could not adopt the decision not to proceed against Germany and France under the form of "Council Conclusions." It should have followed the framework established in regulation 1467/1997, in particular, in article 9 of this piece of legislation. In turn, for the Council, "silence on [its] part did not undermine the credibility of the Stability and Growth Pact."[19]

For its part, the ECJ ruled[20] that the right legal framework was that of article 9 of regulation 1467/1997, and not a Council's conclusion, because the decision not to proceed against Germany and France amounted to holding the excessive deficit procedure "in abeyance."[21] However, the ECJ did not delve into the substantive merits of the case (into whether an exception could be granted to both countries) in what has been considered by commentators a "Solomonic" judgment (Padoa-Chioppa, 2006: 24).

6.3.2 European Council of Brussels of March 2005

Some months after the ruling, in September 2004, the European Commission adopted a Communication proposing a "refocus of the Pact."[22] As with the introduction of the Pact, the Member States later decided to follow a similar procedure: a political document would back the reform of regulations 1466/1997 and 1467/1997 by two other regulations. The political document was the

---

[19] Judgment of the Court of July 13, 2004, *Commission v Council*, Case C-27/04. ECR [2004 I-06649], paragraph 62.

[20] Judgment of the Court of July 13, 2004, *Commission v Council*, Case C-27/04. ECR [2004 I-06649]

[21] See paragraph 97 of the Court's ruling: "The Council's conclusions adopted in respect of the French Republic and the Federal Republic of Germany respectively must consequently be annulled in so far as they contain a decision to hold the excessive deficit procedure in abeyance and a decision modifying the recommendations previously adopted by the Council under Article 104(7) EC."

[22] Communication from the Commission to the Council and the European Parliament Strengthening economic governance and clarifying the implementation of the Stability and Growth Pact. Brussels, 3.9.2004 COM(2004) 581 final

European Council Conclusions of Brussels, March 22–23, 2005,[23] and the legal documents were regulations 1055/2005[24] and 1056/2005.[25]

The political rationale for the reform was the following. To start with, the declared aim of the reform was to reinforce neither rigidity nor flexibility but rather the effectiveness of the SGP. However, right after this statement, the European Council also indicated, "The objective is therefore to enhance the economic underpinnings of the existing framework and thus strengthen credibility and enforcement." In a Union of 25 Member States, economic heterogeneity had largely increased; therefore, the new fiscal framework had to account for it. This framework was a clear departure in tone and flavor but also in content (as seen below) with respect to the Amsterdam European Council of 1997, with its insistence on a rule-based approach. The European Council Conclusions referenced the Lisbon strategy. The Lisbon strategy had been adopted in March 2000, not only as a response to the 2000 crisis but also as a way to address long-term economic challenges in Europe, as seen in the last chapter of this book. Lisbon was a plan for steering economic growth and creating new jobs. Specifically, the European Council of Brussels included the first revision of the Strategy, which had delivered only limited results thus far. In any case, the point that I want to stress here is that the Conclusions explicitly linked the SGP and the Lisbon strategy. Clearly, the reform headed towards flexibility; in much the same vein as the Lisbon strategy, the European Council conclusions (Annex II) spoke now of the importance of "peer support and peer pressure" for fiscal coordination purposes (paragraph 1.4).

More specifically, the main reforms, as announced by the new Pact, were the following. First, MTOs were to consider the different economic situations of Member States. Therefore, from now on, there would not be a "one-size-fits-all" MTO policy but rather different MTOs for different economic realities (paragraph 2.1). This approach might appear obvious today, but at the time, adopting it was a large step in the direction of flexibility. Rigidity was, however, not totally absent; Member State MTOs should range from –1 percent GDP to close to balance or surplus. The logic of this requirement was that in "good times," Member States should make a consolidation effort (stronger in those countries with worse fiscal perspectives, and lighter in those countries with better ones). The adjustment should be of 0.5 percent GDP per year "as a benchmark" (paragraph 2.2).

---

[23] European Council Brussels, March 22 and 23, 2005, Presidency Conclusions. Brussels, March 23, 2005 (04.05) 7619/1/05. See Annex II, "Improving the implementation of the Stability and Growth Pact" – Council Report to the European Council.

[24] Council Regulation (EC) No 1055/2005 of June 27, 2005, amending Regulation (EC) No 1466/97 on the strengthening of the surveillance of budgetary positions and the surveillance and coordination of economic policies. OJEU L 174/1 of 7.7.2005.

[25] Council Regulation (EC) No 1056/2005 of June 27, 2005, amending Regulation (EC) No 1467/97 on speeding up and clarifying the implementation of the excessive deficit procedure. OJEU L 174/5 of 7.7.2005.

A second important point is that both a multi-pillar pension reform (paragraph 2.3) and "the unification of Europe" should be considered[26] (paragraph 3.3). To be sure, the first was a nod to France, and the second a nod to Germany. Third, the European Council now said that the aim of the preventive arm of the SGP was to "assist, rather than to punish" Member States (paragraph 3). A fourth point is that the so-called "golden rule" (excess in deficit could be justified for public investment reasons) (paragraph 2.1) was again emphasized as a fiscal criterion. Fifth, and this is also a crucial indicator of flexibility, the exceptions to the application of the SGP rigors were now considered "too restrictive"; therefore, the 1997 regulations must be amended on this particular point (paragraph 3.2). Among the relevant factors that the EU institutions must now look at when considering exceptions, the European Council cited in its conclusions "international solidarity" and "European policy goals." Finally, deadlines were further enlarged throughout the preventive and corrective arm procedures (paragraph 3.6).

6.3.3 Two Council Regulations of 2005

Council Regulation 1055/2005 was addressed to amend regulation 1466/1997. The main changes were therefore the following. Right from the beginning, in the Preamble to the Act, the flexibility overtones of the new regulation were evident. Paragraph 3 spoke of the new "peer support and peer pressure" accent of the reformed SGP, whereas paragraph 5 mentioned the "heterogeneity" of the EU and therefore the need to have "differentiated" MTOs.

Consequently, article 2a said that Member States would have differentiated MTOs, within the range of –1 percent to close to balance or in surplus. The reference to the 3 percent target was kept; however, the reference to the 60 percent limit disappeared (despite the European Council in Brussels stressing the importance of keeping both) (paragraph 3.1). The new regulation also said that an MTO could be revised when major structural reforms were being implemented. This approach was in fact a recurrent theme of this regulation; the two major exceptions now to "temporary" deviations from MTO were structural reforms and pension reform that followed the multi-pillar model (article 5). Finally, a new article 5.1 second paragraph indicated that the yearly consolidation effort should be of 0.5 percent GDP as a benchmark.

In turn, regulation 1056/2005 reformed regulation 1467/1997. The preamble of this act clearly established that the Commission should always examine whether "exceptions" applied before initiating the corrective arm of the SGP. The most important reform included in regulation 1056/2005 was precisely the one affecting the issue of exceptions. "All the relevant factors" that the EU institutions had to consider were, according to article 2.3, potential

---

[26] The multi-pillar pension reform model is analyzed by the World Bank (2008).

Table 6.3: SGP evolution until 2011

Items	Maastricht	SGP	Regulation 1466/1997	Regulation 1467/1997	Regulation 1055/2005	Regulation 1056/2005
Reference value	Reference values: 3% and 60%	CTBOS criterion	3% disappears; safety margin; CTBOS	Idem	3%; safety margin. Consolidation effort 0.5% GDP per year, "benchmark"	Does not mention 3% or 60%. Consolidation effort 0.5% GDP per year, "benchmark"
MTO	No reference to medium-term objectives	MTO close to balance or in surplus	MTO close to balance or in surplus. Safety margin	Idem	Differentiated MTOs; range from (−)1% of GDP and close to balance or surplus, in cyclically adjusted terms	Appropriately take into account developments in MTOs
Deadline to lower deficit	"Given period" and "time limit" to reduce deficits	1 year to correct deficit unless special circumstances		1 year to correct deficit unless special circumstances		1 year to correct deficit unless special circumstances
Exceptions	"Unless" vague clauses	Severe recessions: 0.75% drop in GDP (but also mention of "unless . . . special circumstances")		Severe recessions: 2%. From 0.75% to less than 2%, an exception is discretionary	Major exceptions: structural reforms and pension reform	"All the relevant factors" and "any other factors"

growth of the concerned Member State, the prevailing cyclical conditions, the execution of the Lisbon agenda, and the implementation of research, development and innovation policies. The margin of discretion that the EU institutions might enjoy was however further increased, because the was aforesaid relevant factors were not meant to be a closed list; the Commission must give due consideration to "any other factors" which, *in the opinion of the Member State concerned*, were relevant to judge any excess over the reference value. Among other factors, the Commission should consider Member States' fostering of international solidarity, the achievement of European policy goals, and the unification of Europe. Pension reform was mentioned later (in articles 2.5 and 2.7) as a circumstance that should also be considered.

Article 2.2 was also important because it provided a new interpretation of the concept of an exceptional excess over the reference value. An exceptional excess would be acceptable if the excess resulted from a negative annual GDP growth rate or from a prolonged accumulated loss of output relative to its potential. Both factors were a significant departure compared with the previous regulation, which quantified the downturn with specific numbers (–2 percent as a rule).

In procedural terms, the new regulation also made changes. I will not insist on those changes that affected deadlines and periods, which were generally enlarged. The second reform considered the need for the Council to adopt "revised" recommendations and notices. This input was from case C-27/04, *Commission v Council*, previously examined. Concerning the former, the Council might decide to adopt a revised recommendation under article 104.7 of the EC Treaty if unexpected adverse economic events with major unfavorable consequences occurred after the adoption of the original recommendation. Concerning the latter, the Council could also decide to adopt a revised notice, if the same exceptional circumstances occurred, under article 104.9 of the EC Treaty.

BIBLIOGRAPHY

Armstrong, K. A. 2013, "The new governance of EU fiscal discipline," *European Law Review*, vol. 38, no. 5, pp. 601–617.

Artis, M. J. & Buti, M. 2000, "'Close to Balance or in Surplus': A Policy Makers Guide to the Implementation of the Stability and Growth Pact," EUI Working Papers. RSC no. 2000/28, pp. 1–38.

Bastasin, C. 2015, *Saving Europe: Anatomy of a Dream*, 2nd edn., Brookings Institution, Washington, D.C.

2012, *Saving Europe: Anatomy of a Dream*. Brookings Institution, Washington, D.C.

Briotti, G. 2004, "Fiscal adjustment between 1991 and 2002: stylised facts and policy implications," *ECB Occasional Paper Series*, vol. 9, pp. 1–38.

Brunnermeier, M., James, H., & Landau, J. 2016, *The Euro and the Battle of Ideas*, Princeton University Press, Princeton, N. Jersey.

Buiter, W. 2005, "The 'Sense and Nonsense of Maastricht' Revisited: What Have We Learnt about Stabilization in EMU?," CEPR (Centre for European Policy Research) Discussion Paper, no. 5405.

Buiter, W., Corsetti, G., & Roubini, N. 1993, "Maastricht's fiscal rules," *Economic Policy*, vol. 8, no. 16, pp. 58–100.

Buiter, W. & Grafe, C. 2004, "Patching up the Pact: some suggestions for enhancing fiscal sustainability and macroeconomic stability in an enlarged European Union," *Economics of Transition*, vol. 12, no. 1, pp. 67–102.

Buti, M., Franco, D., & Ongena, H. 1998, "Fiscal discipline and flexibility in EMU: the implementation of the Stability and Growth Pact," *Oxford Review of Economic Policy*, vol. 14, no. 3, pp. 81–97.

Craig, P. 2012, "The Stability, Coordination, and Governance Treaty: principle, politics and pragmatism," *European Law Review*, vol. 37, no. 3, pp. 231–248.

De Grauwe, P. 2016, *Economics of Monetary Union*, 11th edn., Oxford University Press, Oxford.

    2008, "On the need to renovate the Eurozone," *International Finance*, vol. 11, no. 3, pp. 327–333.

De Grauwe, P. & Yuemei, J. 2013, "Mispricing of sovereign risk and multiple equilibria in the Eurozone," *Journal of International Money and Finance*, vol. 34, April, pp. 15–36.

European Commission. 2002, "The EU Economy: 2002 Review," *European Economy* no. 6.

European Court of Auditors. 2016, "Further Improvements Needed to Ensure Effective Implementation of the Excessive Deficit Procedure," *Special Report*, vol. 10.

Ferguson, N. 2002, "Public debt as a post-war problem: the German experience after 1918 in comparative perspective" in *Three Postwar Eras in Comparison: Western Europe 1918–1945–1989*, eds. C. Levy & M. Roseman, Palgrave Macmillan UK, Basingstoke, pp. 99–119.

Haan, J., Berger, H., & Jansen, D. 2004, "Why has the Stability and Growth Pact failed?," *International Finance*, vol. 7, no. 2, pp. 235–260.

Hallerberg, M., Strauch, R. R., & von Hagen, J. 2010, *Fiscal Governance in Europe*, Cambridge University Press, Cambridge.

Heipertz, M. & Verdun, A. 2010, *Ruling Europe. The Politics of the SGP*, Cambridge University Press, Cambridge.

Ioannou, D. & Stracca, L. 2011, "Have the Euro Area and EU Economic Governance Worked? Just the Facts," ECB Working Paper Series, no. 1344.

Krugman, P., Obstfeld, M., & Melitz, M. 2015, *International Economics: Theory and Policy*, 10th edn., Pearson, Boston, Mass.

Lledó, V., Yoon, S.-W, Fang, X-M., Mbaye, S., & Kim, Y. 2017, "Fiscal Rules at a Glance," International Monetary Fund, www.imf.org/external/datamapper/fiscal rules/Fiscal%20Rules%20at%20a%20Glance%20-%20Background%20Paper.pdf.

Schelkle, W. 2007, "EU fiscal governance: hard law in the shadow of soft law?," *Columbia Journal of European Law*, vol. 13, pp. 705–731.

Sinn, H.-W. 2014, *The Euro-Trap: On Bursting Bubbles, Budgets and Beliefs*, Oxford University Press, Oxford.

Stiglitz, J. 2010, "Lessons from the global financial crisis of 2008," *Seoul Journal of Economics*, vol. 23, no. 3, pp. 321–339.

Wolf, M. 2015, *The Shifts and the Shocks: What We've Learned – and Have Still to Learn – from the Financial Crisis*, Penguin Books, New York.

World Bank. 2008, *The World Bank Pension Conceptual Framework*, World Bank, Washington, D.C.

7

The Stability and Growth Pact under the Crisis - and Beyond

Introduction

In this chapter, I will describe and analyze the reform of the SGP that has occurred due to the crisis that exploded in 2008. I will also take stock of the most recent developments in this domain. The chapter is supplemented by an analysis of how the SGP has been implemented over the years, with an explicit reference to the counterfactual situation (what would have occurred in the absence of the SGP). The last section of this chapter serves to connect the current chapter with the preceding one because I will reflect on several points concerning the credibility of the SGP.

7.1 Economic Situation before the 2011 Reform of the SGP

The Eurozone grew from the time when reform of the SGP began (2004) until the significant recession of 2008, although not at spectacular levels: average growth was 2.5 percent of GDP during this period. In turn, the countries responsible for the first important amendment of the SGP grew significantly but at lower rates than the rest of the Eurozone. While Germany's average growth clearly lagged behind that of the Eurozone as a whole (2.2 percent), France fared only slightly better, at an average rate of 2.3 percent. It is important to remember that the Lisbon strategy had set the marker of 3 percent average growth for the European Union from 2000 to 2010. In the first lustrum, this level of growth could not be achieved due to the sudden explosion of the IT crisis in the US. Moreover, as seen, this objective could not be reached in the first years of the second lustrum (see Figure 7.1).

Recall that, according to Sapir et al.'s (2003) data (see Table 7.1), the EU had only reached that level (on average) in the period from 1970 to 1980. It is also interesting to note the difference in growth levels between the EU and the US: the US effectively reached (and surpassed) the 3 percent target from the 1970s to 2000, whereas the EU only did so, as has been hinted before, in the 1970s, and thereafter experienced steadily decreasing growth.

The above is the background against which the 2008 crisis exploded. In essence, the crisis had its origin in the collapse of the subprime mortgage

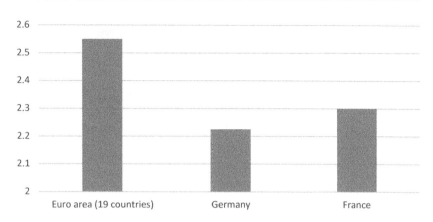

Figure 7.1: Average GDP growth, 2004–2007 (Eurozone, Germany, France)
Source: Eurostat (2016)

market in the USA. The crisis had a name and a surname; the name was Dick Fuld. Dick Fuld (Lehman's CEO) was a broker who made headway in the 2000s by profiting from legal loopholes in the US financial rulebook, which allowed him to sell subprime products. The surname (one that has already become part of the popular imagination due, among other things, to documentaries such as *Inside Job*, movies such as *Margin Call*, and books such as *The Devil's Casino*) was that of Lehman Brothers.[1] The collapse of Lehman on September 15, 2008, marked the beginning of what would soon be dubbed the "big global recession," the worst crisis since the crash of 1929.

The collapse of Lehman spread first in the American financial market and then to the rest of the world (Stiglitz, 2010; Krugman, 2012; Wolf, 2015). In a matter of weeks, financial institutions stopped trusting one another, and interbank credit almost came to a halt. Later, States came to the rescue of financial institutions, of banks in particular. However, because the dimensions of the crisis were larger than expected – as financial institutions had over-sized their risk – it soon became clear that the bailout operations would be much larger than originally thought. Financial markets reacted to this expansion by raising

[1] *Inside Job* makes a direct reference to Lehman Brothers and the company's collapse. *Margin Call* does not refer directly to any particular company or broker, but as its director has repeated on numerous occasions, he took inspiration from the events that prompted the collapse of Lehman Brothers. See Julia La Roche, "The Director of 'Margin Call' Reveals The Event That Inspired The Film" in *Business Insider*, October 24, 2001. The link to the interview with J. C. Chandor (the movie's director) is at www.businessinsider.com/director-j-c-chandor-2011-10. Vicky Ward's *The Devil's Casino* is the inside story of the collapse of Lehman Brothers, with a psychological portrait of Dick Fuld at its core.

Table 7.1: Growth of GDP, labor input (annual number of hours worked), and labor productivity (GDP per hour) (% per annum)

	GDP		Labour		Labour productivity	
	EU	US	EU	US	EU	US
1970-1980	3.0	3.2	−0.5	1.8	3.5	1.4
1980-1990	2.4	3.2	0.0	1.7	2.4	1.4
1991-2000	2.1	3.6	0.3	1.9	1.8	1.7
1991-1995	1.5	3.1	−0.9	1.8	2.4	1.3
1995-2000	2.6	4.1	1.2	2.0	1.4	2.0

Source: European Commission, AMECO database and OECD Employment Outlook (various years). 1970-1990 includes former West Germany: 1991-2000 includes Germany.

Source: Sapir Report (2003), table 4.3, page 25

the risk premia of the sovereigns; they started to discount, anticipating that some States would default. In Europe, this increase provoked the virtual collapse of the Greek economy, which infected other EU countries, essentially those on the periphery of the Eurozone. Thus, the risk premia of Spain, Ireland, Italy, and some other periphery countries increased to almost unsustainable levels. As will be analyzed in Chapters 8 and 9, EU bailouts, which were initially negated in the European economic governance system, had to be performed in some of these countries.

To better grasp why the third reform of the SGP occurred, it is important to examine here for a moment some of the issues that are reviewed in more detail in the next two chapters. As has been mentioned before, bailouts were ruled out in the EU economic governance system. When Member States and the EU institutions understood that, in violation of the Treaty, they must perform bailouts, they realized at the same time that they had to request something difficult in exchange for the assistance that would be given to the beneficiary Member States. This request was made to avoid throwing the credibility of the EU economic governance system into question. Thus, the new rules – the new turn to rigidity – were not an absolute necessity. They were only intended to compensate for the violation of the Treaty rules that banned bailouts.

Figure 7.2 perfectly illustrates the sawtooth form that the 2008 crisis took (and by comparing the German and the Greek cases, it shows the asymmetrical characteristics of the crisis with particular clarity). It is possible to differentiate two moments in the crisis: a first moment (from 2008 to 2010) in which the crisis was a financial crisis and Member States rescued the financial sector, and a second moment (from 2010 onwards) in which the financial crisis turned into a debt crisis. At the latter point, the EU institutions and Member States (Germany and France in particular) decided that Member States in difficulty would be rescued in exchange for the EU fiscal framework being made more stringent.

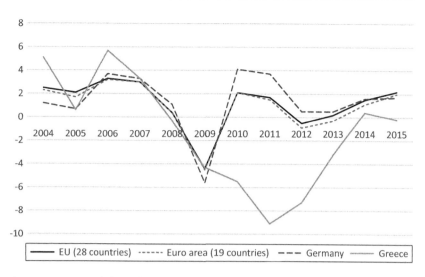

Figure 7.2: GDP growth during the crisis
Source: Eurostat (2016)

7.2 How the EU Reacted to the Crisis in the Fiscal Domain

It is interesting to trace back and reconstruct the course of events of the two crisis periods and how the EU responded to it. Stage 1 of the crisis started when Lehman collapsed in September 2008, which immediately provoked financial turmoil. The European Council of October 15 and 16, 2008,[2] reacted by endorsing the "action plan" that the Eurozone countries had adopted on October 12, 2008.[3] The Euro-group (the recently created euro-summits) clearly observed the financial crisis as a liquidity problem and urged Member States to inject liquidity into their respective financial systems in a coordinated fashion. Interestingly, this European Council did not speak of stimulating the economy. However, when the G20 leaders met in Washington in November 2008, the change in tone and language was clear; the G20 summit declaration openly spoke of the need to "use fiscal measures to stimulate domestic demand to rapid effect, as appropriate, while maintaining a policy framework conducive to fiscal sustainability." This decision by the European Council of December 11 and 12, 2008[4] was made at the EU level. In the conclusions of this European Council, the Member States approved a

---

[2] Brussels European Council 15 and 16 October 2008. Presidency Conclusions. Brussels, October 16, 2008, 14368/08. CONCL 4.

[3] Declaration on a Concerted European Action Plan of the Euro Area Countries of October 12, 2008, available at ec.europa.eu/economy_finance/publications/publication13260_en.pdf.

[4] Brussels European Council 11 and 12 December 2008. Presidency Conclusions. Brussels, February 13, 2009. 17271/1/08. REV 1. CONCL 5.

European Economic Recovery Plan, equivalent to approximately 1.5 percent of the GDP of the European Union (a figure amounting to approximately €200 billion), which had previously been proposed by the European Commission.[5] The Plan was foreseen as a conjoint Member States and EU enterprise. However, concerning the EU's economic involvement, both the Commission communication and the European Council conclusions remained silent.

Following the G20 and European Council recommendations, some Member States, for example Spain, used stimuli to boost their economy. The halt in credit that had occurred due to the fall of Lehman in the US burst the housing bubble that had been inflated in the previous, bonanza years in Spain. Therefore, the Spanish government approved a Plan of approximately €100 billion to shore up its economy (Estella, 2015). It is important to remember that Spain had a surplus when the 2008 crisis started, which the country used to combat that crisis.

Stage 2 of the crisis started on April 23, 2010, when the Greek Prime Minister George Papandreou acknowledged in Castelorizo that his country had lied and that its deficit would be double that originally announced.[6] We could say that this moment is when the financial crisis turned into a debt crisis. Member States, France and Germany in particular, had to face the cold fact that in the absence of a bailout, Greece would default, which in turn could have disastrous consequences for the whole of the Eurozone. Therefore, on May 2, 2010, the Euro-group unanimously agreed to activate stability support to Greece via bilateral loans centrally pooled by the European Commission.[7] Furthermore, on May 7, 2010, the heads of state or governments of the euro area[8] endorsed the Euro-group agreement but added, on the one hand, that a financial stabilization mechanism would be created and, on the other hand, that the SGP would be strengthened, "including more-effective sanctions." In turn, the European Council of June 17, 2010,[9] endorsed all of the previous changes, agreed on the first efforts towards the reform of the SGP, decided on the introduction of the so-called "European Semester," and adopted the "Europe 2020 Strategy."

---

[5] Commission of the European Communities Brussels, November 26, 2008, COM(2008) 800 final Communication from the Commission to the European Council "A European Economic Recovery Plan."

[6] See Prime Minister Papandreou's statement at http://archive.papandreou.gr/papandreou/content/Document.aspx?d=6&rd=7739474&f=1722&rf=-1850948134&m=12893&rm=20504593&l=1.

[7] Statement by the Eurogroup on Greece of May 2, 2020, available at www.consilium.europa.eu/en/press/press-releases/?fn%5b%5d=780&p=10.

[8] Statement of the Heads of State or Government of the Euro Area, May 7, 2010, available at www.consilium.europa.eu/en/european-council/euro-summit/documents-2010-2013/.

[9] European Council, 17 June 2010. Conclusions. Brussels, July 13, 2010. EUCO 13/1/10 REV 1 CO EUR 9 CONCL 2.

Between this European Council and the one on October 28 and 29, 2010, Chancellor Merkel and President Sarkozy met in the "old fashioned" (Brunnermeier, James, & Landau, 2016: 29) resort of Deauville to inject new impetus into the strategy to handle the crisis. This meeting was a decisive moment; despite the Treaty rules on bailouts, *a larger* rescue package must be created. Member States in addition to Greece had also run out of firepower and needed the help of the EU institutions and other Member States to address the crisis. Germany and France's response included three pillars: (1) a reform of the SGP, (2) a strong bailout mechanism for Member States in difficulty, and (3) private involvement in the crisis.[10]

The last pillar (in the European jargon, the so-called "PSI," or private sector involvement) meant a haircut and implied the acceptance of a partial default on Member State debts. Alarm bells rang all over the planet once its main leaders read the Deauville declaration, particularly in Washington. Timothy Geithner, Secretary of the US Treasury, immediately called his European counterparts to force them to make public bailouts and limit private losses as much as possible (thus, to retain pillars 1 and 2 of the Deauville declaration but drop the third). His bold reaction, apparently his exact words when he was informed of Deauville's outcome, is reproduced in Box 7.1. Ultimately, PSI was circumscribed to Greece and later abandoned. However, it also prompted a reform of the European rescue and resolution mechanisms for banks, which introduced the principle that "bail-ins go first" to rescue or resolve banks (see Chapter 5 above). From an institutional perspective, the Deauville summit was important because, for some commentators, it definitively shifted power from the EU supranational institutions to Paris and Berlin, and thereafter only to Berlin (Brunnermeier, James, & Landau, 2016).

After the Deauville declaration, events unfolded incrementally but rapidly. The European Council of October 28 and 29, 2010,[11] took stock of the Deauville summit and stressed that "a fundamental shift in European economic governance is required." It endorsed the report of the Task Force on European Economic Governance that had been created by the European Council of March 25 and 26, 2010.[12] In line with the Deauville outcome, the Task Force proposed a stronger Stability and Growth Pact and a robust framework for crisis management. Interestingly, the Task Force gave a lesser role to private involvement in the new rescue mechanism: "issues to be addressed for such a new future permanent mechanism *may include* the role of the private sector." Geithner's voice had been heard in Brussels.

---

[10] Statement for the France–Germany–Russia Summit, Deauville – Monday, October 18, 2010, available at: www.eu.dk/~/media/files/eu/franco_german_declaration.ashx?la=da.

[11] European Council, 28 and 29 October 2010. Conclusions. Brussels, November 30, 2010. EUCO 25/1/10 REV 1 CO EUR 18 CONCL 4.

[12] European Council 25 and 26 March 2010. Conclusions. Brussels, May 11, 2010. EUCO 7/1/10 REV 1 CO EUR 4 CONCL 1.

Box 7.1: Geithner's reaction to Deauville

"That was, like, [an] incredible miscalculation for damage. They had a summit in Deauville, France, where Sarkozy, in order to get Merkel to back off her 'fiscal union' stuff, which was very hard for him politically because, you know, France in that [was] agreeing to come under the thumb of Germany on fiscal policy – at least that's what the French politics was. He, Sarkozy, agrees to back Merkel on this haircut stuff . . .

"I was on the Cape [Cod] for Thanksgiving and I remember doing a G7 call from the Cape and being in my little hotel room. And I basically, and Trichet did the same thing, I was, I'm sure I was rude and I said: basically, if you guys do that, you will, you know, all you will do is accelerate the run from Europe. No one will lend a dollar, a euro to a European government if they're weak in that context because the fear will be, if they need money, you've got to force some restructuring, haircut [garbled]. It completely inverts the incentives you want to create. I was fucking apoplectic about it and I said it may be that you're going to have to – I can't remember how I said it – you may be, if you're going to restructure Greece, but until you have the ability to in effect protect or guarantee the rest of Europe from the ensuing contagion, this is just [a] metaphor for our fall of '08. You can't do that . . .

"At that point, Trichet was completely apoplectic about these guys, [and] said that you cannot afford to have all this loose haircut talk until you are in a better position to be able to guarantee and protect the rest of Europe from the contagion and the run of what happened."

Source: http://blogs.ft.com/brusselsblog/2014/11/11/draghis-ecb-management-the-leaked-geithner-files/

Furthermore, the European Council of December 2010[13] agreed on a reform of article 136 TFEU to introduce a larger and permanent rescue mechanism, the ESM (see Chapter 8). The tradeoff between rescue mechanism and reinforcement of the Stability and Growth Pact is made clear in this passage of the Conclusions of the European Council of February 2011:[14]

The European Council called on the Council to reach in March a general approach on the Commission's legislative proposals on economic governance, ensuring full implementation of the recommendations of the Task Force, so as to reach a final agreement with the EP by the end of June. *This will allow*

---

[13] European Council, 16 and 17 December 2010. Conclusions. Brussels, January 25, 2011. EUCO 30/1/10 REV 1 CO EUR 21 CONCL 5.
[14] European Council, 4 February 2011. Conclusions. Brussels, March 8, 2011. EUCO 2/1/11 REV 1 CO EUR 2 CONCL 1.

strengthening the Stability and Growth Pact and implementing a new macro-economic framework.

[paragraph. 27; my emphasis]

The European Council of March 2011[15] took a further step in the reform of EU economic governance and adopted a "comprehensive approach" in this domain. The comprehensive approach included strengthening governance, the Euro Plus Pact, restoring the health of the banking sector, and strengthening the stability mechanisms of the euro area.

Concerning the first item, strengthening governance, the European Council announced a major reform of the SGP, the so-called "six-pack." The Council also mentioned for the first time the idea according to which fiscal consolidation would require in most cases an annual *structural adjustment* "well above" 0.5 percent of GDP. In turn, the Euro Plus Pact was intended as an umbrella under which all of the other reforms would be grouped. It had four pillars (competitiveness, employment, sustainability of public finance, and financial stability) and advanced for the first time the idea of inserting EU fiscal rules (and in particular, a "debt brake" provision) into Member State national legislation (and, if possible, constitutions). Important as the previous measures were, the European Council of March 2011 took a decisive step for the European Union governance system by agreeing on the "Term Sheet" on the ESM. The new overall bailing-out fund for Eurozone Member States was therefore born.

The European Council of March 1 and 2, 2012,[16] saw a further crucial step in shaping the new EU economic governance system when it adopted, although "at the margins," the Treaty on Stability, Coordination and Governance in the EMU, the so-called "Fiscal Compact." This sequence of crucial European Councils concluded with the European Council of October 18 and 19, 2012,[17] which announced that a "two-pack" would supplement the "six-pack."

The resulting scheme was the following: (1) the SGP was reformed through the six- and two-packs; (2) the Member States adopted the ESM, but outside of the EU legal system; and (3) the Member States adopted the Fiscal Compact, also outside the EU legal system. These reforms were supplemented by the European Semester, the Euro Plus Pact, and the "Europe 2020 Strategy."[18]

---

[15] European Council, 24 and 25 March 2011. Conclusions. Brussels, April 20, 2011. EUCO 10/1/11 REV 1 CO EUR 6 CONCL 3.

[16] European Council, 1 and 2 March 2012. Conclusions. Brussels, May 8, 2012. EUCO 4/3/12 REV 3 CO EUR 2 CONCL 1.

[17] European Council, 18 and 19 October 2012, Conclusions. Brussels, October 19, 2012. EUCO 156/12 CO EUR 15 CONCL 3.

[18] A good summary of the new EU economic governance system is provided in paragraph 4 of the European Council Conclusions of October 23, 2011: "The European Union now has more powerful tools to enhance its economic governance and to ensure that the required measures are taken to pull Europe out of the crisis: the Europe2020 strategy continues to guide the Union

7.3 SGP Reforms of 2011 and 2013

7.3.1 Fiscal Compact

The Fiscal Compact[19] was signed by 25 Member States (all of them except the UK and the Czech Republic) on March 2, 2012. It entered into force on January 1, 2013.[20] According to Armstrong (2013), "there is no obvious reason why such a tightening of the rules could not have been achieved within the legislative framework of the SGP." However, the reason appears to be political rather than legal (Craig, 2012); the UK, followed by the Czech Republic, vetoed the original French and German intention to amend the Lisbon Treaty.[21] The main elements of the Fiscal Compact are the following.

and the Member States in promoting the delivery of growth-enhancing structural reforms; the European semester will help ensure that they remain on track in implementing these reforms in a coordinated manner; and the Euro Plus Pact will achieve a new quality of economic policy coordination amongst the participating Member States. The package of six legislative acts on economic governance agreed last month will allow a much higher degree of surveillance and coordination, necessary to ensure sustainable public finances and avoid the accumulation of excessive imbalances. The European Council emphasizes its determination to implement this new framework in order to ensure that it is fully and effectively applied. In this context, we welcome the intention of the Commission to strengthen, in the Commission, the role of the competent Commissioner for closer monitoring and additional enforcement."

[19] Treaty on Stability, Coordination and Governance in the Economic and Monetary Union between the Kingdom of Belgium, the Republic of Bulgaria, the Kingdom of Denmark, the Federal Republic of Germany, the Republic of Estonia, Ireland, the Hellenic Republic, the Kingdom of Spain, the French Republic, the Italian Republic, the Republic of Cyprus, the Republic of Latvia, the Republic of Lithuania, the Grand Duchy of Luxembourg, Hungary, Malta, the Kingdom of the Netherlands, the Republic of Austria, the Republic of Poland, the Portuguese Republic, Romania, the Republic of Slovenia, the Slovak Republic, the Republic of Finland and the Kingdom of Sweden (not published in the OJEU). See www.consilium.europa.eu/en/history/#40802201049.

[20] See European Parliament Table on the ratification process of amendment of article 136 TFEU, ESM Treaty and the Fiscal Compact: www.europarl.europa.eu/webnp/cms/pid/1833.

[21] With respect to the legal nature of the Fiscal Compact, this answer was provided by former President of the European Commission Barroso to a question from the European Parliament on this point: "The Fiscal Compact is contained in Article 3 of the Treaty on Stability Coordination and Governance in the EMU (TSCG). The TSCG is an international Treaty concluded inter se by some EU Member States outside the EU legal order. The European Union is not a party to the TSCG. Because it is an international treaty, it is subject to customary international laws on treaties as codified by the Vienna Convention of 1980. However, the TSCG has strong links with EC law. It refers to EC law instruments and partially relies on the EU institutional framework. The TSCG also provides that the necessary steps will be taken in order to incorporate the content of the TSCG into the EU legal order (Article 16 TSCG). By virtue of the principle of primacy of EC law, the TSCG must comply with the provisions of EU primary and secondary law. This is confirmed by Article 2 of the TSCG which provides that the TSCG applies only insofar as it is compatible with EC law." Answer provided by Mr Barroso on behalf of the Commission, February 17, 2014.

To start with, the nuclear part of the Fiscal Compact is its article 3. This article begins by restating the rule "close to balance or in surplus."[22] However, immediately after this restatement, the article defines how that rule is now to be understood: according to the Fiscal Compact, that rule is to be respected if the budgetary position of a Member State (of a contracting party) remains at the lower limit of a structural deficit of 0.5 percent GDP. Member States' progress towards their respective MTOs must adopt the structural deficit as "a reference." Further, the same article supplements this new rule by adding that if a Member State has a debt significantly below 60 percent, then it will be allowed to reach a structural deficit of at most 1 percent. Therefore, the new benchmark is the structural deficit, which superposes and acquires more importance than the nominal one (3 percent). Second, the new fluctuation margin is not –1 percent to close to balance or surplus in cyclically adjusted terms but from 0.5 percent to 1 percent of structural deficit, depending upon whether the Member State is faring well in terms of public debt. The Treaty adds that when a Member State exceeds the 60 percent limit, then that State must reduce its debt at an average rate of 1/20 per year (article 4). Finally, concerning the period to lower deficits, this action is to be proposed by the European Commission "taking into consideration country-specific sustainability risks" (article 3.1(b)).

The second important reform that the Fiscal Compact establishes is that Member States must introduce the previous amendment to the SGP in their own legal orders. The Fiscal Compact goes as far as to establish *a preference* on this point: constitutions are preferred to other legal instruments (article 3.2). Therefore, if possible, Member States should establish the previous rules (what is known as the golden rule of the Fiscal Compact[23]) in their constitutions.[24] Member States had to take this action within one year after the entry into force of the Fiscal Compact. The Commission is empowered by the Treaty to monitor Member States' compliance and write a report (article 8); if Member States have not implemented the golden rule in their own legal orders, a contracting party can bring an action before the ECJ based on the Commission's report. The Commission's report does not however preclude a Member State from bringing actions against the failing Member State. They can still bring actions, even when they do not agree with the Commission's

---

[22] The exact words of article 3.1 (a) are, "the budgetary position of the general government . . . shall be balanced or in surplus," which could be interpreted as a new twist in the direction of rigor; "balanced" is more stringent than "close to balance."

[23] There is a certain degree of confusion concerning what the "golden rule" is. In principle, the golden rule is that the deficit should be equivalent to public investments in a country. However, this rule is not the golden rule that is included in the Fiscal Compact (although informally it is also called the golden rule of the Fiscal Compact). The latter refers to the structural deficit limit and not necessarily to public investments, although certain public investments can be of a structural type.

[24] For an approximation of Member States' implementation of the Fiscal Compact golden rule in their respective legal orders, see IMF (2015).

viewpoint.[25] Moreover, a system of sanctions is foreseen by the Fiscal Compact; if the ECJ's ruling declaring that the Member State failed to implement this article of the Fiscal Compact were not implemented, then a Member State could bring a second action before the ECJ requesting the imposition of a sanction based on article 260 TFEU (article 8.2). In turn, the ECJ could impose on the failing Member State either a lump sum penalty or one that cannot exceed 0.1 percent of its GDP.

Two further rules supplement the whole new package: first, the provision for an automatic correction mechanism "in the event of significant observed deviations" from the path to fiscal balance that Member States must put in place at the national level based on "common principles" established by the European Commission[26] (article 3.2); and second, the establishment of a national independent agency whose major task is to monitor the observance of the "golden rule" at the national level (ibid.).

Finally, in yet another proof of the tradeoff that exists between the establishment of a bailout system in the EU (of the setting up of the ESM, in particular) and the strengthening of the SGP via the Fiscal Compact, the preface of the Fiscal Compact indicates the following:

> The granting of financial assistance in the framework of new programmes under the European Stability Mechanism will be conditional, as of 1 March 2013, on the ratification of the [Fiscal Compact].

The Fiscal Compact represents therefore an unprecedented turn to rigidity in the history of the evolution of the SGP. It is unprecedented, above all, because it sets the concept of structural deficit as the new mother of all benchmarks for the EU system of fiscal governance. It is also unprecedented because it specifies a numerical value (0.5 percent) that in fact lowers the original 3 percent limit. Concerning the latter, there is not a solid and robust economic reason why 0.5 percent should be preferred to other (higher) limits. For example, Artis and Buti (2000a) argue that a limit of 1.5 percent of structural deficit would have done as well.[27] However, the most problematic aspect is related to the former remark (selection of the structural deficit criterion). It is problematic for two reasons. First, economists do not agree on a formula to compute the structural deficit of countries. Second, even were they to agree on a formula, the problem with the computation of the structural deficit would be that it is very volatile.

---

[25] For an alternative interpretation, see Craig (2012).

[26] See Communication from the Commission "Common principles on national fiscal correction mechanisms" Brussels, 20.6.2012 COM (2012) 342 final.

[27] Their words are the following: "The IMF (1998) and the OECD (1997) find that a structural deficit in the range of 0.5% to 1.5% GDP . . . would be enough to allow the automatic stabilizers to operate without breaching the 3% GDP threshold even in periods of pronounced cyclical slowdown" (Artis & Buti, 2000b: 17). Interestingly, these words disappear from their article in the *Journal of Common Market Studies* (Artis & Buti, 2000a).

> ## Box 7.2: De Grauwe (2011) on "balanced-budget fundamentalism"
>
> "The problem with this rule [structural deficit] is that it will be very difficult to implement. The reason is that economic science is not sufficiently reliable to be able to determine what the structural and cyclical components of the budget are. Ask economists today what these structural and the cyclical components of the government budget deficit are and you will probably get a very different answer from each of them. This lack of reliable knowledge makes it possible for governments to cook up the numbers. They will always find reputable economists to back up these numbers.
>
> "A final problem with the balanced-budget rule is that it is based on a cynical view of what governments actually do. The rule implies that in the long run the debt-to-GDP ratio moves towards zero. The reason is that with a balanced-budget rule, the government cannot issue new debt (over the business cycle). Since GDP increases, the debt-to-GDP ratio must decline and ultimately go to zero.
>
> "There is no sound economic reason to back up such a rule . . ."
>
> Source: (CEPS [Centre for European Policy Studies] Commentary, September 5, 2011, p. 2)

In T1, one might calculate the structural deficit of a country and determine that the country in fact has a deficit, and in T2 (let us say, one year later) one might compute the same number and determine that the country actually had a surplus. This phenomenon results from the fact that the computation of the structural deficit is very sensitive to the particular moment at which it is performed. This aspect is rather paradoxical because the structural deficit is a concept that attempts to provide a more certain measure of a country's deficit in a given moment. However, the result is instead the converse: the statistic augments (rather than decreases) uncertainty on this point (see Box 7.2).

7.3.2 Six-Pack

This unprecedented turn to rigidity, in which the Fiscal Compact set the structural deficit as the new benchmark for EU fiscal governance, is supplemented by the so-called six-pack and two-pack legislation. Concerning the first, the starting point is regulation 1175/2011.[28] The main reform that this piece of legislation introduces into the SGP is the concept of structural balance. According to this regulation, MTOs must now be oriented towards

---

[28] Regulation (EU) No 1175/2011 of the European Parliament and of the Council of November 16, 2011, amending Council Regulation (EC) No 1466/97 on the strengthening of the surveillance of budgetary positions and the surveillance and coordination of economic policies. OJEU L 306/12 of 23.11.2011.

a structural balance objective "as a reference" (article 5.1 third indent and article 6.3). It has been shown that the Fiscal Compact further concretizes this objective by adding the already-known specific objective of 0.5 percent of structural deficit. However, the step prior to the introduction of that specification is to be found in this regulation.

Other aspects of interest in this regulation are the following. First, it regulates with some detail the so-called European Semester (section 1 A) and the Economic Dialogue (section 1 Aa). Concerning the former, regulation 1175/2011 says that, for coordinating the economic policies of Member States, the ES refers to the following: (1) the formulation and surveillance of the broad guidelines of economic policies, (2) the formulation and the examination of the employment guidelines, (3) the submission and assessment of the stability and convergence programs, (4) the submission and assessment of the national reform programs, and (5) surveillance to prevent and correct macroeconomic imbalances. The Council shall offer its guidance on all of these exercises; in turn, failure by Member States to follow the Council's guidance may result in further recommendations, a warning, and even "measures" under regulation 1467/1997 (the regulation which regulates sanctions in the framework of the SGP).

The Economic Dialogue is an instrument to foster and enhance institutional dialogue on matters related to fiscal governance among the EU institutions (in particular, among the European Parliament, the Council, and the Commission). The European Parliament may invite the presidents of the Commission, the Council and the European Council and the Euro-group to appear before the competent parliamentary committee to discuss issues related to the European Semester and, in general, matters related to Member States' economic and fiscal coordination.

A second aspect of importance that this piece of legislation introduces is the surveillance missions that the European Commission may undertake in Member States for economic and, in particular, fiscal coordination. There are two modalities: missions (article 11.1) and enhanced missions (article 11.2). Missions are the rule; enhanced "surveillance" missions may be undertaken when Member States are subject to recommendations for significantly deviating from the adjustment path towards MTOs (articles 6.2 and 10.2) and for "on-site" monitoring.

The second piece of legislation that is part of the six-pack is regulation 1177/2011.[29] This regulation is addressed to clarify the sanctions' scheme of the SGP. Article 11 of this regulation establishes that fines shall be preferred "as a rule," overturning old article 11 of regulation 1467/97, which said that a non-interest-bearing deposit was, as a rule, required. Therefore, if read in conjunction with article 126.11 TFEU, fines are the rule, and non-interest-bearing

---

[29] Council Regulation (EU) No 1177/2011 of November 8, 2011, amending Regulation (EC) No 1467/97 on speeding up and clarifying the implementation of the excessive deficit procedure. OJEU L 306/33 of 23.11.2011.

deposits are the exception (that is, non-interest-bearing deposits are not barred from the new SGP's system of sanctions). In turn, article 12 regulates how to calculate the fine; it shall be composed of a fixed and a variable component. The fixed component is 0.2 percent GDP, and the variable component must amount to one-tenth of either the difference between the sanctioned Member State's deficit in the preceding year and the deficit it should have had or the government balance in the same year if "non-compliance" with budgetary discipline includes the debt criterion. Furthermore, article 12.2 indicates that the Council "shall" intensify sanctions by imposing an additional fine if the failing Member State does not comply with the Council's notice "in each year following that in which [the original fine was imposed]"; this fine must be calculated using the same method noted above. Finally, article 12.3 establishes a limit of 0.5 percent GDP that no single fine can exceed. Recall that sanctions are only imposed on Eurozone Member States, as paragraph 22 of regulation 1177/2011 recalls, by remitting to article 136 TFEU.

Regulation 1177/2011 is supplemented by regulation 1173/2011,[30] which streamlines the sanctions scheme of the Union for euro-area Member States. In essence, this regulation establishes and reinforces the system of sanctions for euro-area Member States both in the preventive and corrective limbs of the SGP. Sanctions in the preventive phase of the SGP take the form of interest-bearing deposits (article 4), whereas sanctions in the corrective phase may take the form of either interest-bearing deposits or fines (articles 5 and 6). In my interpretation, the rule established in regulation 1177/2011 applies for euro-area Member States; therefore, fines should be preferred to interest-bearing deposits. This interpretation appears adequate if we bear in mind that the 2011 and 2012 reform of the SGP goes in the direction of rigidity and not flexibility. The amount of interest-bearing deposits, non-interest-bearing deposits and fines shall have a fixed and a variable component along the lines of regulation 1177/2011. The above is at least what paragraph 22 of the preface of regulation 1173/2011 says; however, the dispositive part of the regulation only refers to the fixed component (see articles 4.1, 5.1, and 6.1). Naturally, the dispositive part takes precedence over the declarative part of the regulation; therefore, one must interpret that for the Eurozone Member States, the three types of sanction that this regulation foresees shall amount to 0.2 percent of a Member State's GDP in the preceding year. If anything, this inconsistency in the regulation and in general in the sanctioning scheme of the SGP (if we compare this regulation with regulation 1177/2011) is an illustration of the different philosophies and perspectives that cohabit with respect to the optimal rules for fiscal governance in the EU.

---

[30] Regulation (EU) No 1173/2011 of the European Parliament and of the Council of November 16, 2011, on the effective enforcement of budgetary surveillance in the euro area. OJEU L 306/1 of 23.11.2011

In the context of the general sanctions scheme of the SGP, consider regulation 1303/2013 on Structural and Investment Funds (ESI Funds).[31] Article 23 of this regulation empowers the Commission to propose that the Council suspend, partially or totally, transfers of ESI funds to Member States in specific cases, as a means of sanctioning Member States. In particular, when a Member State is under an excessive deficit procedure, the Commission can propose to the Council a level of suspension that can increase gradually up to a maximum of 100 percent of the commitments relating to the next financial year. If the Member State in question is under an excessive imbalance procedure (see below), the level of suspension can increase to up to 50 percent of the commitments (see Box 7.4).

Regulation 1173/2011 also establishes sanctions for lying; that is, sanctions for "manipulating" Member States' fiscal statistics. This regulation foresees two cases: intentionally manipulating statistics or cases of serious negligence in preparing statistics (deficit and debt data). In today's world, it is difficult to see what the second case could be, although this difference most likely redirects us to an evidence-finding problem: it might be difficult to prove that a Member State voluntarily cooked its books, but it could be easier to show that, irrespective of whether there was intention, the books were incorrect. In any case, the fine for either cannot exceed the 0.2 percent GDP limit that the regulation establishes for other sanctions (article 8).

One important innovation of this regulation is that it establishes what is known as "reversed qualified majority voting." This point applies to all three types of sanctions. In this system, the Commission recommends a sanction, and if the Council does not reject it by a qualified majority vote, then the sanction shall be deemed adopted (see articles 4.2, 5.2, and 6.2).[32] Consider that the Fiscal Compact speaks of "automatic" sanctions (article 3 1(e)).[33] Under regulation 1173/2011, sanctions are not exactly automatic, but to this end, they require the Council to react to a Commission recommendation. This requirement is as close to automaticity as was possible to achieve in this field (Armstrong, 2013).

A final point that this regulation establishes is that sanctions have a European administrative nature (article 9). This point is important, not only

---

[31] Regulation (EU) No 1303/2013 of the European Parliament and of the Council of December 17, 2013, lays down common provisions on the European Regional Development Fund, the European Social Fund, the Cohesion Fund, the European Agricultural Fund for Rural Development, and the European Maritime and Fisheries Fund. It also lays down general provisions on the European Regional Development Fund, the European Social Fund, the Cohesion Fund, and the European Maritime and Fisheries Fund and repeals Council Regulation (EC) No 1083/2006. OJEU, 20.12.2013. L 347/320.

[32] In turn, the Fiscal Compact sets up another instance of reversed qualified majority voting in its article 7.

[33] The Fiscal Compact is ambivalent on this point; it speaks of automatic sanctions in article 3.1 (e)) in general terms, but in turn, article 3.2 appears to leave the establishment of automatic sanctions to the Member States, as was stated in Section 4.2.

because it places the entire fiscal sanctioning scheme for the Eurozone members in the field of administrative law explicitly but also because it provides a further argument showing that the EU acts here as the administration and the EU members (in this case, the Eurozone members) as the administered bodies. This argument connects with the idea that the *permissum videtur* principle and its reverse, *permissae prohibita*, apply in the field of EU economic governance (which includes monetary and fiscal governance), as discussed in Chapter 3 above. Apparently, the fiction that the EU functions as the administration and Member States as though they were the administered bodies is also assumed by the drafters of the EU legislation on European economic governance.

As a final point, recall that the previous scheme occurs within the framework of article 126 TFEU, which sets the basic procedural traits of the EDP. This procedure is detailed in Box 7.3.

Directive 2011/85[34] is the fourth tendon of the six-pack legislation. It harmonizes the characteristics that Member State budgetary frameworks must have. It obliges Member States to use numerical rules in their respective budgetary exercises (article 5). It also instructs them to use the ESA 95[35] standard to prepare data to draft their budgets (article 3.2(b)). Finally, it insists on the idea that the national budgetary exercises must not have an annual basis but rather must be understood as a multiannual exercise, much in line with the MTO concept (articles 2e and 9). In reality, directive 2011/85 is a miscellaneous construct of some of the basic ideas that rule the coordination of the EU system of fiscal governance, in particular in the field of budget preparation by Member States.

Of more importance are the two remaining pieces of the six-pack legislation. These are, respectively, regulation 1176/2011,[36] on the prevention and correction of macroeconomic imbalances, and regulation 1174/2011,[37] on the correction of excessive macroeconomic imbalances in the Eurozone. Both imply a shift and a further turn to rigidity in the EU's system of fiscal governance because they add new checks on Member States and Eurozone members by adding macroeconomic stability to overall fiscal governance.

The first regulation, regulation 1176/2011, emulates the preventive and corrective sides of the SGP and establishes a preventive and corrective prong

[34] Council Directive 2011/85/EU of November 8, 2011, on the requirements for budgetary frameworks of the Member States. OJEU L 306/41 of 23.11.2011.

[35] See Council regulation no 2223/96, of June 25, 1996, on the European systems of national and regional accounts in the Community.

[36] Regulation (EU) No 1176/2011 of the European Parliament and of the Council of November 16, 2011, on the prevention and correction of macroeconomic imbalances. OJEU L 306/25 of 23.11.2011.

[37] Regulation (EU) No 1174/2011 of the European Parliament and of the Council of November 16, 2011, on enforcement measures to correct excessive macroeconomic imbalances in the euro area. OJEU L 306/8 of 23.11.2011.

Box 7.3: Article 126 Excessive Deficit Procedure: basic traits

Commission makes a proposal on the existence of an excessive deficit in a Member State and sends it to the Council

On the basis of the Commission proposal, the Council decides that an Excessive Deficit exists

The Commission adopts a recommendation to end the excessive deficit

The Council adopts a recommendation, on the basis of the previous Commission's recommendation, on ending the excessive deficit, and sends it to the Member State

The Council makes the recommendation public if it understands that the Member State did not abide by the Council's recommendation

The Council decides that the Member State takes measures to bring down deficit

The Council decides to sanction the Member State, if the Member State fails to comply with the Council's decision

of what it refers to as "macroeconomic imbalances." Macroeconomic imbalances are defined as macroeconomic trends adversely affecting, or with the potential to adversely affect, the proper functioning of the economy of a Member State, the economic and monetary union or the Union as a whole (article 2.1). In turn, an "excessive" imbalance means a severe fiscal disparity, one that jeopardizes or risks jeopardizing the proper functioning of the economic and monetary Union (article 2.2). Therefore, this second situation is defined in more restrictive terms than the first one.

The aim of this regulation is therefore to "broaden" the scope of fiscal surveillance and extend it to the macroeconomic dynamics of the Member States. It attempts therefore to close a surveillance circle. On the one hand, this attempt implies a more ample understanding of the very concept of fiscal governance because it integrates a deeper view of the macroeconomic fundamentals of Member States; on the other hand, it does so in a very rule-based fashion. The flavor of numerical targets and limits that is so present in the nuclear parts of the SGP is also in place here. In this sense, the core of the mechanism is the so-called "scoreboard." This instrument is defined in article 4 of the regulation as a set of indicators that should be in place to facilitate an early identification and monitoring of imbalances. In principle, regulation 1176/2011 does not establish numerical limits. It only refers to general indicators that the Commission must set up and include in the scoreboard. These are, for example, economic growth, employment and unemployment performance, and nominal and real convergence inside and outside the euro area. However, article 4.4, second paragraph, says that the scoreboard shall include indicative upper and lower alert "thresholds."

Regulation 1176/2011 defines a macroeconomic imbalance procedure. The whole system works as follows. It first establishes an alert mechanism (article 3) whose central piece is a Commission's annual report that contains a qualitative economic and financial assessment of Member States' performance that is made based on the scoreboard. An element of flexibility is that the Commission cannot base its conclusions on a "mechanical reading" of the scoreboard indicators. In turn, article 3.5 says that the Council and the Euro-group shall discuss the Commission's annual report. This examination prompts what is called the "in-depth" review (article 5); based on the previous Council and Euro-group's discussions, the Commission undertakes an in-depth review of particular Member States that can be affected by imbalances. If, based on the previous exercise, the Commission considers that a country is experiencing imbalances, it can issue a recommendation to the Council that, in turn, can address a recommendation to the Member State in question (article 6.1). This option is what the regulation calls "preventive action." However, the regulation opens up another option, which is that the Commission might recommend that the Council initiate an excessive imbalance procedure against the Member State in question (article 7). Upon this Commission recommendation, the Council might establish the existence of an excessive imbalance in a particular Member State via a recommendation.

Once the Member State in question receives the Council's recommendation, it then must design a corrective action plan. The Council must then endorse or reject the plan. If the plan is rejected, then the Member State in question must submit another corrective action plan, and so forth. If, alternatively, the Council agrees on the plan, then it endorses the plan through a recommendation. Regulation 1176/2011 also provides for the monitoring and assessment of the corrective action plan as endorsed by the Council's recommendation. Concerning monitoring (article 9), the corrected Member State must present to the Council and the Commission, at regular intervals, progress reports, which might even lead to the Member State in question submitting a revised corrective action plan. Concerning assessment (article 10), the article includes what could be called the "sanctioning" side of the whole procedure. The corrective arm of the excessive deficit procedure (for Member States outside the Eurozone) only includes sanctions based on naming and shaming. If the EU institutions detect noncompliance with the recommended corrective action, the Council shall adopt a decision establishing noncompliance and shall make public the conclusions of the surveillance missions based on which the noncompliance decision was adopted. Note that a system of reversed qualified majority voting is also in place here (article 10.4(2)); the Council's decision is based on a Commission recommendation that the Council can therefore reject. This procedural quagmire is supplemented by the possibility of closing the excessive imbalance procedure as soon as the Council decides that the Member State in question is no longer affected by an excessive imbalance (article 10.5).

Regulation 1174/2011 reinforces the previous sanctioning scheme for the Eurozone members. Whereas regulation 1176/2011 established, as has been commented on, a system of naming and shaming for the rest of the Member States, this regulation sets up real sanctions for Eurozone members. In fact, paragraph 16 of this regulation states that the imposition of sanctions on Eurozone Member States must be the rule and not the exception, which implies that the naming and shaming system of regulation 1176/2011 can also be applied to Eurozone members, although as a default procedure. Regulation 1174/2011 therefore takes precedence over regulation 1176/2011 in the Eurozone.

The sanctions that this piece of legislation foresees are of two types: interest-bearing deposits and fines. The first type is to be imposed when Member States do not take the corrective action that is recommended by the Council. In turn, fines shall be imposed when two successive Council recommendations have been adopted in the same imbalance procedure and the Council considers that the corrected Member State's corrective plan is insufficient or when two successive Council decisions have been adopted stating that the corrected

Box 7.4: Sanctioning scheme for Eurozone Member States under current SGP

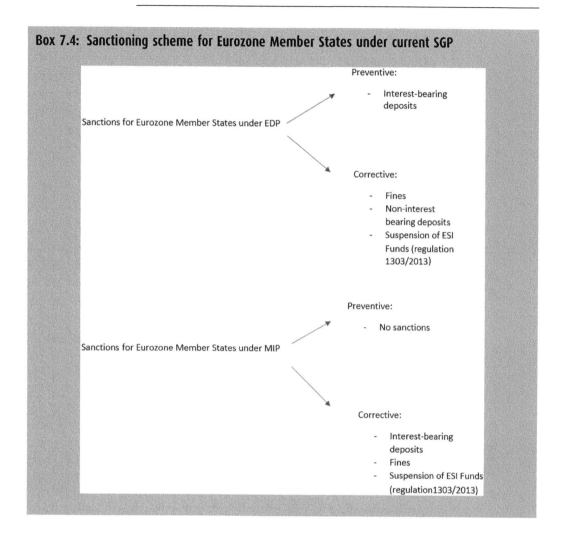

Member State did not comply with the Council's recommendation. Again, a system of reversed qualified majority voting is established here; the Commission makes the appropriate sanctioning recommendations, which can be lifted if the Council rejects them by a qualified majority vote. Furthermore, article 3.5 of the regulation establishes the amount of the two types of sanctions (0.1 percent of the corrected Member State's GDP in the preceding year). Finally, another element of flexibility within rigidity is established here, because the European Commission might propose that the Council reduce (or even cancel) both types of sanctions in two cases: if exceptional circumstances occurred or if the corrected Member State issued a reasoned request to the Commission in this sense. Although the regulation does not clarify this point, in my opinion, article 3.3 (Council's reversed qualified majority voting) also applies here.

7.3.3 Two-Pack

The second leg of what is now the SGP is the so-called "two-pack" legislation. The two-pack is formed by regulations 472/2013[38] and 473/2013.[39] The first piece of legislation regulates the situation in which Eurozone Member States are placed under "enhanced surveillance" by the European Commission. This situation can occur in two cases: when Member States are experiencing or threaten to experience serious financial difficulties or when they are subject to a bailout program (articles 2.1 and 2.3). Member States under an enhanced surveillance program are subject to a number of obligations, above all of a reporting type, to the EU institutions, particularly the EU Commission (see articles 3 to 9 of the regulation).

Article 3 of the regulation sets up what is known in lay language as the "Troika"; "enhanced surveillance" shall be conducted by the Commission (as said previously) in cooperation with the ECB and (if appropriate) the IMF (in addition to the ESAs and the ESRB; see chapter 5). In addition to placing bailed-out Member States in an enhanced surveillance program, regulation 472/2013 imposes on these Member States the obligation to draft macroeconomic adjustment programs (article 7). Macroeconomic adjustment programs shall "build on and substitute" economic partnership programs under regulation 473/2013 (see below). Briefly, Member States must indicate in their macroeconomic adjustment programs how they plan to return to economic normality once they have been subject to a bailout program. The program is to be approved by the Council based on a proposal from the Commission. Note that the program must be consistent with MOUs. According to article 7.2 second indent, the Commission is responsible for ensuring coherence in this domain.

The program must also be consistent with other parts of the EU system of economic and fiscal governance. With respect to the SGP (*stricto sensu*), regulation 472/2013 establishes that the Member State in question must integrate the stability program into its macroeconomic adjustment program (article 10.1); therefore, such Member State shall be exempt from its obligation to submit the stability program separately. Neither shall regulation 1176/2011 (macroeconomic imbalance procedure) apply to the Member State in question, with the exception of the scoreboard indicators, which shall be integrated into the monitoring of the macroeconomic

---

[38] Regulation (EU) No 472/2013 of the European Parliament and of the Council of May 21, 2013, on the strengthening of economic and budgetary surveillance of Member States in the euro area experiencing or threatened with serious difficulties with respect to their financial stability. OJEU L 140/1 of 27.5.2013.

[39] Regulation (EU) No 473/2013 of the European Parliament and of the Council of May 21, 2013 on common provisions for monitoring and assessing draft budgetary plans and ensuring the correction of excessive deficit of the Member States in the euro area. OJEU L 140/11 of May 27, 2013.

adjustment program (article 11). Additionally, the Member State under a macroeconomic program shall be exempted from the European Semester obligations (established by regulation 1466/97) (article 12) and from producing the so-called "economic partnership programmes" (established by regulation 473/2013) (article 13).

Article 14 of regulation 472/2013 establishes what is referred to as "Post-programme surveillance." A Member State shall be subject to this program to the extent that a minimum of 75 percent of the bailout moneys have not been repaid to the respective bailing-out funds whence the moneys came. In essence, a country under post-program surveillance must comply with a number of obligations, essentially of a reporting type, along much the same lines as those that Member States under an enhanced surveillance program must implement.

In turn, regulation 473/2013 reinforces monitoring of budgetary policies for the Eurozone members and, in particular, the preventive side of the SGP. Initially, this regulation establishes a number of deadlines. First, medium-term national fiscal plans (which can be the same document as the stability program) must be made public by Eurozone Member States between April 15 and April 30 each year (article 4). Second, the draft government budgets of Eurozone Member States must be made public no later than October 15 (article 6). They must also submit this document to the European Commission within that deadline. Third, the central government budgets must be adopted no later than December 31 (article 4.3).

Once the draft budget is submitted by the Member States to the European Commission, a budget assessment process starts. Therefore, the Commission must adopt opinions on each of the draft budgets no later than November 30 (article 7). This Commission opinion must be sent to the Euro-group, which shall discuss it. The results of such discussions must be made public "where appropriate," says article 7.5. Finally, the Commission's opinion can have an effect when the Commission itself recommends the imposition of a non-interest-bearing deposit or when the Council is deciding whether an excessive deficit exists (see article 12.1).

Regulation 473/2013 creates yet another document that Eurozone Member States must produce, the so-called "economic partnership programme" (article 9). Therefore, when the Council decides that an excessive deficit exists in a Member State, this Member State must produce this document and send it to the Commission and the Council. In this document, the Member State in question must describe all of the measures (e.g., structural reforms) that it intends to take to reduce its deficit. Recall that this requirement is an important innovation with respect to the "standard" excessive deficit procedure. In the standard excessive deficit procedure, Member States must only comply with the Council's decisions on deficit reduction. Instead, under regulation 473/2013, Eurozone Member States must create plans (the economic partnership programs) indicating

Table 7.2: Six-pack plus two-pack legislation: summary

Regulation 1175/2011	Amends regulation 1466/97
	Structural balance as the reference
Regulation1177/2011	Amends regulation 1467/97
	Basic traits of sanctions
Regulation1173/2011	Streamlines sanctions for Eurozone members
Directive 2011/85	Budgetary frameworks for Member States
	Numerical fiscal rules
Regulation 1176/2011	Macroeconomic imbalances
	Preventive and corrective arms
Regulation 1174/2011	Sanctions macroeconomic imbalance procedure for
	Eurozone members
Regulation 472/2013	Enhanced surveillance for Eurozone members under bailout
	or experiencing serious difficulties
Regulation 473/2013	Deadlines for budget process Eurozone members
	Economic partnership programs in the case of excessive
	procedure

through which measures and reforms they will reduce the excess of deficit. In turn, the Council must adopt an opinion on the economic partnership program. Member States must implement the economic partnership program in the light of such an opinion. In turn, article 9.5 of this regulation states that corrective action plans (plans that Member States must design if immersed in a macroeconomic imbalance procedure) can replace, if properly amended, the economic partnership programs. However, if the economic partnership program is submitted before the corrective action plan, then the measures included in the former can be incorporated in the latter, if appropriate. Finally, article 13 establishes that a Member State subject to a macroeconomic adjustment program (that is, when it is receiving a bailout) shall be exempted from submitting the economic partnership program. The details of the economic partnership program would go into the macroeconomic adjustment program, as was mentioned previously.

7.4 Future Perspectives on Reform: The Commission Communication of 2015

In recent times, the Commission has proposed a new interpretation of the SGP's rules in the direction of flexibility. The origin of this new twist towards flexibility is to be found in the Political Guidelines for the new Commission, which its president, Jean-Claude Juncker, presented to the European

Table 7.3: SGP evolution until 2013 (in italics, the SGP's main hallmarks)

Items	Maastricht	SGP	Regulation 1466	Regulation 1467	Regulation 1055	Regulation 1056	Fiscal Compact
Reference value	*Reference values: 3% and 60%*	CTBOS criterion	3% disappears; safety margin; CTBOS	Idem	3%; safety margin Consolidation effort 0.5% GDP per year, "benchmark"	Does not mention 3% or 60% Consolidation effort 0.5% GDP per year, "benchmark"	*0.5% structural deficit*
MTO	No reference to medium-term objectives	MTO close to balance or in surplus	MTO close to balance or in surplus. Safety margin	Idem	*Differentiated MTOs*; range from (−)1% of GDP and close to balance or in surplus, in cyclically adjusted terms	Appropriately take into account developments in MTOs	Country-specific MTOs
Deadline to lower deficit	"Given period" and "time limit" to reduce deficits	1 year to correct deficit unless special circumstances	1 year to correct deficit unless special circumstances	1 year to correct deficit unless special circumstances		1 year to correct deficit unless special circumstances	Time frame proposed by the Commission taking into account country-specific sustainability risks Reduction excess of public debt 1/20 per year Regulation 1177/2011: 1 year to correct deficit unless special circumstances
Exceptions	"Unless" vague clauses	Severe recessions: 0.75% drop in GDP (but also mention of "unless… special circumstances")	Severe recessions: 2%. From 0.75% to less than 2%, an exception is discretionary		Major exceptions: structural reforms and pension reform	"All the relevant factors" and "any other factors"	1% structural deficit when government debt significantly below 60%

Parliament on July 15, 2014,[40] before the vote on the Commission College occurred. On this occasion, the president stated the following:

> As regards the use of national budgets for growth and investment, we must – as reaffirmed by the European Council on 27 June 2014 – respect the Stability and Growth Pact, while making the best possible use of the flexibility that is built into the existing rules of the Pact, as reformed in 2005 and 2011. I intend to issue concrete guidance on this as part of my ambitious Jobs, Growth and Investment Package.

Thus, flexibility is the new buzzword in Brussels, at least with respect to the SGP. Furthermore, in its 2015 Annual Growth Survey,[41] the Commission signaled investment, structural reforms and fiscal responsibility as the key elements of the Union's new economic strategy to create jobs and growth. In this document, the Commission said the following:

> To strengthen the link between structural reforms, investment and fiscal responsibility, the Commission will also provide further guidance on the best possible use of the flexibility that is built into the existing rules of the Stability and Growth Pact.

In turn, the European Council of December 2014 indirectly endorsed this Commission stance.[42] Following this endorsement, the European Commission published the Communication "Making the best use of the flexibility within the existing rules of the stability and growth pact" of January 13, 2015.[43]

In essence, the European Commission divides its Communication into three parts, not without reminding in its introduction that its aim is to "provide further guidance on the best possible use of the flexibility that is built into the existing rules of the SGP without changing these rules." The three parts to which I refer are investment, structural reforms, and cyclical conditions. The Commission proposes, therefore, a new approach to implementing the SGP's rules concerning these three particular aspects, but not others. However, the

---

[40] "A New Start for Europe: My Agenda for Jobs, Growth, Fairness and Democratic Change Political Guidelines for the next European Commission Opening Statement in the European Parliament Plenary Session Strasbourg, 15 July 2014," available at https://ec.europa.eu/commission/sites/beta-political/files/juncker-political-guidelines-speech_en_0.pdf.

[41] Communication from the Commission to the European Parliament, the Council, the European Central Bank, the European Economic and Social Committee, the Committee of the Regions and the European Investment Bank. Annual Growth Survey 2015. Brussels, 28.11.2014 COM (2014) 902 final.

[42] "The European Council takes note of the favourable position the Commission has indicated towards such capital contributions in the context of the assessment of public finances under the Stability and Growth Pact, necessarily in line with the flexibility that is built into its existing rules." See European Council Conclusions, 18 December 2014, paragraph 1 a.

[43] Communication from the Commission to the European Parliament, the Council, the European Central Bank, the Economic and Social Committee, the Committee of the Regions and the European Investment Bank, Strasbourg, 13.1.2015 COM(2015) 12 final provisional.

third item, cyclical conditions, is a sort of general category in which other uses of flexibility, which might not fall into the first two items, can find accommodation.

The first, investment, is linked to the new European Fund for Strategic Investment (EFSI).[44] The EFSI is part of the so-called "Investment Plan for Europe."[45] Consider that the design, development and implementation of this Plan were among the main political commitments of President Jean-Claude Juncker when he took office in November 2014.[46] The Plan was a way to mark distance from Barroso's Commission and the materialization of the new, friendlier outlook, which the new Commission was adopting towards the citizens of the European Union.[47] The idea behind the Investment Plan for Europe was to mobilize up to €315 billion. The original plan was thereafter to be increased to €500 billion,[48] which does not mean that the European Fund for Strategic Investment amounted to €500 billion. In fact, the original plan endowed the Fund with only a small fraction of the whole investment plan (€31 billion). More than a real investment plan, the EFSI rested on the multiplier idea: investment from the EU institutions would multiply investment efforts from other partners.[49] Furthermore, the moneys of the Fund came from other, pre-existing, parts of the EU budget (€21 billion) plus from the European Investment Bank (€5 billion).[50] These funds are now redirected to steer investment in the EU; however, there is no trace of new, fresh, money.

[44] See Regulation (EU) 2015/1017 of the European Parliament and of the Council of June 25, 2015, on the European Fund for Strategic Investments, the European Investment Advisory Hub and the European Investment Project Portal and amending Regulations (EU) No 1291/2013 and (EU) No 1316/2013 – the European Fund for Strategic Investments. OJEU L 169/1 of 1.7.2015.

[45] Communication from the Commission to the European Parliament, the Council, the European Central Bank, the European Economic and Social Committee, the Committee of the Regions and the European Investment Bank. An Investment Plan for Europe. Brussels, 26.11.2014 COM (2014) 903 final.

[46] See "A New Start for Europe: My Agenda for Jobs, Growth, Fairness and Democratic Change" Political Guidelines for the next European Commission. Opening Statement in the European Parliament Plenary Session. Strasbourg, July 15, 2014.

[47] Barroso set up the so-called "European Recovery Plan" in November 2008. However, this plan was conceived as an economic stimulus to boost the economy in the first years of the crisis. Furthermore, the funding came, above all, from the Member States. See my remarks on the European Recovery Plan in Chapter 10 below.

[48] See Proposal for a Regulation of the European Parliament and of the Council amending Regulations (EU) No 1316/2013 and (EU) 2015/1017 concerning the extension of the duration of the European Fund for Strategic Investments and the introduction of technical enhancements for that Fund and the European Investment Advisory Hub {SWD(2016) 297 final} {SWD(2016) 298 final}. Brussels, 14.9.2016 COM(2016) 597 final 2016/0276 (COD).

[49] According to regulation 2015/1017, the EU's resources are therefore an "EU guarantee," not a direct investment.

[50] See Communication from the Commission to the European Parliament, the Council, the European Central Bank, the European Economic and Social Committee, the Committee of the Regions and the European Investment Bank. An Investment Plan for Europe. Brussels, 26.11.2014. COM(2014) 903 final, at page 7. The proposal for a regulation of the European

Nevertheless, what the Commission proposes concerning the EFSI is that "national contributions [to this Fund] will not be taken into account when defining the fiscal adjustment under either the preventive or the corrective arm of the [SGP]." The idea is therefore that Member State contributions to the EFSI will not be considered an excess of deficit. Furthermore, concerning "other investments under the preventive arm of the Pact" (which would go beyond the EFSI), the Commission's new interpretation is that they will be allowed if a number of conditions are fulfilled, among which, notably, is the requirement that the investor Member State does not overshoot the 3 percent deficit ceiling. In this domain, eligible investments are Member State investments in projects co-funded by the EU under the Structural and Cohesion policy, Trans-European Networks and the Connecting Europe Facility, and national co-financing of projects also co-financed by the European Fund for Strategic Investments.

Concerning the second area in which the European Commission proposes to implement flexibility and structural reforms, the Commission will from now on consider the "positive fiscal impact" of structural reforms (i.e., pension reform) under the preventive arm of the SGP provided that they are "major," that "they have verifiable, direct long-term positive budgetary effects," and "are fully implemented." Furthermore, concerning structural reforms under the corrective arm of the SGP, the Commission will consider a number of factors before initiating an EDP or in later stages of an EDP that has already been opened. One of these factors is the adoption of a "dedicated" structural reform plan. In particular, concerning pension reform, the Commission even goes as far as to state that an EDP might be closed even when the deficit overshoots the 3 percent ceiling, provided that the excess of deficit is "wholly due" to the costs of implementing the pension reform.

Finally, concerning the third area in which the Commission intends to apply flexibility, cyclical conditions, the Commission states that it will apply a new matrix (established in Annex 2 of the Communication) to better consider the effect that the business cycle has on the preventive arm of the pact. In the annex, the Commission differentiates among five different scenarios, ordered as a function of their economic gravity: exceptionally bad times, very bad times, bad times, normal times, and good times. Then, the Commission projects two different types of situations on each of these scenarios: a situation in which debt is less than 60 percent and a situation in which debt is greater than 60 percent. The type of fiscal adjustment effort that Member States must undertake depends therefore upon the specific scenario that they are experiencing and upon the situation in terms of the debt levels at which

Parliament and of the Council amending Regulations (EU) No 1316/2013 and (EU) 2015/1017 proposes to raise the endowment of the EFSI from €16 billion to €26 billion. See page 6.

they find themselves, whether the consolidation effort is higher as the scenario improves in the first situation or smaller as the scenario worsens in the second situation. The point is that in exceptionally bad times, which are defined as real growth being below zero or output gap being below –4 percent GDP, no adjustment is needed at all, independently of whether a Member State has a debt above or below 60 percent GDP.

The Commission also considers, within the general heading of cyclical conditions, two further cases: the case of unexpected fall in economic activity under the corrective arm of the SGP and the case of severe economic downturn in the Eurozone or in the Union as a whole. In the first case, the Commission intends to differentiate between fiscal consolidation actions and fiscal consolidation outcomes. The latter are, in the Commission's interpretation, "often" influenced by exogenous developments outside the control of national governments. Thus, the Commission will be more flexible with Member States in these cases, giving, for example, additional time to correct the excessive nominal deficit without incurring any financial sanctions or a suspension of commitments or payments of the European Structural and Investment Funds. With respect to the second case, severe economic downturn, the Commission reports that "this provision [of article 3 of regulation 1467/97] has so far never been applied"; now, the Commission proposes to use it "when necessary," although the Commission acknowledges that it was *de facto* implemented when this institution redesigned the fiscal adjustment paths of some Member States during the worst part of the 2008 crisis.

In conclusion, many of the changes now proposed by the Commission are in one way or another present in the motley SGP regulatory landscape. However, what the Commission is now announcing is to employ the more open parts of the SGP to instill more flexibility in its implementation in what is a new turn – but surely not the last one – in the life of the Pact.

7.5 Implementation of the SGP

What is the status of the implementation of the SGP? Has the Pact been successful in limiting fiscal profligacy in Member States? The first point that is important to have in mind with respect to the implementation and effectiveness of the SGP is that no sanctions have been imposed thus far under the EDP (European Court of Auditors, 2016: 73), whereas the excessive imbalance procedure has not been implemented to date (European Commission, 2016). For institutions (see the European Court of Auditors, above) and most commentators (see for example Heipertz & Verdun, 2010; Hann, Berger, & Jensen, 2004), this omission clearly called into question not only the effectiveness of the SGP but also its credibility (see below). For others, it instead proved the inherent flexibility of the entire system (Buiter et al., 1993; Buiter & Grafe, 2004).

However, the real question that must be asked is whether, despite sanctions not having been imposed, the whole system yields results. I believe that this question is much more appropriate than the question of trying to measure the effectiveness of the SGP from the purely legalistic perspective of sanctions. Perhaps sanctions were not imposed because it was not ultimately necessary to impose them. From this perspective, the nonimposition of sanctions would not be proof of the SGP's failure but evidence of its success. In other words, the right question to be asked here is about the counterfactual situation. Would the fiscal stance of Member States (above all of Eurozone Member States) have improved, remained the same, or worsened without the SGP?

The academic literature that has addressed this issue is not aligned on this point. For example, Ioannou and Stracca (2011) find that the SGP was neutral with respect to Member States' fiscal policy; that is, it had no effect upon them. "Our results indicate that the SGP has not delivered according to its strictest benchmark," say these authors. For de Grauwe (2008), the problem lies in the lack of accountability of the Commission, which in turn makes the SGP unsustainable. Thus, each time a conflict arises between the Commission and the national governments, the former is bound to lose. According to de Grauwe, this result occurred in 2003 when Germany and France forced a reform of the SGP to make it more flexible. "It will happen again when conflicts arise between the Commission and the national governments." Thus, for the author, the SGP is a fragile institutional construction that is unlikely to yield results. Hallerberg, Strauch, and Von Hagen (2010) indicate that the data suggest that the SGP was not effective in maintaining the deficit below 3 percent. "At the same time, this is not the whole story" because some Member States fared better than others did in this respect. The puzzle would be therefore to find an answer to the question of why, within this general landscape of an unsuccessful implementation of the SGP, some national budgets deteriorated more than did others.

In turn, Koehler and König (2014) directly address the counterfactual question and offer a more nuanced account of the effectiveness of the SGP. These authors compare eleven Eurozone members with a control group of nonmembers of the Eurozone to check the counterfactual. They measure the overall SGP performance with respect to the debt criterion (not the deficit one[51]). According to them, the SGP was successful with respect to the donor Member States but played a much lesser role concerning the recipient countries. In other words, the donor countries were better off with the euro and the SGP than without it, whereas the recipient countries would have been better off without the euro and the SGP in fiscal terms (in particular, with respect to the control of public debt). Among the second group there are however

---

[51] This point might clearly bias the entire counterfactual exercise because the debt criterion has played a secondary role as a fiscal objective until recently, as has been discussed in this and the previous chapter.

differences: whereas the effect of the euro and the SGP was most likely more positive for countries such as Spain and Ireland, it was clearly negative for the rest of the recipient Member States (Greece, Portugal, and Italy). In other words, the latter group would have been better off in terms of their fiscal performance without the SGP rather than with the SGP.

However, these results must be interpreted with caution, first because, different from what the authors imply in their conclusions, this outcome would reveal a failure, rather than a success, of the SGP. That is, those countries that would benefit more from the SGP would precisely be those countries that would need it less, the rich countries of the EU. Recall that the SGP was, among other things, an attempt by northern countries (Germany in particular) to fiscally discipline periphery Member States in exchange for their participation in the euro in the first round (Sinn, 2014). If Koehler and König's analysis were further empirically backed, then the whole operation would have been problematic because those countries that need it more are the countries that would control their fiscal stance better outside the euro and the SGP. Second, caution should also be exercised because in their analysis it is difficult to differentiate between the effects of being part of the Eurozone (and there- fore, of having delegated monetary policy to a central agency such as the ECB) and the effect of the SGP's implementation by itself, independently of the euro.

A different perspective is provided by the mechanism shown in Chapter 6 of this book. This mechanism implies that the SGP would have the effect of being a signal that the markets would use in their decisions concerning whether to penalize a given Member State, which would be the actual benchmark against which the SGP should most likely be measured. Thus, markets would take the SGP's ceilings as a signal of good or bad economic fiscal and economic performance (independently of whether these ceilings make sense and reveal more fundamental economic developments). Therefore, if a Member State did not respect these ceilings, the markets would penalize it, and if it did, then the markets would prime it. As de Grauwe (2016) has noted, the markets only started to differentiate among Member States once the 2008 crisis erupted.[52]

Thus, the markets did not focus on these ceilings before the crisis (and thereby revealed a lack of effectiveness of the SGP), whereas they woke up and did notice them during the crisis, in principle revealing a more effective use of

---

[52] De Grauwe points out the following (2016: 226): "At the start of the eurozone in 1999, the devaluation risk disappeared; the spreads dropped to close to zero and remained in that position until 2008. Thus, during this period the financial markets considered that investing in, say, a Greek government bond carried the same risk as investing in a German government bond. In other words, the markets perceived the default risk on Greek government bonds to be the same as on German government bonds. In 2008, perceptions dramatically changed, and spreads increased and reached levels that were higher than in the 1990s. Thus, suddenly, the markets perceived huge default risks on the government bonds of countries such as Ireland, Portugal, Greece and Italy." His point is that markets are not efficient. From this perspective the SGP would never work, due to how markets' rationality (or lack of it) works.

the SGP. However, the hypothesis is that for this system to keep working, it would be important to keep it simple and clear. The idea would be that, to the extent that the ceilings change (and we have shown how they do change, for example with the Fiscal Compact insistence on the structural deficit of 0.5 percent rather than employing the 3 percent and 60 percent limits) and to the extent that the SGP's rules are further complicated, the markets would be unable to develop a clear picture of the Member States' fiscal performance. Confirmation of this perspective by future evidence on the performance of the SGP would indicate a failure rather than a success of the SGP in terms of its effectiveness. In turn, if this effectiveness problem was detected and further confirmed, it would clearly serve to undermine the overall credibility of the SGP.

7.6 SGP from the "Law as Credibility" Perspective

Now that the evolution of the SGP has been described, in this and the preceding chapter, it is important to analyze it from the perspective of law as credibility. As the European Commission itself says in the Communication of 2015, which has been analyzed above, "the credibility of the agreed [SGP] rules is key for the sustainability of public finances and for the financial stability in the euro area and in the EU as a whole ... The existence and respect of the rules have been essential to restore trust and confidence" (European Commission, 2015: 4). However, the Commission's efforts not-withstanding, the summary of what has been shown in this and the previous chapter is clear: the SGP has been subject, since its inception, to constant and continuous amendments. Obviously, this symptom clearly suggests that the SGP is not an equilibrium: when the players of a game have incentives to modify the status quo and in fact modify it, then the system (in this case, the SGP) is far from credible. The SGP has been modified into solely a function of Member State short-term interests, coupled with the economic context that those Member States were experiencing at particular junctures of the EU's history. Interests plus a varied array of contingencies have therefore marked the life of the SGP. In my opinion, it is possible to make the following prediction: the SGP will be prone to new amendments, modifications, and updates in the future.

The reason why the SGP is not an equilibrium and will most likely not be one in the near future has very little to do with either rigidity or flexibility. A new turn to flexibility (as the Commission is advocating for now), or a further twist in the rigidity traits that the SGP is showing at present, would not do. This problem is not the core problem of the SGP. Instead, the problem relates to the current structure of the EU economic and, more specifically, the fiscal governance system.

Figure 7.3 plots a geometric representation of what the EU's structure of economic and fiscal governance should look like. This triangle is formed by

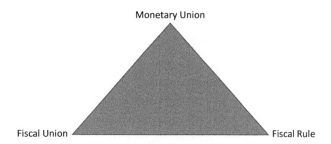

Figure 7.3: Economic and fiscal governance in equilibrium

three vertexes: the vertex of monetary union at the top, the vertex of fiscal rules at the right-hand side of the triangle, and the vertex of fiscal or transfers union at the left-hand side of the triangle. This model is for example currently in place in the USA (Fabbrini, 2016). The vertex "monetary union" is represented by the dollar and the Fed in the US; the vertex "fiscal rules" is essentially represented by the no-bailout requirement, which (as seen in Chapter 8 below) is more a custom than a legally binding norm in this country; and the vertex "transfers union" is represented by the US federal government budget.

The system works as follows. When a State of the Union experiences serious financial problems, it defaults. At that point, two systems are activated: on the one hand, the Fed activates quantitative easing; on the other hand, and this point is important in this context, the federal government makes transfers (which take different forms; for example, the federal government covers at least part of the unemployment benefit burden of the State which defaulted, and/or it makes tax cuts). Therefore, the system works. The no-bailout rule makes sense in a legal and fiscal context in which the federal government has the muscle to make transfers and alleviate the shock in the State that is suffering from the crisis. Second, this function is accompanied by a not precisely aloof willingness of the Fed to use its resources to alleviate the shock, as was shown during the 2008 crisis.

In this specific context, hard fiscal rules make little or almost no sense. The US Constitution does not include aspects similar to the EU's SGP quagmire. One must dive into the States' constitutions to find fiscal rules that are, in general terms, of a general character, in particular, the so-called "balanced budget" rule. The American National Association of State Budget Officers (2015: 39) reports the following:[53]

> The vast majority of States (46) reported having a constitutional or statutory balanced budget requirement. The governor is required to submit a balanced

---

[53] For a very good summary of the current balanced-budget rules in the US, see the National Conference of State Legislatures' "Appendix to State Balanced Budget Requirements: Provisions and Practice" at www.ncsl.org/research/fiscal-policy/state-constitutional-and-statutory-requirements-fo.aspx.

Box 7.5: Article IV, Section 12, California Constitution: the balanced-budget rule

(a) Within the first 10 days of each calendar year, the Governor shall submit to the Legislature, with an explanatory message, a budget for the ensuing fiscal year containing itemized statements for recommended state expenditures and estimated state revenues. If recommended expenditures exceed estimated revenues, the Governor shall recommend the sources from which the additional revenues should be provided.

...

(g) For the 2004–05 fiscal year, or any subsequent fiscal year, the Legislature may not send to the Governor for consideration, nor may the Governor sign into law, a budget bill that would appropriate from the General Fund, for that fiscal year, a total amount that, when combined with all appropriations from the General Fund for that fiscal year made as of the date of the budget bill's passage, and the amount of any General Fund moneys transferred to the Budget Stabilization Account for that fiscal year pursuant to Section 20 of Article XVI, exceeds General Fund revenues for that fiscal year estimated as of the date of the budget bill's passage. That estimate of General Fund revenues shall be set forth in the budget bill passed by the Legislature.

budget in 44 states, the legislature is required to enact a balanced budget in 41 states and the budget signed by the governor is required to be balanced in 40 states. Eleven states indicated that they are permitted to carry over a budget deficit in certain circumstances.

One example of a balanced-budget rule is found in Box 7.5.

As Henning and Kessler (2012) report, US balanced-budget rules vary in terms of their degree of detail and complexity, but in general terms they are rather broad – particularly if compared with the SGP's rules. In any case, the bottom line is that rules of this type might make sense in a context in which it is for the federal government, through the federal budget, to act countercyclically in the case of an economic downturn. As was hinted before, a significant factor is that the US Constitution lacks a balanced-budget rule. Thus, the States of the Union can adhere to the balanced-budget rule because the federal government will make transfers to alleviate their economic situation. What does not make sense is to have a slim budget in Brussels coupled with strict fiscal rules not only in the center but also in Member States – as occurs now, above all after the Fiscal Compact has been adopted. In other words, the lack of the third vertex in the EU economic and fiscal governance structure causes the whole system to be prone to permanent instability, regardless of how hard or flexible the fiscal rules are. Figure 7.4 represents this situation graphically.

A counterfactual analysis is apropos here. Would the SGP's current rules make sense were the situation different – for example, if the EU had a

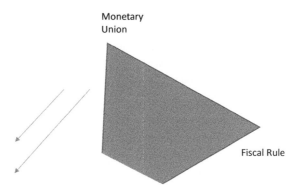

Figure 7.4: EU economic and fiscal governance system without equilibrium

Transfers Union? As previously discussed, the first counterfactual rule is plausibility. In the current state of affairs of the EU, it is very unlikely that the EU would increase the size of its budget to the point at which a Transfers Union would be possible. Nevertheless, even were a Transfers Union put in place, the SGP's rules would still not make sense and therefore would not be an equilibrium, at least in its current form.

The main reason for this situation is that in the presence of a monetary union and a Transfers Union, a State or structure such as the EU does not actually need detailed fiscal rules; the no-bailout rule (or custom) would most likely be sufficient to discipline the State in question, as occurs in the US. Therefore, the only fiscal rules that should be established were the counter-factual to become a factual situation should be very general and broad guidelines (such as the balanced-budget rules of the States of the Union) coupled with, at a maximum, procedural rules to coordinate the budget cycle of the Member States and that of the Union. It should be emphasized that the US rules never set numerical targets or define specifically how to understand their respective fiscal rules. As was stated in Chapter 6, the establishment of numerical targets only serves as a sort of self-fulfilling prophecy, which the markets might use to penalize Member States independently of their real macroeconomic performance. In summary, even were the EU to adopt a Transfers Union, the fiscal rules of the EU should be rather generic and of a procedural type to be an equilibrium.

BIBLIOGRAPHY

Armstrong, K. A. 2013, "The new governance of EU fiscal discipline," *European Law Review*, vol. 38, no. 5, pp. 601–617.

Artis, M. J. and Buti, M. 2000b, "'Close-to-balance or in surplus': a policy-maker's guide to the implementation of the Stability and Growth Pact," *JCMS: Journal of Common Market Studies*, vol. 38, pp. 563–591.

Artis, M. J. & Buti, M. 2000a, "'Close to Balance or in Surplus': A Policy Makers Guide to the Implementation of the Stability and Growth Pact," EUI (European University Institute) Working Papers, RSC no. 2000/28.

Aust, A. 2014, *Modern Treaty Law and Practice*, 3rd edn., Cambridge University Press, Cambridge.

Brunnermeier, M., James, H., & Landau, J. 2016, *The Euro and the Battle of Ideas*, Princeton University Press, Princeton, N. Jersey.

Buiter, W., Corsetti, G., & Roubini, N. 1993, "Maastricht's fiscal rules," *Economic Policy*, vol. 8, no. 16, pp. 58–100.

Buiter, W. & Grafe, C. 2004, "Patching up the Pact: some suggestions for enhancing fiscal sustainability and macroeconomic stability in an enlarged European Union," *Economics of Transition*, vol. 12, no. 1, pp. 67–102.

Cisotta, R. & Gallo, D. 2014, "The Portuguese Constitutional Court Case Law on Austerity Measures: A Reappraisal," Luiss Guido Carli Academy, Working Paper 4/2014, pp. 1–11.

Craig, P. 2012, "The Stability, Coordination, and Governance Treaty: principle, politics and pragmatism," *European Law Review*, vol. 37, no. 3, pp. 231–248.

De Grauwe, P. 2016, *Economics of Monetary Union*, 11th edn., Oxford University Press, Oxford.

2011, "Balanced budget fundamentalism," CEPS (Centre for European Policy Studies) Commentary, September 5, 2011. http://aei.pitt.edu/32338/1/De_Grauwe_on_Balanced_budget_fundamentalism_September_2011.pdf.

2008, "On the need to renovate the Eurozone," *International Finance*, vol. 11, no. 3, pp. 327–333.

De Haan, J., Berger, H., & Jansen, D. 2004, "Why has the Stability and Growth Pact failed?," *International Finance*, vol. 7, no. 2, pp. 235–260.

Estella, A. 2015, "Potential exit from the Eurozone: the case of Spain," *Indiana Journal of Global Legal Studies*, vol. 22, no. 2, pp. 335–377.

European Commission. 2016, "The Macroeconomic Imbalance Procedure. Rationale, Process, Application: A Compendium," European Economy Institutional Paper 039, November.

2002, "The EU Economy: 2002 Review," *European Economy* no. 6.

European Court of Auditors. 2016, "Further Improvements Needed to Ensure Effective Implementation of the Excessive Deficit Procedure," *Special Report*, vol. 10.

Fabbrini, F. 2016, *Economic Governance in Europe: Comparative Paradoxes and Constitutional Challenges*, Oxford University Press, Oxford.

Fasone, C. 2014, "Constitutional Courts Facing the Euro Crisis. Italy, Portugal and Spain in a Comparative Perspective.," Max Weber Programme, MWP 2014/25.

Hallerberg, M., Strauch, R. R., & von Hagen, J. 2010, *Fiscal Governance in Europe*, Cambridge University Press, Cambridge.

Heipertz, M. & Verdun, A. 2010, *Ruling Europe. The Politics of the SGP*, Cambridge University Press, Cambridge.

Henning, R. & Kessler, M. 2012, "Fiscal federalism: US history for architects of Europe's fiscal union," Peterson Institute for International Economics Working Paper 2012-1.

Hinarejos, A. 2015, *The Euro Area Crisis in Constitutional Perspective*, Cambridge University Press, Cambridge.

Koehler, S. & König, T. 2014, "Fiscal governance in the Eurozone: how effectively does the Stability and Growth Pact limit governmental debt in the euro countries?," *Political Science Research and Methods*, vol. 3, no. 2, pp. 329–351.

Krugman, P. 2012, *End this Depression Now!*, W. W. Norton & Co., New York; London.

National Association of Budget Officers. 2015, "Budget Processes in the States." https://higherlogicdownload.s3.amazonaws.com/NASBO/0f09ced0-449d-4c11-b787-105 05cd90bb9/UploadedImages/Reports/2015%20Budget%20Processes%20-%20S.pdf.

Reinhart, C. & Rogoff, K. 2009, *This Time Is Different: Eight Centuries of Financial Folly*, Princeton University Press, Princeton, N. Jersey.

Sapir, A., Aghion, P., Bertola, G., Hellwig, M., Pisani-Ferry, J., Rosati, D., Viñals, J., & Wallace, H. 2003, "An agenda for a growing Europe: Making the EU Economic System Deliver. Report of an Independent High-Level Study Group established on the initiative of the President of the European Commission." http://citeseerx.ist .psu.edu/viewdoc/download?doi=10.1.1.618.5034&rep=rep1&type=pdf

Sinn, H.-W. 2014, *The Euro-Trap: On Bursting Bubbles, Budgets and Beliefs*, Oxford University Press, Oxford.

Stiglitz, J. 2010, "Lessons from the global financial crisis of 2008," *Seoul Journal of Economics*, vol. 23, no. 3, pp. 321–339.

Wolf, M. 2015, *The Shifts and the Shocks: What We've Learned – and Have Still to Learn – from the Financial Crisis*, Penguin Books, New York.

Zettelmeyer, J., Trebesch, C., & Gulati, M. 2013, "The Greek Debt Restructuring: An Autopsy," CESifo Working Paper no. 4333.

8

European Union Bailouts (I):
General Aspects

Introduction

The economic crisis that unfolded in Europe after September 15, 2008, which is the exact date on which Lehman Brothers collapsed and filed for what is known under US law as "Chapter 11" bankruptcy protection, prompted eight bailouts of Member States of the European Union. The purpose of this chapter is to analyze this crucial European rescue program, addressed to both members and non-members of the Eurozone.

To assess the significance of EU bailouts, it is important to consider that at the time of writing, the EU has approved an amount equivalent to €525 billion in bailouts, of which approximately €380 billion has already been disbursed.[1] This figure is without considering either the standard or nonstandard measures that the ECB has taken throughout the crisis, which amounted to over €3 trillion at the peak of the crisis (May 2012) (Micossi, 2015: 12). We are discussing here the most ambitious international financial rescue operation in the history of humanity; the IMF bailouts to Latin American countries of the 1980s and the IMF Asian bailouts of the 1990s pale in comparison to the EU bailouts. It is therefore important to understand the issues that EU bailouts have posed from an intertwined legal and economic perspective.

In legal terms, the basic difficulty with EU bailouts has been the fact that, as will be discussed in this chapter, EU (or Member State) rescue operations to Member States that are in distress are ruled out by the EU Treaties. In fact, article 125 TFEU – together with article 123 TFEU – prohibited in a very clear fashion the conducting of bailouts. The main question that must therefore be addressed is how it was then possible to conduct eight (not one or two, but eight) bailouts of EU Member States in the amount previously noted. In part, the answer is provided by the fact that the EU legal and, above all, constitutional EU bailout edifice was profoundly transformed during the crisis. However, what remains to be seen is whether the emerging system will be stable – or to use this book's nomenclature, what remains to be seen is whether the emerging system is an equilibrium from a "law as credibility" perspective.

---

[1] For a summary, see Table 9.1 in Chapter 9.

To address this question, this chapter will proceed as follows. In the next section, I briefly describe and analyze the EU bailout regime that existed before the crisis. In Section 8.2, I analyze the crisis amendments to the EU bailout system. Section 8.3 is more analytical in scope because it attempts to understand the EU bailout regime from a "law as credibility" perspective. I leave for the next chapter the analysis of the specific bailouts that have been provided to Member States and an examination of the legal nature of MOUs.

8.1 EU Bailout Regime Prior to the Crisis

8.1.1 Prohibition of Bailouts

Article 125.1 TFEU stated (and still states) the following:

> The Union shall not be liable for or assume the commitments of central governments, regional, local or other public authorities, other bodies governed by public law, or public undertakings of any Member State, without prejudice to mutual financial guarantees for the joint execution of a specific project. A Member State shall not be liable for or assume the commitments of central governments, regional, local or other public authorities, other bodies governed by public law, or public undertakings of another Member State, without prejudice to mutual financial guarantees for the joint execution of a specific project.

Although the ECJ has not ruled on the direct effect of this TFEU provision, the truth of the matter is that article 125.1 is rather clear and precise – it prohibits bailouts. In other words, neither the EU nor its Member States can assume the outstanding debts that a Member State (or its subnational units, or else its other authorities governed by public law) might have assumed. The wording of this article and its redundancies (it says the same thing twice, the first time referring to the EU and the second time to its Member States) provide little room for interpretation on this point.

Two questions rapidly emerge once it is clearly established that article 125.1 rules out bailouts. First, what exactly is a bailout? Second, what logic underlies this article? Both are legal but also economic questions.

States (or their subnational units) borrow moneys from the international markets to finance their policy programs. Although the question is most likely more complex than this statement implies, suffice it to say for the moment that they must do so because their tax revenues are not sufficient to pay for all of the public goods that they offer to their citizens. The EU Member States are no exception to this rule; they also borrow money from the financial markets to pay for the public goods they deliver. In other words, because spending is greater than revenues, the deficit that is generated must be financed through borrowing. This result has one advantage: States can offer more public goods, and of better quality, than they would if they ran no deficits. It however also creates problems, the main one being that in certain circumstances, States might have difficulty honoring their debts. Therefore, if they have difficulty paying back the moneys lent to them, they can either default on their debt (not such an unusual event as one might think, as Reinhart and Rogoff (2009) report in their analysis of State defaults from 1800 to 2010) or request a bailout. A bailout is, therefore, a financial assistance intervention program that comes from an actor alien to the borrower State. Internationally, this actor is, typically, the IMF. In the EU setting, before the 2008 crisis unfolded, and because article 125.1 ruled out bailouts, there was no specific agency or fund designed to conduct bailouts.

Who pays for the bailouts? In the last instance, the bailouts are paid for by the taxpayers. Therefore, if the bailout is an international bailout (as EU bailouts are), the taxpayers of other countries will pay for it. If instead the bailout is a national bailout, the taxpayers of that particular State will pay for it. However, it is important to mention at this point that bailouts are not the only option available; for example, to rescue financial institutions. For example, instead of a bailout, a bail-in can be decided on. In bail-ins (for example, in a bail-in to a bank) it is the bank shareholders and creditors who suffer the loss from the rescue operation.

Having stated the above, what article 125.1 states is that if a Member State experiences financial difficulties, then the EU institutions (of other Member States) will not be legally allowed to alleviate its debt burden. In other words, the derailed Member State should try to rescue itself (for example, through increasing taxes), its creditors should accept haircuts, or both. If these two options were impossible to implement, then that Member State in distress must default on its debt. However, it could not expect any assistance whatsoever from either the Union as a whole or the rest of the Member States, acting together or separately.

The second question we must address is, why are bailouts prohibited by the EU Treaties? Is this just? Does it make sense, from a legal and an economic viewpoint? To answer this question, I must introduce one further concept: *moral hazard*. A direct answer to the previous question is that bailouts are forbidden to avoid the moral hazard problems that would result if they were not. Let me first explain what moral hazard is.

Moral hazard is a concept with an economic dimension but that can also be approached from other perspectives, such as from a philosophical viewpoint, and from still others (see below). In economic terms, moral hazard is a concept that comes from the world of insurance. In this context, "moral hazard" is defined as the excessive risk-taking behavior of an insurer whenever there is a situation of "excess insurance" (Arrow, 1963; Pauly, 1968). For example, health insurance covers the insured for all health risks at a given constant premium. Therefore, the insured takes advantage of this constant premium and both uses and abuses the insurance by going as much as she can to the doctor (because, for example, she suffers from hypochondria). Further, the negative externality produced by the insured (increase in health costs) is distributed among the other insured (past and future) such that the insured premium is kept at a low level. This situation illustrates a typical "moral hazard."

In the sovereign debt markets, moral hazard is defined as the temptation of debtor countries to engage in profligacy, that is, in excessive debt and deficit risk-taking (knowing that at a certain point, that risk will be imposed upon third parties). The whole idea of excluding bailouts is understood precisely by reference to the origins of the idea of moral hazard, seen previously; a bailout would act as a sort of "excess" insurance, which would be precisely ruled out in the EU framework to place a further limit on this type of behavior.

However, the concept is more complex than it might appear at first sight. Both the debtors *and the creditors* alike can indulge in excessive risk-taking behaviors (the debtors by accepting too much credit, the creditors by lending too much). From this perspective (and setting aside the possibility of other insurance mechanisms, such as collateral or CDSs), a bailout also works as a sort of insurance not only for the debtor but also for the creditor; if the creditor knows that there will be bailouts, she will not care about moral hazard. Therefore, it can be argued that the EU also ruled out bailouts as a means of disciplining creditors rather than only debtors.

Finally, from a philosophical perspective, the moral hazard concept poses issues of distributive justice (Braynen, 2013; Hale, 2009); here, the question would be, under what conditions would it be fair to disseminate the negative externalities of a debtor having taken too much credit. Arnott and Stiglitz (1990) suggest that because the debtor behavior is conditioned, at least in part, by exogenous variables such as prices, it is not completely clear that these externalities should be borne only by the debtors. In other words, this situation would appear to justify at least some degree of public intervention in this field.

8.1.2 Prohibition of ECB Bailouts

Article 123.1 TFEU reads as follows:

> Overdraft facilities or any other type of credit facility with the European Central Bank or with the central banks of the Member States (hereinafter referred to as "national central banks") in favour of Union institutions, bodies, offices or agencies, central governments, regional, local or other public authorities, other bodies governed by public law, or public undertakings of Member States shall be prohibited, as shall the purchase directly from them by the European Central Bank or national central banks of debt instruments.

Article 123 TFEU is a provision that duly supplements article 125 TFEU. As seen in Chapter 4 of this book, it prohibits the monetization of Member State debt. In other words, it prohibits a bailout from occurring from the side of the European Central Bank. Thus, article 123 forbids the ECB from acting as a lender of last resort for Member States. Therefore, the point is that without article 123 TFEU, article 125 would be devoid of its very substance; the EU and its Member States would be barred from conducting bailouts, but if the ECB could conduct bailouts, then the moral hazard problem that article 125 TFEU tries to combat would reemerge. Both debtors and creditors would know that they could count on the "insurance" provided by the ECB.

Some authors such as Paul de Grauwe (2016) defend an interpretation of article 123 that includes qualifications to the previous stance. According to this author, article 123 prohibits the ECB from providing credit to the Member States but not the ECB from providing liquidity to them. Thus, the ECB could act as a lender of last resort for Member States to provide liquidity but not credit. However, it is clear that the line between credit and liquidity operations is very fine (Zilioli, 2015: 5). In fact, it would be very difficult to differentiate between when the ECB is providing liquidity and when the ECB is providing credit. We can therefore say that the prohibition against the ECB acting as a lender of last resort has a strict and a light interpretation. Under the strict interpretation, the ECB could not act as a lender of last resort. Under the light interpretation, it could not do so with respect to credit operations, but it could do so with respect to liquidity operations. The *Gauweiler* case (analyzed in Chapter 4 of this book) illustrates well that it is not entirely clear whether the ECB has respected this rule, at least in its strict sense, throughout the crisis.[2]

The second important rule that article 123 TFEU introduces is that the ECB cannot buy sovereign bonds in primary markets. No one disputes this restriction. Therefore, the ECB can only buy sovereign debt in secondary markets; in other words, it cannot buy public bonds directly from a State, its subnational units, or other public law bodies. The ECB has respected this rule throughout the crisis, although it is debatable whether the OMT announcement (see again Chapter 4 for analysis) was a violation of this prohibition.

8.1.3 Exception of Article 122 TFEU

Article 122.2 states:

> Where a Member State is in difficulties or is seriously threatened with severe difficulties caused by natural disasters or exceptional occurrences beyond its control, the Council, on a proposal from the Commission, may grant, under certain conditions, Union financial assistance to the Member State concerned. The President of the Council shall inform the European Parliament of the decision taken.

This article foresees the possibility that "financial assistance" may be granted to a Member State that is experiencing severe difficulties. The article does not specify what these difficulties might be, but it cites, in particular, natural

---

[2] C-62/14, *Gauweiler and others*, Judgment of the Court (Grand Chamber) of June 16, 2015, ECLI: EU:C:2015:400.

disasters and, more generally, "exceptional occurrences" beyond its control. Clearly, this article does not contemplate a deep economic recession such as the one that unfolded in Europe after 2008, but nor does it discard such an event. Thus, article 122.2 can be considered an exception to the rule established in article 125.1; plain bailouts are ruled out, but financial assistance could be granted to Member States in economic distress (Borger, 2013a).

8.1.4 Exception of Article 143 TFEU

Article 143.1 and 2 read as follows:

> Where a Member State with a derogation is in difficulties or is seriously threatened with difficulties as regards its balance of payments either as a result of an overall disequilibrium in its balance of payments, or as a result of the type of currency at its disposal, and where such difficulties are liable in particular to jeopardize the functioning of the internal market or the implementation of the common commercial policy, the Commission shall immediately investigate the position of the State in question and the action which, making use of all the means at its disposal, that State has taken or may take in accordance with the provisions of the Treaties. The Commission shall state what measures it recommends the State concerned to take. If the action taken by a Member State with a derogation and the measures suggested by the Commission do not prove sufficient to overcome the difficulties which have arisen or which threaten, the Commission shall, after consulting the Economic and Financial Committee, recommend to the Council the granting of mutual assistance and appropriate methods therefor.
>
> The Commission shall keep the Council regularly informed of the situation and of how it is developing.

In turn, article 143.2 says the following:

> The Council shall grant such mutual assistance; it shall adopt directives or decisions laying down the conditions and details of such assistance, which may take such forms as:
>
> (a) a concerted approach to or within any other international organisations to which Member States with a derogation may have recourse;
> (b) measures needed to avoid deflection of trade where the Member State with a derogation which is in difficulties maintains or reintroduces quantitative restrictions against third countries;
> (c) the granting of limited credits by other Member States, subject to their agreement.

This article applies to Member States that do not belong to the Eurozone. It provides legal ground for the creation of a specific assistance mechanism for countries that might experience a balance of payments (BOP) crisis. This mechanism is MTFA (Medium-Term Financial Assistance), a financial facility that assists non-Eurozone Member States in difficulty. This financial vehicle was created in 1988 by regulation 1969/88 and reformed in 2002 by regulation

332/2002. This regulation was in turn amended during the crisis by Council Regulation (EC) No 431/2009.[3] This modification raised the total amount of the loans that could be granted to Member States to €50 billion.

A BOP crisis is defined by Pisani-Ferry, Sapir and Wolff (2013: 19) as occurring when

> private markets stop financing viable borrowers because of the country they belong to. Because it is within the confines of its jurisdiction, the state, as the ultimate insurer of private agents – notably banks – tends to concentrate risk incurred by households, companies and banks. Banks with assets that are not diversified internationally also concentrate risks resulting from the potential insolvency of private agents as well as of the sovereign. As they rely on the state as their backstop, they transfer the risk to it ... This perspective in turn weakens private agents that hold large quantities of government paper. This web of interdependence between the state, banks and non-financial agents may lead markets to price country risk and, in the extreme, to shun all agents located in a particular country, irrespective of their individual financial health.

In summary, a BOP crisis occurs when a State is unable to service its debt repayments. For these cases, article 143 is activated; therefore, it is another exception to article 125.

The resulting scheme is therefore the following:

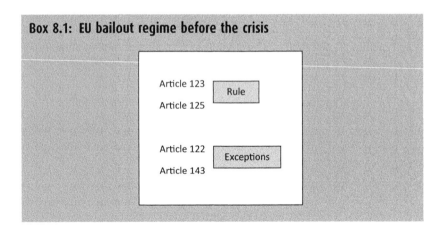

Box 8.1: EU bailout regime before the crisis

8.2 EU Bailout Regime after the Crisis

During the crisis that started in 2008, the EU bailout regime that was studied in the previous section experienced a radical transformation. It can even be argued that the system that was set prior to the crisis was completely turned

---

[3] Council Regulation (EC) No 431/2009 of May 18, 2009, amending Regulation (EC) No 332/2002 establishing a facility providing medium-term financial assistance for Member States' balances of payments. OJEU L 128/1 of 27.5.2009.

upside down after the crisis. However, it is important to clarify that the regime described in the previous section *has also been maintained after the crisis*. Therefore, article 125, which rules out bailouts, remains in place and has not been derogated from the EU Treaties but has been supplemented by the measures that I will analyze in this section.

There have been three important changes during the crisis. The first was the establishment of a (limited) rescue Fund under article 122 TFEU. The second was the amendment of article 136 TFEU. The last change was the adoption of the ESM, the European Stability Mechanism, which is a bailout mechanism. I will describe these reforms in turn.

8.2.1 Fund of Article 122 TFEU

The EU decided to create a rescue Fund in May 2010, on the legal basis of article 122, for the benefit of all Member States. This fund is the European Financial Stabilisation Mechanism (EFSM henceforth).[4] It has a volume of €60 billion. In principle, it is a nonpermanent rescue mechanism; however, based upon a Commission recommendation (which has taken the form of a communication), the EU institutions have thus far retained it.[5] It has been used for the rescue operations of Ireland and Portugal and for the bridge loan of July 2015 to Greece.

8.2.2 Reform of Article 136 TFEU

Article 136 TFEU was amended in 2011. In particular, Decision 2011/199/EU[6] introduced a third paragraph in article 136. It reads as follows:

> The Member States whose currency is the euro may establish a stability mechanism to be activated if indispensable to safeguard the stability of the euro area as a whole. The granting of any required financial assistance under the mechanism will be made subject to strict conditionality.

[4] See Council Regulation (EU) No 407/2010 of May 11, 2010, establishing a European financial stabilization mechanism (OJ L 118/1, May 12, 2010). It was amended by Council Regulation (EU) 2015/1360 of August 4, 2015, amending Regulation (EU) No 407/2010 establishing a European financial stabilization mechanism (OJ L 210/1, August 7, 2015).

[5] See Communication from the Commission to the Council and the Economic and Financial Committee on the European Financial Stabilization Mechanism. Brussels, 30.11.2010 COM (2010) 713 final.

[6] European Council Decision of March 25, 2011, amending Article 136 of the Treaty on the Functioning of the European Union with respect to a stability mechanism for Member States whose currency is the euro (2011/199/EU). OJEU L 91/1 of April 6, 2011. This modification of the TFEU was made based on article 48.6 of the TEU, which establishes a "simplified revision procedure" of the provisions of Part Three of the Treaty on the Functioning of the European Union, which relate to the internal policies and action of the Union. Such revisions are adopted by the European Council, by unanimity, but do not require a Convention for Treaty reform to be convened, as the ordinary Treaty revision procedure (article 48.2 EUT) establishes. Article 136 TFEU, in effect, belongs to Chapter IV of Title VIII of Part III of the TFEU.

This amendment entered into force on May 1, 2013, after the EU Council's secretary-general received notification from the Czech authorities of the completion of the ratification procedure in this Member State.[7]

A number of interpretative points must be made concerning this new provision. The first is that although it says that the Member States "may establish" a stability mechanism, this one is already established (although outside the EU legal order); it is the European Stability Mechanism, which will be analyzed later in this chapter. A second point is that article 136.3 refers to, and only to, Eurozone Member States. Therefore, in principle, only Eurozone members could benefit from the ESM. However, this interpretation is more formal than substantive. In fact, in my opinion, non-Eurozone members could also benefit from the ESM. If, for example, the UK experienced serious financial trouble, that could in turn spill over into the Eurozone; therefore, the ESM could be activated to rescue the UK as a means of protecting the euro (Estella, 2016).[8] The third and most important point is that this provision references the concept of "strict conditionality." Only members that accept being subject to "strict conditionality" will benefit from the ESM.

"Strict conditionality" is a new concept in the EU jargon, one that has emerged during the 2008 crisis. Before the crisis, the EU Treaties did not refer at all to this concept. First, the concept was absent from article 136 itself. Second, in the framework of the EU bailout regime prior to the crisis, the closest references to this concept could be found in articles 122 and 143. In particular, article 122 stated, "the Council, on a proposal from the Commission, may grant, *under certain conditions*, Union financial assistance to the Member State concerned" (my emphasis). The notion of "conditions" is unclear in this framework, but it can be argued that article 122 TFEU is referring to the "terms" under which the aid should be granted to the beneficiary Member State rather than to "conditionality" in the sense in which article 136.3 is speaking. Furthermore, article 143.2 says, "The Council shall grant ... mutual assistance; it shall adopt directives or decisions laying down the conditions and details of such assistance." Again, the sense in which this article is referring to "conditions" is unclear, but it can also be argued that the Treaty is speaking here more to the "terms" of financial assistance than to "strict conditionality."

Strict conditionality is a value-laden concept, whereas that of "conditions" is more neutral and technical. Conditions, as terms, can be of any

---

[7] See "Table on the ratification process of amendment of art. 136 TFEU, ESM Treaty and Fiscal Compact" by the Directorate General for the Presidency, Directorate for Relations with National Parliaments Legislative Dialogue Unit (Brussels, September 27, 2013), at www.europarl.europa.eu/webnp/cms/pid/1833.

[8] Article 3 of the ESM Treaty sets its purpose, which is "to safeguard the financial stability of the euro area as a whole." To continue with the British example, in my opinion, such interpretation would be independent of Brexit.

type to which both the EU and the beneficiary Member State might agree. They might or might not include austerity measures; the choice will depend upon the specific terms that are fixed in the assistance agreement. "Strict conditionality" is however referring to austerity measures. An interpretation of the ESM and of the MOUs (the Memoranda of Understanding that bailed-out Member States must sign to be the recipient of financial assistance) offers legal ground to sustain this point, as will be shown later in Chapter 9.

Therefore, "strict conditionality" or, *rectius*, "austerity measures," have been constitutionalized through the reform made to article 136 TFEU. The point is not solely that austerity is the price that a Member State must pay for being the recipient of financial assistance from the Union. The point is, more profoundly, that austerity has emerged during the crisis *as the primary guiding principle for the Union* when it addresses financial crises and bailouts. Austerity is, however, a very controversial program to address financial crises. As authors such as Blyth have forcefully argued, austerity is "a dangerous idea" (Blyth, 2013). Blyth's argument is simple: in an economic downturn, austerity not only does not work but also further complicates the situation. In support of his argument, Blyth even cites a number of IMF policy papers that were produced during the 2008 crisis. It is worth recalling that the IMF was once the world's austerity champion. Notwithstanding the above, austerity is now at the core of the new EU bailout regime.

A second point that can be made is that, as will be shown later, conditionality, or austerity; that is, that Member States that need financial assistance must accept austerity measures in exchange, is very controversial not only in itself but also because it further calls into question the effectiveness of the new EU bailout regime. In fact, Member States might prefer to default or to exit the euro rather than accept a bailout with conditionality. The story (the drama, I would rather call it) of the third Greek bailout is a very good example of this point, as will be shown later.

Therefore and to summarize, austerity is constitutionalized in article 136.3; it is, however, a controversial idea as a means to address crises. Finally, austerity might even compromise the effectiveness of bailouts.

8.2.3 European Stability Mechanism

The Treaty establishing the ESM was signed on February 2, 2012 by the 19 members of the Eurozone.[9] The ESM draws on the experience accumulated

---

[9] Latvia and Lithuania signed the Treaty and acceded to the ESM at a later stage. In particular, the Republic of Latvia, which joined the euro area on January 1, 2014, became the eighteenth member of the ESM on March 13, 2014. The Republic of Lithuania became the nineteenth member of the ESM on 3 February 2015, after this Member State adopted the euro on January 1, 2015.

through the operation of both the EFSM[10] and the EFSF[11] and integrates with the latter in a single bailing-out mechanism.[12] The total capital stock of the ESM is approximately €700 billion (€701 billion). Of this amount, the paid-in capital is approximately €80 billion. Therefore, the rest (€620 billion) is "callable" capital. The ESM Member States are committed to making extra disbursements if need be. Finally, its maximum lending capacity is €500 billion (Tomkin, 2013; Borger, 2013b).

Two points are relevant concerning this major bailout mechanism: first, the organization of the Mechanism's decision-making process, and second, the issue of conditionality. Concerning the first, all relevant decisions are made unanimously by the Board of Governors (which is composed of one governor per ESM member) or by the Board of Directors (which is composed of one representative of each governor per member of the ESM). For example, the decision to grant financial assistance is accorded by the Board of Governors by unanimity (article 5.6(f)). Not only is the first tranche of financial assistance to be decided by unanimity but also the disbursement of subsequent ones (article 16.5). In this domain, article 4.4 opens up a way out from the gridlock that unanimity can bring about by establishing a qualified majority for adopting both decisions when a failure to grant financial assistance would "threaten the economic and financial sustainability of the euro area." However, qualified majority is defined by the same article as 85 percent of the votes cast. In other words, without Germany, France or Italy, a qualified majority vote cannot be attained. Thus, these three countries hold a "veto-player" position in the ESM governance.

Concerning conditionality, it is interesting to note that this word is mentioned sixteen times in the text of the ESM Treaty. The idea is therefore clear: bailouts are only possible if subject to strict conditionality or an austerity program.

The sacrifices implied by austerity can range from a macroeconomic program to the continuous respect of preestablished eligibility conditions, as article 12.1 of the ESM Treaty states (see also Chapter 7 on macroeconomic adjustment programs and the SGP). If one examines the eight bailouts that have occurred to date, but in particular, the five Eurozone bailouts, conditionality has rather taken the form of a macroeconomic adjustment program, as

---

[10] European Financial Stabilisation Mechanism. See Council Regulation (EU) No 407/2010 of May 11, 2010, establishing a European financial stabilization mechanism (OJ L 118/1, May 12, 2010). It was amended by Council Regulation (EU) 2015/1360 of August 4, 2015, amending Regulation (EU) No 407/2010 establishing a European financial stabilization mechanism (OJ L 210/1, August 7, 2015). See also the Communication from the Commission to the Council and the Economic and Financial Committee on the European Financial Stabilisation Mechanism (Brussels, November 30, 2010). COM(2010) 713 final

[11] European Financial Stability Facility. See the EFSF Framework Agreement of June 7, 2010, at www.efsf.europa.eu/about/legal-documents/index.htm.

[12] However, it does not integrate the EFSM, which remains in place.

shown later. MOUs (Memoranda of Understanding) are the "legal" instrument through which specific conditionality has been established for bailed-out Member States. One of the main points here is that the beneficiary Member State must recover the path of fiscal sustainability, as defined by the so-called Fiscal Compact. This requirement means, in particular, that a Member State that has received a bailout must evolve, in the timeframe marked by its specific MOU, towards a fiscal position in which its structural deficit is not greater than 0.5 percent of its GDP. In turn, the specific MOU must be in line with both the excessive deficit procedure and the macro-imbalance procedure (analyzed in Chapter 7 of this book) to which the beneficiary Member State might be subject.

In summary, the resulting EU bailout after the crisis is as follows:

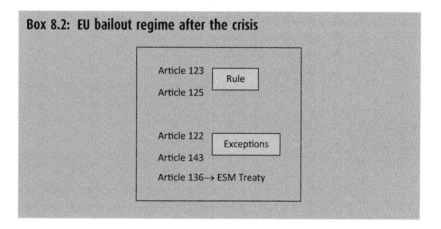

Box 8.2: EU bailout regime after the crisis

Article 123
Article 125 — Rule

Article 122
Article 143 — Exceptions

Article 136→ ESM Treaty

8.3 Bailouts and Credibility

In view of the preceding description of the old and new EU bailout regimes, the first question that we can ask is whether the rule has become the exception and the exception, the rule. This question is even more legitimate if we consider the eight bailouts that have occurred during the economic crisis. On this point, the ECJ has ruled in the *Pringle* case[13] that there is no incompatibility whatsoever between Articles 125 and 136 TFEU as amended (or, therefore, between the ESM and Article 125) insofar as two conditions are met: first, that financial assistance is subject to strict conditionality; and second, that it is oriented towards a sound budgetary policy (Borger, 2013b).

Therefore, although formally speaking the golden rule of the EU bailout regime is that no bailouts will occur, it is clear that if a new deep economic

---

[13] Judgment of the European Court of Justice of November 27, 2012, Case C-370/12, *Thomas Pringle* v. *Government of Ireland, Ireland, The Attorney General.*

downturn occurred, a doubt would emerge concerning the probable behavior of EU institutions vis-à-vis Member States in financial distress.

In particular, it can be argued that the system prior to the economic crisis was clearly not an equilibrium from a "law as credibility" perspective. The "mix" between rigidity and flexibility that was represented by articles 125, 123 and 122 TFEU was not, as the events that unfolded after 2008 showed, a good fix. As the crisis deepened, and despite the pronouncements of political leaders and some central banks' governors that sovereign bailouts would not occur (Bastasin, 2015: 1 and 406), the EU rapidly moved to modify the *ex ante* status quo and established bailout programs, initially timidly but thereafter more decisively. All indications appear to support the idea that markets had discounted that bailouts would occur in the midst of the crisis (ibid.: 170). The question that we must answer now is whether the new system represents an equilibrium point between rigidity and flexibility.

It could be argued that the new EU bailout regime is closer to equilibrium because, although it still rules out bailouts as a general approximation to this problem, it also provides sufficient flexibility to the system to be able to conduct bailouts if circumstances demand them. Therefore, the equilibrium point of the system before the crisis would have moved downwards to instill the flexibility that the system needed and did not have previously.

However, on a second (and more subtle) reading, it can be argued that, despite the improvements with respect to the system prior to the crisis, the current system is also not an equilibrium. In some respects, it can be argued that the new system is even more problematic, from a credibility perspective, than was the previous one. The reasons for this result are the following.

First, the previous system had at least the advantage of being clear. Although as has been remarked in Chapter 2 of this book, credibility and clarity are two different things, it is also evident that clarity is an important part of credibility. Bailouts were ruled out in the EU context. This choice was perhaps an unrealistic assumption, but at least, before the crisis, it could be argued that the EU would not conduct bailouts. Whether this position affected the evolution of sovereign bond prices is open to debate, but it is possible to argue that perhaps in the first epoch of the euro it might have had a positive effect (de Grauwe, 2016).

Second, after the crisis, the resulting system has gained flexibility. However, in exchange, it has lost coherence and has increased its contradictory character. On the one hand, the current system rules out bailouts; on the other hand, it establishes a massive bailing-out mechanism. However, it also inserts in the very core of the EU bailout system conditionality, or austerity. All of these policies together can yield strange outcomes such as for example that the EU might be interested in providing a bailout (despite the prohibition), whereas the potential recipient Member State might not want one (despite the fact that it would be its first beneficiary) due to conditionality. In turn, markets can react oddly to this possible outcome, with increased uncertainty and volatility.

In fact, it is noteworthy that the historic experience of the IMF's bailouts tells us that neither were the main objectives of such bailouts (economic growth) achieved nor did the conditionality linked to those rescue programs have a high degree of implementation. According to some authors, impaired growth and the conditions were largely ignored in general bailouts (Przeworski & Vreeland, 2000; Dreher, 2006 and 2009). In this context, this experience concerns countries in development or at most emerging states but not developed countries such as the EU Member States. In other words, the IMF's record with past bailouts need not be replicated in the EU context. However, it is also true that this story projects a gloomy shadow on prospects for EU bailouts (Estella, 2016).

This upside-down result (the EU being interested in giving a bailout, whereas a Member State is interested in not being bailed out due to conditionality) is very well illustrated by the case of the third bailout to Greece.

The facts that led to the third Greek bailout are the following. First, Syriza (a left-wing political party with an anti-austerity platform) defended a policy in which a third bailout would be rejected unless conditionality changed and a deep haircut was accepted by the EU institutions. Markets anticipated Syriza's victory, and in December 2014 the Greek risk premium began tending to increase. Second, Syriza won the national election by an ample majority on January 25, 2015. The Greek risk premium continued its tendency to increase. Third, the EU offered Greece a third bailout. Syriza announced that a referendum on the third bailout package would occur in July. Syriza defended the "no" vote, and opinion polls appeared to indicate that the "no" would win. The Greece risk premium upward tendency increased further. Fourth, three days after the referendum (the outcome of which was a "no" vote), Syriza's government requested a third bailout, on July 8, 2015. The Greek risk premium plummeted after the government made the announcement (see Figure 8.1).

This case appears to suggest the following points. First, it confirms our prediction according to which markets prefer (and discount) bailouts. In the middle of a deep crisis such as the Greek one, they prefer a bailout to a default and/or a euro-exit. Second, the transformation of the EU bailout regime, which was performed during the crisis, appeared worthless. That article 136 was amended and an ESM mechanism was introduced apparently had no calming effect on the markets. With the new scheme, as occurred with the old scheme, markets only calmed when a bailout was actually requested and/or implemented. The spectacular drop in the Greek risk premium after the third bailout, announced on July 8, 2015 (from more than 2,000 basis points to approximately 600 in two weeks), appears to be an indication of this calming. Third, the counterfactual is a case in point here; are we better off with this new scheme than with the pre-crisis (no-)bailout scheme? The answer is difficult to provide because, since the crisis unfolded, a bailout system was created in the EU (irrespective of the no-bailout clause); in other words, there is no parallel example in the EU in which there was a grave financial crisis and bailouts were

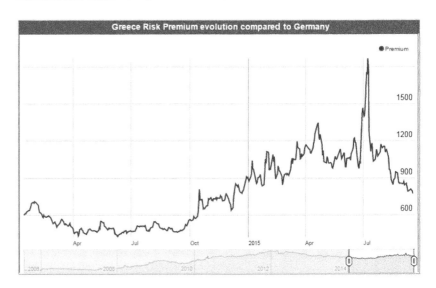

Figure 8.1: Greece risk premium 2015
Source: http://countryeconomy.com/risk-premium/greece (last accessed on September 17, 2015)

not implemented to compare with the current situation. However, if we consider the evolution of the Greek risk premium since the crisis started, it would appear that a similar pattern emerges: risk premium increase until a bailout is conducted. Then, they decrease after the bailout. However, if markets understand that a new bailout is going to be needed, then the increasing tendency starts over again. In summary, the new system does not appear to have a preventive function. Moreover, it increases its contradictory characteristics.

Although this book's purpose is not to make policy recommendations, we can at least discuss a bailout model that could represent an equilibrium point from the perspective of law as credibility. That model is the US system. Henning and Kessler (2012), speaking of the US tradition in this area, explain that in the American legal context, there is no equivalent to article 125 TFEU. Neither the Federal Constitution nor the States' respective constitutions formally prohibit bailouts. However, since more or less 1840, there have been no bailouts in this country. According to Kelemen and Teo (2012), nine US states have in fact defaulted since then. Therefore, the no-bailout rule is more a constitutional convention than anything else. The same authors also argue that there are no general bailing-out funds in the US. Rather, the no-bailout tradition has been compensated for by strong federal fiscal powers and a strong federal budget, which rescue states that are in financial difficulties either directly or indirectly through a variety of transfer mechanisms.

In particular, in the 2008 economic crisis, the most important federal program that was adopted in the US to assist states in distress was the

---

Box 8.3: An example: Florida and Spain compared

A (very crude) measure of the differences between the US and the EU is given by Krugman (2012), who compares Florida and Spain during the crisis. According to the author, "between falling tax payments without any corresponding fall in federal benefits, plus safety-net aid – not counting Medicaid, which would make the number even bigger – Florida received what amounted to an annual transfer from Washington of $31 billion plus, or more than 4 percent of state GDP. That's a transfer, not a loan." Of course, one should consider, to have a complete picture, the €41 billion that Spain received as a bailout from the ESM. However, this would be a loan, not a transfer.

American Recovery and Reinvestment Act (ARRA), with an amount of $804 billion.[14] Feyrer and Sacerdote (2011) indicate that ARRA's spending can be categorized into three groups: (1) education and police, (2) support to low-income individuals, and (3) new infrastructure projects. In terms of types of funds available, ARRA establishes the following types: (1) contracts, grants, and loans; (2) entitlements; and (3) tax credits. Therefore, most ARRA funds were direct or indirect transfers or direct spending from the federal government; there were also loans to be repaid by the recipient, although under very good conditions, but these loans were not the majority of ARRA funds. Furthermore, there is a lot of debate in the US about how efficient the ARRA has been. Although I believe that its effectiveness is beyond any doubt, if compared with the counterfactual (not having any stimulus federal program at all, which is what occurred in the EU), the same authors understand that ARRA had a multiplier effect on the US economy of between 0.5 and 2.0 (see Box 8.3).

The lessons that can be extracted from the American experience are therefore the following: (1) it is not necessary to have a no-bailout legal rule; rather it is sufficient that the no-bailout rule be a political commitment that can, over time, be translated into a constitutional convention. (2) Strong fiscal powers in the center coupled with a strong federal budget are better approaches than a permanent rescue mechanism to help states that are undergoing financial stress. The American experience appears to provide an equilibrium point between flexibility and rigidity whose arrangement in this area appears to be more credible than the EU one.

Therefore, the only option available to the EU to make credible its commitment not to bail out would be a much higher degree of fiscal coordination and cooperation at the EU level, in which the EU budgetary powers and resources

---

[14] American Recovery and Reinvestment Act. See all of the relevant information on this program at www.recovery.gov/Pages/default.aspx.

would be sufficiently strong to make internal transfers from the center to the states if a new economic calamity arose. In the absence of such a mechanism, the EU commitment not to bail out will not be credible. The existence of article 125 TFEU, together with a bailout regime based on conditionality, will only serve to generate doubts in the markets concerning what policy the EU will finally follow in a new crisis. Market lack of coordination would in turn generate financial volatility and economic distress.

BIBLIOGRAPHY

Arnott, R. & Stiglitz, J. 1990, "The Welfare Economics of Moral Hazard," NBER (National Bureau of Economic Research) Working Paper Series, no. 3316.

Arrow, K. 1963, "Uncertainty and the welfare economics of medical care," *American Economic Review*, vol. 53, pp. 941–973.

Athanassiou, P. 2011, "Of past measures and future plans for Europe's exit from the sovereign debt crisis: what is legally possible (and what is not)," *European Law Review*, vol. 4, pp. 558–575.

Aust, A. 2014, "MOUs" in *Modern Treaty Law and Practice*, 3rd edn., Cambridge University Press, Cambridge, pp. 28–54.

Baird, D., Gertner, R., & Picker, R. 1998, *Game Theory and the Law*, Harvard University Press, Cambridge, Mass, & London.

Bast, J. 2014, "'Don't act beyond your powers': the perils and pitfalls of the German Constitutional Court's ultra vires review," *German Law Journal*, vol. 15, no. 2, pp. 167–182.

Bastasin, C. 2015, *Saving Europe: Anatomy of a Dream*, 2nd edn., Brookings Institution, Washington, D.C.

Beckert, J. 2013, "Imagined futures: fictional expectations in the economy," *Theory and Society*, vol. 42, no. 3, pp. 219–240.

Beukers, T. 2013, "The new ECB and its relationship with the Eurozone: between Central Bank independence and Central Bank intervention," *Common Market Law Review*, vol. 50, no. 6, pp. 1579–1620.

Borger, V. 2013b, "The ESM and the European Court's predicament in Pringle," *German Law Journal*, vol. 14, no. 1, pp. 113–140.

2013a, "How the debt crisis exposes the development of solidarity in the euro area," *European Constitutional Law Review*, vol. 9, no. 1, pp. 7–36.

Blyth, M. 2013, *Austerity: The History of a Dangerous Idea*, Oxford University Press, Oxford.

Braynen, W. 2013, "Moral dimensions of moral hazards," *Utilitas*, vol. 26, no. 1, pp. 34–50.

Buti, M. & Pench, L. 2012, "Fiscal austerity and policy credibility," VoxEU.org, April 20, www.voxeu.org.

Chiti, E. & Texeira, P. G. 2013, "The constitutional implications of the European responses to the financial and public debt crisis," *Common Market Law Review*, vol. 50, no. 3, pp. 683–708.

Craig, P. 2013, "Pringle and use of EU institutions outside the EU legal framework: foundations, procedure and substance," *European Constitutional Law Review*, vol. 9, no. 2, pp. 263–284.

De Grauwe, P. 2016, *Economics of Monetary Union*, 11th edn., Oxford University Press, Oxford.

2011, "The European Central Bank: Lender of Last Resort in the Government Bond Markets?," CESifo Working Paper no. 3569.

De Gregorio Merino, A. 2012, "Legal developments in the Economic and Monetary Union during the debt crisis: the mechanisms of financial assistance," *Common Market Law Review*, vol. 49, no. 5, pp. 1613–1645.

de Witte, B. 2011, "The European Treaty Amendment for the Creation of a Financial Stability Mechanism," Swedish Institute for European Policy Analysis.

de Witte, B. & Beukers, T. 2013, "The Court of Justice approves the creation of the European Stability Mechanism outside the EU legal order: Pringle," *Common Market Law Review*, vol. 50, no. 3, pp. 805–848.

Di Fabio, U. 2014, "Karlsruhe makes a referral," *German Law Journal*, vol. 15, no. 2, pp. 107–110.

Dreher, A. 2009, "IMF conditionality: theory and evidence," *Public Choice*, vol. 141, pp. 233–267.

2006, "IMF and economic growth: the effects of programs, loans, and compliance with conditionality," *World Development*, vol. 34, no. 5, pp. 769–788.

Dresser, R. 2003, "Precommitment: a misguided strategy for securing death with dignity," *Texas Law Review*, vol. 81, no. 7, pp. 1823–1847.

Eijsbouts, W. T. & Michel, B. 2013, "Between Frankfurt and Karlsruhe: the move, the law and the institutions ," *European Constitutional Law Review*, vol. 9, no. 3, pp. 355–357.

Elster, J. 2003, "Don't burn your bridge before you come to it: ambiguities and complexities of pre-commitment," *Texas Law Review*, vol. 81, no. 7, pp. 1755–1787.

1984, *Ulysses and the Sirens*, Cambridge University Press, Cambridge.

Estella, A. 2016, "European Union bailouts and credibility: the constitutional dimension," *European Public Law*, vol. 22, no. 3, pp. 507–540.

2008, "Law as credibility: the case of Presidential Term Limits," *European Journal of Legal Studies*, vol. 2, no. 1, pp. 116–142.

Feyrer, J. & Sacerdote, B. 2011, "Did the Stimulus Stimulate? Real Time Estimates of the Effects of the American Recovery and Reinvestment Act," NBER (National Bureau of Economic Research) Working Paper no. 16759.

Hale, B. 2009, "What's so moral about the moral hazard?," *Public Affairs Quarterly*, vol. 23, pp. 1–25.

Henning, R. & Kessler, M. 2012, "Fiscal Federalism: US History for Architects of Europe's Fiscal Union," Bruegel Essay and Lecture Series, pp. 1–44.

Kelemen, D. & Teo, T. K. 2012, "Law and the Eurozone Crisis," APSA (American Political Science Association) 2012 Annual Meeting Paper.

Micossi, S. 2015, "The Monetary Policy of the European Central Bank (2002–2015)," CEPS (Centre for European Policy Studies) Special Report No. 109.

Pauly, M. 1968, "The economics of moral hazard: comment," *The American Economic Review*, vol. 58, pp. 531–537.

Pisani-Ferry, J., Sapir, A., & Wolff, G. 2013, "EU–IMF assistance to euro-area countries: an early assessment," Bruegel Blueprint, vol. 19.

Przeworski, A. & Vreeland, J. R. 2000, "The effect of IMF programs on economic growth," *Journal of Development Economics*, vol. 62, pp. 385–421.

Reinhart, C. & Rogoff, K. 2009, *This Time Is Different: Eight Centuries of Financial Folly*, Princeton University Press, Princeton, N. Jersey.

Tomkin, J. 2013, "Contradiction, circumvention and conceptual gymnastics: the impact of the adoption of the ESM Treaty on the state of European democracy," *German Law Journal*, vol. 14, no. 1, pp. 169–190.

Zilioli, C. 2015, "Introduction" in European Central Bank (ed.) *ECB Legal Conference 2015: From Monetary Union to Banking Union, on the Way to Capital Markets Union: New Opportunities for European Integration.* European Central Bank, Frankfurt, pp. 49–52, www.ecb.europa.eu/pub/pdf/other/frommonetaryuniontobankingunion201512.en.pdf.

9

European Union Bailouts (II): Bailouts of Member States and MOUs

Introduction

In this chapter, I address the eight bailouts of Member States that have occurred since the 2008 crisis began. A second point will be to delve into the legal nature of Memoranda of Understanding (MOUs), the master legal piece around which bailouts revolve.

9.1 EU Bailouts of Member States

As has been mentioned previously, since the crisis started in 2008, there have been eight bailouts of EU Member States. In the following, I will briefly describe and analyze the eight bailouts that have been conducted on Member States, with a particular focus on the Eurozone Member State bailouts. The amount of money approved and actually disbursed for bailing-out purposes is summarized in Table 9.1.

9.1.1 Bailouts of Non-Eurozone Member States

Bailouts of non-Eurozone Member States constitute a minor part of the bailing-out effort that the EU has undertaken in recent years: the total amount of money that has been disbursed is equivalent to €13.4 billion, whereas the volume approved is €16.6 billion; these amounts constitute 3.5 percent and 3.15 percent of the total, respectively. All bailouts to non-Eurozone Member States are considered BOP programs, as stated previously in Chapter 8 (Louis, 2010).

Economically speaking, the most important (and first) bailout of a non-Eurozone member was that of *Hungary*, which requested a BOP assistance program from the EU in October 2008 (Gyorffy, 2015). The program was approved in November 2008. In exchange, Hungary had to sign an MOU, in which significant austerity measures were imposed on that country.[1]

---

[1] Memorandum of Understanding between the European Community and the Republic of Hungary of November 19, 2008, available at http://ec.europa.eu/economy_finance/publications/pages/publication13495_en.pdf.

Table 9.1: EU bailouts (€ billion) (2008–2015)[2]

Article I. Country	Article II. Approved	Article III. Disbursed
Ireland	40.2	39.4
Greece	308	231.18
Spain	100	41.3
Portugal	52	50.3
Latvia	3.1	2.9
Hungary	6.5	5.5
Romania	7	5
Cyprus	9	5.8
TOTAL	**525.8**	**381.38**

Note: Does not take into account IMF or other contributors.
Source: European Commission (EC), ESM, and EFSF.

In November 2011, Hungary requested a second BOP assistance program, this time of a precautionary nature. At the same time, Hungary was subject to post-program surveillance (PPS). The PPS was discontinued in January 2015, when Hungary repaid more than 70 percent of the loan.

The second most economically important bailout of a non-Eurozone Member State was that of *Romania* (IMF, 2010). In spring 2009, Romania requested a BOP assistance program from the EU. This assistance was granted in May of that year. As in the previous cases, Romania had to sign a stringent adjustment program in the form of an MOU.[3] The program for Romania has, however, been less successful than were the cases of Hungary and of Latvia, which will be examined next. In February 2011, a precautionary BOP assistance program was requested by Romania. This assistance was granted by the EU in May 2011. However, in 2013, Romania had to request a second precautionary BOP assistance program. Although the moneys granted by the EU in October 2013 have not yet been disbursed, Romania has not yet officially exited the program (June 2015).

Latvia (currently a member of the Eurozone) was the third non-Eurozone Member State to be bailed out. In November 2008, Latvia requested a BOP assistance program. This assistance was granted in December of that year. To this effect, Latvia signed an MOU,[4] in which strong austerity measures were imposed on the country in exchange for the assistance. It is important to note that during the crisis, Latvia was one of the hotspots of the intense debate that

---

[2] As of September 30, 2015.

[3] Memorandum of Understanding between the European Union and Romania of June 23, 2009, available at http://ec.europa.eu/economy_finance/articles/financial_operations/article15406_en.htm.

[4] Memorandum of Understanding between the European Community and the Republic of Latvia of January 26–28, 2009, available at https://ec.europa.eu/info/sites/info/files/ecfin_mou_bop_latvia_en.pdf.

occurred between the advocates and the detractors of austerity. Because the Latvian slump was so intense, even the IMF (including Olivier Blanchard, the director of the IMF Research Department; Blanchard, 2012) understood that Latvia should devalue its currency rather than adopt stringent austerity measures. However, the country did not devalue, instead opting for an intense program of internal devaluation. The outcome is that today Latvia is a member of the euro; therefore, the Latvian case is usually adduced as a successful example of the good that austerity policies are able to do for a country. However, its detractors argue that the Latvian recovery was too painful, that the same results could have been obtained with less pain for the population, and that the Latvian recovery is founded on a weak basis and therefore unsustainable (Blanchard, Griffiths, & Gruss, 2013; Krugman, 2013; Weisbrot & Ray, 2010).

9.1.2 Bailouts of Eurozone Member States

Bailouts of Eurozone Member States constitute the lion's share of the bailout efforts that the EU has undertaken since 2008. In terms of volume, we are speaking of €509.2 billion (€367.98 billion disbursed). In percentage terms, this amount represents more than 96 percent of the total approved amount. However, bailouts have been important in the EU framework because of not only the considerable amount of money that they have involved but also their prompting of intense structural reforms in the Member States that have received the bailouts. Due to the bailouts and the associated conditionality, many beneficiary Member States have been transformed institutionally, legally, economically, and in terms of the extent and scope of their respective welfare states. Whether all of these changes have been for the good is something that remains to be seen. Only time will tell.

The first and by far the most important bailout that has occurred throughout the crisis years has been the bailout of *Greece* (Panagiotarea, 2013; see in general Tsoukalis, 2016). In many senses, the Greek bailout has been a laboratory for the rest of the bailouts for Eurozone Member States, particularly concerning the push for austerity programs in the EU. As Figure 8.1 above illustrates, the Greek risk premium started an escalating trend at the end of 2008, some months after the collapse of Lehman Brothers in the USA. Greek interest rates for senior sovereign bonds rose more sharply than in other countries in distress such as Portugal, Ireland, or Spain. From the perspective of GDP growth and employment, Greece presented good numbers before the crisis started. However, from a fiscal perspective, the country entered the crisis with a rather gloomy outlook; Maastricht's public debt and deficit ceilings were constantly overshot. This issue might be part of the reason why financial markets experienced exacerbated fury against this country. On April 8, 2010, the two-year bond spreads had reached 652 basis points, and the ten-year bond spreads had reach 430 basis points. On April 23, 2010, Greece requested financial assistance from the IMF and the EU, once Greek Prime Minister George Papandreou acknowledged in Castelorizo that his country had lied and that its deficit would be double what that had been originally announced, as seen above in Chapter 7. The agreement among this Member State, the ECB, the European Commission, and the IMF was reached on May 2, 2010. Because the EU lacked a financial support mechanism for this type of case, it had to activate the agreement via bilateral loans centrally pooled by the European Commission (Greek Loan Facility Agreement). The approved amount was €80 billion (EU)[5] plus €30 billion (IMF).

In exchange for help, Greece had to sign an MOU[6] that, as will be argued below, has in my opinion a clear, legally binding nature. In any case, all MOUs follow a similar structure. They are usually composed (as in the Greek case) of four headings: Fiscal Consolidation, Structural Fiscal Reforms, Financial Sector Regulation and Supervision, and Growth-Enhancing Structural Reforms. Most of the Greek MOU measures were, on the one hand, very detailed, and on the other, definitively intrusive with respect to national sovereignty. For example, the first Greek MOU instructed the Greek government to reduce the "public wage bill by reducing the Easter, summer and Christmas bonuses and allowances paid to civil servants, with net savings amounting to EUR 1500 million for a full year (EUR 1100 million in 2010)." The point to be stressed is that ulterior disbursements were made conditional on the MOU's implementation. For the first rescue package, Greece was required to sign up to five updates of the first MOU.

The first Greek rescue package was, to say the least, unsuccessful. Greek macroeconomic fundamentals deteriorated further over time. The Greek risk premium also increased; thus on May 1, 2012, the Greek risk premium was at 3,445 basis points.[7] Therefore, Greece had to request a second bailout on March 11, 2012. The bailout was granted two days later, on March 14. The approved amount was of €130 billion, to be financed by the European Financial Stability Facility (EFSF). The amount later increased to €144.7 billion through the end of 2014 (the period was later extended until the end of June 2015). In turn, the IMF-approved contribution was of €19.8 billion.[8]

---

[5] Slovakia decided not to participate in the Greek Loan Facility Agreement. Therefore, the previous amount was reduced by €2.7 billion.

[6] Greece: Memorandum of Understanding on Specific Economic Policy Conditionality May 3, 2010, available at http://ec.europa.eu/economy_finance/publications/occasional_paper/2010/pdf/ocp61_en.pdf.

[7] http://countryeconomy.com/risk-premium/greece.

[8] There was also a PSI (Private Sector Involvement), which implied a bond swap in the amount of €197 billion. According to this Euro-group statement, this amount equaled a 53.5 percent nominal haircut. See www.consilium.europa.eu/uedocs/cms_data/docs/pressdata/en/ecofin/128075.pdf. Zettelmeyer, Trebesch and Gulati (2013) argue that the "present value haircut" was 64.6 percent. A critical view on the PSI operation, by Yanis Varoufakis, former Greek Minister of Finance, can be found at http://yanisvaroufakis.eu/2014/03/12/lessons-from-the-greek-psi/.

Once again, Greece had to sign a new MOU[9] in exchange. As in previous Greek MOUs, the document included the already familiar four headings mentioned above. It further reinforced the liberalization-cum-privatization flavor that had started in previous MOUs, affecting, for example, airports, energy, railways, defence, and water. It also imposed upon the Greek authorities a freeze on 2012 minimum wages in nominal terms for three years.

The second Greek bailout was more successful than the first, in the sense that a relaxation of the Greek risk premium was observed as disbursements were occurring. Draghi's WIT (Whatever it Takes)[10] statement of July 26, 2012, also most likely affected its success (Estella, 2016). As was argued in Chapter 8, it appeared that the markets had discounted the bailouts, despite the EU Treaties' prohibition of the same. However, in terms of fiscal sustainability, or growth prospects, the second bailout was, once again, a failure. The Greek public deficit rose from €8.7 billion in 2012 to €12.3 billion in 2013, decreasing thereafter to €3.5 billion in 2014. Public debt dynamics was even more alarming; it rose from 156.9 percent GDP in 2012 to 175 percent GDP in 2013 and 177.1 percent GDP in 2014. Finally, concerning growth prospects, in 2012, Greece's growth was –6.6 percent; it was –3.9 percent in 2013. Only in 2014 did it have a weak positive value of 0.8 percent.

Greece had four reviews of its second bailout program, with subsequent amendments and adjustments to its initial MOU. In January 2015, a legislative election occurred in the country, and the far left-wing party Syriza won a majority of the seats in the Greek parliament. Syriza's platform was to renegotiate the bailout terms and negotiate an in-depth debt restructuring with both private and public Greek creditors. However, the EU pushed the new Greek government hard to respect the terms of the previous bailout deals and even tried to force Greece to request a third bailout. The Greek government was left alone with its demands; no other EU Member State (not even periphery Member States) supported the new Greek government's platform (Varoufakis, 2016). Therefore, to regain political impetus, the Greek government called a referendum on the terms of the EU proposal for a third bailout. The referendum result went against the EU proposal: a majority of 61.32 percent of the votes cast were in favor of rejecting the agreement. The Greek government then started negotiations with the EU to strike a new deal. However, before this deal was definitively struck, the Greek government had to request a third bailout on July 8, 2015, because the country's financial situation was rapidly

---

[9] Greece Memorandum of Understanding on Specific Economic Policy Conditionality of March 11, 2012, available at http://ec.europa.eu/economy_finance/publications/occasional_paper/2012/pdf/ocp94_en.pdf.

[10] Speech by Mario Draghi, President of the European Central Bank, at the Global Investment Conference in London, July 26, 2012. Available at www.ecb.europa.eu/press/key/date/2012/html/sp120726.en.html. Draghi's exact words were, "Within our mandate, the ECB is ready to do whatever it takes to preserve the euro. And believe me, it will be enough."

deteriorating. The signature of the corresponding MOU was preceded by a political agreement on August 14, 2015 that granted Greece a bailout of €86 billion. Its most relevant paragraph was the following:[11]

> The debt sustainability assessment was conducted by the Commission, in liaison with the ECB, as foreseen in Article 13(1) of the ESM Treaty. The analysis concludes that debt sustainability can be achieved through a far-reaching and credible reform programme and additional debt related measures without nominal haircuts. In line with the Euro summit statement of 12 July, the Eurogroup stands ready to consider, if necessary, possible additional measures (possible longer grace and repayment periods) aiming at ensuring that Greece's gross financing needs remain at a sustainable level. These measures will be conditional upon full implementation of the measures agreed in the ESM programme and will be considered after the first positive completion of a programme review. The Eurogroup reiterates that nominal haircuts on official debt cannot be undertaken.

Therefore, although a haircut was expressly discarded, "possible longer grace and repayment periods" for Greek sovereign debt were included in the deal. The new MOU of August 19, 2015,[12] included the familiar headlines previously noted, but it also included a new one on "A modern State and public administration." Its rhetoric was generally less aggressive than in previous MOUs (for example, it addressed more clearly the social problems that the country was experiencing), but the substance remained very similar to that of old MOUs. The combination of liberalization and privatization still had a prominent role in the new MOU. Even the privatization of Piraeus port, which was the subject of a heated public debate before the third bailout, was not removed from the new MOU.[13] Nor was conditionality, or austerity, substantially relaxed in this case. Finally, after three bailouts, in 2014 Greece had a government deficit of –3.5 percent and a public debt of 177.1 percent.

In terms of amount, the second most important bailout was that of *Spain*. The approved size of this bailout was €100 billion, although €41.3 billion was ultimately disbursed. Of the bailed-out countries, Spain is the most important economically, being the fifth-largest economy in the EU and the fourth-largest in the Eurozone.[14] Therefore, Spain was an economic "red line," the crossing

---

[11] Eurogroup statement on the ESM programme for Greece, August 14, 2015, www.consilium.europa.eu/en/press/press-releases/2015/08/14-eurogroup-statement.

[12] Memorandum of Understanding between the European Commission acting on behalf of the European Stability Mechanism and the Hellenic Republic and the Bank of Greece of August 19, 2015, available at https://ec.europa.eu/info/sites/info/files/01_mou_20150811_en.pdf.

[13] See Tom Mitchell and Kerin Hope, "Chinese investors wary of filling Greece's golden begging bowl," *Financial Times*, June 25, 2015.

[14] Eurostat, Gross Domestic Product at market prices, in million euro (2014), http://ec.europa.eu/eurostat/tgm/table.do?tab=table&init=1&language=en&pcode=tec00001&plugin=1.

of which would most likely have amounted to a collapse of the Eurozone (Estella, 2015).

However, the situation in Spain, until the crisis unfolded in 2008, was very different from that of Greece. In 2007, Spain was in good health from the perspective of both its macroeconomic fundamentals and fiscal position. In 2007, its growth rate was 3.8 percent. Its unemployment rate (the main Spanish hobbyhorse) was at 8.2 percent. More importantly, Spain had a fiscal surplus in 2007 of 2 percent GDP and a public debt of 35.5 percent GDP, much lower than was established by the Maastricht parameters.

However, the situation dramatically changed in Spain after the collapse of Lehman Brothers and the virtual halt of interbank credit. The Spanish housing bubble, which had been fed during the bonanza years, burst in a matter of months. The government reaction was to adopt a recovery plan (the so-called "E" plan) to reinforce the housing market, in the hope that the crisis would not be as deep as it later proved to be, following the recommendations of the G20 that occurred in Washington on November 15, 2008.[15] Thus, from 2008 to 2010, Spain pumped approximately €100 billion into the economy. However, the global economic slump continued. Growth rates decreased, and unemployment started increasing. In a matter of months, Spain overshot the Maastricht ceilings: government deficit was at 4.4 percent in 2008 (reaching 11 percent in 2009), and public debt reached the 60 percent limit in 2010 (60.1 percent). Consequently, the Spanish risk premium started an escalating trend. In May 2010, the month during which Greece requested the first bailout, the Spanish risk premium was at 162 basis points (May 7, 2012). However, in June 2012, it had already reached approximately 500 basis points. The EU and other countries' authorities suggested to the Spanish government that a bailout should be requested.[16] Spain made this request on June 25, 2012. However, its risk premium only started a decreasing tendency after Draghi's "WIT" statement.

The peculiarity of the Spanish bailout is that it bails out the banking sector rather than the sovereign. However, from the beginning, differences between the former and the latter blur. First, the loan granted by the EU (by the ESM) goes to the Spanish government, which then uses it to recapitalize Spanish banks in distress. Second, although the Spanish MOU indicates that conditionality is only "financial-sector specific," in reality it affects areas that go well

---

[15] See point 7 of the Declaration of the Summit on Financial Markets and the World Economy in Washington, D.C., November 15, 2008: "As immediate steps to achieve these objectives, as well as to address longer-term challenges, we will: . . . Use fiscal measures to stimulate domestic demand to rapid effect, as appropriate, while maintaining a policy framework conducive to fiscal sustainability." See the Declaration at www.g20.utoronto.ca/2008/2008declaration1115.html#actions.

[16] "G20 leaders urge Spain to make formal bank bailout request," *El País*, June 19, 2012. http://elpais.com/elpais/2012/06/19/inenglish/1340131940_182486.html.

beyond the financial sector and that are mentioned in the MOU itself. The key paragraphs are the following:

> There is a close relationship between macroeconomic imbalances, public finances and financial sector soundness. Hence, progress made with respect to the implementation of the commitments under the excessive deficit procedure, and with regard to structural reforms, with a view to correcting any macroeconomic imbalances as identified within the framework of the European semester, will be regularly and closely monitored in parallel with the formal review process as envisioned in this MoU.[17]

Therefore (*inter alia*):

> Regarding structural reforms, the Spanish authorities are committed to implement the country-specific recommendations in the context of the European semester. These reforms aim at correcting macroeconomic imbalances, as identified in the in-depth review under the Macroeconomic Imbalance Procedure (MIP). In particular, these recommendations invite Spain to: 1) introduce a taxation system consistent with the fiscal consolidation efforts and more supportive to growth, 2) ensure less tax induced bias towards indebtedness and home-ownership, 3) implement the labour market reforms, 4) take additional measures to increase the effectiveness of active labour market policies, 5) take additional measures to open up professional services, reduce delays in obtaining business licences, and eliminate barriers to doing business, 6) complete the electricity and gas interconnections with neighbouring countries, and address the electricity tariff deficit in a comprehensive way.[18]

Therefore, although the hard core of the Spanish MOU affected the Spanish financial sector, the previous reference to the MIP indirectly amounted to requiring Spain to take additional, non-financial-sector related measures. Austerity was also enshrined in the MOU[19] when it referred to the EDP (excessive deficit procedure) recommendations to Spain.[20] Formally, Spain exited the program on December 31, 2013. In 2014, its government deficit was –5.8 percent and its public debt was 97.7 percent.

The next most economically important bailout after Spain was that of *Portugal* (Moury & Freire, 2013). This case is different from the two cases previously reviewed. First, Portugal suffered from persistently low GDP growth in the decade before the 2008 economic crisis; thus, in the years 2001–2008, average annual real GDP growth was only 1 percent (the second

---

[17] Memorandum of Understanding on Financial-Sector Policy Conditionality (Spain) of July 20, 2012, available at http://ec.europa.eu/economy_finance/publications/occasional_paper/2012/pdf/ocp118_en.pdf, paragraph 29.

[18] Memorandum of Understanding on Financial-Sector Policy Conditionality (Spain) of July 20, 2012, paragraph 31.

[19] Memorandum of Understanding on Financial-Sector Policy Conditionality (Spain) of July 20, 2012, available at http://ec.europa.eu/economy_finance/publications/occasional_paper/2012/pdf/ocp118_en.pdf.

[20] Memorandum of Understanding on Financial-Sector Policy Conditionality (Spain) of July 20, 2012, paragraph 30.

lowest of the twenty-seven EU Member States). Second, Portugal also pre-sented important problems in terms of productivity, competitiveness, and exports. Third, in the years before the crisis Portugal had an unemployment rate below the European average. However, the introduction of the euro almost coincides with the reversal of this trend of low unemployment rates; beginning in 2001, Portugal initiated an upward unemployment trend that was aggravated by the crisis. However, even in the midst of the crisis, the Portu-guese unemployment rate, although well above the European average, was not as bad as those of Greece or Spain.

Concerning its fiscal position, Portugal entered the economic crisis with a relatively balanced situation in terms of government deficit (–1.9 percent GDP in 2007). However, in the years prior to 2007, Portugal consistently overshot the Maastricht 3 percent deficit ceiling. Public debt was not dramatically high but was out of sync with the Maastricht limits; the average from 2003 to 2007 was 65.14 percent GDP. Both government deficit and public debt figures further deteriorated from 2008 onwards.

Portugal's risk premium started an increasing tendency in 2008. This increase further accelerated in April 2010, coinciding with the first Greek bailout. On April 1, 2011, the Portuguese risk premium was at 513 basis points. To stop this trend, the Portuguese government requested a bailout on April 7, 2011. As shown in Table 9.1, the final approved amount was €52 billion, and €50.3 billion was disbursed.

Portugal signed the corresponding MOU.[21] The MOU's main headings were Fiscal policy; Financial sector regulation and supervision; Fiscal structural measures, labor market and education; Goods and services markets; Housing market; and Framework conditions. The usual liberalization-cum-privatization mix was also present. However, the MOU also went well beyond that mix, for example commanding the Portuguese authorities to make reforms in the judicial system of the country. Portugal had eleven updates of its MOU. The country formally exited the program on May 18, 2014. In that year, Portugal had a government deficit of –4.5 percent and a public debt of 130.2 percent.

The Portuguese case is particularly interesting from a legal perspective. In a series of landmark judgments that began in July 2012, the Portuguese Consti-tutional Court (PCC) struck down a number of cuts included in the Portu-guese Budget Laws. These cuts were implemented in Portugal as a direct consequence of the conditionality linked to the Portuguese rescue package. Thus, in its ruling no. 353/2012 of July 5, 2012,[22] the Court found that "the norms that provided for a measure under which the Christmas-month (13th month) and holiday-month (14th month), or any equivalent, payments

---

[21] Portugal Memorandum of Understanding on Specific Economic Policy Conditionality of May 17, 2011, available at http://ec.europa.eu/economy_finance/publications/occasional_paper/2011/pdf/ocp79_en.pdf.

[22] A summary of the ruling, in English, can be consulted at www.tribunalconstitucional.pt/tc/en/acordaos/20120353s.html.

were suspended in 2012–2014, both for persons who receive salary-based remunerations from public entities and for persons who receive retirement pensions via the public social security system, are unconstitutional." The PCC based its ruling on the principle of proportional equality. Accordingly, "there should have been limits to the difference between the extent of the sacrifice made by the persons who were affected by this measure and the sacrifice of those who were not; and the inequality caused by the difference in situations should have been the object of a degree of proportionality." In other words, the cuts in public wages and pensions would only be deemed legal if paralleled by equivalent cuts in the private sector and if they had been less significant. However, because the implementation of the 2012 Portuguese budget was well underway, the Court restricted the effects of the declaration of unconstitutionality and did not apply them to the suspension of payment of the Christmas and holiday bonuses or any equivalent payments with respect to 2012. The next decision was PCC ruling no. 187/2013 of April 5, 2013.[23] In this ruling, the Court declared unconstitutional the suspension of the additional holiday month of salary or equivalent for public administration staff on the same grounds (principle of proportional equality). On this occasion, the Court did not restrict the effects of its judgment. As Fasone (2014) reports, the latter judgment "resulted in a shock at the institutional level" because the PCC was perceived by the EU institutions as a potential risk to the fiscal stabilization plans of the country. In fact, in the seventh update of the Memorandum of Understanding on Specific Economic Policy Conditionality of May 2013, the Portuguese government was instructed to "take a number of steps aiming at mitigating the legal risks from future potential Constitutional Court rulings." The Court nevertheless did not retrench, and it adopted similar decisions in 2014.[24] In summary, the most serious legal challenge to the austerity measures implemented in bailed-out Member States came from Portugal.

The next bailout in economic importance was that of *Ireland* (IMF, 2015; Hardiman et al., 2016). The Irish case bears some resemblance to the Spanish one. Beginning in the early 1990s, a bubble in the housing market started emerging. This bubble was further inflated by Irish membership in the Eurozone. Credit interest rates were low. Furthermore, a seductive fiscal policy of low taxes designed to attract foreign investment diverted savings from the central Members of the Eurozone to Ireland, which were in turn channeled to the construction sector. Because credit expanded substantially faster than did deposits, Irish banks had to close the gap with heavy borrowing from the international markets. When the crisis started in 2007, the housing bubble burst, and nonperforming loans started increasing; these events directly

---

[23] A summary of the ruling, in English, can be consulted at www.tribunalconstitucional.pt/tc/en/acordaos/20130187s.html.

[24] See, in particular, ruling no 413/14 of May 2014. An English language summary of this ruling can be consulted at www.tribunalconstitucional.pt/tc/en/acordaos/20140413s.html.

affected the balance sheet of national banks. Thereafter, when Lehman Brothers collapsed, an interbank credit ended, and the Irish government had to rescue the most impaired national banks, both guaranteeing their liabilities and strengthening their capital base. The fates of the banks and the government financial situation thus became interlinked. The country's fiscal position deteriorated to an alarming extent in just a few months. In 2007, the Irish government deficit was 0.7 percent GDP. By 2010 it had soared to –32.5 percent. Whereas in 2007 public debt was at 24 percent GDP, by 2010 it had increased to 87.4 percent GDP.

In this economic context, Ireland requested a bailout on December 3, 2010. As shown in Table 9.1, the approved amount was €40.2 billion, and the actual disbursed amount was €39.4 billion. The funds were pooled from the EFSM and the EFSF (plus IMF and bilateral tenders). In exchange, Ireland had to sign the corresponding MOU,[25] which included the following headings: Fiscal consolidation; Financial sector reforms; Structural reforms; and Structural fiscal reforms. Although the program was largely focused on fiscal adjustment and the reform of the Irish banking sector, it also included other liberalization measures (such as the reduction of the minimum wage, and pension reform) and privatization (of state-owned assets in the transport, energy, broadcasting, and forestry sectors). On December 8, 2013, Ireland officially exited the program. In 2014, its government deficit was of –4.1 percent GDP and its public debt was at 109.7 percent.

One final bailout was that of *Cyprus* (Zenios, 2013). This Member State enjoyed steady growth during the whole of the 2000s, with an average GDP growth of 3 percent. Due to very lax and attractive tax and bank deposit regulation, the country's financial sector was able to attract funding capacity from the nonresident segment of depositors. The domestic financial system channeled this investment to steer a housing bubble and to invest abroad, in Greece in particular, a Member State through which Cyprus became highly exposed. Therefore, when economic turbulence and financial distress started in Greece, these events directly affected Cyprus' financial system. In parallel, nonperforming loans started increasing in 2010. In September 2011, Cyprus was *de facto* cut off from the financial markets when its risk premium peaked to 2,548 basis points. This risk placed untenable stress on domestic financial institutions, which virtually collapsed. Furthermore, the fiscal position of the country was in dire straits. Cyprus had a surplus in 2007 of 3.3 percent GDP that became a deficit in a matter of months. When the country requested the bailout in 2012, its government deficit was at –5.8 percent, and public debt was at 79.5 percent but soaring rapidly.

The country therefore requested a bailout on June 25, 2012. The approved amount was €9 billion, of which €5.8 billion was actually disbursed.

---

[25] Ireland. Memorandum of Understanding on Specific Economic Policy Conditionality of December 3, 2010, available at http://ec.europa.eu/economy_finance/articles/eu_economic_situation/pdf/2010-12-07-mou_en.pdf.

In exchange for the rescue moneys, Cyprus had to sign the corresponding MOU.[26] The main program's headings were: Financial sector reform; Fiscal policy; Fiscal-structural measures; Labor market; and Goods and services markets. Although the program was very much focused on the reform of the Cypriot financial system (it included, for example, anti-money-laundering reforms), it also inserted the classical liberalization (pensions and minimum wage) and privatization (telecom, electricity, and ports) program. In 2014, the fiscal position of Cyprus was far from being consolidated (–8.8 percent government deficit and 107.5 percent of public debt), and the country had not yet returned to growth (–2.3 percent GDP in 2014). Therefore, Cyprus remains under the bailout program.

9.2 Legal Nature of MOUs

The question of the legal nature of MOUs is a crucial one in the context of the EU bailout programs (Kilpatrick, 2014). If they did not have a legally binding nature, then Member States would not be obliged to follow MOUs strictly; therefore, the EU institutions could not attempt any legal challenges to Member States' failure to implement them. Conversely, if MOUs had a legally binding nature, then Member States would be legally obliged to implement them, and the EU institutions could not only suspend ulterior disbursements but also bring to the courts (national, European, and international) the defaulting Member State. A third dimension (and perhaps the most important one, as seen later) is that of citizens and markets; if MOUs had a legally binding nature, then citizens and markets could bring actions before the courts based on them.

However, from a different, more in-depth perspective, the problem posed by the legal nature of MOUs returns us to the discussion of law as credibility. A means of showing the challenges posed by the legal nature of MOUs is that we have all possible answers to the question of whether such instruments are legally binding. These challenges can be illustrated through the national and EU Court case law on this issue. Thus, the ECJ had ruled, until *Ledra*,[27] that MOUs lack any link with EU law; it had therefore refused to pronounce itself on the legal nature of these instruments.[28] However, the Court has clearly departed from this position in *Ledra*. In this case (September 2016), the Court

---

[26] Memorandum of Understanding between the European Commission acting on behalf of the European Stability Mechanism and Cyprus of April 26, 2013, available at http://ec.europa.eu/economy_finance/publications/occasional_paper/2013/pdf/ocp149_en.pdf.

[27] See Joined cases C-8/15 P to C-10/15 P, *Ledra*, Judgment of the Court of September 20, 2016, in particular, paragraphs 59 to 61.

[28] For a review of the ECJ case law pre-*Ledra*, see Hinajeros (2015), in particular, chapter 8. In fact, the ECJ reverses here a previous ruling of the General Court, which unadmitted the actions for annulment of the appellants against the Cyprus MOU.

admitted a legality and constitutionality control of the Cyprus MOU, therefore indirectly backing its legally binding nature. Furthermore, for the Greek Council of State, MOUs lack a legally binding nature, therefore being not more than political guidelines that orient the rescued Member State's behavior. Finally, for other Courts, such as the Portuguese Constitutional Court, MOUs are legally binding, which grants jurisdiction to the Court to review the constitutionality of the national measures that are adopted in its implementation, as explained in a previous section.

The different Courts' approach to the legal nature of MOUs more or less mirrors the different perspectives that are adopted by legal academics on this issue. The point of departure here is Aust (2014), who argues, based on the Vienna Convention on the Law of the Treaties, that MOUs are "gentlemen agreements" (political pacts). This position is the traditional, International Law approach to this issue. However, he leaves the door open to a more legally stringent interpretation of these instruments, which could be derived from the "intentions" of the parties to the agreement. In turn, Hinarejos (2015: 153) appears to validate the ECJ's treatment of MOUs when she says, "National Courts may be better placed to choose the level at which social rights should be protected in a situation of financial instability." Finally, for Cisotta and Gallo (2014: 5), MOUs are legally binding instruments because they are "inserted in a wider legal mechanism" that is to be considered "the Treaty."

A number of considerations emerge if we approach the issue from a "law as credibility" perspective. To start with, it is evident that Member States and the EU institutions sought a type of flexibility that they would not otherwise have if they had selected a more explicit legal instrument, such as an International Treaty. Flexibility was therefore an important concern here. To avoid the stringent procedural constraints of Treaty ratification that could emerge in some Member States, they decided to use MOUs, which is understandable in the context of an emergency situation. The challenge is to ascertain the exact degree of flexibility that the Member States and the EU institutions wanted to give to conditionality through MOUs – that is, whether this degree was greater than rigidity or whether it was high but not greater than rigidity.

Considering this question, let us conduct a counterfactual thought experiment and imagine two scenarios: one in which rigidity was slightly greater than flexibility, and another in which rigidity was slightly less than flexibility. In the first case, we would remain in the "law world," and in the second case, we would be in the "political realm." In both simulations, Member States, EU institutions, markets, and citizens are the main actors whose expectations about both scenarios interest us. In the first case (law world), the citizens would expect that the government would be obliged to implement the cuts inserted in the MOUs – but at the same time, they would be able to bring legal actions against social cuts (as in the Portuguese cases or the *Ledra* ECJ case). Concerning markets, in the first case (legal world), they would lend (to the ESM, for example) knowing that if Member States did not comply with austerity, they would be able to bring legal actions against, in this case, the financial vehicle in question. Member States would expect to use the argument that MOUs are legally binding and that their hands are tied as a means of justifying social cuts. However, the drawback under this scenario would be that they must accept lawsuits from citizens, markets, or even the EU institutions if they did not comply with the MOU. Finally, the expectations of the EU institutions under this scenario would be that they would be able to place more pressure on national governments to implement social cuts, with the major drawback being that they could be obliged to make disbursements if Member States implemented the MOUs.

Conversely, in the second scenario (political realm), citizens would understand that the government could escape from conditionality; however, the price to be paid would most likely be that the EU would stop disbursements. This decision would be political, not automatic, as in the legal realm scenario. Conversely, if the government applied conditionality, citizens would also know that they could not bring legal actions against it. The markets' expectation would be that they would lend to the financial vehicle in question, knowing that if conditionality was not implemented and the disbursements continued, they could not bring any legal actions against it. Member States could not use the legally binding character of MOUs as an alibi to make social cuts; further, they could not bring actions against the EU institutions if conditionality was implemented but disbursements stopped. Finally, EU institutions could no longer pressure Member States to implement cuts using the argument that MOUs are legally binding; however, in exchange they would have the flexibility to stop disbursements whenever they saw fit.

The problem in this game is how to provide payoffs under the different possibilities that we can envision in the two scenarios. However, considering the number of legal suits that citizens (and other actors) have brought against social cuts above all in domestic courts, it is possible to argue that they value the first option (legal world) more than the second one (political realm). In fact, the consideration of MOUs as legal instruments has proved interesting in certain States, such as in Portugal, as a way of placing a brake on social cuts. The markets' choice is more indecisive because they could stop lending to the financial vehicle in question. It is also clear that any attempt to have their moneys returned via a legal suit due to a Member State failure to comply with conditionality would be complex and protracted. Let us say that markets would be indifferent with respect to both scenarios, although slightly more inclined towards the first than to the second (they would prefer somewhat less uncertainty, although uncertainty would be sufficiently high even under the first scenario). Third, it is clear that for Member States it would be more interesting to be in the first scenario than in the second one because they could use the argument that cuts are inevitable in the domestic arena. Finally, the choice by EU institutions is also more indecisive because, on the one hand, they could use the argument that MOUs are legally binding instruments to place additional pressure on Member States to make cuts. Conversely, that they can stop disbursements when they see fit under the second scenario is most likely more effective than any other legal argument in placing pressure on Member States. In summary, a counterfactual analysis appears to add flesh to the bones of the argument that MOUs are legally binding objects for citizens and Member States, whereas markets would be indecisive about it and EU institutions would most likely prefer the political realm scenario. In other words, the only actors really interested in being in the political realm scenario would be the EU institutions. For the rest of the actors, being in the legal realm scenario would do.

Given the above (there appear to be more actors interested in the legal scenario than in the opposite, political one), a second step would be to try to understand what type of norm MOUs are. The argument that I will advance in the following is that MOUs are international contracts between the Member States and the EU institutions. This argument has a number of steps.[29]

First, let us examine this statement by Ross Leckow, Assistant General Counsel of the IMF, on May 7, 2002:[30]

> The Fund arrangement creates legal rights for the member and provides the member with a level of certainty as to what has to be done in order to receive financial assistance. At the same time, it does not subject the member to legal obligations to meet the conditions of the arrangement. To the extent that the member fails to meet a condition under an arrangement, the only legal consequence which ensues is that the member will not be able to purchase from the Fund. To understand what a Fund arrangement is, you have to understand what it is not. As a unilateral decision of the Fund, an arrangement is not a contract between the Fund and the member. The Fund sought to avoid subjecting a member to contractual obligations to implement their programs and putting the member in the unenviable position of being in breach of a legal obligation if it failed to meet a condition. To provide incentives to members, the Fund sought to minimize the legal consequences attached to failure. A member is free to walk away from its program and the arrangement at any time.

This statement is paradoxical, at least in certain ways. For one, Leckow acknowledges that the arrangement with the IMF creates "legal rights" for the member. These rights are that if the member complies with conditionality, then it is entitled to receive disbursements. Conversely, if it does not, then it

---

[29] The ECJ examines the European Commission responsibility in the *Ledra* case under the banner of "non-contractual" liability. This context would appear to indicate that for the ECJ, MOUs are legally binding instruments – but not private contacts. However, this conclusion must be qualified because it is derived from the fact that the ECJ understands (in a previous paragraph of the ruling) that MOUs are not acts that "can be imputed to [the EU institutions]." The question therefore remains open; the ECJ says in *Ledra* that MOUs have a legally binding nature. However, what it does not say is what type of legal acts MOUs specifically are.

[30] "Conditionality in the International Monetary Fund," www.imf.org/external/np/leg/sem/2002/cdmfl/eng/leckow.pdf.

cannot claim disbursements. Second, complying does not create "legal obliga-tions." This point apparently means that the member cannot be obliged to make cuts. However, there is a consequence: if conditionality is not fulfilled, then the disbursements will not be made.

This structure very much resembles a private contract structure. As Leckow quickly says in the next sentence, an arrangement "is not a contract between the Fund and the member." Again, this stance appears very much as though *excusatio non petita accusatio manifesta* ("he who excuses himself, accuses himself"). A private contract of this type works under the *do ut des* principle: the parties to the contract commit themselves to give or do something in exchange for another giving or doing. If one of the parties does not give or do, the other immediately escapes from her commitment to do or give. This point is exactly what Leckow is describing; if the member does not comply with conditionality, then the Fund is entitled not to disburse the funds.[31]

The parallelism between Leckow's statement and MOUs is evident. MOUs are directly inspired by the IMF's arrangements. Therefore, one could argue that they create certain legal commitments in the sense that if the Member State complies with the conditionality, it cannot be denied the funds; the EU institutions will not be legally entitled not to disburse. The question is, can we go beyond this conclusion?

Yes, we can. For example, if certain disbursements have been made, hoping for an ulterior implementation of certain MOU commitments, the EU insti-tutions can ask the courts to enforce the contract and oblige the Member State to implement it. Conversely, as stated previously, if certain conditions have been met, but the EU institutions refuse to make disbursements, the Courts could enforce the contract. Similarly, citizens, or markets, could ask the courts to enforce the contract in similar situations.

The second consideration that we must address is that the proposed solu-tion complies with the need for flexibility that both the EU institutions and the Member States were seeking, without entering into a situation in which rigidity is less than flexibility. As was analyzed in Chapter 2 of this book, private law can be precisely defined as the last situation after which flexibility becomes higher than rigidity. Viewing MOUs as contracts appears to strike an equilibrium point between flexibility and rigidity without abandoning the law realm.

The last point we must address is the following: if MOUs are contracts, to what jurisdiction should they be made subject? And a related one: what is the law that this jurisdiction must apply? The answer to these questions is twofold; first, MOUs are normally silent on this point. Second, we must therefore look somewhere else for a clue on this particular point. Here, the situation varies.

---

[31] The "contract" between the EU institutions and the Member State in question would be a "sui generis" contract; public because the parties to the contract are public institutions, and private in the sense that the contract would be subject to private law.

For example, in the first Greek bailout, the moneys came from Member States individually. The funds were pooled by the European Commission in what is called the "Greek Facility Agreement."[32] Article 14(1) of the Agreement establishes that the Agreement "shall be governed by and shall be construed in accordance with English law." However, article 14(2) says that any dispute among the parties about "the legality, validity, interpretation or performance" of the Agreement shall be submitted to the jurisdiction of the Court of Justice of the European Union. Concerning the corresponding MOU, the Agreement Preamble states, that "The support granted to Greece is made dependent on compliance by Greece amongst others with measures consistent with such act and laid down in a Memorandum of Economic and Financial Policies, Memorandum of Understanding on Specific Economic Policy Conditionality and Technical Memorandum of Understanding." Consequently, in this particular case, the jurisdiction to judge on the MOU would lie with the ECJEU, which should employ English law as a source to interpret the terms of the MOU as a contract among the parties. In the second Greek bailout, the solution provided for in the Master Financial Assistance Facility Agreement is the same one.[33]

In other cases, the situation is somewhat different, although the outcome is similar. For example, in the third Greek bailout, the Financial Assistance Facility Agreement is silent on this point. However, this agreement and the other agreements that have been adopted under the ESM framework are related to the ESM Treaty. Article 37 of the ESM Treaty grants jurisdiction to the ECJEU to judge "any dispute arising between an ESM Member and the ESM, or between ESM Members" in connection with "the interpretation and application of this Treaty, including any dispute about the compatibility of the decisions adopted by the ESM with this Treaty." This article would therefore indirectly grant jurisdiction to the ECJEU to judge these Agreements and therefore MOUs.

To summarize, for reasons of credibility, MOUs appear to have a legally binding nature. They adopt the particular form of contracts between Member States and the EU institutions. In general, the jurisdiction to judge these contracts will be that of the ECJEU (although specific arrangements might alter this rule). Concerning the applicable law, unless otherwise indicated (as in the case of the Greek Loan Facility), the Court must use EU law in addition to the laws of Member States (which will normally be English law, which is the traditional legal forum for this type of financial contract) to judge the case.

---

[32] The text of the agreement can be consulted at www.irishstatutebook.ie/eli/2010/act/7/enacted/en/pdf.

[33] See article 15 of the MFAFA, which text can be consulted at www.efsf.europa.eu/attachments/efsf_greece_fafa.pdf.

BIBLIOGRAPHY

Aust, A. 2014, "MOUs" in *Modern Treaty Law and Practice*, 3rd edn., Cambridge University Press, Cambridge, pp. 28–54.

Blanchard, O. 2012, "Lessons from Latvia." https://blogs.imf.org/2012/06/11/lessons-from-latvia/.

Blanchard, O., Griffiths, M., & Gruss, B. 2013, "Boom, Bust, Recovery: Forensics of the Latvia Crisis," Brookings Papers on Economic Activity, pp. 325–388.

Cisotta, R. & Gallo, D. 2014, "The Portuguese Constitutional Court Case Law on Austerity Measures: A Reappraisal," Luiss Guido Carli Academy, Working Paper no. 4/2014, pp. 1–11.

Estella, A. 2016, "European Union bailouts and credibility: the constitutional dimension," *European Public Law*, vol. 22, no. 3, pp. 507–540.

2015, "Potential exit from the Eurozone: the case of Spain," *Indiana Journal of Global Legal Studies*, vol. 22, no. 2, pp. 335–377.

Fasone, C. 2014, "Constitutional Courts Facing the Euro Crisis. Italy, Portugal and Spain in a Comparative Perspective," Max Weber Programme, MWP 2014/25.

Gyorffy, D. 2015, "Austerity and growth in Central and Eastern Europe: understanding the link through contrasting crisis management in Hungary and Latvia," *Post-Communist Economies*, vol. 27, no. 2, pp. 129–152.

Hardiman, N., Blavoukos, S., Dellepiane, S., & Pagoulatos, G. 2016, "Austerity in the European periphery: the Irish experience," UCD Geary Institute for Public Policy, Discussion Paper no. WP2016/04.

Hinajeros, A. 2015, *The Euro Area Crisis in Constitutional Perspective*, Oxford University Press, Oxford.

IMF 2015, "Ireland: Lessons from Its Recovery from the Bank-Sovereign Loop," European Department, International Monetary Fund.

2010, "Romania – Staff Report for the 2010 Article IV Consultation, Fourth Review Under the Stand-By Arrangement, and Requests for Modification and Waiver of Nonobservance of Performance Criteria – Staff Report; Staff Supplement; Public Information Notice and Press Release on the Executive Board Discussion; Statement by the Executive Director for Romania," IMF Country Report no. 10/227, July.

Kilpatrick, C. 2014, "Are the bailouts immune to EU social challenge because they are not EU law?," *European Constitutional Law Review*, vol. 10, pp. 393–421.

Krugman, P. 2013, ""The Conscience of a Liberal," September 19. https://krugman.blogs.nytimes.com/2013/09/19/latvian-adventures/.

Louis, J.-V. 2010, "Guest editorial: the no bail-out clause and rescue packages," *Common Market Law Review*, vol. 47, pp. 971–986.

Moury, C. & Freire, A. 2013, "Austerity policies and politics: the case of Portugal," *Pôle Sud*, vol. 2, pp. 35–56.

Panagiotarea, E. 2013, *Greece in the Euro: Economic Delinquency or System Failure?*, ECPR Press, Colchester.

Tsoukalis, L. 2016, *In Defence of Europe: Can the European Project Be Saved?* Oxford University Press, Oxford.

Varoufakis, Y. 2016, *And the Weak Suffer What They Must? Europe, Austerity and the Threat to Global Stability*, The Bodley Head, London.

Weisbrot, M. & Ray, R. 2010, "Latvia's Recession: The Cost of Adjustment with an 'Internal Devaluation,'" Center for Economic Policy Research, February. http://cepr.net/documents/publications/latvia-recession-2010-02.pdf.

Zenios, S. 2013, "The Cyprus debt: perfect crisis and a way forward," *Cyprus Economic Policy Review*, vol. 7, no. 1, pp. 3–45.

Zettelmeyer, J., Trebesch, C., & Gulati, M. 2013, "The Greek Debt Restructuring: An Autopsy," CESifo Working Paper no. 4333.

10

The EU Economic Strategy

Introduction

In the year 2000, the Member States and the European institutions realized that, although the European Union had adopted a common currency and an incipient set of fiscal rules, there remained a missing link in the overall European economic governance structure – an economic strategy. To close this gap, the EU adopted in 2000 the so-called Lisbon agenda. Furthermore, in 2010, the EU revisited the Lisbon agenda and adopted the so-called 2020 Strategy. The aim of this chapter is to describe and analyze the process that started in Lisbon.

The major point that this chapter will make is that, despite the social flavor that the economic strategy of the Union had had since its inception in the 2000s, both the Lisbon agenda and the 2020 Strategy have always been rather subordinated to the rigors of the Union's fiscal rules, as established by the Stability and Growth Pact.

Furthermore, note that since its inception the European economic growth strategy has embraced the so-called "open method of coordination." Thus, the Lisbon agenda and then the 2020 Strategy were initially based upon a complex system of naming and shaming rather than on a rule-based approach. As will be argued in this chapter, we are therefore speaking here of bureaucratic or administrative compromises rather than of commitments encapsulated in law. This controversial approach to regulation has implications for the credibility of the whole system of EU economic governance.

10.1 The 2000 Lisbon Agenda

At the beginning of the year 2000, the European Union was facing its future economic prospects with relative optimism. The economy was growing, the euro was being introduced in the EU according to the original plan, and there were no major macroeconomic shadows on the horizon. We already know that, as has already been discussed (see in particular Chapter 6), European and world prospects were soon to change because of the bursting of the IT bubble in the United States in the first semester of the same year. Prior to that, however, and the ensuing economic slump, the EU regarded itself as being in rather good economic shape. It was therefore time to address the long-delayed question of adopting an in-depth economic strategy for the Union.

Before Lisbon, other European Councils had raised the issue of the need to establish an economic and growth strategy for the Union. Fragmentary, important hallmarks of this point included the European Council of Essen of 1994,[1] which further elaborated on the recommendations of the Commission's White Paper of 1993 on "Growth, Competitiveness and Employment";[2] the Luxembourg Extraordinary European Council of November 1997,[3] which established the so-called Luxembourg process, aimed at developing a European Employment Strategy; the Cardiff European Council of June 1998,[4] which established the Cardiff process, aimed at integrating environmental issues in EU policies in different fields; and the European Council of Cologne of June 1999,[5] which initiated the Cologne process, aimed at establishing a macroeconomic social dialog at the EU level. Note that a Commission communication served as an important basis for the future Lisbon strategy: Agenda 2000, which was adopted by the European Commission in 1997.[6]

However, not until the European Council of Lisbon, which was held in March 2000,[7] did the EU envisage and adopt an *overall* strategy on this issue. At this important European Council, the EU Member States declared, somewhat pompously, the objective that the Union would become "the most competitive and dynamic knowledge-based economy in the world, capable of sustainable economic growth with more and better jobs and greater social cohesion."

At the outset, the Lisbon agenda fixed only a few concrete targets. These were full employment and an average growth rate of 3 percent GDP for the "coming years." It also spoke of an open method of coordination as the new key approach to attain the Lisbon agenda objectives. The document was divided into three main headings: (1) Preparing the transition to a competitive, dynamic, and knowledge-based economy; (2) Modernizing the European social model by investing in people and building an active welfare state; and (3) Putting decisions into practice: a more coherent and systematic approach.

---

[1] European Council Meeting on 9 and 10 December 1994 in Essen. Presidency Conclusions.

[2] European Commission. Growth, competitiveness, and employment. The challenges and ways forward into the 21st century. White Paper. COM (93) 700 final. Brussels: 05.12.1993.

[3] Extraordinary European Council Meeting on Employment Luxembourg, 20 and 21 November 1997. Presidency Conclusions.

[4] Cardiff European Council 15 and 16 June 1998. Presidency Conclusions.

[5] Presidency Conclusions Cologne European Council 3 and 4 June 1999. 150/99 REV 1 EN CAB.

[6] Agenda 2000. For a Stronger and Wider European Union. Brussels, 15.07.1997. COM(97) 2000 final.

[7] Presidency Conclusions Lisbon European Council 23 and 24 March 2000.

Each of these headings was divided into subheadings, each covering more or less specific objectives. Under the first heading came: (1) an information society for all, which included objectives such as all schools in the Union should have access to the Internet and multimedia resources by the end of 2001, and all of the teachers needed should be skilled in the use of the Internet and multimedia resources by the end of 2002; (2) the establishment of a European Area of Research and Innovation, which implied objectives such as the removal of obstacles to the mobility of researchers in Europe by 2002 and attracting and retaining high-quality research talent in Europe; (3) the creation of a supportive environment for starting up and developing innovative businesses, particularly small and medium-size enterprises (SMEs), with objectives such as the redirecting of European Investment Bank (EIB) and European Investment Fund (EIF) funding towards the support of business start-ups, high-tech firms, and microenterprises, and other risk-capital initiatives proposed by the EIB; (4) economic reforms for a complete and fully operational internal market, which implied the removal of barriers to the free circulation of services, the liberalization of gas, electricity, postal services, and transport, and the updating of public procurement rules, among other objectives; (5) efficient and integrated financial markets, with objectives such as the implementation by 2005 of the Financial Services Action Plan; and (6) the coordination of macroeconomic policies: fiscal consolidation and quality and sustainability of public finances, which included objectives that were in line with SGP requirements.

The second set of subsections were: (1) education and training for living and working in the knowledge society. This subsection included objectives such as the reduction by one-half by 2010 of the number of eighteen- to twenty-four-year-olds with only lower-secondary level education who were not in further education and training; (2) more and better jobs for Europe – development of an active employment policy. This subsection included another specific objective (besides the overall full employment objective) – to raise the employment rate from an average of 61 percent to as close as possible to 70 percent by 2010 and to increase the number of women in employment from an average of 51 percent to more than 60 percent by 2010; (3) modernizing social protection, with objectives, *inter alia*, such as giving particular attention to the sustainability of pension systems in different time frameworks up to 2020 and beyond; and (4) promoting social inclusion. This sub section included objectives such as the eradication of poverty by setting adequate targets.

Finally, under the third heading came subsections on: (1) improving the existing process; (2) an open method of coordination; and (3) mobilizing the necessary means. The first of these subsections started with the paradoxical statement that "no new process is needed" because the "existing Broad Economy Policy Guidelines and the Luxembourg, Cardiff and Cologne processes offered the necessary instruments, provided they were simplified and better coordinated, in particular through other Council formations contributing to the preparation by the ECOFIN Council of the Broad Economic Policy Guidelines." However, immediately thereafter, the second subsection specific-ally revolved around a new method for the coordination of Member State economic growth policies, the so-called open method of coordination. According to Lisbon, the new method of coordination involved four main items. The first was to fix the guidelines for the Union, together with specific timetables for achieving the goals that they had set for the short, medium and long terms. The second item was to establish quantitative and qualitative indicators and benchmarks "against the best in the world" and tailored to the needs of different Member States and sectors as a means of comparing best practices. The third item was to translate these European guidelines into national and regional policies by setting specific targets. The fourth and final item comprised periodic monitoring, evaluation, and peer review. I will even-tually return to these different aspects of the open method of coordination (OMC hereinafter).

Concerning the third subsection, mobilizing the necessary means, Lisbon mentioned that the EIB should proceed with its plans to make an additional €1 billion available for venture capital operations for SMEs and its dedicated lending program of €12–15 billion over the next three years for the priority areas. Thus, the new EU grand economic design for growth and jobs was born, once again, in the absence of new resources. We will show in this chapter that this lack is one of the main issues with the EU overall approach to growth: it is an economic strategy without a budget. This approach calls into question not only the efficiency but also the credibility of the whole exercise.

As referred to above, the most important innovation of the Lisbon agenda was the introduction of the OMC. The Council, together with the Commis-sion, progressively developed a number of indicators to measure Member States' performance in the different areas included in Lisbon. Approximately 100 indicators were developed, and the Kok report selected the fourteen most important (Kok report, 2004: 10; see Section 10.2).[8] These indicators are largely superseded by the 2020 Strategy new set of indicators, so I will not insist on their analysis.

It is important to have a clear idea of the main foundation on which the OMC rested. This foundation was to place the Member States' economic performance in competition. This approach would be possible through the establishment of indicators and targets that would show Member States' different behaviors in a varied array of areas. The idea was to generate a certain impetus by way of comparison; those Member States whose perform-ance was less good than that of other Member States would be spurred to ameliorate their score and become closer to the best students in the class.

---

[8] However, the Kok report actually included fifteen indicators.

The approach was not top-down, but bottom-up; the indicators and targets did not "bind" Member States in any meaningful sense of this word. Instead, it was just expected that Member States would be "shamed" by the better performance of other members and that this mechanism would catalyse national reforms (under the guidance of the EU institutions), which in turn would lead to better performance in the future.

Therefore, in terms of our "law as credibility" paradigm, the OMC is a regulatory technique that does not rely on legally binding commitments. Thus, in the OMC, flexibility is greater than rigidity. The point is whether this technique has worked to align Member States' respective economic policies, or, in other words, whether the OMC has been a credible arrangement for the EU and its Member States. Since the 2020 Strategy also relies on the OMC, this argument will be explored in the final section of this chapter.

10.2 The Kok Report of 2004

The European Council of March 2004[9] established a High-Level Group and entrusted it with performing a review of the first years of operation of the Lisbon agenda. The group was chaired by Mr Win Kok of the Dutch Labor Party, a former prime minister of the Netherlands. The report was delivered in November.

The Kok report did not exactly refrain from criticizing the Lisbon agenda. "Clearly, there are no grounds for complacency" (Kok report, 2004: 11). Nonetheless, it recommended continuing with that agenda. "Ambition is needed more than ever," said the report. Among the problems noted were an overload of the Lisbon agenda, poor coordination of actions and targets, conflicting priorities, and, above all, a clear lack of political determination to implement Lisbon. Some exogenous factors were also mentioned: the bursting of the IT bubble in the US had occurred at the very beginning of the period of implementation of the Lisbon agenda (see Chapter 6); furthermore, the September 11, 2001, terrorist attacks had most likely not helped generate trust in a sudden economic recovery. Nevertheless, the report did not use these factors as excuses for the failure of Lisbon. The root of the problem was found in how Lisbon had been conceived and the paths that the EU and Member States had established for implementing the agenda.

The report divided its main recommendations for reinvigorating the Lisbon agenda into three blocks. It also devised five main policy areas in which urgent action was recommended. It established three main lines along which Lisbon should be refocused, and the third block was an institutional block.

In the first block, the Kok report recommended implementing urgent measures in the following fields:

---

[9] Brussels European Council 25 and 26 March 2004 Presidency Conclusions. Brussels, 19 May 2004 9048/04 POLGEN 20 CONCL 1.

- **the knowledge society**: increasing Europe's attractiveness for researchers and scientists, making R&D a top priority and promoting the use of information and communication technologies (ICTs);
- **the internal market**: completion of the internal market for the free movement of goods and capital, and urgent action to create a single market for services;
- **the business climate**: reducing the total administrative burden; improving the quality of legislation; facilitating the rapid start-up of new enterprises; and creating an environment more supportive of businesses;
- **the labor market**: rapid delivery on the recommendations of the European Employment Taskforce; developing strategies for lifelong learning and active aging; and underpinning partnerships for growth and employment;
- **environmental sustainability**: spreading eco-innovations and building leadership in eco-industry; pursuing policies that lead to long-term and sustained improvements in productivity through eco-efficiency.

Concerning the second block, the Kok report recommended that the new phase of the Lisbon agenda should be refocused along the following three major lines:

- More coherence and consistency between policies and participants
- Improve delivery by involving national parliaments and social partners in the Lisbon process
- Clearer communication of objectives and achievements.

Finally, concerning the institutional block, the Kok report proposed that

- the **European Council** take the lead in progressing the Lisbon strategy;
- the **Member States** prepare national programs to commit themselves to delivery and engage citizens and stakeholders in the process;
- the **European Commission** review, report and facilitate progress and support it by its policies and actions;
- the **European Parliament** play a proactive role in monitoring performance;
- the European **social partners** assume their responsibility and actively participate in the implementation of the Lisbon strategy.

Two further points are of interest concerning the Kok report. First, it reflected in a clear fashion the economic philosophy underlying the economic growth strategy that Lisbon advocates. Second, it made a number of remarks concerning one of the main innovations of Lisbon, which is the OMC.

Concerning the first item, the Kok report said,

Actions by any one Member State . . . would be all the more effective if all other Member States acted in concert; a jointly created economic tide would be even more powerful in its capacity to lift every European boat. The more the EU could develop its knowledge and market opening initiatives in tandem, the stronger and more competitive each Member State's economy would be.

> The Lisbon strategy, as it has come to be known, was a comprehensive, interdependent and self-reinforcing series of reforms.
>
> (Kok report, 2004: 8)

The saying "a rising tide lifts all boats" is generally attributed to President John F. Kennedy, who made it in a speech in Arkansas on October 3, 1963. It is interesting to retrieve Kennedy's whole sentence: "As this State's income rises, so does the income of Michigan. As the income of Michigan rises, so does the income of the United States. *A rising tide lifts all the boats* [my emphasis] and as Arkansas becomes more prosperous so does the United States and as this section declines so does the United States."[10] Applied to the EU context, this concept would imply that, for example, if Germany grows, so would the UK, and if the UK does, so would the EU.

This stance, according to which as the economic tide rises, all of the boats in that sea will benefit, has provoked an intense debate in the economic discipline in general terms, not only with respect to the EU. Some economists find evidence that this premise is true (for example, Hines et al., 2001), others that it is not (Freeman, 2001). The latter argue above all, that not all groups in society benefit equally from the rise of the tide and that some groups do not benefit from it at all. All economists understand, however, that, even with a rising tide, in the absence of at least some public intervention not all boats will be lifted. More recently, the debate has revolved around what type of public intervention is needed to lift all, or most, of the boats. For the neo-Keynesian school of thought, what is needed is strong public intervention to spread the benefits of economic growth to all. For neoliberals, growth would produce a sort of trickle-down effect; thus, public intervention should be limited to tax cuts for the top earners, which would promote economic growth and therefore better spread its benefits. There are many doubts concerning the theoretical foundations of the second line of thought (Stiglitz, 2015). However, this point is not the one that I wish to make here. The question is, rather, to which of the two philosophies the Lisbon strategy adheres.

In this connection, it is obvious that the Lisbon agenda is silent on the issue of taxation. Taxation policy is a competence of the Member States, and therefore the EU can only make, at most, recommendations on this point. In this area, the Lisbon strategy and, similarly, the Kok report are silent. However, two points might provide clues as to the philosophical orientation of the Lisbon strategy: first, the absence of a budget for the implementation of the Lisbon strategy; and second, Lisbon's insistence on structural reforms and fiscal discipline.

Concerning the first, even the Kok report is silent. Among all of the criticisms that the Kok report makes of the Lisbon strategy, the most obvious

---

[10] See the whole speech in the "The American Presidency Project," www.presidency.ucsb.edu/ws/index.php?pid=9455.

one, which is that Lisbon is a growth strategy without even a minor budget in place, is completely absent from the report. Concerning the second, recall that this approach is part and parcel of so-called "supply-side" economics.[11] Structural reforms will make States become more competitive and therefore grow. In short, the argument is not that both the Lisbon strategy and the Kok report are exercises in trickle-down economics but simply that their respective flavors very much recall the neoclassical economic model. Whether this aspect is due to the policy limitations of the EU, particularly in the taxation domain, is most likely another story.

As mentioned previously, the Kok report also made a number of points about the OMC. "The open method of coordination has fallen far short of expectations," said the report. The problem was that Member States "do not enter the spirit of mutual benchmarking." The central elements of the OMC, which are peer pressure and benchmarking, were not working properly because of a lack of political will. Accordingly, the Kok report proposed a radical improvement of the process.

In particular, it argued that more than 100 indicators had been associated with the Lisbon process, which made the whole instrument rather ineffective. Member States could use this cloud of indicators at their convenience; if one did not fit them, they could easily find another one that would. "Simplification is therefore vital," said the report. In this vein, it proposed to reduce all of these indicators to approximately the fourteen (fifteen) indicators presented in Table 10.1. It also recommended that the European Union institutions should make regular updates to the previous indicators. Moreover, Member States should be ranked from 1 to 25. The essence of the radical improvement proposed by the Kok report could be synthetized in the idea of "praising and castigating" – praise good performance and castigate bad performance, what the report refers to as "naming, shaming and faming." The report was also sensitive to the fact that not all Member States started from the same position; for example, new Member States were generally further behind compared to older Member States. The new system should consider this point and praise those Member States that, although far away from the fulfillment of actual targets, had made an adequate evolution towards them. More than the accomplishment of the targets themselves, the new OMC should positively evaluate correct trajectories towards them.

10.3 The 2020 Strategy

At the European Council of June 2010,[12] the EU decided to adopt a new strategy for jobs and smart, sustainable, and inclusive growth. Because the

---

[11] For the link between trickle-down economics and supply-side economics, see Galbraith (1982).
[12] European Council 17 June 2010 Conclusions. Brussels, 13 July 2010 EUCO 13/1/10 REV 1 CO EUR 9 CONCL 2.

Table 10.1: Lisbon indicators and targets selected by the Kok report

Indicator	Target
GDP per capita (PPS, EU-15 = 100)	
Labor productivity per person employed (PPS, EU-15 = 100)	
Employment rate (%)	70.0
Employment rate females (%)	60.0
Employment rate of older workers (%)	50.0
Educational attainment (20–24) (%)	
Research and development expenditure (% of GDP)	3.0*
Business investment (% GDP)	
Comparative price levels (EU-15 = 100)	
At-risk-of-poverty rate (%)	
Long-term unemployment rate (%)	
Dispersion of regional employment rates	
Greenhouse gas emissions (index base year = 100)	92**
Energy intensity of the economy	
Volume of transport	

*Target introduced in the European Council of Barcelona, March 15 and 16, 2002 (paragraph 47)
**Target introduced into the EU by the signature on April 29, 1998 by the EU of the 1997 Kyoto Protocol. See Kyoto Protocol reference manual on accounting of emissions and assigned amount http://unfccc.int/resource/docs/publications/08_unfccc_kp_ref_manual.pdf

objective was to achieve a number of economic objectives for the year 2020, the strategy was nicknamed "the 2020 Strategy." The 2020 Strategy was built up based on previous experience with the design and implementation of the Lisbon agenda. It was intended to correct all of the errors detected in the previous Lisbon exercise and to propel the entire economic strategy of the Union a step forward. For the European Council, the aim of the 2020 Strategy was not only to recover from the 2008 crisis but also above all to emerge "stronger" from it through the introduction of medium- and longer-term economic reforms.

However, and notwithstanding its declared aim, the European Council made clear from the outset that the 2020 Strategy was subordinate to the EU's fiscal objectives. According to the European Council:

> Priority should be given to growth-friendly budgetary consolidation strategies mainly focussed on expenditure restraint. Increasing the growth potential should be seen as paramount to ease fiscal adjustment in the long run.[13]

[13] European Council 17 June 2010. Conclusions, paragraph 2, page 2.

Thus, it can be argued that the 2020 Strategy is part of the wider attempt of the EU to impose further fiscal discipline on Member States (particularly Eurozone Member States), rather than fiscal discipline serving the purposes of economic growth. It cannot be by chance that the 2020 Strategy was launched by the same European Council that adopted the decision to re-reform the SGP, as discussed in Chapter 7 above.

The 2020 Strategy established five "headline targets." These targets were already present, in one way or another, in the Lisbon agenda; but the 2020 Strategy, by setting five overall objectives, had the merit of clarifying right from the outset what the principal economic objectives were for the Union. These targets were established in an Annex to the Conclusions of the European Council of June 2010 and were the following:

- **Employment**: raise to 75 percent the employment rate for women and men aged twenty to sixty-four
- **Research and development**: raise combined public and private investment levels in this sector to 3 percent of GDP
- **Environment**: These targets are the so-called 20, 20, 20 objectives – reducing greenhouse gas emissions by 20 percent compared with 1990 levels; increasing the share of renewables in final energy consumption to 20 percent; and moving towards a 20 percent increase in energy efficiency. The EU also committed itself to making a decision to move on a reciprocity basis to a 30 percent emissions reduction by 2020 compared with 1990 after 2012.
- **Education**: reduce school drop-out rates to less than 10 percent and increase the share of thirty- to thirty-four-year-olds having completed tertiary or equivalent education to at least 40 percent
- **Social inclusion**: lift at least 20 million people out of the risk of poverty and exclusion.

The principal socioeconomic targets for the Union were now translated into numerical objectives, as had been proposed by the Kok report. The next step was for the EU institutions to translate these targets into more-specific indicators. Thus, one of the EU agencies, Eurostat, published the document "Smarter, Greener, More Inclusive? – Indicators to Support the Europe 2020 Strategy" in 2013. In this document, Eurostat spoke of eight headline indicators and "three sub-indicators." The three subindicators were all related to the social inclusion target: at-risk-of poverty, material deprivation, and jobless household. They were all included in the Conclusions of the June 2010 European Council. However, the European Commission and Eurostat made them operational by converting them into the three following, more specific, indicators: (1) monetary poverty (people at risk of poverty after social transfers);[14]

---

[14] Monetary poverty is measured by the indicator "People at risk of poverty after social transfers." The indicator measures the share of persons with an equivalent disposable income below the

(2) material deprivation ("severely materially deprived people");[15] and (3) low work intensity ("People living in households with very low work intensity").[16]

Furthermore and for clarification, there are a number of key instruments in the context of the 2020 Strategy. These instruments are the Broad Policy Guidelines, the Guidelines of Employment Policies, the National Reform Programs, and the European Semester already mentioned in Chapter 7 of this book.

First, the "Broad guidelines for the economic policies of the Member States and of the European Union" have their origin in article 121.2 of the TFEU. This article says that

> The Council shall, on a recommendation from the Commission, formulate a draft for the broad guidelines of the economic policies of the Member States and of the Union, and shall report its findings to the European Council. The European Council shall, acting on the basis of the report from the Council, discuss a conclusion on the broad guidelines of the economic policies of the Member States and of the Union. On the basis of this conclusion, the Council shall adopt a recommendation setting out these broad guidelines. The Council shall inform the European Parliament of its recommendation.

In turn, Council recommendation 2015/1184 established the broad economic policy guidelines.[17] These four main guidelines on economic policy are addressed to the Member States. They are the following: promoting investment, enhancing growth through Member States' implementation of structural reforms, removing key barriers to sustainable growth and jobs at the Union level, and improving the sustainability and growth-friendliness of public finances.

Second, the guidelines for employment policies for the Member States also have their origin in the TFEU. In particular, its article 148.2 states the following:

> On the basis of the conclusions of the European Council, the Council, on a proposal from the Commission and after consulting the European Parliament,

---

risk-of-poverty threshold. This threshold is set at 60 percent of the national median equivalent disposable income after social transfers. Social transfers are benefits provided by national or local governments, including benefits relating to education, housing, pensions, or unemployment.

[15] Material deprivation covers issues relating to economic strain, durables and housing, and environment of the dwellings. Severely materially deprived persons have living conditions greatly constrained by a lack of resources and cannot afford at least four of the following: to pay their rent or utility bills, to keep their home warm, to pay unexpected expenses, to eat meat, fish or other protein-rich nutrition every second day, a week's holiday away from home, to own a car, a color TV or a telephone.

[16] Very low work intensity describes those people aged 0 to 59 living in households in which the adults worked less than 20 percent of their work potential during the past year.

[17] Council Recommendation (EU) 2015/1184 of July 14, 2015, on broad guidelines for the economic policies of the Member States and of the European Union. OJEU 18.7.2015. L 192/27.

the Economic and Social Committee, the Committee of the Regions and the Employment Committee referred to in Article 150, shall each year draw up guidelines which the Member States shall take into account in their employment policies. These guidelines shall be consistent with the broad guidelines adopted pursuant to Article 121(2).

In turn, the Council decision of October 21, 2010, set the first employment guidelines after the 2020 Strategy was adopted.[18] These were the following: increasing labor market participation of women and men, reducing structural unemployment and promoting job quality; developing a skilled workforce responding to labor market needs and promoting lifelong learning; improving the quality and performance of the education and training systems at all levels and increasing participation in tertiary or equivalent education; and promoting social inclusion and combating poverty. These were updated by the Employment Guidelines of 2015.[19]

Both the Broad Economic Guidelines and the Employment Guidelines constitute what the European Council of June calls the Integrated Guidelines for Economic and Employment Policies. Therefore, the economic and employment guidelines must be read in conjunction and form part of the same pack. They also constitute the basis upon which the Member States must draw up their National Reform Programmes.

Third, the National Reform Programmes are therefore the documents in which the Member States indicate not only how the Integrated Guidelines for economic and employment policies will be implemented but also, more broadly, how the 2020 Strategy objectives will be met on a yearly basis.

Finally, the European Semester is the yearly cycle of economic policy coordination. It is therefore the instrument that connects all of the different limbs previously examined together with the six- and two-packs that form the Stability and Growth Pact. In other words, it is the instrument that connects the European Union economic strategy with its fiscal strategy (see also Chapter 7). The timeline of the European Semester is summarized in Figure 10.1.

10.4 Midterm Commission Review of the 2020 Strategy

The European Commission conducted the corresponding midterm review of the 2020 Strategy in its Communication of 2014 "Taking stock of the Europe 2020 strategy for smart, sustainable and inclusive growth."[20] Because the

---

[18] Council Decision of 21 October 2010 on guidelines for the employment policies of the Member States (2010/707/EU) OJEU L 308/46 of November 24, 2010.

[19] Council Decision (EU) 2015/1848 of October 5, 2015, on guidelines for the employment policies of the Member States for 2015 OJEU L 268/28 of 15.10.2015.

[20] Communication from the Commission to the European Parliament, the Council, the European Economic and Social Committee and the Committee of the Regions. Taking stock of the Europe 2020 strategy for smart, sustainable and inclusive growth. Brussels, 19.3.2014 COM (2014) 130 final/2.

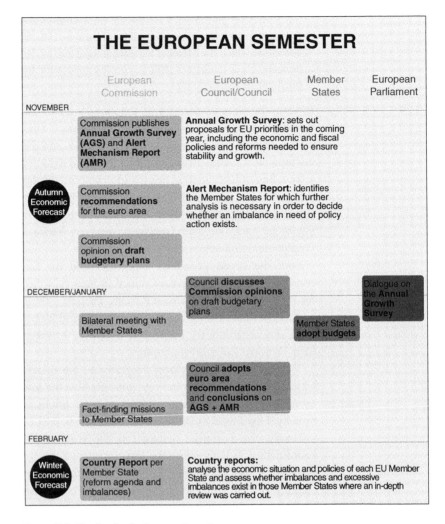

Figure 10.1: Timeline for the European Semester
Source: European Commission, http://ec.europa.eu/europe2020/making-it-happen/index_en.htm.
(Last accessed on December 15, 2016).

initial implementation of the 2020 Strategy began in the worst years of the crisis that started in 2008, the European Commission analysis was not particularly positive: "Progress towards the Europe 2020 targets has inevitably been mixed," said the Commission's communication. More specifically, the Commission summarized its view on the progress towards the 2020 objectives as follows:

> The crisis has had a clear impact, particularly on employment and levels of poverty, and has constrained progress towards the other targets, with the exception of its effect on the reduction of greenhouse gas emissions. It has also exacerbated the differences in performance between Member States in several

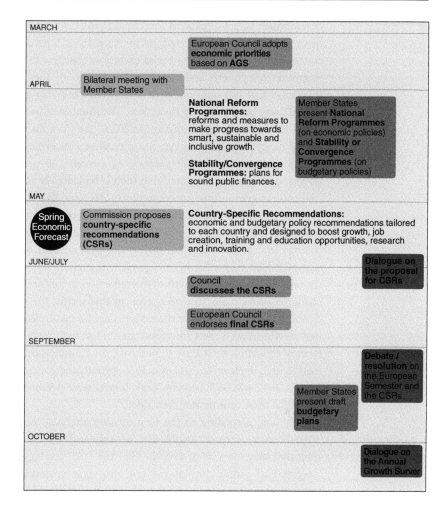

Figure 10.1: (*cont.*)

areas, such as employment and R&D. Progress has also been affected by the varying degree of policy response across the EU.

Therefore, except for some of the environmental objectives, which were established by the 2020 Strategy and whose achievement was most likely a consequence of the slowdown of economic activity, the remaining targets had been missed (if not worsened) by 2014–2015.

More specifically, concerning the five main objectives that the 2020 Strategy had established, the Commission's review established the following. First, concerning the employment objective (75 percent employment rate in 2020), the Commission said that employment was expected to increase to approximately 72 percent in 2020 and that "the fulfilment of national targets" would bring it to 74 percent. Second, concerning the research and development target (3 percent investment), the Commission stated that investment for R&D was expected to increase by 2.2 percent by 2020. Third, concerning the poverty and social exclusion objective (96.4 million of people removed from poverty and social exclusion by 2020), the Commission said that this target had not only not been approached but also that the EU had even drifted away from it during the crisis. "The number of people at risk of poverty might remain close to 100 million in 2020," the Commission concluded.

The outcome was, however, more positive concerning the two remaining targets. Concerning the 20 percent, 20 percent, 20 percent environmental targets, the Commission stated that the EU had already achieved an 18 percent reduction in greenhouse gas emissions in 2012 and that it was expected that by 2020 this figure would be improved to 24 percent. Concerning the share of renewables, the share by 2020 could even be 21 percent. Concerning the primary energy consumption target, the Commission was less optimistic; it acknowledged that a further 6.3 percent reduction would be needed to meet the target and that a large part of the reduction in this area had been due to the economic slowdown. However, even in this sector, the Commission did not discount the possibility that the target could be met by 2020. Finally, concerning the education targets (dropout rates to less than 10 percent and completed tertiary education to at least 40 percent), the Commission stated that concerning the first, the level in 2012 was 12.7 percent, and concerning the second, the level in 2012 was 35.7 percent. Both targets were deemed "broadly achievable by 2020," the Commission concluded.

Although, according to the Commission analysis, three out of five of the 2020 Strategy targets would not be achieved by 2020, the Commission indicated that the sort of exercise that the 2020 Strategy implied was useful. Targets had certain limitations but also clear advantages. Concerning the latter, the targets were illustrative of "dynamic change," they served as "policy anchors," and they were "easy to monitor." Concerning the former, the Commission critically noted that the targets "were not exhaustive," that "qualitative assessment was necessary," and that they were only "politically – and not legally – binding." The latter was the only comment that the Commission made concerning the Open Method of Coordination. Without mentioning it specifically, the Commission clearly recommended a more rule-based approach to targets and used the SGP as the model to be followed; "Contrary to the SGP, or even the new macro-economic imbalance procedure, where reference values or benchmarks are set in a legally binding framework including possible sanctions, the Europe 2020 targets are essentially political objectives." I will return to this point in the last section of this chapter.

Two points are striking concerning the Commission 2014 analysis. First, there was no reference whatsoever to the fact that the Strategy once again lacked any specific budget. The only references that the Commission made to the crucial issue of funding were the following: (1) it mentioned the European

Economic Recovery Plan; (2) it mentioned the so-called European flagship initiatives; and (3) it referred to the EU budget.

Concerning the first, the Commission said that in November 2008 the EU launched the European Economic Recovery Plan with a volume of €200 billion (1.5 percent EU GDP).[21] Irrespective of the fact that the EU Recovery Plan has been criticized for being clearly insufficient to serve as a Europe-wide stimulus package,[22] the point is that the Commission was here counting the European Recovery Plan as part of the 2020 Strategy – which it was not. As mentioned previously, the EERP was an EU limited stimulus package whose aim was to supplement the national stimulus packages; it therefore cannot be counted as the specific budget or funding of the 2020 Strategy.[23] The so-called flagship initiatives[24] were "sometimes backed by EU funding."

---

[21] See Communication from the Commission to the European Council. "A European Economic Recovery Plan" Brussels, 26.11.2008 COM(2008) 800 final. This stimulus package was made up of a budgetary expansion by Member States of €170 billion (approximately 1.2 percent of EU GDP), and EU funding in support of immediate actions of the order of €30 billion (approximately 0.3 per cent of EU GDP). However, the EU budget was not expanded to this end. Rather, old budgetary commitments were now used to boost the economy, and parts of the EU budget which were not spent were now reoriented to stimulate the EU economy under the European Recovery Plan.

[22] "EU leaders to reject calls for greater fiscal stimulus." EurActiv.com. March 19, 2009. Available at www.euractiv.com/section/euro-finance/news/eu-leaders-to-reject-calls-for-greater-fiscal-stimulus.

[23] See my remarks in Chapter 7 concerning the European Fund for Strategic Investment and the Investment Plan for Europe (2014). As was argued there, both rely on preexisting EU budget funding and do not imply new, fresh moneys.

[24] The 2020 Strategy's "Flagship Initiatives" were announced at the European Council of June 2010 and progressively adopted by the Commission. They supplement the 2020 Strategy and, in particular, the five headline targets that the Strategy sets. The flagship initiatives are the following: (1) A digital agenda for Europe (Communication from the Commission to the European Parliament, the Council, the European Economic and Social Committee and the Committee of the Regions "A Digital Agenda for Europe," Brussels, 19.5.2010 COM(2010)245 final); (2) Innovation Union (Communication from the Commission to the European Parliament, the Council, the European Economic and Social Committee and the Committee of the Regions "Europe 2020 Flagship Initiative Innovation Union" SEC(2010) 1161); (3) Youth on the move (Communication from the commission to the European parliament, the Council, the European economic and social committee and the committee of the regions "Youth on the Move An initiative to unleash the potential of young people to achieve smart, sustainable and inclusive growth in the European Union" COM(2010) 477 final); (4) Resource efficient Europe (Communication from the Commission to the European Parliament, the Council, the European Economic and Social Committee and the Committee of the Regions "An Integrated Industrial Policy for the Globalisation Era Putting Competitiveness and Sustainability at Centre Stage" SEC(2010) 1272 SEC(2010) 1276); (5) An industrial policy for the globalization era (Communication from the Commission to the European Parliament, the Council, the European Economic and Social Committee and the Committee of the Regions "An Integrated Industrial Policy for the Globalisation Era Putting Competitiveness and Sustainability at Centre Stage" SEC(2010) 1272 SEC(2010) 1276); (6) Agenda for new skills and jobs (Communication from the Commission to the European Parliament, the Council, the European Economic and Social Committee and the Committee of the Regions "An Agenda for new skills and jobs: A European contribution towards full employment." Strasbourg, 23.11.2010 COM(2010) 682 final); (7) European Platform against poverty and social exclusion (Communication from the

This statement is true for some flagship initiatives, but this point does not mean that there was additional funding for these; when funding for the flagship initiatives existed, it came from the EU general budget.[25] Finally, concerning the EU budget, the Commission speaks of what can be called the "twenty-fication" of the EU budget: "the new EU financial framework for 2014–2020 is closely aligned to the priorities of the Europe 2020 strategy." This statement is most likely true (Estella & de Sola, 2010), but it is important to recall that the EU budget was reduced concerning the previous financial perspectives (2007–2013) and that, once again, no new specific funding was added to support implementing the 2020 Strategy in the EU budget.[26] Despite the Commission's cheerful optimism, the 2020 Strategy remained, as had occurred with its genitor, the Lisbon strategy, an economic growth plan without an associated budget.

The second striking aspect of the Commission analysis relates to what the Commission referred to as "long-term trends affecting growth." When the Commission wrote its communication, these trends were, indeed, alarming. The mere passage of time has made them even more pressing. According to the Commission, they are as follows: the process of Europe's population aging (the estimate is that in 2050 the average age of the European population could reach 52.3 years); immigration (which now accounts for two-thirds of Europe's population growth); inequality (the top 20 percent earned 5.1 times more than the bottom 20 percent in 2012, and the trend is increasing); productivity (EU output stands at approximately 70 percent of US per capita GDP, compared with 90 percent in 1980; again, the most worrisome aspect of this statistic is the trend which, according to the Commission, was worsening); and the environment (although the environment is part of a wider, global trend; for example, the Commission reports that 60 percent of the world's major ecosystems have already been depleted to unsustainable levels).

Commission to the European Parliament, the Council, the European Economic and Social Committee and the Committee of the Regions "The European Platform against Poverty and Social Exclusion: A European framework for social and territorial cohesion" SEC(2010) 1564 final). For a summary, see http://ec.europa.eu/europe2020/europe-2020-in-a-nutshell/flagship-initiatives/index_en.htm.

[25] The best example is the H2020 program, which is included in the flagship initiative "Innovation Union." This effort is the largest EU Research and Innovation program of the EU, with nearly €80 billion of funding available over seven years (2014–2020). However, this funding is not new; H2020 is already foreseen in the latest EU financial perspectives for 2014–2020. H2020 is included in heading 1 "Smart and inclusive growth" and subheading 1a "Competitiveness for growth and jobs" of the EU budget.

[26] The previous EU's multiannual framework (2007–2014) had a total amount of 1.12 percent GNI; the current one (2014–2020) is 1.04 percent GNI. See the data at http://ec.europa.eu/budget/figures/fin_fwk0713/fwk0713_en.cfm.

As mentioned previously, these concerns were and are very well founded, the first three ones in particular. What is striking is not that the Commission refers to them. What is striking is that, in its review of the 2020 Strategy, these concerns are largely absent in the Commission's recommendations, with the exception of the environmental aspects. Granted, the growth, education, R&D, poverty, and social exclusion targets all relate in some way or another to the long-term problems that the Commission detected. However, none of these targets addresses these concerns directly. For example, the EU manifestly lacks a plan for addressing what is most likely its most important problem: aging.[27] It is also clear that the EU simply lacks a common vision on how to address in a systematic and coordinated manner what could be one of the main factors for the resolution of this problem, which is immigration.[28] The EU is also short of a plan on how to address the problem of inequality and fairness.[29] In any case, what is most shocking is that the Commission was silent on the need to reorient the 2020 Strategy towards the resolution of these particularly acute problems.[30]

[27] The ECOFIN Council of February 14, 2006, assigned the European Commission to "undertake a comprehensive assessment" of the demographic trends of the Union. This assessment has given rise to the so-called "Ageing Reports." The European Commission published its first Ageing Report in 2009; the latest, most up-to-date one was published in 2015. The Commission's reports are simple projections of the demographic trends of the Member States upon the sustainability of their public financial stance. See all of the reports at http://ec.europa.eu/economy_finance/publications/european_economy/ageing_report/index_en.htm.

[28] The European Commission has adopted an Agenda on Migration in 2015. See Communication from the Commission to the European Parliament, the Council, the European Economic and Social Committee and the Committee of the Regions. "A European Agenda on Migration." Brussels, 13.5.2015. COM(2015) 240 final. The Commission acknowledges in its Communication that "decisions on the volume of admissions of third country nationals coming to seek work will remain the exclusive competence of Member States." For a thorough critique of the EU's policy stance on immigration, see Hampshire (2016).

[29] See Salverda (2015). According to this author, "[EU policies] are found wanting because of their narrow focus on risk of poverty and the absence of a role for considering poverty and inequality in policy made at the European level. Instead [Salverda] advocates mainstreaming inequality concerns in broad areas of policy making and suggests starting an annual Inequality Assessment of the Union." To my knowledge, this report has not been produced to date.

[30] As part of the midterm review of the 2020 Strategy, the Commission launched a public consultation on the Strategy. The public consultation on the Europe 2020 strategy was held between May 5, 2014, and October 31, 2014. It was addressed to a varied number of both public and private stakeholders. A total of 755 contributions were received from twenty-nine countries. Social partners, interest groups, and nongovernmental organizations were the most represented categories of respondents, followed by Member States' governments and public authorities, individual citizens, think-tanks, academia, foundations, and companies. The outcome of the public consultation on the 2020 Strategy is published in the Communication from the Commission to the European Parliament, the Council, the European Economic and Social Committee and the Committee of the Regions "Results of the public consultation on the Europe 2020 strategy for smart, sustainable and inclusive growth" Brussels, 2.3.2015 COM (2015) 100 final.

10.5 Subordination of the 2020 Strategy to the Rules of European Fiscal Governance

Is the Union's economic strategy an umbrella that covers the rest of the limbs of the EU economic governance system (monetary and fiscal policy)? Or is it the other way around; is the Union's economic strategy subordinated to the other aspects of the EU economic governance system? I will show in this section that, despite the social flavor of the EU's strategy, this is in reality part of an economic plan that serves the needs of fiscal policy – and not the other way around.

To start with, the Lisbon agenda was already rather vocal concerning which limb of the EU system of economic governance led and which one followed. In paragraph 3 of the Conclusions of the Lisbon European Council of March 2000, the European Council stated that

> The Union is experiencing its best macro-economic outlook for a generation. As a result of stability-oriented monetary policy supported by sound fiscal policies in a context of wage moderation, inflation and interest rates are low, public sector deficits have been reduced remarkably and the EU's balance of payments is healthy. The euro has been successfully introduced and is delivering the expected benefits for the European economy. The internal market is largely complete and is yielding tangible benefits for consumers and businesses alike. The forthcoming enlargement will create new opportunities for growth and employment. The Union possesses a generally well-educated workforce as well as social protection systems able to provide, beyond their intrinsic value, the stable framework required for managing the structural changes involved in moving towards a knowledge-based society. Growth and job creation have resumed.

The idea was clear: growth would come after fiscal consolidation had succeeded, not before. The point was repeated, this time even more clearly, in a later passage of the Lisbon Conclusions: "the opportunity provided by growth must be used to pursue fiscal consolidation more actively and to improve the quality and sustainability of public finances." The final *raison d'être* was not economic growth and social development by themselves but rather growth as a driver for fiscal consolidation.

As has been reported previously, what was mentioned in Lisbon rather implicitly was made even clearer in the renewal of the Lisbon agenda, the 2020 Strategy. It is worth reproducing again the following passage of the European Council of June 2010:

> Priority should be given to growth-friendly budgetary consolidation strategies mainly focussed on expenditure restraint. Increasing the growth potential should be seen as paramount to ease fiscal adjustment in the long run.

To be sure, the economic strategy of the Union had been tinged, since the beginning of this process in Lisbon, with a clear social flavor. As mentioned in other sections of this chapter, one of the paramount objectives of Lisbon was "more and better jobs" and "social cohesion." This objective was instantiated, *inter alia*, by setting specific targets for example in the field of employment and by a firm commitment to fight against social exclusion and poverty. In turn, the 2020 Strategy took the social side of the Union's economic strategy a step forward by establishing more ambitious objectives for employment and set specific targets for education and social inclusion.

All of these aspects have been interpreted by some authors as a way to enhance the legitimacy of the whole economic plan for the Union in an area in which the EU lacked a clear pack of competences (Dehousse, 2002; 2004; 2011). More plausibly, it is possible to argue that the Union was taking stock of the fact that no economic strategy would be possible without introducing into the plan the social side of any strategy for economic progress, particularly in a context, such as the European one, with a strong social-welfare State tradition. The point is that the social side of the economic strategy for the Union was most likely a compensation for the fact that the whole strategy, social aspects included, was rather considered a means to a major end that would be the fiscal consolidation objectives of the Union.

Three further factors appear to point in this direction. First, that the economic strategy of the Union is devoid of a budget, or at least of a funding plan, is illustrative of the secondary importance that the economic plan played, in reality, in the whole system of European economic governance. Second, as shown in Section 2 of this chapter, the Lisbon agenda and its progeny, the 2020 Strategy, adhere to a very particular economic philosophy in which public economic intervention plays, at most, a secondary role. Third, the SGP and in general the rules of fiscal governance of the Union are, for the most part, "hard law" (in fact, as seen in Chapters 6 and 7, its level of "legalification" is most likely beyond equilibrium), whereas the economic strategy of the Union belongs, at most, to the world of "soft law," illustrating the same trend. The EU economic strategy is subordinate to and follows the EU rules of fiscal governance.

To summarize this point graphically, the whole system of EU economic governance should have appeared as in Figures 10.2 and 10.3.

10.6 OMC and Credibility

The OMC has been criticized, in the academic studies that have examined this issue, on different fronts. One of the most salient criticisms relates to the credibility of the instrument. Armstrong (2016), for example, argues that "overall, agreeing objectives and guidelines is intended to sign political commitment to the coordination process. How credible is that commitment is debatable." Concerning targets and credibility, he argues that "while the aim of targets is to increase political commitment, conversely, missed targets tend to

Figure 10.2: Ideal EU economic governance structure

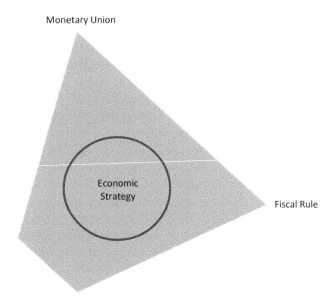

Figure 10.3: Current EU economic governance structure

undermine the credibility of those commitments." Dehousse (2002) says, "Thanks to its relative stability and involvement in all areas covered by the OMC, it could be the laboratory where such a synthesis is prepared. However, to do so, two conditions would need to be met: its internal coordination capacity must be reinforced, and its credibility in the national capitals must be restored." Therefore, although not equating the lack of binding force of the OMC with a generalized caveat concerning the instrument in credibility terms, he appears to relate the credibility of the OMC to how seriously national governments take the whole exercise of coordination that the OMC implies. Overall, what is clear is that the credibility of the OMC is a common concern in the literature that addresses this issue.

The "law as credibility" framework offers an apt model through which we can examine the issue of credibility of the OMC. First, with the OMC, we are in a world in which the main condition on which the law as credibility paradigm rests ($R > F$) ceases to exist. In fact, with the OMC, the following is true:

$$R < F$$

The OMC is therefore in the nonlegal domain. There is consensus on this point. Therefore, we know what the OMC is not. However, the fact that there is a consensus around what the OMC is not does not mean that there is agreement on what it is. Are we seeing a political commitment? Is the OMC a moral commitment? Is the OMC a customary commitment?

This question is relevant because these different credibility structures all have their own logic and, therefore, generate credibility in very different forms. On its face, it would appear that the OMC is neither a moral commitment nor a customary one. Therefore, the OMC would appear to belong to the category of political commitments, which is Armstrong's point; he calls the OMC a "political commitment." However, it is difficult to adhere to the characterization of OMC as a plain political commitment, at least in the usual sense of this concept. A political commitment is for example a commitment that a politician makes not to run for a third mandate in the next general election. It is, as in the game-theory ultimatum game, the commitment of the dictator to share, up to a certain point, any given amount of money with the people. Political commitments also constitute political parties' platforms in elections. The highly bureaucratic flavor of the OMC (indicators, targets, objectives, processes, and the like) appears to conform not particularly well to the conventional representation that we have of political commitments. Furthermore, although they belong to the nonlegal world, it is also true that they have certain traits that would make them resemble law. These traits are why some authors refer to the commitments (in a not entirely acute fashion, in my opinion) as "soft law" instruments (Trubek, Cottrell & Nance, 2006; Trubek & Trubek, 2005; for a very accurate critique, see Armstrong, 2013). Moreover, they not only set an objective (as in "I will not run for President a third time") but also are occasionally much more about a process or a path than a specific outcome. The best example of this process is the European Semester, which is about process coordination beyond law, although it does incorporate legally binding elements. Therefore, we can refer to the OMC as bureaucratic or administrative commitments, that is, a new form of commitments which are more than political commitments but less than law and that occasionally include (secondary and less important) legally binding elements, although not in all cases.

The setting of standards, targets, indicators, and the like is becoming a common by-product of what is being referred to as the emerging "global administrative *law* " (Krisch Kingsbury, 2006 my emphasis). To be sure, law is italicized because these new instruments would all, at best, be at the fringes of law and not within the legal realm. The OMC would be but the vanguard in the EU context of this new approach to doing things in the sphere of administrative law and policy at a global level. Examples of this wider trend would be, for example, the OECD or IMF indicators, reports, and targeting systems.

The structure of bureaucratic commitments differs very much from its sister-in-arms, political commitments. If a political actor does not fulfill a political commitment, then she will be punished electorally. This result is the "sanction" in the political realm. However, to speak of this type of sanctioning system in the world of OMC can be done only if a great deal of voluntarism is included in the whole exercise of attempting to systematize what OMC is and how it functions. If a Member State's government does not comply with, for instance, an employment target to which it committed, then it could be sanctioned electorally, as Dehousse (2002: 14) suggests in his analysis of OMC. However, for this result to occur, the mere existence of the target would not do; for example, it would most likely be necessary to add a strong political commitment from the politician's side. "I promise I will stick to the 2020 Strategy employment commitments; judge my performance as a politician based on that." It would be the political commitment – and not the bureaucratic one – that would provoke an electoral reaction, although the bureaucratic commitment would be a necessary condition for the whole commitment to stand.

The sanctioning system in bureaucratic commitments therefore seems to be of a different type. It relates to naming and shaming, which amounts to saying that the sanction here is in terms of reputation. If targets, objectives, or ends are not complied with, or if indicators are systematically violated, then the Member State will lose reputation. Reputation might be important, for example, in economic terms; if markets perceive that economic targets are not being met, then they can punish the Member State in question. In this sense, the retributive system of the OMC is very similar (and in fact is tailored-made on its model) to that of the SGP, which is why I argued in Chapters 6 and 7 that the SGP's rule-based approach most likely forces the whole SGP system out of equilibrium. A mere system of naming and shaming, such as the OMC, would most likely have sufficed. A different matter is how rational markets are and how closely they actually examine Member States' accomplishment of targets.

In the OMC, the structure of the commitment works as follows. Consider for instance the example of the 3 percent GDP growth in 2020, which was the baseline commitment in the Lisbon Strategy (and although the 2020 Strategy is silent on this point, we can assume that this commitment still holds, at least as a desideratum). This structure is very similar to the syllogistic structure that legal commitments normally have. In law, commitments take the following shape: if you commit a crime, you will be punished. The 3 percent commitment implies that if you do not reach the 3 percent target, then you will be shamed by your peers and you will lose reputation. There is therefore an antecedent and a consequent.

The next questions to be solved, as Armstrong (2016: 46) correctly asks, are who the author of the OMC commitment is, who the maker of the commitment is, and who the addressee of the commitment is. These questions are relevant because it is in the nature of OMC commitments to be adopted in a coordinated, horizontal, way rather than in a hierarchical one. Therefore, OMC commitments are made by the EU institutions together with the Member States. However, formally speaking, the EU institutions (and in particular, the European Council, aided in this process by the European Commission and Eurostat) make the commitment, which is then addressed to the Member States. Although the reality is somewhat more complex than described, the OMC commitment structure can be simplified and represented as a game between the EU institutions and the Member States: the EU institutions adopt the commitment, which is then addressed to the Member States, who must fulfill it. As in legal commitments, OMC commitments have a certain degree of self-referentiality: "If you commit a crime, you will be punished" means in reality that I, public authority, commit myself to use my resources to punish you in the event that you commit a crime. In OMC commitments, this structure takes a different shape: if you don't achieve the target, you will lose reputation. In other words, your loss of reputation will occur by itself; it will not be necessary that the EU institution take any particular action to make you suffer the loss. Here, we are speaking more of a process than of a particular action that is taken in the case that a violation of the commitment occurs. For example, the EU institution might "report" that you did not reach the target of 3 percent. This report implies an action, of course, but this action has a very different nature from an action to punish, which is connatural with legal commitments. This consequence is the main difference between legal commitments and OMC bureaucratic-like commitments.

Another matter that is related to the credibility of the OMC system is the question of its efficiency. Did the OMC system work? On its face, we could say that it did not; we have shown already that, according to the Kok report and the Commission 2004 report on the Lisbon and 2020 Strategies, the targets were largely missed, in many cases at least. However, we should ask here, again, about the counterfactual situation: would the Union be better off, worse off, or the same in the absence of the OMC? To my knowledge, no serious study exists that has put the question to the test. However, there is agreement in the literature that has examined the issue that such an exercise places Member States into a certain dynamic towards the achievement of the targets in the absence of which those targets would be much more difficult to achieve (Borrás & Radaelli, 2010: 30). I tend to agree with this impressionistic view, although the question remains open to empirical validation. The point is that showing that the OMC system worked would enhance its credibility; failure to show that it worked would undermine it.

The final question is whether the OMC represents an equilibrium. Recall once again that, from the "law as credibility" perspective, it makes no sense to speak in general terms of "an equilibrium" of a given system. The idea of equilibrium is only meaningful with respect to specific commitments. However, it is also true that OMC commitments all take a very similar shape: "You must reach X target in time T; otherwise, you will lose reputation." Therefore, some general remarks can at least be attempted.

A key point here is that, as has been recurrently mentioned in this chapter, the Lisbon agenda first and then the 2020 Strategy are both economic plans for Europe – with no particular budget or funding. That we face an economic strategy without a funding plan makes establishing legally binding targets, objectives, and ends less than credible. Therefore, establishing a system such as the OMC, which is, on the one hand, voluntary, but which, on the other hand, has a certain cost for those Member States that do not achieve the targets, is the best that the EU could afford, given the circumstances. The OMC system is therefore a system that represents an equilibrium, and all efforts that attempt to legalize it, that is, to give the OMC more legal flesh,[31] are bound to fail. In fact, few incentives exist to change the nature of the OMC process; it has been rather stable over time, as Dehousse (2014: 20) contends. For example, what the 2020 Strategy does, in reality, is to stream-line and clarify many of the objectives and targets that were already put in place in the Lisbon agenda. However, the nature of the process, and its main tool, the OMC, are not seriously called into question by the players of the OMC game.

In fact, it could be argued that the SGP should most likely have taken the same shape taken by the economic strategy of the Union. If the legal ambition of the SGP had been reduced, as occurred concerning the Union's economic plan, and a system of naming and shaming had been put in place, then we should also have most likely witnessed more stability in the fiscal domain. It would have been a different matter had the Union a strong budget, allowing it to make social transfers and adequately fund its economic

---

[31] See Communication from the Commission to the European Parliament, the Council, the European Economic and Social Committee and the Committee of the Regions. "Taking stock of the Europe 2020 strategy for smart, sustainable and inclusive growth" 19.3.2014 COM(2014) 130 final/2, p. 15.

strategy. However, in the world as we now know it, the OMC could become a model that other sectors of the EU economic governance system would be well advised to emulate.

BIBLIOGRAPHY

Armstrong, K. A. 2016, "The Open Method of Coordination: Obstinate or Obsolete?," University of Cambridge Legal Studies Research Paper Series, vol. 45.

2013, "New Governance and the European Union: An Empirical and Conceptual Critique," Queen Mary University of London, School of Law Legal Studies Research Paper, no. 135.

Borrás, S. & Radaelli, C. 2010, "Recalibrating the Open Method of Coordination: Towards Diverse and More Effective Usages," Swedish Institute for European Policy Studies (SIEPS) 2010/7.

Dehousse, R. 2011, *The Community Method: Obstinate or Obsolete?*, Palgrave Macmillan, New York.

2004, *L'Europe sans Bruxelles: une analyse de la méthode ouverte de coordination*, L'Harmattan, Paris.

2002, "The Open Method of Coordination: A New Policy Paradigm?," paper presented at the First Pan-European Conference on European Union Politics "The Politics of European Integration: Academic Acquis and Future Challenges," Bordeaux, September 26–28.

Estella, A., & de Sola, M., 2010, "La Estrategia 2020. Del Crecimiento y La Competitividad a la Prosperidad y la Sostenibilidad," Fundación Ideas para el Progreso, February 1.

Eurostat. 2016, "Smarter, Greener, More Inclusive? – Indicators to Support the Europe 2020 strategy," revd edn. http://ec.europa.eu/eurostat/documents/3217494/7566774/KS-EZ-16-001-EN-N.pdf/ac04885c-cfff-4f9c-9f30-c9337ba929aa.

2013, "Smarter, Greener, More Inclusive? – Indicators to Support the Europe 2020 Strategy." http://ec.europa.eu/eurostat/documents/3217494/5777461/KS-02-13-238-EN.PDF/1a6fa7e5-85b7-40aa-987e-6a6d049ad723.

Freeman, R. 2001, "The rising tide lifts …?," NBER (National Bureau of Economic Research) Working Paper Series 8155.

Galbraith, J. K. 1982, "Recession economics," *New York Review of Books*, February 4, p. 34.

Hampshire, J. 2016, "Speaking with one voice? The European Union's global approach to migration and mobility and the limits of international migration cooperation," *Journal of Ethnic and Migration Studies*, vol. 42, no. 4, pp. 571–586.

Hines, J., Hoynes, H., & Krueger, A. 2001, "Another look at whether a rising tide lifts all boats," NBER (National Bureau of Economic Research) Working Paper Series 8412.

Kok report. 2004, "Facing the Challenge The Lisbon Strategy for Growth and Employment." Report from the High Level Group chaired by Wim Kok November 2004. http://europa.eu.int/comm/lisbon_strategy/index_en.html.

Krisch, N. & Kingsbury, B. 2006, "Introduction: global governance and global administrative law in the international legal order," *European Journal of International Law*, vol. 17, no. 1, pp. 1–13.

Salverda, W. 2015, "EU Policy Making and Growing Inequalities," *European Economy* Discussion Papers no. 8.

Stiglitz, J. 2015, *Reduce Inequality, Increase Economic Growth: A Conversation with Joseph Stiglitz*, New York University Press, New York & London.

Trubek, D., Cottrell, P., & Nance, M. 2006, "'Soft law', 'hard law' and EU integration" in *Law and New Governance in the EU and the US*, eds. G. De Burca & J. Scott, Hart Publishing, Oxford & Portland, Ore.

Trubek, D. & Trubek, L. 2005, "'The open method of co-ordination and the debate over 'hard' and 'soft' law'" in *The Open Method of Co-ordination in Action: The European Employment and Social Inclusion Strategies*, eds. J. Zeitlin & P. Pochet, PIE Peter Lang.

Index

Inside Job, 161
institutional selection, 25
Integrated Guidelines for Economic and
    Employment Policies, 245
Intergovernmental Agreement on the Transfer
    and Mutualisation of Contributions to the
    SRM, 126, 129
Investment Plan for Europe, 185
Ioannou, R., 188
Ireland, 162, 189, 203, 224–225
Ismihan, M., 75
Israel, Bank of, 73
IT bubble, 148, 160
Italian Central Bank, 131
Italy, 15, 100, 130–132, 140, 148, 162, 189, 206
    constitution, 20
Ivory Coast, 8

James, H., 48
Japan problem, 75
judges, 32–34
Juncker, Jean-Claude, 182

Kelemen, D., 210
Kelsen, Hans, 54–56
Kennedy, John F., 240
Keynes, Maynard, 70
Klamert, M., 59–60
Koehler, S., 188–189
Kok report (2004), 238–241
Kok, Win, 238
Kolb, R., 53, 55–56, 58–59
Krugman, Paul, 3, 6, 70, 211
Kyoto Protocol, 242

Larosière Group, 107–108
Larosière report, 108, 110
Larosière, Jacques de, 107
Lastra, Rosa M., 39, 42–43, 50
Latin America
    bailouts, 196
    crisis, 102
Latvia, 48, 205, 216–217
law
    and credibility, 22–25
    as credibility model, 18, 23–24, 28, 134
    preference for, 26
law as credibility, xvii, 1, 4, 18–34, 73, 88, 94,
    109–110, 132, 134, 196
    bailout model, 210
    commitment, 19

conditions, 29–30
counterfactuals, 33
courts, 32
equilibrium, 23, 258
law as an institutional technology, 22–23
legal nature of MOUs, 226–227
OMC, 238, 255
pre-crisis EU system, 208
public law vs. private law, 28
role of citizens, 31
SGP, 190–193
Leckow, Ross, 229–230
Ledra case, 226
legal norms
    as commitments, 19
Lehman Brothers, 161, 163, 196
Lenaerts, K., 57
Lisbon Agenda, 154
Lisbon Agenda (2000), 234–238, 252–253, 258,
    See also Kok report
    2020 Strategy, 242
Lisbon Strategy, 160
Lisbon Treaty, 43
Lithuania, 48, 89, 205
Louis, Jean Victor, 39, 42, 50

M'batto, 8
Maastricht Treaty
    public debt and deficit ceilings, 217
Maastricht Treaty, 43, 138–143, *See* Treaty on
    European Union (TEU)
    article 104c, 140
    article 109k, 140
Macroeconomic Imbalance Procedure, 222
Malta, 48
Mandela, Nelson, 7
Margin Call, 161
markets, legal conceptualization of, 21
Marx, Karl, 4
Master Financial Assistance Facility
    Agreement, 231
material deprivation, definition, 243
maximizing, 10
Medium-Term Financial Assistance, 201
Medium-Term Objective (MTO), 142
Memorandum of Understanding (MOU)
    Cyprus, 226
    flexibility, 227
    Greece, 218–219
    Ireland, 225
    Portugal, 223–224